Linguistics Out of the Closet

Interdisciplinary Linguistics

Editor
Allison Burkette

Volume 3

Linguistics Out of the Closet

The Interdisciplinarity of Gender and Sexuality
in Language Science

Edited by
Tyler Everett Kibbey

DE GRUYTER
MOUTON

ISBN 978-3-11-221385-8
e-ISBN (PDF) 978-3-11-074251-0
e-ISBN (EPUB) 978-3-11-074264-0
ISSN 2626-9228

Library of Congress Control Number: 2023932400

Bibliographic information published by the Deutsche Nationalbibliothek
The Deutsche Nationalbibliothek lists this publication in the Deutsche Nationalbibliografie;
detailed bibliographic data are available on the internet at http://dnb.dnb.de.

© 2025 Walter de Gruyter GmbH, Berlin/Boston
This volume is text- and page-identical with the hardback published in 2024.
Cover image: Steve Johnson on Unsplash
Typesetting: Integra Software Services Pvt. Ltd.
Printing and binding: CPI books GmbH, Leck

www.degruyter.com

To WRC

Entreat me not to leave thee, or to return from following after thee; for whither thou goest, I will go, and where thou lodgest, I will lodge. Thy people shall be my people, and thy God my God. (Ruth 1:16)

Acknowledgements

This collection would not have been possible without the support and mentorship of Allison Burkette, Rusty Barrett, and Jessi Grieser. I am greatly indebted also to the many colleagues who have engaged with, over the years, on projects focused on promoting gender and sexual diversity within and beyond the discipline of linguistics. This work would not have been possible without support from the Collaborative Research Center for Register Studies in Berlin as well as the support of my friend and colleagues there. Gefördet durch die Deutsche Forschungsgemeinschaft (DFG) – SFB1412, 416591334.

Thank you. *Vielen Dank.*

Contents

Acknowledgements —— VII

Tyler Everett Kibbey
A queer(ed) science of language —— 1

Intersection

Chris VanderStouwe
Theoretically queer, practically straight —— 13

Dominique A. Canning
Unbreakable —— 35

Ping-Hsuan Wang
Identity and desire in gay Indian immigrants' definition of coming out in the U.S. —— 63

Brenton Watts
Mountain magic —— 89

Integration

J Calder
Towards a queer and trans sociophonetics —— 117

Bryce McCleary
Queer+ Trans folk linguistics —— 139

Lex Konnelly
Transmedicalisms, transnormativities, and semantic authority —— 169

Institution

William Leap
Queer language before —— 197

Tyler Everett Kibbey
The state of Tennessee and the Kingdom of God —— 215

Nicholas Mararac
Queering the military —— 235

Rusty Barrett and Kira Hall
Closet monsters —— 259

Index —— 277

Tyler Everett Kibbey
A queer(ed) science of language
On the failures and futures of discipline

1 Introduction

Discipline is not an immutable monolith of intellectual life; nor is interdisciplinarity a panacea for the institutional problems of the contemporary academy. This becomes especially clear when intellectual lives and institutions are forced to contend with gender and sexual diversity, either among their peers and colleagues or within the context of their scholastic activities. The intellectual project of discipline as it emerged in the long(er) nineteenth century still yet betrays much of the Western interests in these projects when they were first coming into being. While these colonial, imperial, and moral facets of discipline are ubiquitous to the following discussion and the extant literature on the myriad manifestations of discipline (e.g., interdisciplinarity, multidisciplinarity, etc.), much yet remains beyond the scope of this introduction. Yet, by looking at discipline from without, by occupying the liminality of queer experience, we may yet better come to understand discipline as both an intellectual and institutional project that is frequently, if not always, at odds with queer experience. In effect, queering language science both for the sake and at the expense of discipline.

In brief, if it is demonstrable that discipline is both an intellectual and institutional project and if such projects are immediately at odds with queer experience, then what is the position of queer experience within and beyond discipline? In being peripheralized within discipline, forced to the very edge of what is acknowledged as acceptable academic inquiry, are queer projects inherently interdisciplinary? Is it even accurate to refer to queer work as disciplinary in the first place? And depending on how we answer these questions, what then is the future of the queer academy? In this introduction, following a survey of research on disciplinarity and my discussion of these questions, I briefly outline at the conclusion of this chapter the subsections of this collection – Intersection, Integration, Institution – the chapters of which each explore in dynamic fashion the position of queer and trans experience within and beyond the contemporary discipline of linguistics.

Tyler Everett Kibbey, University of Kentucky & Humboldt-Universität zu Berlin

2 Within and without discipline

First, *discipline* entails both intellectual and institutional projects (Kibbey 2020). These disciplinary projects are wide-ranging, discipline specific, and likewise differentiated by their intellectual or institutional loci. Thus, it is impossible to catalogue them all here, especially as they interact between and amongst competing disciplines. Attempts to synthesize the definition of discipline, in addition to attempts in parallel to define interdisciplinarity, are as varied as the disciplines themselves and often do not differentiate between the intellectual and institutional aspects of such. So, for our purposes *intellectual discipline* refers to the intrinsic products and activities of intellectual work within a historiographically defined area of study: the formulation of questions, the search for answers to those questions, the communication of the results of those inquiries, and so on – the intangible aspects of discipline. In parallel, *institutional discipline* refers to the concrete, tangible aspects of discipline: why and how questions are prioritized, research is funded, results are published; who is allowed to ask questions and who is allowed to answer them; and where the project of discipline is physically located. From the classroom of the university to the call for proposals from a journal or conference, institutional discipline indexes not only the tangible aspects of academic life but also, more simply, the manner in which discipline is instituted in the world.

Discipline as an intellectual project has been defined as an epistemological framework for organizing research and knowledge on discipline-specific objects. While rarely differentiated from institutional discipline, writing on intellectual discipline constitutes the vast majority of the literature. In a historiographical sense, discipline as an intellectual project emerged from the needs of the nineteenth century academy. As Western colonial-imperial institutions facilitated the exploitation and plunder of the world's (intellectual) history, the impulse to cleave natural philosophy from theology matured into a more systematic, albeit decidedly Western, division of human knowledge (Dear 2009; Goldsmith & Laks 2019; Kibbey 2019). The nascent disciplinary system of the nineteenth century demanded categories of knowledge-making which could provide a means of curating the immense volume of knowledge that was beginning to overwhelm the university as a political and academic institution.

Kramnick (2017) defines the contemporary disciplinary impulse of academia in pluralistic terms, as a way of accumulating and creating deep knowledge on a particular subject matter as it is either socially constituted or physically manifested within the world. As an apologetic, he dismisses historiographical arguments against discipline as antidisciplinary and characterizes interdisciplinary endeavours as artificial attempts to create new epistemological orders. Reference is sparingly made to the institution of discipline or its embodied consequences.

Newell (2001), on the other hand, argues that interdisciplinarity is necessary for understanding complex systems with multi-faceted, non-linear relationships between their discipline-specific objectification. The irreducible complexity of the world demands interdisciplinarity, demands for connections to be made in order to facilitate a more holistic knowledge of a particular object. While he does mention the institution of interdisciplinarity (i.e., how interdisciplinarity is made present in the university through the formalization of programs of study or establishment of specific pedagogical initiatives), Newell similarly glosses over the manner in which discipline is instituted already.

With respect to intellectual discipline and its relationship with interdisciplinarity, Kuhn (1970) first surveyed the nature of intellectual progress within the academy in his foundational work on the structure of scientific revolutions, which were prefigured by what he referred to as *paradigm shifts*. While the complexity of knowledge may change radically over time, along the same lines that Newell (2001) argues, the core nature of human knowledge does not.

> We may, to be more precise, have to relinquish the notion, explicit or implicit, that changes of paradigm carry scientists and those who learn from them closer and closer to the truth [. . .] The developmental process described in this essay has been a process of evolution *from* primitive beginnings – a process whose successive stages are characterized by an increasingly detailed and refined understanding of nature. But nothing that has been or will be said makes it a process of evolution *toward* anything. (170–171)

In linguistics, for example, Saussure's (1986) operationalization of the sign can be seen as demarcating a shift from a pre-Saussurian to a post-Saussurian language science (Lukin 2018; Williamson 2007) just as Herder's (1772) essay on the natural origins of human language can be seen as demarcating a theology-based and a philosophy-based approach to the study of language. Yet these paradigmatic shifts do not necessarily mean that everything which came before should be so quickly discarded or ignored, nor is it to imply that prior works are based on poorly formulated questions (Kramnick 2017). It is true that the questions posed by Lucretius, Aristotle, and Aquinas are not immediately legible to the modern reader as a science of language, but this does not mean that the questions posed are not themselves well-formulated or not insightful. By Kuhn's (1970) accounting, they only differ by orders of complexity, and by Newell's (2001) appraisal, this increasing complexity demands interdisciplinarity.

The disciplinary project of linguistics, both intellectually and institutionally, began in earnest during the early twentieth century, what Goldsmith and Laks (2019) refer to as an *acceleration* of professional development. Up until Saussure's (1916) formalization of the linguistic sign as an object of empirical study, the study of language had remained a multidisciplinary area of inquiry. Bloomfield

(1925), writing on the formation of the Linguistic Society of America (i.e., the preeminent institution of linguistics as a discipline in the United States, if not but for its history), posed the question *Why a linguistic society?*:

> In our country are scholars who for a generation or more have worked in linguistics and have never met [. . .] For ourselves this is answer enough, but for the layman it is no answer at all, and leads him only to restate the question: Why should So-and-so want to meet So-and-so? and What have you, after all, in common? and Why will not the existing societies, Philological, Oriental, Modern Languages, Anthropological, Psychological, and what not, serve you as meeting places? (1)

To institute linguistics as a distinct disciplinary project during this time, the study of language had to be excised from the other, competing disciplinary projects in which it had been involved: philology, anthropology, psychology, and so on. The articulation of linguistics as a fully formed science in its own right was paramount, and similar projects were taking place throughout the universities of the West, such as those in Britain, France, and Germany (Goldsmith & Laks 2019).

Yet, the intellectual project of discipline does not only rest on the formulation of questions and historiography but also the way we arrive at certain questions, who is asking the question, and the broader professional tendencies of the body academic. While the Soviet Russian linguist Vološinov (1929) explored the relationship between language and Marxist conceptions of class, explicitly; the American sociolinguist Labov (1972, for example) explores the relationship between language and capitalist conceptions of class, implicitly. The need or lack thereof to make explicit the motivations for why or how a certain question is asked betrays the subtle distinction in the goals of each project: goals which might help us differentiate between a Soviet linguistics and an American linguistics, for example. Similarly, the positionality of the researcher and their programs of research also lends itself to differentiating disciplinary projects along social fault-lines in the same way that disciplines are differentiated amongst different nations, as in the example above. For the study of language, this has frequently skirted around notions of ethno-linguistic and racial identity, both on the part of the research and on the part of the research topic. The most immediate example is the notion of *raciolinguistics* which as a novel sub-discipline represents a centring of the inter-relationship between race and language (Alim, Rickford & Ball 2016; Rosa 2019). As a project, raciolinguistics is a reaction to approaches to language that either ignore critical aspects of ethnicity and race or else trivialize it within the discipline's greater project of institution (Charity Hudley, Mallinson, Bucholtz, Flores, Holliday, Chun & Spears 2018; Charity Hudley, Mallinson & Bucholtz 2020). Similarly, Crip Linguistics has emerged as a critique of approaches to the study of language that marginalize, dehumanize, and disenfranchise disabled, neurodivergent, and neuroqueer language users, centring the lived experience of linguists with disabilities (Henner & Robinson 2021; Smilges 2021).The embodiment of discipline in terms of an individual's gender, sexuality, race, ethnicity, class, neurotypicality, and so on necessarily erodes the boundary between intellectual and institutional discipline.

3 (Inter)disciplinary anxiety

Interdisciplinarity, then, can be distinguished as both an intellectual and institutional endeavour to bridge disciplinary divides (Burkette 2021). Between familial disciplines – such as with linguistics, anthropology, sociology, literature, and history, for example – interdisciplinarity often presents as a form of cross-disciplinary exchange or borrowing. Burkette cites Bott's (1971) social network theory, Lave and Wenger's (1991) practice theory, and Butler's (1990) performativity as but a few exemplars of this practice as it has occurred in linguistics. Building from this, Childs (2021) highlights the integrative nature of interdisciplinarity, emphasizing the broader connections between linguistics and the humanities, social sciences, biological sciences, mathematics, and education. She also emphasizes expansiveness, a common theme in interdisciplinary literature, specifically:

> If we begin to look around not only at the field of linguistics, but expand our gaze more broadly to the pressing questions and concerns in academia and, more importantly, in the public sphere, it is clear that linguistics and, especially, interdisciplinary and transdisciplinary approaches in linguistic research are necessary to provide information and insight that concern contemporary society. (7–8)

Integration and expansiveness differentiate the project of interdisciplinarity from multidisciplinarity or pluridisciplinarity which is characterized by approaching shared question from multiple disciplinary perspectives, often in collaboration with other discipline-external scholars (Childs 2021; Choi & Pak 2007; Hudson & Day 2019). Scholars working on multidisciplinary projects generally stay within the boundaries of their respective disciplines and seek to complement or supplement the contributions of others, rather than integrating each perspective into a single account. In contrast, interdisciplinary research seeks to answer a research question as well as possible through the integration of knowledge from several disciplines so as to either advance our understanding of a particular issue or to address a problem which is beyond the scope of a single disciplinary project (Childs 2021; Klein 1990, 2004). Moving beyond integration, *transdisciplinarity* represents an extension of interdisciplinary and multidisciplinary research within a collaborative framework that looks beyond the discipline as an institutional project (Childs 2021; Klein 2004; Stokol 2006). Transdisciplinary work seeks a connection to broader society and can include the public dissemination of research, education reform, and advocacy on issues relevant to domestic and foreign policy.

However, these conceptions of interdisciplinary projects are grounded, needless to say, in conceptions of disciplinary projects. The same anxiety on the position of language science within the academy as expressed in Bloomfield (1925), the same complexity that compels the paradigm-shifts of Kuhn (1970) and the non-linear relationships of Newell (2001); these conspire with and contribute to the larger projects of discipline, both intellectual and institutional, which peripheralize scholars of all identities, marginalized or elsewise nonnormative. The immediate material effects can be devastating, both for a person's career and for their health. One study of LGBTQ inequality in STEM fields, for example, showed that LGBTQ STEM professionals were more likely to experience frequent health difficulties, professional devaluation, career limitations, social exclusion, and harassment than their cisgender-heterosexual peers (Cech & Waidzunas 2021). Disciplines seek legitimacy because, simply put, those invested in the project of discipline seek security: social, financial, personal. To legitimize itself as a science, Bloomfield (1925) and his contemporaries sought to distance themselves from the less empirical fields in which the study of language had thereunto been situated. With the introduction of social complexity in the production and perception of language, formalists sought to differentiate themselves as more central, more legitimate, and more necessary to the study of language; and likewise sought to elevate their subfields within the discipline while peripheralizing others. And finally, as the academy – as a physical, social, and political institution – began to diversify and include scholars from minority communities, the object of linguistic research was emphasized as more central than the subject conducting the research; queer and trans scholars, to gain proximity to disciplinary legitimacy as well as professional security, are still frequently forced to *tone down* their work, or to subscribe to cis-heteronormative expectations of academic professionalism. This (inter)disciplinary anxiety drives many of the structural problems that the chapters in this collection seek to addresses, so rather than re-hash every single point for every single letter in the expansive LGBTQ+ community, I will leave the final word on this matter to those scholars who have herein contributed chapters on what a queer interdisciplinary linguistics looks like and could look like in the future.

4 Linguistics out of the closet

This collection is motivated by the need to create new spaces for interdisciplinary queer and trans scholarship and the for the exploration of what is means for queer and trans research to be interdisciplinary. Queer linguistics – in its position as both a linguistic science of and for queer and trans folk – is inherently agitating to the disciplinary anxiety of a general linguistic science. It represents, as all queer science does, a disruption of normative modes of knowledge production and a displacement of academic authority. These disruptions and displacements are not, needless to say, well-tolerated within projects of discipline, and the disciplinary impulse to attain greater intellectual and institutional legitimacy forces minority perspectives to the periphery. To bring linguistics out of the closet, then, we must make space for interdisciplinary work on language, gender, and sexuality without prior assumptions about what such work looks like. And then, we must explore that space and make it our own. To help structure this exploration, the collection is divided into three sections: Intersection, Integration, and Institution.

Chapters in **Intersection** explore queer linguistic perspectives on communities that exist either at the intersection or on the periphery of queer experiences. In Chapter 2, Chris VanderStouwe explores the discursive negotiation of identity and ideology among Mormon men who experience same-sex attraction but openly profess to living a heterosexual lifestyle and enter into marriages with Mormon women. His analysis demonstrates how Same-Sex Attraction (SSA) as an identity category among Mormon men represents a queering of sexuality at the margins of our normative understandings of sexual orientation, identity, and practice. In Chapter 3, Domonique Canning presents a sociolinguistic analysis of Titus Andromedon's language usage in *Unbreakable Kimmy Schmidt* as compared to the language usage of Tituss Burgess, the actor, during interviews. Here, Canning complicates intersectional approaches to the performativity of race and sexuality, looking at how Titus(s) uses African American English to negotiate identity though persona-based style shifting. In Chapter 4, Ping-Hsuan Wang explores queer theoretical work on the experience of *coming out* and shows how Indian immigrants living in the US discursively position themselves in relation to this experiential frame. Using narrative analysis to identify microlevel positioning in these coming-out narratives, Wang presents a compelling argument for the centrality of this narrative type in the expression of same-sex desire in cross-cultural contexts. Finally, in Chapter 5, Brent Watts demonstrates how the co-negotiating of folk magic cultural practices create and maintain queer Appalachian communities on social media. Exploring the complexities of regionality, sexuality, gender, and socio-economic status, Watts documents a vibrant, queer folk magic community in an emerging digital Appalachia.

Chapters in **Integration** explore how queer and trans linguists have sought to integrate discipline-external and peripheralized research into new sub-disciplinary projects and programs of research. In Chapter 6, Jeremy Calder outlines, theoretically and historiographically, how the disciplinary goals of a nascent queer and trans sociophonetics complements and diverges from queer linguistics, trans linguistics, and traditional sociophonetics. Calder argues that queer and trans sociophonetics showcases how the body serves an indexical role in the phonetic realization of gender identity, wherein "queer voices emerge from queer bodies". In Chapter 7, Bryce McCleary outlines the disciplinary scope of queer folk linguistics as an emerging subfield at the intersection of dialectology, sociolinguistics, and queer theory through a case study of co-negotiate identity construction among an Oklahoma drag community. Expanding on research looking at folk linguistic discourses, McCleary argues for the importance of centring identity in the study of language regard, both within and beyond LGBTQ+ populations. In Chapter 8, Lex Konnelly outlines a program of transdisciplinary research into the ideologies of transmedicalism and transnormativity. Konnelly shows how issues of authority and authenticity are negotiated linguistically within the trans community through discussion of what it means to be trans.

Chapters in **Institution** explore issues of language, gender, and sexuality as it relates reflexively and critically to institutional programs including the university, the military, and the state. In Chapter 9, William Leap historiographically charts the origins of the study of queer language as distinct political, medical, and intellectual projects of their respective institutions, highlighting how early notions of queer language were used to evaluate the fitness of military servicemen. Leap demonstrates how this institutionalization of queer language science, as it was originally conducted by cis-heterosexual individuals, was complicit in the pseudo-eugenic projects of various early-twentieth century institutions and how the contemporary discipline was influenced by this. In Chapter 10, Tyler Kibbey bridges cognitive linguistic research on metaphor with emerging areas in the cognitive science of religion to delineate gender transcendentalist ideology as it has developed among evangelical Tennessee conservatives, an ideology related to the theo-political regulation of queer and trans language, spaces, and bodies. Kibbey shows how the linguistic realization of ideologies, as wider semiotic systems, play a central role in the maintenance and implementation of anti-LGBTQ+ laws and policies by the Tennessee General Assembly. In Chapter 11, Nicholas Mararac presents an analysis of how ideologies of gender and sexuality affect leadership discourse in the military. Focusing on that narrative identity construction of two naval officers, Mararac takes innovative steps to expand the field of queer linguistic research to include, as an imperative, the lived experiences if queer members of the military. In Chapter 12, Kira Hall and Rusty Barrett interrogate the complex generational and political facets of academic life, showing how the power of language can be deployed both within and beyond the discipline of linguistics to gatekeep and bully those who are different or diverge from an established paradigm, nom, or institution.

When we bring the discipline of linguistics out of the closet, the discipline's skeletons come with it too. One cannot address problems of homophobia and transphobia without also addressing racism, ableism, colonialism, misogyny, and all the rest. And whereas interdisciplinarity has become a more accepted practice for the discipline of linguistics in a general sense, working between and at the borders of discipline has always been a necessity for queer and trans academics. Making these deeper, community-specific traditions of interdisciplinary work legible to the wider discipline, then, is the cruel burden placed upon scholars whose work was formerly deemed illegible purely by association to an unspeakable queerness. A burden that might yet be lifted from future generations of queer and trans linguists.

References

Alim, H. Salim, John R. Rickford & Arnetha F. Ball. 2016. *Raciolinguistics: How Language shapes our ideas about race*. Oxford: Oxford University Press.
Bloomfield, Leonard. 1925. Why a linguistic society? *Language* 1(1). 1–5.
Bott, Elizabeth. 1971. *Family and Social Network*. London: Tavistock.
Burkette, Allison. 2021. Introduction: Why Interdisciplinarity? In Allison Burkette & Tamara Warhol (eds.), *Crossing Border, Making Connections: Interdisciplinarity in Linguistics*, 1–6. Berlin: De Gruyter Mouton.
Butler, Judith. 1990. *Gender Trouble*. London: Routledge.
Cech, Erin A. & Tom J. Waidzunas. 2021. Systematic inequalities for LGBTQ professionals in STEM. *Science Advances* 7. 1–9.
Charity Hudley, Anne H., Christine Mallinson & Mary Bucholtz. 2020. Toward racial justice in linguistics: Interdisciplinary insights into theorizing race in the discipline and diversifying the profession. *Language* 96(4). e200–e235.
Charity Hudley, Anne H., Christine Mallinson, Mary Bucholtz, Nelson Flores, Nicole Holliday, Elaine Chun & Arthur Spears. 2018. Linguistics and race: An interdisciplinary approach towards an LSA statement on race. *Proceedings of the Linguistic Society of America* 3(1). 1–14.
Childs, Becky. 2021. The value of interdisciplinary and transdisciplinary linguistic research. In Allison Burkette & Tamara Warhol (eds.), *Crossing Border, Making Connections: Interdisciplinarity in Linguistics*. 7–21. Berlin: De Gruyter Mouton.
Choi, Bernard & Anita Pak. 2007. Multidisciplinarity, interdisciplinarity, and transdisciplinarity in health research, services, education and policy. *Clinical and Investigative Medicine* 31(1). e41–48.
Dear, Peter. 2009. *Revolutionizing the sciences: European knowledge and its ambitions, 1500–1700* (2nd edn.). Princeton: Princeton University Press.
Goldsmith, John & Bernard Laks. 2019. *Battle in the mind fields*. Chicago: The University of Chicago Press.
Henner, Jon & Octavian Robinson. 2021. Unsettling Languages, Unruly Bodyminds: Imaging a Crip Linguistics. *PsyArXiv*. 1–37.
Herder, Johann Gottfried. 1966. Essay on the Origin of Language. Alexander Gode (trans.). In John H. Moran & Alexander Gode (eds.), *On the origin of language*. 86–176. New York City: Frederick Ungar Publishing.

Hudson, Valerie M. & Benjamin S. Day. 2019. *Foreign policy analysis: Classic and contemporary theory* (3rd edn.). Lanham: Rowman & Little.

Kibbey, Tyler. 2019. Transcriptivism: An ethical framework for modern linguistics. *Proceedings of the Linguistic Society of America* 4(1). 1–13.

Kibbey, Tyler. 2020. Linguistics out of the closet: Comments on a discipline's anxiety. *Cadernos de Linguistica* 2(1). 1–19.

Klein, Julie. T. 1990. *Interdisciplinarity: History, theory and practice*. Detroit: Wayne State University Press.

Klein, Julie T. 2004. Prospects for transdisciplinarity. *Futures* 36. 515–536.

Kramnick, Jonathan. 2017. The interdisciplinary fallacy. *Representations* 140. 67–83.

Kuhn, Thomas S. 1970. *The structure of scientific revolutions* (2nd edn.). Chicago: The University of Chicago Press.

Labov, William. 1972. The social stratification of (r) in New York City department stores. In William Labov (ed.), *Sociolinguistic patterns*. 168–178. Philadelphia: University of Pennsylvania Press.

Lave, Jean & Etienne Wenger. 1991. *Situated learning: Legitimate peripheral participation*. Cambridge: University of Cambridge Press.

Lukin, Annabelle. 2018. *War and its ideologies: A social-semiotic theory and description*. New York City: Springer.

Newell, William H. 2001. A theory of interdisciplinary studies. *Issues in Integrative Studies* 19. 1–25.

Rosa, Jonathan. 2019. *Looking like a language, sounding like a race: Raciolinguistic ideologies and the learning of Latinidad*. Oxford: Oxford University Press.

de Saussure, Ferdinand. 1986. *Course in General Linguistics*. Roy Harris (trans.). Chicago: Open Court Classics.

Smilges, J. Logan. 2021. Neuroqueer literacies; or, against able-reading. *College Composition and Communication* 73(1). 103–125.

Stokol, Daniel. 2006. Toward a science of transdisciplinary action research. *American Journal of Community Psychology* 38. 63–77.

Vološinov, Valentin N. 1986. *Marxism and the philosophy of language*. Ladislav Matejka & I. R. Titunik (trans.). Cambridge: Harvard University Press.

Williamson, Timothy. 2007. Chapter 1: The linguistic turn and the conceptual turn. *The philosophy of philosophy*. 10–22. Boston: Blackwell Publishing.

Intersection

Chris VanderStouwe
Theoretically queer, practically straight
Linguistic negotiations of identity and same-sex attraction among Mormon men

1 Introduction

Contemporary popular representations of sexuality have begun to include more non-exclusively heterosexual conceptualizations of sexual identity. Viral media articles and op-ed pieces have sprung up with claims that "surprising numbers of straight men" have had same-sex encounters, promoting a representation of younger generations coming of age as more frequently rejecting identity labels entirely (e.g., DiDomizio 2016; LGBTQ Nation 2016). Many of the recent statements about this seemingly surprising phenomenon are based on a 2016 report by the Centers for Disease Control and Prevention (CDC) that highlights the disparities between sexual identity and sexual practice in men and women ages 18 to 44 in the United States (Copen, Chandra & Febo-Vazquez 2016). In the report, the authors show evidence that more men claim to have had some level of same-sex "contact" (6.2%) than claim a gay or bisexual identity (3.9% combined). Despite the report's claims that "[s]exual attraction and sexual orientation correlate closely but not completely with reports of sexual behavior," (2016:1) and that women had even higher levels of reported sexual disparity, media reactions focused solely on the discrepancies between sexual practice and sexual identity found among men.

Related to this phenomenon is the rising use of coinages based on male friendship terms such as *bro*, including the now-ubiquitous "bromance" referring to a close friendship between ostensibly heterosexual men, and terms such as *brojob*, a practice in which straight men get together to "help a brother out" by engaging in sexual acts such as fellatio (i.e., blowjobs). This development has led to a greater awareness of shifting conceptualizations of sexuality, and this trend is often framed by liberal news outlets as unsurprising and natural. These news outlets often make frequent allusions to the Kinsey scale (Kinsey, Pomeroy & Martin 1949), which places sexual preference along a linear 0–6 designation with 0 being exclusively heterosexual and 6 being exclusively homosexual and other numbers representing varying amounts of sexual preference for the same or opposite sex.

Chris VanderStouwe, Boise State University

Despite these and other popular claims about reimagining sexuality, dominant ideologies about the relationship between sexual orientation, sexual identity, and sexual practice often remain rigid and naturalized, in which one's gender and sexual identities are mapped onto a binary heteronormative framework that if one is born assigned male, they are expected to be attracted to women, and any deviation from this is placed into specific categories such as gay or bisexual. This chapter explores a unique community of Mormon men who push back against these ideologies both from within their religious community and from the broader secular society. While acknowledging attraction to both men and women, they choose to constrain their sexual practices to be within the confines of monogamous heterosexual marriages. However, they simultaneously reject normalized non-heterosexual identity labels such as gay and bisexual, instead creating a new identity category around their same-sex attraction that more authentically captures their lived experience and their commitment to traditional religious values.

2 Same-sex attraction in "My Husband's Not Gay"

Beginning in late 2014, a controversy arose surrounding a television special that was about to be released by The Learning Channel (now known primarily as TLC) entitled "My Husband's Not Gay." This special was a documentary-style episode of the *TLC Presents* series, which consists of a series of shock-value one-time specials with titles such as "Buying Naked: Nudists Fetch a Home" and "Santa Sent Me to the ER." "My Husband's Not Gay," which aired on January 11, 2015, followed four Mormon men in Salt Lake City, Utah, as they explain what they refer to as same-sex attraction, or SSA. Each of these men, three of whom are married to women, all profess to live a heterosexual lifestyle and together describe the distinction between being gay, which the Mormon church forbids, and experiencing SSA, which they explain as an attraction toward other men that they actively choose not to act upon.

The Mormon church's stance on sexuality, and especially homosexuality, is largely influenced by the church's "law of chastity," which states that "sexual relations are proper only between a man and a woman who are legally and lawfully wedded as husband and wife" (LDS 2011). While the church has historically taught that homosexuality was a curable condition (Kimball 1964; Oaks 1984), more recent church writings have moved away from a goal of trying to cure same-sex attraction and instead have focused on a distinction between attraction and acting upon attraction (LDS 2011, 2012).

The use of the term same-sex attraction, often abbreviated as SSA, in the Mormon church dates at least back to 1991 (Schow & Schow 1991) and possibly earlier. SSA is referenced periodically in Mormon writings since that time (e.g., Oaks 1995,

LDS 2012), beginning first as same-gender attraction and moving to the more contemporary current designation. It is most commonly used in Mormon writings to describe something one *has* but not something one *is*. This is done in order to distinguish between being attracted to those of the same sex, which is not inherently seen as against church teachings, and engaging in physically intimate actions involving those of the same sex, which is forbidden. As I discuss here, the proliferation of SSA as a concept and term among Mormon church members is crucial to the understanding of the men in TLC's documentary and how they agentively construct their sexual identity through language while still being constrained by both religious and secular perceptions of sexuality.

Work in linguistic anthropology, queer studies, and other related fields has explored straight-identified men who engage in same-gender sex acts under varying labels such as MSM (or men who have sex with men) (e.g., Boellstorff 2011; Bogetic 2013; VanderStouwe 2019) and dudesex (Ward 2008, 2015). In these studies, sexuality is often primarily examined in terms of practices and actions, downplaying the differences between sexual identity and sexual activity. In the United States, MSM is predominantly a clinical term used to describe the actions of populations regardless of how they sexually self-identify. SSA stands in contrast to these discussions of sexual practice and highlights the important role of language in enacting sexual identity. Instead of placing the focus on the actions being performed, SSA is specifically designed to refer to those who do *not* act on such desires or attractions. Since the men who claim this term typically present as heterosexual and do not engage in sexual activities with other men, language is therefore the primary way through which an SSA identity is constituted.

Scholars of the link between religion and sexuality throughout history have argued that attraction to others of the same sex existed long before terminology such as 'homosexuality' existed (Boswell 1980), and that attraction and marriage did not always align in such situations. Social constraints on who could partake in which roles in same-sex intimacy were also present, and social expectations of marriage and families were often adhered to even if one's practices did not align with one's familial structure (Boswell 1980). However, as pointed out in Greenberg and Bystryn (1982), many of the historical constraints on same-sex practices are rooted in Christian-based religious dogmas, while other non-Christian religious paradigms may have tolerated or embraced various levels of same-sex intimacy. In the context presented here, same-sex attraction is treated differently from same-sex intimacy, wherein as mentioned above, the Mormon church only condemns acting on such attractions, as the law of chastity only permits sexual intimacy between a man and a woman within the confines of marriage. Thus, while the idea of same-sex attraction existing in the sphere of social and religious constraints is not novel in its existence, the example provided here illustrates a unique manifestation, wherein acting upon such attraction does not take place, and language becomes the only means by which one is known to have such attractions at all.

In this chapter, I analyze footage from the "My Husband's Not Gay" documentary as well as media coverage and comment threads pertaining to the show in order to shed light on the experiences and perceptions of men who identify as SSA. In doing so, I examine the ways that these men's sexual identities are both constructed and constrained through language and the popular ideologies revealed in discussions of this episode.

3 Situating SSA among sexual identity labels

While "My Husband's Not Gay" centers around the struggles of being SSA, only small portions of the show directly address what SSA is and what it means to be SSA, with the rest tackling the challenges faced with how men who identify as SSA share this identity with others in their lives. The show begins with a caption that says, "In Salt Lake City . . . There is a group of Mormons who live their lives a little differently . . . ." This opening leads into cameos of each of the main participants who state things such as, "I like to say I've chosen an alternative to an alternative lifestyle" and "I'm attracted to my wife, sure. But I'm definitely attracted to men too."

In the show, SSA identity is constructed from the point of view of the main male participants and their wives as they work through what it means to be in a heterosexual marriage with someone who experiences SSA, all while maintaining a commitment to their Mormon faith. Jeff and Tanya, who have been married for eight years at the time of filming, explained their relationship as follows:

Example 1. *"Not gay, SSA"*[1]
1 JEFF;   One of the most unique things about our relationship,
2   is I experience SSA,
3   or same-sex attraction.
4 TANYA;   Not gay.
5   SSA.

By making a very clear distinction between SSA and being gay, Tanya and Jeff jointly construct an identification category that allows Jeff to maintain a claim to

---

[1] All video data in this chapter is transcribed according to the basic tenets of Discourse Transcription as outlined by DuBois, Cumming. Schuetze-Coburn & Paolino (1993). Breaths and pauses not relevant for analysis have been omitted for ease of reading.

heterosexuality even while attracted to other men. Although Jeff initially uses the term in line 2 as it is often discussed in the Mormon church – as a trait that one possesses – Tanya expands its meaning and usage by providing a contrasting parallel between being 'gay' and being 'SSA' in lines 4–5. Not only does this contrast work to combat the assumption that an attraction toward other men inherently makes one gay, it also positions SSA as more than just a trait, instead setting it up as on par with a sexual identity such as gay. Further, the couple's co-construction of this concept further illustrates that regardless of his orientation toward same-sex attraction, Jeff is still working to maintain and wishes to remain in his current marriage, a sentiment that is repeated more than once by both partners.

In addition to participants' frequent mentions of choosing to be in a heterosexual relationship, there is a clear attempt to disambiguate between SSA and being gay along ideological and identity lines as well. This is brought out not only in the title of the special, "My Husband's Not Gay," but also among the individuals whose lives are followed throughout the show. For instance, one of the wives Tera remarks, "I think there are so many people in the church that don't know the difference between having a gay lifestyle and having same-sex attraction," an ideological viewpoint that frequently manifests itself not only in the show, but in the media comments about the show as well.

Tera and her husband Curtis also disambiguate SSA from other sexual identity labels when they are discussing the first time that Curtis mentioned his same-sex attraction to Tera, sixteen years into their now over twenty-year marriage:

Example 2. *"What matters is how we act"*
1   CURTIS;   If someone can experience sexual attraction toward both women and men,
2   in mainstream America,
3   they're considered bisexual.
4   PROD;   *(off-screen)* But you don't identify with that word.
5   CURTIS;   I don't necessarily?
6   And if you look at most of the studies that have been done about sexuality,
7   they'll show you that sexuality is fluid,
8   it changes.
9   But ultimately when it comes to our faith and our belief,
10   what matters is how we act.

Notably, Curtis and Tera both mention a frequent confusion between being gay or bisexual and being SSA, and work to create clarity between the two. When Curtis mentions that mainstream America might consider him to be bisexual in lines 2 and 3, the producer asks for clarification about Curtis' stance on the term in his own self-identification in line 4. In response, Curtis tilts his head and says that he doesn't necessarily identify with it (line 5) because sexuality is "fluid" and "changes" (lines 7–8).

Instead, he focuses on his faith and the allowance for same-sex attraction so long as he doesn't act on it (lines 9–10). By contrasting established sexual identity terms with personal experience, Curtis is able to claim SSA without identifying with any of the terms often placed upon them by "mainstream America" through common ideologies of sexuality.

However, participants are not always so steadfast in their distinctions between the labels "gay" and "SSA." Sometimes they are playful about their attraction in ways that evoke gay labels and identity categories, but then complicate them to make it clear they don't actually align with these labels. Tom, notably the only unmarried man featured in the special, explains that he is a basketball player and coach and not active in what he considers "gay" activities. Tom explains why such complexities are necessary:

Example 3. *"Kinda gay"*
1	TOM;	I don't feel like I fit the mold of guys that are attracted to other men.
2		Other than my deep and abiding love for Broadway show tunes.
3		And my attraction to males.
4		Those are the two things that are kinda gay about me.

While this example has previously elicited laughter in response, illustrating a recognition of the pervasiveness of stereotypical associations with gay identities, Tom here is being both playful with the recognition that some of his interests overlap with stereotypes of homosexuality, but also serve to highlight that the similarities stop there, setting himself apart from the other possible associations with gay identities. Thus, while his attraction to males – the SSA part of him – does overlap conceptually with being gay or bisexual, his lifestyle choices and interests do not feature much similarity, allowing him to carve out SSA from other existing sexual orientations and identities.

Tom brings up being labelled as gay again later on in the episode, when he runs into a few former SSA-identified Mormons who now identify as gay. He clarifies, however, that he's not afraid to be called gay, as seen here:

Example 4. *"I'm not afraid"*
1	TOM;	I'm not afraid to be called gay.
2		I just feel like it's not real accurate.
3		I don't feel like the label totally describes me or who I am.
4		And sometimes I feel like when someone says, 'He's gay,'
5		it means that you're in relationships with men,
6		and I'm not.

Tom's playfulness with these sexual identity terms shows an awareness of the cultural ideologies that insist upon a link between attraction and action. However, in this acknowledgement, he also attempts to complicate and challenge such views. Being gay, according to these men, inherently involves not only acting upon same-sex attractions or desires, but more importantly participating in a lifestyle involving other men with aligned interests. Due to their strong desires to engage only in traditional heterosexual relationships, being gay is neither an option nor an accurate description of their own sexualities, creating a gap that allows for the construction of a novel sexual identity category.

4 Linguistically negotiating an SSA identity

The following examples illustrate the ways in which SSA is constructed and productively used as a category of identification much the same ways as "straight" or "gay" are used by others. This identity construction is accomplished through linguistic actions such as commentary about being part of an SSA "community," descriptions of and reactions to 'coming out'[2] as SSA, and the overt ranking of attraction towards other men using a 'danger scale'. While participants waver between identifying *as* SSA and as *having* SSA, the show makes distinctions that separate the lived experiences of these men from both gay experiences and straight ones, which are described as "lifestyles" by the husbands and wives featured in the show. For example, Tera makes this distinction by saying that "gay, to them [their husbands] is a lifestyle choice, and same-sex attraction is just a part of them, a part of who they are." Her remarks parallel those of Tanya, who states multiple times throughout the show that she feels she and her husband are "just like any other heterosexual couple" and that SSA individuals "are attracted to men but want to be in a heterosexual relationship." By framing gay and straight experiences as lifestyle choices one actively chooses to act or not act upon while describing SSA as just "a part of who they are," the participants mark SSA as central to the identity of the husbands, adopting similar discourses to the "born this way" ideologies found in many LGBTQ+ communities, who then choose to live a heterosexual lifestyle instead of a gay one.

---

2 I place 'coming out' in scare quotes as it is not the word used by the individuals on the show, but it parallels the experience as they discuss it.

4.1 The SSA community

Part of the evidence for SSA becoming more than a description and now also an identity is the way in which it is discussed among members who identify as having or being SSA. There are several mentions not only equating SSA with other sexual identity labels such as straight or gay, as seen in the examples above, but also in the way a "community" is discussed, and the fact that there are others for whom the identity also pertains, as seen below in Examples 5 and 6.

Example 5. *"Lots of others"*	
1 TANYA;	I know,
2	Lots of other of my friends,
3	That are in these same type of marriages.
4	That are in good relationships,
5	And none of us feel oppressed.
6	We've chosen to be here.

One example of the ways that SSA has grown to include a sense of identity as opposed to just a description is the mention of an SSA community found in the Salt Lake City area, where other SSA men often come together and spend time together as a social group in what could be considered a community of practice (e.g. Eckert & McConnell-Ginet 1992; Lave & Wegner 1991), although ironically based on the absence of a particular action in their socialization. Jeff explains the nature of their community briefly in Example 6 below.

Example 6. *"An SSA community"*	
1 JEFF;	In Salt Lake City,
2	there is a pretty tight knit SSA community.
3	but not everybody we hang out with,
4	is attracted to men.

That there can be such a "tight knit" community (line 2) in Salt Lake City gives credence to the categorization of SSA; in order to form a community, others with similar experiences and a wish to identify around those experiences often do so with a particular label, such as the gay community and others. Thus, despite the distinction that participants make between SSA as an inherent quality and gay/straight as a lifestyle choice, the men and their wives frequently discuss the importance of SSA in defining the way they live their lives as well, even if it isn't the only defining factor of their social lives (lines 3–4). Nearly every non-interview scene features events highlighting the unique activities in which they partake that, while not necessarily exclusive to SSA individuals, are used to bond and create a community centered around others with similar interests and attractions. Activities such as Bible studies, pick-up basketball games at the park, and other mentions of "guy time" by the wives featured in the special all contribute to the sense of community as well as an identity of being and having SSA. Furthermore, unique linguistic practices are found as well in their group. These practices are central not only to the creation of their community of practice but to an SSA identity more broadly, as the attraction exists in their community without action on it. Thus language is the primary outlet through which they can claim and share their identity.

4.2 "Coming out" as SSA

As with other non-heterosexual sexual identities, a big part of interactions with others are moments where one chooses whether or not to come out as that identity. While typically seen in discourses of gay, bisexual, lesbian, and transgender identities (e.g., Chirrey 2003; Kitzinger & Wilkinson 1995; Sedgewick 1990; Thorne 2013; Zimman 2009), this phenomenon is also present among the SSA-identified individuals in the TLC show as well, as seen in many examples of couples sharing stories of when and how they first told their spouses, to revealing the husbands as having same-sex attraction to other friends within their social groups. This parallel to the ongoing struggle of non-heterosexual individuals to choose when and how to 'come out' to others in their lives on a recurring basis reveals the similarities even in the absence of directly referring to these conversations or moments as 'coming out' moments. However, even without the label of 'coming out' directly used in their explanations of SSA and the men who experience it, there is an interaction toward the end of the show when Tom is about to meet a blind date at a group dinner party and asks the others not to say anything until he decides he is ready to discuss it. In this exchange, Pret, one of the featured men of the show, asks, "So you don't want us to out you?," highlighting the similarities of their experiences with those with other non-heterosexual sexualities and identities.

Being the only single man featured on the show, Tom struggles with the idea of revealing his same-sex attraction throughout the episode, as the blind date toward the end is a commonly discussed theme throughout the show. At one point during their dinner table interactions when some of the others are hinting at the tension of not discussing their same-sex attraction, Tom rhetorically asks in a breakaway interview moment, "How do you say we all know each other through our mutual admiration of men without really saying that?" His anxiety of whether or not to "come out" to his date, Emily, is discussed among the entire group prior to Emily's arrival as well, while standing in Tanya and Jeff's kitchen, where he reveals he's unsure what to do and the others explain that they all feel they waited too long to reveal their attractions, as seen below in Example 7:

Example 7. *"I waited too long"*

```
1   TOM;      (interview) I don't know if I,
2             Want to tell her about it,
3             Early on or?
4             Wait and see how things go.
5             I don't know what I'm gonna do.
6   TOM;      (back in kitchen) I'm tryin to just be,
7             More open with it.
8             Not that it has to be (.) something I tell people,
9             Right away.
10            I don't usually shake hands and say,
11            Sorry that was (.) so soft um,
12  GROUP;    @@
13  TOM;      I'm attracted to men.
14  TERA;     (interview with Curtis) I feel like Tom should be honest with her?
15            But,
16            There's a time and a place to,
17            Share everything about yourself?
18            And I don't think the first date is probably,
19            The ideal time to tell her about everything you struggle with.
20  JEFF;     (back in kitchen) I waited too long.
21            So don't do what I did.
22            I waited what,
23            A year and a half?
24  CURTIS;   I waited too long too.
25            Sixteen years.
26  TOM;      @@Okay.
27  GROUP;    @@@@
28  TOM;      [Alright.]
29  CURTIS;   [After married.]
30            Yeah.
```

The rhetoric of when to come out and the importance of doing so to reveal one's 'true self' is analogous to common views on coming out as gay, and the struggles faced in deciding when to come out in daily life and more broadly as someone either "in the closet" or not. While Tom explains that he wants to "wait and see" and that he's not sure what he'll eventually do (lines 4–5), others have a view that Tom should both be honest about it, such as Tera's statement in line 14, but seek the right time and place for it (lines 16–19). The consensus remains though that one should avoid "waiting too long," as both Jeff and Curtis explain in their views.

Eventually, the episode culminates in the "big reveal" of Tom sharing his same-sex attraction with his blind date, Emily, and the reactions she has to the information. Tom is often quoted throughout the episode as feeling as though he "deals" with SSA, framing it as a facet of his life and a community to which he belongs more than identity marker per se. This facet is portrayed as a part of him that he wants to balance with his religiously motivated desires to get married to a woman and have children and a family. Just before the footage of Tom explaining his SSA to Emily is shown, a short interview clip reveals Tom has decided that he wants to be up front and share with her as soon as possible because he likes her and wants to see her again. As Emily leaves, they walk into the front yard, and Tom begins to open up about his feelings, shown below in Example 8.

Example 8. *"I don't know how to tell you this"*

1	TOM;	(in front yard of Tanya and Jeff's house) Uh.
2		I don't know how to (.) tell you this.
3		Um.
4	EMILY;	Kay.
5	TOM;	I deal with something called same sex attraction?
6		We call it SSA but,
7		Uh.
8		I'm-
9		I'm attracted to men.
10		I'm attracted to women, too?
11	EMILY;	Right.
12	TOM;	I wouldn't be on a blind date with you if I wasn't?
13	EMILY;	Thanks for telling me.
14	TOM;	Yeah.
15		It's kind of a bombshell I realize but,
16		Some of my friends were kind of alluding to it,
17		and joking about it.
18	EMILY;	Oh ok.
19	TOM;	Actually,
20		All of those guys in there,
21		Deal with it too.
22	EMILY;	Right.
23	TOM;	So,
24		Uh,
25	EMILY;	(interview) When Tom did open up to me about the SSA,
26		I,
27		Immediately thought wow this is something,
28		Really brave of him to do.

Emily's response reveals a level of acceptance seen in many ways. She not only thanks him for sharing and nods agreement that the other men at the dinner party are also SSA in lines 13 and 18, but also claims during the interview cutaway placed between portions of their outside conversation that Tom is "really brave" (line 28) for sharing it with her, and so quickly after meeting. In fact, instead of providing any judgment or outward confusion, she immediately asks questions regarding what he is then looking for and why he is choosing to pursue only women, seen below in example 9, which immediately follows the exchange in example 8:

Example 9. *"What is it you want the most?"*

29	EMILY;	(outside) What is it that makes you want to,
30		Continue on in the way you've chosen.
31	TOM;	It's uh- it's just what I've always wanted the most.
32	EMILY;	Mhmm.
33	TOM;	You know what I mean?
34	EMILY;	What is it that you want the most?
35	TOM;	To be married have a wife have [kids have] a family.
36	EMILY;	[Mhmm.]
37	EMILY;	Mhmm.
38	TOM;	Just live the way that I think God wants me to live.
39	EMILY;	I'm glad that(.) you,
40		feel comfortable enough with me to start,
41		things out like that,
42	TOM;	Yeah.

Tom's coming out to Emily reiterates that while SSA is intrinsic for him, he is actively choosing to negotiate and balance this with his commitment to his Mormon faith and his desire to be in a heterosexual relationship. For Tom, it is equally important that he be open about his intrinsic same-sex attraction as it is for him to agentively choose a heterosexual lifestyle, adhering to his faith and seeking what he has "always wanted the most": to be married and have a wife and family.

4.3 The "danger scale"

The balance between acknowledging oneself as SSA and seeking a religiously sanctioned, heterosexual lifestyle happens not only in the men's coming out experiences with those outside the SSA community, but also among each other as well. This is seen in the TLC episode through the men's use of the so-called "danger scale" to discuss their attractions toward other men. The danger scale is a way for them to acknowledge their attractions but also diffuse them through group accountability.

Pret and Jeff explain this in example 10 through pieced-together interview clips that are edited into a scene where they are playing basketball outside on a court with a group of young men. They describe a scale that runs from 0–4 based on the levels of "danger" perceived by the attractiveness of a particular individual.

Example 10. *"Any of 'em dangerous?"*

1	PRET;	(outside on basketball court) Any of 'em dangerous for ya?
2	JEFF;	Maybe one?
3		The tall one.
4		In grey.
5	PRET;	Uh huh.
6		That's who I'd say.
7	PRET;	(interview) When I'm out with the guys,
8		Yeah,
9		We'll- we'll look at other guys.
10		For sure.
11	PRET;	(outside) What's the danger score?
12	JEFF;	Uh-
13	PRET;	(interview) The danger scale is a way to,
14		Bring out some of the inner feelings and,
15		Figure out,
16		Oh okay.
17		that is attractive to me and I didn't even realize it.
18	JEFF;	(separate interview) The danger scale goes from zero to four.
19		A one on the danger scale is you notice,
20		You look.
21	PRET;	A two means,
22		You looked again.
23	JEFF;	A three?
24		You'd be tempted to turn around and look again,
25		And again.
26	PRET;	A four,
27		Pretty much means,
28		You're requiring restraints.
29	JEFF;	(back outside) Two and a half.
30	PRET;	Really?
31	JEFF;	Uh-huh.
32	PRET;	Oh I'd go higher than that.
33	JEFF;	That's some danger.
34	PRET;	That's why the basketball's been fun.

As outlined in example 10, Pret and Jeff separately co-construct the levels of danger as a useful way to "bring out some of the inner feelings" (line 14) in terms that all of the men in their social group understand. That they can discuss the danger as something "fun," as Pret does in line 34, illustrates the power it has to allow the men to bond. Further, their ability to be playful with it and bring it into the open provides an outlet and a way to express their SSA experiences with each other. This aspect of sharing can solidify their experience as a community of practice, as they do not otherwise act on their attractions to men.

The danger scale is a facet of their lives that, while common to them, is not always clearly a part of every wife's experience in their relationships with their husbands. In one scene of the show, Jeff and Tanya meet up with Pret and his wife Megan for an early dinner at a French café in town. When an attractive young waiter comes up and the wives notice him, the conversation quickly turns from joking about the proper French pronunciation for 'Tuna Nicoise' to whether the men noticed their server as an attractive man. The ensuing conversation brings up discussion of the danger scale, which Megan had not heard of before, causing the following interchange between the two couples in Example 11.

Example 11. *"Not everybody's dangerous"*

1	JEFF;	(in café) You know not everybody's dangerous.
2	TANYA;	(nods) 'kay.
3	JEFF;	And that's,
4		good.
5		That's a relief.
6	MEGAN;	So what do you mean by dangerous though?
7	JEFF;	Uh,
8		[Thre]atening.
9	MEGAN;	[Lik-]
10	PRET;	Well not threatening [as]$_2$ much as just tempting.
11	JEFF;	[No.]$_2$
12	MEGAN;	Tem[pting.]$_3$
13	JEFF;	[Yeah.]$_3$
14	TANYA;	[Tempting.]$_3$
15	JEFF;	[Mhmm.]$_4$
16	MEGAN;	[Okay.]$_4$

In this interaction, where Megan first hears about being "dangerous" and the ensuing conversation of the danger scale, Jeff initially suggests that the scale is a measurement of how "threatening" (line 8) someone may be. This is quickly rebutted by Pret who insists that it's not actually about a threat, but that individuals who fall high on the danger scale are more tempting than others (line 10). This downplay of intensity is likely meant to soothe any fears the wives may have hearing about someone being a threat to their marriage. Whereas a danger may indicate something more imminent, a temptation is something that has potential but not actuality. This downgrading of the threat is also in line with the men's previous description of the danger scale as being useful for talking about attractions in a healthy way. Once Megan understands the meaning behind the danger scale, she then presses on with questions about what happens at the top of the scale (which would be a 4.0 on a 0–4 scale):

Example 12. *"Who would be a four?"*

1	MEGAN;	So who would be a d- four on your danger scale.
2	JEFF;	You [naturally.]
3	PRET;	[Well,] hold on a sec[ond.]₂
4	TANYA;	[Ohh,]₂
5		Good answer.
6		Good answer.
7		Good [answer.]
8	PRET;	[No] that's the truth.
9	JEFF;	So, [because-]₂
10	TANYA;	[Glad I'm]₂ a four.
11		[This is good.]₃
12	JEFF;	[Because we've had]₃ sex.
13		A few times.
14		Just a [few.]
15	PRET;	[That's] all?
16	TANYA;	A couple.
17	JEFF;	(interview with Tanya) Yeah women can be on the danger scale too.
18		Obviously my wife's a four point oh given our,
19		relationship.
20		Uh,
21	TANYA;	I've never heard you talk about a woman on the danger scale.
22	JEFF;	Yeah.
23		Yeah.
24		Women- of course,
25		Women can be dangerous to me,
26		But it's just very unusual I mean,
27		Not a lot of women are dangerous to me but there are,
28		Some that are.
29	TANYA;	(raises eyebrows)
30	GROUP;	(back in café) @@
31	MEGAN;	Okay.
32		So who would be the highest guy then if it's not gonna be a four.
33	TANYA;	'Cause you [said you've never] had a [four.]₂
34	JEFF;	[Three point nine.]
35	PRET;	[Three point]₂ nine nine nine.
36	MEGAN;	[Right]₃ but,
37	JEFF;	[Right.]₃
38	TANYA;	So who's the highest that's ever been yours.
39	JEFF;	Three point nine five.

40	TANYA;	Yeah.
41	JEFF;	Mhmm.
(. . .)		
53	TANYA;	(interview with Jeff) I really like,
54		Their danger scale.
55		I like to kinda be able to gauge where he's at there.

The men explain that a 4.0 on the scale would include action (lines 2–13), and therefore is reserved in their minds only for their wives, but that there are men tempting enough to get dangerously close to that level of desire, such as Pret's inclusion of the possibility of a 3.999 (line 35). When pressed, Jeff also explains the highest number he's experienced (lines 38–39); in the elided lines, he tells a quick story of being at the gym and seeing someone he describes as looking just like Superman, which Tanya confirms is a source of his extreme attraction. When the camera shot switches to an interview with Tanya and Jeff immediately after this exchange, Tanya responds in lines 54–55 that the danger scale is useful not only for the men to discuss their attractions in a way that expresses desire without acting on it, but it also provides the wives a way to understand and "gauge" where they are regarding particular individuals and experiences. There is also a sense that, while Jeff insists that "women can be on the danger scale too," (line 17) which Tanya questions the validity of, it is primarily used as an outlet to express their SSA orientations and maintain their community bonds through shared experiences and also accountability.

5 Reactions to "My Husband's Not Gay"

Due to its perceived controversial subject matter, "My Husband's Not Gay" garnered a lot of public attention. This included both news coverage of the show itself as well as op-eds and opinion pieces about the show's material and the subject matter it covered. Notably, the Gay and Lesbian Alliance Against Defamation (known as GLAAD) reacted very strongly to the special, insisting that it was a step back from the progress made in spreading a "born this way" approach to gay sexualities and claiming the episode was dangerous to LGBTQ youth by equating the premise of the show to reparative therapy. As part of this reaction, GLAAD president Sarah Kate Ellis was quoted as saying, "No one can change who they love, and more importantly, no one should have to. By investing in this dangerous programming, TLC is putting countless young LGBT people in harm's way" (Whitehurst 2015).

For the individuals in the show, the struggles of balancing their religious values with same-sex attraction, negotiating their personal lives in public spaces, and justifying their sexual identities to others reveal the difficulty that individuals with non-traditional sexual interests face – even when they exist within otherwise traditional settings such as a heterosexual marriage and within a conservative religious community. Despite consistent ideologies in the SSA community that reject the ascription of other sexuality labels like gay and bisexual to their experiences, public discussions surrounding the documentary and the men themselves were almost exclusively in opposition to their self-proclamations of SSA as a valid identity.

One news article collected for this project was written for *The Atlantic*, an American literary and cultural commentary magazine that frequently addresses political issues. The article, "The profound lack of empathy in 'My Husband's Not Gay'," was written by Emma Green and published the day after the show aired. Green's piece claims that the portrayal of men with same-sex attraction living happy lives despite not identifying as gay hides the "pain that likely defines those men's lives" (Green 2015, 1). Ultimately, Green argues that, despite her criticisms, the show should have aired because the controversy stems from "a sign of just how far gay rights have come in America." Specifically, she notes that the outcry against the show emerges from LGBTQ advocates' fear that representations of the religious stance "that says being and acting gay is a sin" might cause harm (Green 2015, 3).

Additionally, Green takes a strong view that the show focuses only on male agency, leaving women stuck in "traditional roles in their relationships" where "[t]hey're defined by the men in their lives" (Green 2015, 2). Green's stance suggests a separate level of agency and identity provided by religion more broadly: To Green, Mormonism grants agency more directly to men than women. Comments by the wives such as Megan's statement that "he chose me out of all the women . . . and all the men!" are seen by Green as feeble attempts to justify their role in a relationship with someone who is married to them but isn't attracted to them. In this viewpoint, then, those in such relationships – both the men and women – are constrained by the tenets of their religious dogma that prevents them from expressing their gay identities, which ideologically removes the agency these men are linguistically claiming through self-identification. However, this view fails to recognize the pre-existing possibilities of bi- or pansexual individuals in straight-passing relationships that could already conceptually exist within the tenets of the Mormon faith. In fact, Example 2 highlights Curtis' awareness of this possibility by explicitly mentioning bisexuality as a possibility that he also rejects in the construction and discussion of his same-sex attraction.

The comments that accompany Green's article, however, tend to remove agency from both the men and the women in the episode. While the wives (and women in general) are rarely even mentioned, essentially removing them from the conversation entirely, the men's identity is most frequently constructed as different than what they claim it to be. Thus, commentary tends to diverge from Green's assertion of men having all of the agency while aligning with her ideas that the men are "hiding their pain" by challenging their self-assertion of their identity as uniquely different than homosexuality or bisexuality.

The commenters do this by frequently insisting that attraction toward men equates to homosexuality, or at least bisexuality by default. This challenge is seen quite explicitly in several reader comments made on articles written about the show such as, "If it looks like a duck and quacks like a duck, he's gay," "So he's bisexual. People forget that bisexuality exists," or "A Mormon who's 'not gay' but is gay, kinda." In these proclamations, the men's sexuality is defined by essentialized 'truths' that others assign based on their impressions of these individuals; attempts by the men themselves to define their own sexuality, such as the "Not gay, SSA" mantra espoused in the episode, are rejected by these commenters, who insist that the men are still at least "kinda" gay.

6 Discussion

Ideologies about what sexual identity is and how it can be assigned illustrates the struggle faced by individuals who do not align themselves with established norms of sexual identity and orientation, and who must then justify and legitimate their own sexuality in relation to these norms. This presents a challenge to the men in "My Husband's Not Gay," who attempt to create a unique category of identification with which to align themselves, as even in doing so they are not given credence or support for having such an identification. For those individuals who acknowledge same-sex attraction yet seek a highly heteronormative lifestyle, the struggle to gain acceptance for their differences, both among their religious peers and in the public eye, is a difficult path in the face of ideologies that run in direct opposition to their lived experiences.

Despite these challenges, the men take steps not only to dismiss these external assertions about their identity but also to create, claim, and use their own novel identity label of SSA. The validity of this identity label is established through examples in the TV special such as self-identifying as SSA, referring to the "SSA community," and creating distinctions between SSA and other established sexuality labels. Challenging such established systems through the creation of a new one is a highly agentive act that is crucially language-dependent. People who experience same-sex attraction can and often do 'pass' as heterosexual by living within normative structures such as traditional marriage and the nuclear family. It is through language that SSA is established as an identity category in and of itself, and the discourses surrounding the term and the experience of SSA provide an outlet for the expression of this new form of identity.

While this identity formation agentively challenges established sexuality labels, the backdrop of religion in this particular setting complicates the men's agentive capacity. In particular, SSA-identified men are constrained in both in their actions and identities, as the Mormon church prohibits them from acting upon their same-sex attractions and from identifying as gay – whether or not they may even want to. In many ways, these are self-imposed constraints on their agency, thus adding another layer of complexity to the construction of their identity and sexuality. Importantly, however, despite mixed levels of acceptance from the public and the very indoctrinated homophobic policies of the Mormon church, the men and their families continue to linguistically negotiate their own "alternative to an alternative" lifestyle.

Crucially, this analysis shows a process by which the creation of an identity category such as SSA demonstrates a queering of sexuality. In the example presented here, highly religious individuals discursively define their sexuality in a way that not only maintains adherence to their values but also validates alternative forms of sexual expression. Through the men's reactions to the norms of their church, the heteronormative expectations of their relationships, and their rejection of other sexual identity categories and the lifestyles associated with them, these individuals create a new identity category that works both within and on the margins of normative understandings of sexual orientation, sexual identity, and sexual practice. For those who embody or are allied with LGBTQ identities, the desire to support homonormative ideologies of being 'born this way' and needing to 'find one's true self' can interfere with the ability to validate individuals who acknowledge same-sex attraction without a desire to act on it due to personal and religious values that constrain such actions. At the same time, these personal and religious constraints provide a way to construct a distinct sexual identity while maintaining a lifestyle that is seen as traditional through religious marital institutions.

Throughout the analysis presented here, understandings of sexuality and sexual identity were challenged and queered by the complications faced by this group of men. In "My Husband's Not Gay," the men had identity claims that can be seen as being "practically straight," in which the men maintained a heterosexual lifestyle while also acknowledging additional aspects of the sexual self in their desires or attraction toward other men. This complexity illustrates the queering of sexuality as well as understandings of sexual identity categories, because for these men, identity categories are constructed as useful points of reference without being bound to the limited nature of being "boxed" into a particular category. This perspective challenges both the essentialized sexual ideologies found in mainstream society while also acknowledging the semiotic associations with such categories, as seen in the men's manipulation and negotiation of the labels and the ideals represented by such labels in constructing their own sense of the sexual self. In this way, it is specifically through language that this construction and negotiation takes place. In the agentive absence of action on sexual interest and desire, their identities as *being* or *having* SSA are only seen in their linguistic interactions and descriptions and rely on their rejection of existing sexual identity labels and their use of a novel categorization to situate themselves in the complexities of sexuality.

A final factor emerges in theorizing sexuality more broadly: for these men, the complicated nature of their sexualities works to both employ and challenge established sexuality labels such as straight, gay, bisexual, and others. In many ways, this exhibits a queering of sexuality that pushes beyond labels while still employing them as a reference both for their own identity presentations as well as the variations on them that they portray in their lives. Thus, despite not identifying as "queer" themselves, the linguistic and semiotic resources employed by these men prove useful for furthering a "theoretically queer" understanding of what queerness is, how it can be studied, and how to analyze constructions of sexuality in ways that recognize the usefulness of using the term *queer* as an umbrella term for all non-normative sexual experiences, while acknowledging the limitations of placing a label on individuals who many not themselves identify as queer. Queerness can be seen in theoretical terms as a process employed to break from or negotiate around established categorizations of sexuality regardless of whether it becomes used as a label itself. Understanding how sexuality can be read as queer even among men who claim a heterosexual lifestyle is crucial to expanding the way that language, gender, and sexuality scholars explore categories of identification and groups of individuals who construct unique sexualities outside of the realm of a queer identity.

References

Boellstorff, Tom 2011. But do not identify as gay: A proplectic genealogy of the MSM category. *Cultural Anthropology* 26(2). 287–312.

Bogetic, Ksenija. 2013. Normal straight gays: Lexical collocations and ideologies of masculinity in personal ads of Serbian gay teenagers. *Gender and Language* 7(3). 333–367.

Boswell, John. 1980. *Christianity, social tolerance, and homosexuality: Gay people in Western Europe from the beginning of the Christian Era to the Fourteenth Century*. Chicago: University of Chicago Press.
Chirrey, Deborah A. 2003. 'I hereby come out': What sort of speech act is coming out? *Journal of sociolinguistics* 7(1). 24–37.
Church of Jesus Christ of Latter-Day Saints (LDS). 2011. Chapter 39: The Law of Chastity. *Gospel Principles*. 224–232.
Church of Jesus Christ of Latter-Day Saints (LDS). 2012. Same-Sex Attraction. *LDS Church Perspective on Chastity*. Retrieved: 1 Nov 2015. (https://www.lds.org/topics/same-gender-attraction?lang=eng#print)
Copen, Casey E., Anjani Chandra & Isaedmarie Febo-Vazquez. 2016. Sexual behavior, sexual attraction, and sexual orientation among adults aged 18–44 in the United States: Data From the 2011–2013 National Survey of Family Growth. *National health statistics reports* no 88. Hyattsville, MD: National Center for Health Statistics.
DiDomizio, Nicolas. 2016. A surprising number of straight men are having sex with other men, says the CDC. Published 8 January, 2016. *Mic Network*. Retrieved 1 June, 2016. (https://mic.com/articles/132129/a-surprising-number-of-straight-men-are-having-sex-with-other-men-says-the-cdc#.Eoqqa5vEl)
DuBois, John W., Susan Cumming, Stephen Schuetze-Coburn & Danae Paolino. 1993. Outline of discourse transcription. In Jane Edwards & Martin D. Lampert (eds.), *Talking data: Transcription and coding in discourse research*. 45–89. Hillsdale, NJ: Lawrence Erlbaum.
Eckert, Penelope and Sally McConnell-Ginet. 1992. Think practically and look locally: Language and gender as community-based practice. *Annual review of anthropology* 21(1). 461–488.
Green, Emma. 2015. The profound Lack of Empathy in *My Husband's Not Gay*. Published 12 January 2015, The Atlantic. Retrieved: 26 January 2015. (http://www.theatlantic.com/entertainment/archive/2015/01/the-profound-lack-of-empathy-in-my-husbands-not-gay/384414/)
Greenberg, David F. & Marcia H. Bystryn. 1982. Christian intolerance of homosexuality. *American Journal of Sociology* 88(3). 515–548.
Kimball, Spencer. 1964. A Counselling problem in the church. *Address to Seminary and Institute Faculty*, 10, July 1964. Provo, Utah: BYU.
Kinsey, Alfred C., Wardell B. Pomeroy & Clyde E. Martin. 1949. Sexual behavior in the human male. *The Journal of Nervous and Mental Disease* 109(3). 283.
Kitzinger, Celia & Sue Wilkinson. 1995. Transitions from heterosexuality to lesbianism: The discursive production of lesbian identities. *Developmental Psychology* 31(1). 95–104.
Lave, Jean, and Etienne Wenger. 1991. *Situated learning: Legitimate peripheral participation*. Cambridge university press.
LGBTQ Nation. 2016. CDC Survey: A surprising number of heterosexual men have had gay sex. Published 7 January, 2016. *LGBTQ Nation*. Retrieved 1 June, 2016. (http://www.lgbtqnation.com/2016/01/cdc-survey-a-surprising-number-of-heterosexual-men-have-had-gay-sex/)
Oaks, Dallin H. 1984. *Principles to govern possible public statement on legislation affecting rights of homosexuals*. Manuscript on Homosexuality by LDS leader. Retrieved 21 July 2016. (http://www.ldspapers.faithweb.com)
Oaks, Dallin H. 1995. Same-gender attraction. *Ensign Magazine*, October.
Schow, Ron. L. & Wayne Schow. 1991. *Peculiar people: Mormons and same-sex orientation*. Salt Lake City: Signature Books.
Sedgwick, Eve 1990. *Epistemology of the closet*. Berkeley: University of California Press.
Thorne, Lisa. 2013. 'But I'm attracted to women': Sexuality and sexual identity performance in interactional discourse among bisexual students. *Journal of Language and Sexuality* 2(1). 70–100.

VanderStouwe, Chris. 2019. "'Straight-ish': Agency, constraints, and the linguistic negotiation of identity and desire in online personal advertisements among men seeking men" *Gender and Language* 13(1). 122–145.

Ward, Jane. 2008. Dude-sex: White masculinities and 'authentic' heterosexuality among dudes who have sex with dudes. *Sexualities* 11(4). 414–434.

Ward, Jane. 2015. *Not gay: Sex between straight white men*. New York: New York University Press.

Whitehurst, Lindsay. 2015. Gay advocates assail new TV show 'My Husband's Not Gay'. Published: 7 January 2015, Yahoo! TV. Retrieved: 26 January 2015. (https://www.yahoo.com/tv/s/gay-advocates-assail-tv-show-husbands-not-gay-172733674.html)

Zimman, Lal. 2009. 'The other kind of coming out': Transgender people and the coming out narrative genre. *Gender and Language* 3(1). 53–80.

Dominique A. Canning
Unbreakable
What Titus Andromedon teaches us about race, sexuality, and intersectionality in sociolinguistics

1 Introduction

As a field, sociolinguistics has focused on a number of varieties and styles, often connecting styles to different identities or personas (Eckert 2008; Podesva et al. 2002). One such style, gay men's speech, has been a topic of interest since the early 20th Century, with research initially focusing on sexual vocabulary and signs of "gender deviance" in gay men's language (Barrett 2006, p. 317). While contemporary sociolinguistic research has shifted towards questions around structural and social properties of gay men's speech, this research has often focused on a particular type of gay speaker – white, middle class, and English speaking – leading to an unintentional flattening of what constitutes gay sounding speech (GSS) (Podesva 2007). Similar claims have been made about the study of African American Language (AAL) and African American Vernacular English (AAVE).[1] While widely studied, research on AAL has, often strategically, assumed a uniformity of the variety and its speakers (Wolfram 2007). The two varieties have been studied in interaction, most notably in Barrett's (1998, cited in Barrett 2017) work on African American Drag Queens, in which drag queens alternated between features of white women's speech and AAVE to index social class, gender, and race in their performances.

Language research has also focused on media, which is widely accessible and acts as a means to spread linguistic features and ideologies, as well as social information and expectations (Bednarek 2010; Queen 2015). Using the Netflix show *Unbreakable Kimmy Schmidt* as an example, the present study aims to further understand the complexity of language and the role of indexicality in identity performance as it occurs in popular media.

---

1 I primarily use *AAVE* to refer to the language variety (or varieties) described by linguists as being characterized by a particular set of linguistic features, while AAL is used as an umbrella term for language used by African American communities more generally (Lanehart et al. 2015, 3).

Dominique A. Canning, University of Michigan

1.1 Andromedon, Burgess, & Unbreakable Kimmy Schmidt

In March of 2015, Netflix premiered *Unbreakable Kimmy Schmidt*, a show about a woman (Kimmy) discovering the world after spending her teen and adult life in an underground bunker. Despite its set up, the show is billed as a combination of comedy and drama. Kimmy moves to New York City from Durnsville, Indiana, where she meets Titus Andromedon, a Black gay man trying to make it in show business. *Unbreakable Kimmy Schmidt* ended in January 2019 after four seasons.

Though Andromedon is a side character in the first season, he is a clear fan favorite, known for his songs, catchphrases, and over the top personality. (Some Andromedon highlights include his Season 1 song *Peeno Noir* and an homage to Beyonce's *Lemonade* in Season 3.) Tituss Burgess, the actor who portrays Andromedon, parallels his character in some ways. He identifies as gay, is from a Southern state (Georgia, while Andromedon is from Mississippi), and has had a successful career as a performer, both on and off Broadway.

This study uses media as a lens through which linguistic and social identities can be examined by analyzing and comparing the language between Andromedon and Burgess. Though Andromedon's lines are scripted, the performance of those lines relies in part on Burgess' understanding of not just Andromedon as a character, but also on his own understanding of Black gay identity and language. Every person involved with bringing *Unbreakable Kimmy Schmidt* and its characters to life carries their own social positioning, biases, and expectations, which then impact how they decide a character's speech, behavior, and appearance should be portrayed. And, while this study does discuss Andromedon and Burgess as if they are two separate people, they are performed by the same person. This, along with the parallels between actor and character discussed above, provides an opportunity to observe how a single speaker may avoid or enhance linguistic features when indexing a Black gay male identity in different contexts.

2 Background

2.1 Language & media

In a field that is particularly interested in naturalistic speech, it may seem strange to focus on media for linguistic research. TV shows and films are highly scripted situations, very far from the spontaneous communication many sociolinguists are interested in (Bednarek 2010). This is a valid observation, but it does not discredit the valuable insight that can be gained from examining television and other scripted media. Media does not exist separately from the society in which it is created; writers bring their social experience to their scripts, and actors use their own social knowledge to portray their characters (Bednarek 2010). These creations are then watched by millions of viewers around the world, who then discuss the story and the characters with each other, adding their own social knowledge to the mix (Bednarek 2010). Media can also tell us about the societal hierarchies that are in place at the time of creation, particularly in the case of marginalized groups.

Black characters in American television shows made up only 13% of the total number of 813 series regulars in the 2014–2015 season (GLAAD 2014,17). Of the total 813 regulars, only 32 (4%) were LGBT identified (GLAAD 2014, 4). In the same season, there were 105 regular and recurring[2] LGBT characters announced, and of these characters, specifically Black LGBT characters made up 10%, compared to white LGBT characters who made up 66% (GLAAD 2014, 18). The low number of Black, LGBT, and Black LGBT characters requires considering not only whether an identity is being represented on screen, but also what sorts of representations are considered acceptable and available (Kohnen 2016). This motivates the use of more stereotypical representations that reinforce often harmful societal norms, stereotypes, and expectations (Bucholtz & Lopez 2011; Queen 2015).

Bucholtz and Lopez (2011) discuss stereotypical representations of Blackness through the use of AAVE by white actors in American film. This usage of AAVE is described as "linguistic minstrelsy," calling back to a time of blackface performances (Bucholtz & Lopez 2011, 681). The purpose of this linguistic minstrelsy, frequently paired with visual cues of stereotypical Black masculinity, is often to highlight a (usually) white male character's inauthentic and inadequate performance of a masculine "hip-hop" identity (Bucholtz & Lopez 2011). "Mock AAE" was found to favor the most stereotypical phonological features of the variety, as well as features that are considered generally non-standard such as nasal fronting (Bucholtz & Lopez 2011, 686). Grammatical features of "mock AAE" were found to be simplified and used less frequently compared to real-life examples of AAVE use (Bucholtz & Lopez 2011). The grammatical features that *did* appear were often used incorrectly, as is the often case with habitual *be,* or may be altogether ungrammatical in AAVE (Bucholtz & Lopez 2011; Queen 2015).

Gay characters in media have historically been restricted in different ways than Black characters. The creation of the Hollywood Production Code (also called

---

2 "Recurring characters" are characters who are not in every episode of a TV show, but who do appear from time to time throughout the season or series (Epstein 2006). Season regulars are characters who appear in all episodes.

the Hays Code) in 1934 limited the representation of heterosexual intimacy on screen and outright banned the explicit representation of "transgressive" relationships, such as interracial and same-sex romance (Kohnen 2016, 44). Banning the explicit representation of gay relationships led to "connotative" representations, such as men who were "too feminine" or women who were "too masculine"(Kohnen 2016, 47), a pattern that still exists despite the original Hays Code being replaced by the MPAA Rating System in 1968. For example, Cartei and Reby (2012) found that actors playing gay male characters pitched their voices higher and used more pitch variation than when playing straight male characters, an effect that was exaggerated in comedy films (87). These performances of gender and sexuality, however, do not account for aspects of race.

Kohnen (2016) discusses the intersection between race and sexuality in the media, focusing primarily on the fact that there is very little. Drawing from previous work by Eve Kosofsky Sedgwick on the Closet as a regulating force for how queer knowledge is filtered and circulated through culture, Kohnen proposes the term "Closet as screen," which highlights the use of the screen as both a "projecting and filtering" of queerness and queer knowledge (2016, 3). "Closet as screen" leads to the projection of queerness onto the "blank surface" of whiteness (2016, 12), marking racialized queerness as further deviant within an already marginalized community. This further constrains the representation of queer characters of color.

For example, many early gay characters in Black media were stereotypically masculine and reified homonormative[3] ideologies, purposefully positioning typically masculine Black gay men as normal, "regular guys" in opposition to characters whose gender expression deviated from normative masculinity (Martin 2015). This tension between gay identity, masculinity, and Blackness may manifest in which linguistic styles are used by a character. This may motivate the avoidance of AAVE by a Black character whose gay identity does not include normative performances of masculinity. This avoidance of AAVE may lead to higher use of Mainstream US English (MUSE) and GSS, which are both styles highly associated with whiteness. These linguistic performances are just one way that Black queer identity may become less about Blackness and more about projecting an acceptable queerness onto a blank slate.

---

3 *Homonormativity* refers to "a politics that does not contest dominant heteronormative assumptions and institutions, but upholds and sustains them" (Duggan 2003, qtd in Martin 2015, 653).

2.2 African American Vernacular English & gay sounding speech

Though these two styles have been widely studied, they are most frequently studied as indexing separate, isolated identities. While this does allow for the identification of features particular to each style, it does not provide information on how these styles may interact within an individual's life, or which features are salient in different contexts.

Research on GSS has focused primarily on white gay men, following a common positioning of gay identity as white by default (Cornelius 2016, 40; Johnson 2005, 4). This association between whiteness and gayness (and more broadly queerness) is likely motivated by a long tradition of excluding minoritized populations from research and academia, tensions between fields and their ideologies, and by the conceptualization of which identities are considered "marked" compared to others. An example of this is seen in Queer Studies, where many argued that much of the work being done in the field failed to account for race as a dimension of oppression (Johnson 2005, 4). At the same time, scholars outside of queer studies had analyses that incorporated race, exploitation, and oppression, but avoided discussions of sexuality and heteronormativity (Cohen 1997, 443). These and similar situations led to the creation of fields such as *Quare Studies* and *Black Queer Studies,* which directly tied experiences of racial oppression to those linked to classism, heterosexism, homophobia, and transphobia (Cohen 1997; Johnson 2005). Linguistics has followed this trend towards interdisciplinary research through the creation of fields like raciolinguistics, queer linguistics, and trans linguistics, among others.

Within sociolinguistics, the focus on white gay men's speech is likely also driven in part by the racialization of MUSE and other standardized forms as "white language," and its speakers as the unmarked norm to which speakers of other language varieties are compared (Flores & Rosa 2015, 150). This variety is also quietly connected specifically to *men's* speech, with questions around gender and language originally focusing on the ways women *didn't* speak like men (Eckert & McConnell-Ginet 2003, 188; Gal 1995, 171). Gender performance was also a key motivation for research on gay men's speech, as seen in the focus on "deviant" linguistic features that inadequately indexed white American masculinity (Barrett 2006, 317). These ideologies around language, gender, and race impacted AAVE research, providing a basis for the prototypical AAVE speaker: young Black men who lived in larger cities (King 2020; Wolfram 2007). In this case, the main marked feature was the speakers' Blackness, not necessarily their presumed gender or sexuality. These single-axis approaches to identity and language research have resulted in the unintentional exclusion of several demographics of speakers, but most relevantly to this chapter, it has led to frequent exclusion of Black gay men.

That's not to say AAVE hasn't been studied in relation to gay identity. Barrett (2017) discusses his past research on the language of African American Drag Queens (AADQs), where the humor in performances done by the AADQs often relied on switching between AAVE and a middle-class white women's style. This alternation involved using features from both varieties; for example, one commonly used tactic was the use of careful, hyperstandard phonology and AAVE phonology (47). Though there was some overlap between the AADQs and Black gay men in the area, Barrett notes that the stereotypical women's speech used among AADQs was not as common among the gay Black men he observed (2017, 47).

Cornelius & Barrett (2020) discuss pressures faced by gay Black men as they move through Black spaces and gay spaces. Within Black spaces, homophobia and concepts of "appropriate" masculinity lead to the policing of certain linguistic and behavioral features deemed "too feminine" (Cornelius & Barrett 2020, 325). An overt form of linguistic policing and awareness can be seen in "marking," in which ". . . speakers take on caricatures or dramatized personas of the victim (or referent) to make fun of them" (Cornelius & Barrett 2020, 325). Features often mocked in marking are the "gay lisp", higher pitch, and gestures like hair flipping, dramatic hip swinging, and finger snapping (325).

In white gay spaces, Black gay men face (often hypersexualized) racism and stereotyping, while once again navigating spaces where their racial and sexual identities are considered separate and opposing. There's also the issue of appropriation of Black language by white gay men, partially due to popularization of shows like *RuPaul's Drag Race*, and through the adoption of a "sassy Black woman" persona, allowing white gay men to perform a form of femininity that doesn't conform to normative expectations of (white) femininity (Cornelius & Barrett 2020, 327). To discourage racism, stereotyping, and appropriation, some gay Black men may avoid using AAVE features in white gay spaces. However, there are of course some Black gay men who embrace the various roles and stereotypes, especially if they feel they align with their sense of self (328).

Regardless of how they position themselves, Black gay men are often required to be able to shift between different linguistic styles depending on their environment and identity presentation. For example, Cornelius & Barrett (2020) find that Bakari, a Black gay man, displays a continuum of features related to AAVE and GSS while speaking about his own identities. Though Bakari moves closer to GSS – raising his pitch and using more standardized forms – when talking about his sexuality, he also increasingly uses features of AAVE over the course of the interview (Cornelius & Barrett 2020, 332). Cornelius & Barrett, along with

Bakari's own explanations, suggest that to keep himself safe, Bakari moves *between* his identities, not fully "choosing" one or the other (333).

2.3 Language, identity, and performance

This chapter builds upon linguistic approaches to the study of marginalized identities, specifically Blackness and gayness, as they coexist within a single individual. Studying the intersection of identities is intrinsic to the application of identity research to real world situations. Kimberlé Crenshaw (1989) calls attention to this in her discussion and application of *intersectionality*, or the interaction of oppression based on two or more marginalized identities, within legal studies. While describing Black women's difficulties in legally challenging workplace discrimination as laws focus on either racial *or* gender discrimination, Crenshaw (1989) shows that one marginalized identity does not exist in isolation from another; rather, an individual's experiences of oppression based on one marginalized identity may be compounded by another, while also influencing how a person portrays their sense of self to the world.

The need for this application of intersectionality as interacting forms of oppression has also been highlighted within sociolinguistics and discussions of variation. For example, Lanehart (2009) discusses the positioning of men and whiteness as the "norm," leading to the underrepresentation of Black women's language within sociolinguistics research, as white women represent prototypical women's speech and Black men represent prototypical Black American speech. Rickford & King (2016) show the role intersectionality played in the 2013 George Zimmerman trial as they analyze Rachel Jeantel's speech and discuss the reactions to her testimony. Despite Jeantel being the star witness in the case, she and her testimony were discredited and disregarded as people instead focused on her perceived lack of linguistic ability. Though Rickford & King discuss that there *may* have been a genuine intelligibility issue for those who were unfamiliar with the language varieties Jeantel spoke, they also call attention to how the public's perception of Jeantel was likely motivated by structural racism, classism, sexism, and other existing negative stereotypes and ideologies around Black women and Black language (2016, 971–978).

In this study, intersectionality is assumed to contribute to differences in understandings of identity and identity performance, particularly between Black and white gay men. For example, the ways a Black gay man performs his gayness is likely to be influenced by his Blackness and vice versa, resulting in a different kind of gayness (and/or a different kind of *indexing* of gayness) than would be performed by a white gay man or a straight Black man. This portrayal of identity comes through social and cultural cues such as clothing, embodiment, and most relevantly to this chapter, language. The intersection between language, personal identity, and group membership have long been considered promoting factors in language variation within a community (e.g., Eckert 1989, 2008; Labov 1972). Though often discussed in regard to production, social information and social *expectation*, in tandem with social identity, have also been shown to influence the way speakers perceive their own and others' language (e.g., Craft, Wright, Weissler & Queen 2020; Niedzielski 1999).

2.4 Indexicality & style

The linguistic construction of identity is often attributed to the use of a particular style of speech coinciding with an identity. Though *style* has a range of definitions and usages throughout sociolinguistics, its use in this chapter parallels the definition given in Podesva et al. (2002), in which they define style as the "... situational use of linguistic resources ... to negotiate one's place in the local communicative context as well as in society in general" (178). This definition is especially relevant to this paper, where the two linguistic styles in question (i.e., AAVE & GSS) are both associated with socially marginalized communities. Social marginalization may act as a motivating factor in the use of less obvious cues (linguistic or otherwise) to index one's group membership and may also motivate a more complex usage of features as the speaker moves between interlocutors and environments.

Sociolinguistics, at its core, looks to describe the relationship between language and society through a linguistics framework. Unfortunately, this does often mean that nuanced social explanations for linguistic variation may be oversimplified or overlooked altogether. This issue of nuanced explanation was addressed in one way through Michael Silverstein's (2003) proposal of *indexical order*, a way to relate "... the micro-social to the macro-social frames of analysis of any sociolinguistic phenomenon" (193). This approach more clearly provides a connection between the broader societal structures in place and the association of linguistic features with certain locations, cultures, or social identities.

Eckert (2008) expands Silverstein's proposal through the use of an *indexical field*, a "constellation of ideologically related meanings, any one of which can be activated in the situated use of the variable" (454). This allows a variable, such as word-final aspirated /t/ release, to index more than one meaning – articulateness, intelligence, but also annoyance and even "prissiness." These meanings are then applied to the context in which the variable is used. For example, aspirated /t/ release, when used by a group of nerd girls in high school may index intelligence (Bucholtz 2001), while when used by a gay man, aspirated /t/ release may be part of a diva persona built on a perception of "prissiness" and elegance (Podesva 2007).

The aim of this chapter is not to assign a social identity to the use of a particular feature, but to explore the complex relationship between a set of features and the sociolinguistic contexts in which they are used. Additionally, this chapter aims to explore the combination and avoidance of certain linguistic features within identity performance. Through considering the construction of linguistic style as a type of "stylistic bricolage," rather than the work of a single variable, it is possible to explore how multiple styles and identities are navigated by a speaker in different contexts (Eckert 2004, 43; Eckert 2008, 456). Comparing Tituss Burgess' use of linguistic features in his performance as Titus Andromedon in episodes of *Unbreakable Kimmy Schmidt* to his use of language out of character in interviews has the potential to show just how linguistic features may work in tandem to index Black gay identity for one speaker in two very different contexts.

2.5 Features of gay sounding speech and African American Vernacular English

2.5.1 Gay sounding speech

The use of the term *gay sounding speech* (GSS) (Podesva, Roberts & Cambell-Kibler 2002, 176) is motivated by the recognition that there are many ways to "sound gay", as well as the recognition that there are many people who may "sound gay" while not actually identifying as such. That being said, there are features that have repeatedly been found to lead to percepts of gayness.

One such feature is the perception and production of sibilants, most frequently /s/. Previous sociophonetic perception research has observed connections between perception of a speaker's gender and the perception of sibilants (Munson 2011; Strand 1999). An example of this is seen in Munson (2011), who found that participants' perceptions of /s/ and /ʃ/ tokens changed based on whether they were shown a picture of a man or woman (2633). When paired with a male face, tokens were perceived as more /s/-like than when the same tokens were paired with a female face (Munson 2011, 2633).

Percepts of gayness have also been associated with the placement (fronting or backing), duration, and center of gravity for /s/ (Campbell-Kibler 2011). In her own study, Campbell-Kibler found that fronted /s/ increased perceptions of gayness while lowering perceptions of masculinity (2011, 58). Levon (2007) investigated the relationship between /s/ duration and pitch range as indexes of gay men's speech. Listeners' ratings of "gayness" changed from "extremely gay" to "gay" when pitch range was narrowed, regardless of whether sibilant durations were shortened, indicating that pitch range was working independently of sibilant duration in percepts of gayness (Levon 2007, 546). In ratings for masculinity, however, sibilant duration was only found to significantly affect percepts of masculinity in combination with pitch range; cases where sibilant duration was shortened *and* pitch range was narrowed were rated as significantly more masculine (Levon 2007, 545). The above research suggests that production and perception of sibilants can be affected by perceptions of gender, which then interact with ideologies around male sexuality, specifically the perceived masculinity of gay men.

Other phonemes addressed in relation to GSS are word-final stops. Most relevant to this paper is /t/, which in American English can be pronounced in a variety of ways word-finally (Zsiga 2013). This variation makes word-final released /t/ particularly interesting to the study of speech styles, where released /t/ has been shown to carry social meaning. For example, Bucholtz (2001) examines this feature as used by high-school nerd girls, who use hyperarticulation in their own speech to set themselves apart from their peers; while Benor (2004) examines its use by Orthodox Jewish men, where intelligence, specifically "learnedness," indexes masculinity (Benor 2004, cited in Podesva & Kajino 2014, 113). Higher rates of word-final voiceless stops (including released /t/) were also found in the speech of a lawyer for Lambda Legal in a radio debate about a gay-related topic than in his opponent (Podesva & Kajino 2014). In this case, the use of released consonants is suggested to have been used to perform a gayness that was not flamboyant but was still not straight. Like the nerd girls and the Orthodox Jewish men discussed above, the lawyer's use of released /t/ also indexed intelligence – in other words, this person speaks articulately because he is well-educated, but also happens to be gay (Podesva & Kajino 2014, 113).

Socially, it has often been assumed that gay men have higher pitched voices than their straight counterparts, but this has not been observed in linguistic research (Gaudio 1994; Podesva, Robert & Campbell-Kibler 2002). However, there have been findings that suggest a wider pitch range *does* carry percepts of gayness, most frequently when paired with other features, such as longer /s/ duration and greater pitch variation (Levon 2007). Voice quality must also be considered, as perceptions of creaky voice and falsetto rely on pitch information. Podesva's (2007) study of a gay man (Heath) found that creak and falsetto tended to co-occur in his participant's speech, suggesting that the two voice qualities were used in tandem to expand the vocal range in both directions (2007, 489).

2.5.2 African American Vernacular English

The study of African American Vernacular English has been intertwined with sociolinguistics since its earliest days, focusing on population-wide linguistic trends rather than on an individual's use of features. Early sociolinguistic research on AAVE was also based in affirming the systematicity of the language variety through comparisons to Mainstream US English (Lippi-Green 1997; Wolfram 2007), research often done in direct opposition to discrimination in education, housing, and criminal justice (Wolfram 2007, 293). In short, the purpose of early research on AAVE was to reinforce its validity as a language variety existing in a system that so heavily places value on an unattainable American English linguistic standard.

Though many features of AAVE are discussed in this paper as stylistic tools, the goal here is not to undermine or minimize the legitimacy of AAVE as a language variety. Instead, the goal is to show the complex interaction between linguistic features and identity in socially motivated speech. Much like gay sounding speech, the use of AAVE is argued to assist in the performance of Black identity, specifically a particularly *masculine* Black identity (Bucholtz 1999). As discussed above, this use of AAVE has also been employed by non-Black individuals to perform a type of hypermasculinity based on images of Blackness seen throughout American media.

2.5.3 Phonological features of AAVE

Though there are several phonological features within AAVE, only a small subset will be examined in this paper, which focuses primarily on consonant cluster reduction (CCR) and intonation, specifically the L+H* pitch accent.

Intonation, defined here as "the use of pitch and other suprasegmental features to convey discourse-level meaning" (Zsiga 2013, 392), has been a primary cue mentioned in the identification of AAVE speakers, even those who do not use other marked grammatical or phonological features (Spears 1988, cited in Holliday 2016). For example, participants in a 1972 study by Rickford found that for read phrases, listeners correctly identified the race of a reader 86% of the time (Rickford 1972, cited in Rickford & Rickford 2002, 102). Listeners cited inflection, intonation, timbre, and pitch variation as cues they used to identify speaker race (Rickford & Rickford 2002, 102). This supports the suggestion that something in AAVE prosody is saliently different from MUSE prosody, but what that *something* is has proved difficult to pin down (Thomas 2015).

Previous research has found that AAVE speakers may show differences in pitch at the end of yes/no questions, with some using a falling or level tone at the end of an intonational phrase (IP) where MUSE speakers would typically rise (Thomas 2015). Intonational differences have also been identified within the IP, particularly regarding the placement of pitch accents, which are used to mark prominence within a phrase (Beckman, Hirschberg & Shattuck-Hufnagel 2004; Thomas 2015). The high pitch accent (H*) in the final word of a yes/no question, for example, was placed at the onset of the word for AAVE speakers rather than in the final syllable, as was seen for MUSE speakers (Jun & Foreman 1996, cited in Thomas 2015).

A frequently explored pitch accent in AAVE research is the "sharp rise," or L+H* accent. The L+H* pitch accent in AAVE has been found to be used at a greater rate than in MUSE and in places where MUSE speakers would typically use the H* pitch accent (Thomas 2015). McLarty (2011), in examining change in AAVE over time, found that AAVE speaking men used more L+H* compared to AAVE speaking women and white American English speakers, regardless of the time of recording (cited in McLarty 2018). Focusing more on language and identity performance, Holliday (2016) examined the use of L+H* in the speech of Black/White Individuals (BWIs), finding that the participants who tended to shift between racial identities based on social context and those who identified as exclusively Black generally used fewer H* pitch accents than those who identified consistently as biracial. Further, the rates of H* and L+H* usage fluctuated for some speakers based on whether their interlocutor was Black or white (Holliday 2016). This research supports that, not only are there salient intonational differences between MUSE and AAVE, but that these differences are deployed stylistically depending on a speaker's goals and position within a conversation.

While the claim that AAVE speakers have either higher or lower F0 than MUSE speakers is unsupported, the use of a wider pitch range as been identified as a possible feature of AAVE (Thomas 2015). Use of a wider pitch range also includes the use of falsetto, though this usage has been argued to be used only in specific contexts, such as in competitive speech acts like *playing the dozens* and *signifying* (Morgan 1996; Thomas 2015). Much like in GSS, the use of falsetto may be acting as a tool for expanding the pitch range even further for increased dramatic effect. The use of creaky voice has been understudied in AAVE research, but it has been found in some cases that less jitter in a speaker's voice leads to higher perceptions of Blackness (Holliday & Villarreal 2019).

2.5.4 Grammatical features of AAVE

Grammatical features of AAVE are noticeably different from MUSE features and are often described as particularly marked relative to phonological features of

AAVE. These features are also prone to misinterpretation by MUSE speakers, particularly features that deal with tense and aspect. Only a subset of grammatical features that differ between MUSE and AAVE were part of the planned analysis in this study: habitual *be*, null copula, negative concord, and the omission of third-person singular and possessive *-s* (Rickford & Rickford 2002). These grammatical features will not be discussed at length in this chapter, due to their not being observed in the data.[4]

3 Research methodology

In this section, I first focus on the selection of the episodes that provided the data for Andromedon, then on the selection of the interviews that provided the data for Burgess. Then, I discuss the analyzed linguistic features and how they were identified and labelled. Finally, I present the predictions and results for the statistical analyses.

3.1 Data selection & analysis

The first set of data analyzed in this project comes from four episodes from the first season of *Unbreakable Kimmy Schmidt* and was used to examine Titus Andromedon's speech. Each episode was selected based on both Andromedon's presence and storyline in the episode and was edited to include only the scenes in which Andromedon was present. All episodes were released on Netflix in March 2015 ("Episode List," 2015). The chosen episodes were *Kimmy Goes Outside* (Episode 1), *Kimmy Kisses a Boy* (Episode 5), *Kimmy is Bad at Math* (Episode 8), and *Kimmy's in a Love Triangle* (Episode 10). Episode 1 was chosen because it is the episode in which the audience, through Kimmy, is first introduced to the character Titus Andromedon (Queen 2015). Both episodes 5 and 10 were chosen due to their dealing with gay identity in some way – episode 5 sees Andromedon trying to prove to Kimmy that her best friend's boyfriend is actually a gay man, and in episode 10, Andromedon hires a "straight coach" after being told that he is unable to pass as straight while acting. Episode 8 was chosen because of the way Andromedon interacts with his identity as a Black man, deciding to "live as a werewolf" after noticing

---

[4] Negative concord was the only grammatical AAVE feature observed in the data. It was used once by Burgess in the interview data, after Stephen Colbert asked if Burgess had any kids. Burgess' response was an emphatic, "I ain't got no kids."

differences in how he is treated by the people around him as he travels to work in his costume makeup. Though this interaction with race is brief and meant to be comedic, it is one of the few times in Season 1 where Andromedon's race is directly discussed. Each episode was categorized as either "gay" or "not gay" according to the overall theme of the episode's plot. Episodes 1 and 8 were categorized as "not gay," while episodes 5 and 10 were categorized as "gay." The combined length of analyzed episode data, excluding overlapping speech, was 26 minutes and 9 seconds. A summary of Andromedon's role in each episode, as well as the categorization and the analyzed video length, is available in Table 1 below.

Table 1: Episode Information.

Ep. #	Title	Summary	Theme	Video Length (m:ss)
1	"Kimmy Goes Outside!"	Titus and Kimmy meet and become roommates. Titus tries to convince Kimmy to leave New York City and return to Indiana.	Not Gay	7:50
5	"Kimmy Kisses a Boy!"	Titus is determined to prove that Kimmy's friend's boyfriend is a gay man pretending to be straight.	Gay	2:01
8	"Kimmy is Bad at Math!"	Titus, performing as a werewolf for his job at a spooky bar, decides to "live as a werewolf" after realizing he is treated better in costume than he is as a Black man.	Not Gay	8:36
10	"Kimmy's in a Love Triangle!"	Titus hires a straight coach after being passed over for a promotion at his job and is told the reason is because he doesn't "pass as straight."	Gay	7:42

The data for Tituss Burgess comes from two filmed interviews with the actor. The interviews were chosen based on availability and chronological similarity. The first interview, which took place on *The Late Show with Stephen Colbert* in September 2016, focused on *Unbreakable Kimmy Schmidt*, the upcoming Emmy Awards, and Burgess' upbringing and love of cooking. The second interview took place with the *LA Times* in May 2017 with Sarah Rodman and focused on the new season of *Unbreakable Kimmy Schmidt*, in addition to other aspects of Burgess' life as an entertainer. Due to a large difference in length between the interviews, only the middle 15 minutes of the *LA Times* interview was analyzed to better balance the samples, while still keeping the duration of the interview segments comparable to the duration of the analyzed segments from *Unbreakable Kimmy Schmidt*. Focusing solely on Burgess' speech, the combined length of analyzed interview data was

10 minutes and 54 seconds. Further information about the interviews is available in Table 2 below.

Table 2: Interview Information.

Title	Interviewer	Video Length (m:ss)
Lemonading with Tituss Burgess	Sarah Rodman	6:31
Tituss Burgess is Totally Crushing It!	Stephen Colbert	4:23

3.1.1 Analyzed features

Phonological features examined for AAVE were consonant cluster reduction (CCR) and pitch accents, most notably the L+H* pitch accent (Rickford & Rickford 2002; Thomas 2015). The features analyzed for gay-sounding speech were primarily phonological: aspirated /t/ release, word final /s/ duration and center of gravity, use of falsetto and creaky voice, and pitch range. Though wide pitch range has also been identified as a feature of AAVE in previous research (see Thomas 2015), it was analyzed here as a feature of GSS. This follows previous research on GSS linking pitch range with other features like creak and falsetto, which involve low and high pitch correlates (see Levon 2007; Podesva 2007).

The edited videos were all transcribed using ELAN 5.2 (Nijmegen 2017). After transcription, the videos were further annotated for grammatical features of AAVE. Once annotation was complete, acoustic annotation of phonological and prosodic features was done in Praat (Boersma & Weenink 2018). Acoustic analysis was used to determine pitch range and word final /s/ measurements, while ToBI analysis (described below, Beckman & Elam 1997) was used to determine pitch accents. Word-final aspirated /t/ release, monophthongization, and phonation type (creaky voice, modal voice, and falsetto) were coded perceptually. While CCR was also coded primarily by ear, all CCR tokens were double checked using the waveform provided in Praat to determine if both consonants were present.

3.1.2 Acoustic analysis

Pitch was measured in Hertz for all intonational phrases, determined by the presence of a pitch accent and boundary tone. Minimum, maximum, and mean pitch were extracted for all utterances. Sections containing creak or errors in the pitch track were omitted to prevent inaccuracies in pitch measurement. For similar reasons, overlapping speech and sections with background music were also omitted from the pitch analysis. Falsetto was not omitted from the pitch analysis, as it did not lead to errors in the pitch track in the way creaky voice did and so was considered part of the overall pitch range. Minimum, maximum, and mean pitch were recorded for all utterances across an episode or interview. An average minimum, maximum, and mean pitch were calculated for each video, and average pitch range (the variable of interest) was then found by subtracting the average minimum from the average maximum pitch across an episode or interview.

Pitch accents were coded using the Tone & Break Indices system for Mainstream American English (MAE_ToBI) (Beckman & Elam 1997). MAE_ToBI was used for prosodic analysis due to an unavailability of a ToBI system specific to AAVE, making MAE_ToBI the most relevant system available. Though phrase accents and boundary tones were coded, as were break indices, they were not considered in the final analysis. The boundary tone data was used primarily to determine intonational phrases. The pitch accents were labeled as L* (low), H* (high), !H* (down-stepped high), L+H*, and L*+H, using both the audio and pitch track in Praat. For periods with falsetto, maximum pitch was adjusted from 450Hz to 700Hz.

For /s/ measurements, only word-final tokens were considered to allow for comparisons to previous research on /s/ in GSS, which primarily focused on word-final and word-initial tokens. Word-final tokens were chosen as the focus due to there being a higher number of them in the data. Occurrences where /s/ was present word-finally as part of a reduced word-final consonant cluster were omitted, as were tokens that were immediately followed by a word-initial /s/. To avoid the effect of phrase-final lengthening, /s/ tokens that occurred at a phrase boundary were also omitted. All tokens were measured acoustically using Praat. Duration was measured by hand based on signs of frication and voicelessness in the waveform and concentration of energy at higher frequencies in the spectrogram (Ladefoged 2003). Center of gravity was measured at the midpoint of the token. It must also be noted here that some /s/ measurements were affected by the use of false teeth in episode 8. Though this didn't impact the overall findings, described in more detail below, some of the measurements do show differences.

3.2 Predictions and statistical analyses

Continuous data were analyzed using simple linear regression models, while categorical data were analyzed as rates of occurrence. Data comparisons discussed here were conducted based on video type (episode or interview), episode theme (gay or not gay), and interview (*Late Show* or *LA Times*). Rates of aspirated /t/-

release, consonant cluster reduction, phonation type (creaky, falsetto, modal), and pitch accents (H* and L+H*) were compared by video type, episode theme, and interview type. Linear regression models of pitch range and /s/ measurements were compared by the same categories. Two primary hypotheses will be discussed in this chapter. The first hypothesis it that all features will occur in both the *Unbreakable Kimmy Schmidt* episodes and in interviews, though at differing rates. Features associated with GSS are expected to occur more frequently in the *Unbreakable Kimmy Schmidt* episodes than in the interviews, due to Andromedon's gay identity being such a big part of his characterization. Second, features associated with AAVE are expected to occur less frequently in the *Unbreakable Kimmy Schmidt* episodes, based on findings of AAVE features acting as indexes for hypermasculinity in the media. Rates of features associated with AAVE and GSS are expected to vary based on episode theme. Episode themes categorized as "gay" are expected to show higher rates of GSS features and lower rates of AAVE features, again based on the indexing of hypermasculinity through use of AAVE, which directly contradicts Andromedon's gay identity in the show.

A third hypothesis addressing stylistic variation and convergence based on interview type was also examined but will not be discussed in this chapter, but the factor (interview type) remains part of the statistical analysis.

3.3 Results

All statistical tests were performed in R 3.5.0 (R Core Tea, 2018) using the *dplyr* (v0.7.6; Wickham, François, Henry, & Müller 2018), *lme4* (Bates, Maechler, Bolker & Walker 2015), and *psych* (v1.8.4; Revelle 2018) packages. The independent variables (video type, episode theme, and interview) were used to test all dependent variables, but in separate tests. The results are organized as follows. I first present the categorical data that showed no significant difference based on any of the independent variables: consonant cluster reduction, aspirated /t/ release, and pitch accent. The rest of the section focuses on the data that showed significant differences based on the independent variables: pitch range, /s/ duration and center of gravity, and phonation type.

3.3.1 Consonant cluster reduction, aspirated /t/ release, and pitch accent

There were no significant differences found in CCR, aspirated /t/ release, or pitch accent based on the independent variables. Figures 1–3 provide the raw counts for each feature by Episode & Theme. For proportions, please see Table 3. In all figures, the categories *Gay* and *Not Gay* represent the Show data (Andromedon's speech), while the category *None* represents the interview data (Burgess' speech).

Figure 1 provides the rates of CCR by Episode & Theme. All categories showed more occurrences of reduced clusters than unreduced clusters.

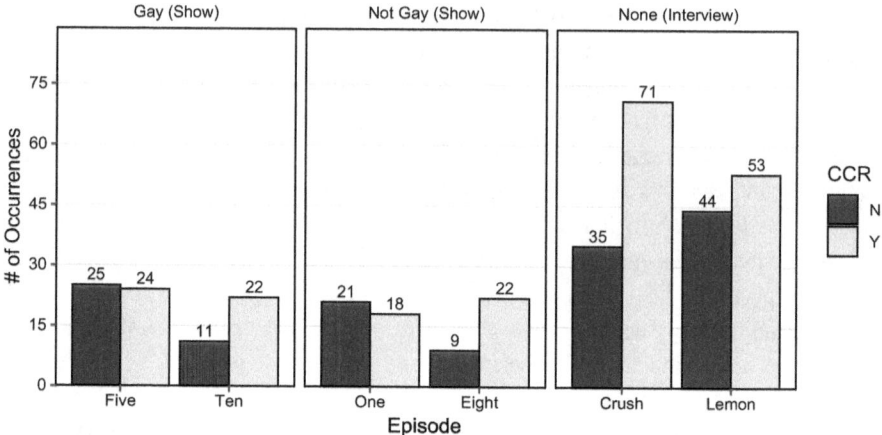

Figure 1: Rates of Consonant Cluster Reduction by Episode & Episode Theme (Raw Numbers).

Figure 2 shows the rates of word-final released /t/ by Episode & Theme. The categories are the same as in Figure 1. In all categories, word-final /t/ was unaspirated more frequently than it was aspirated.

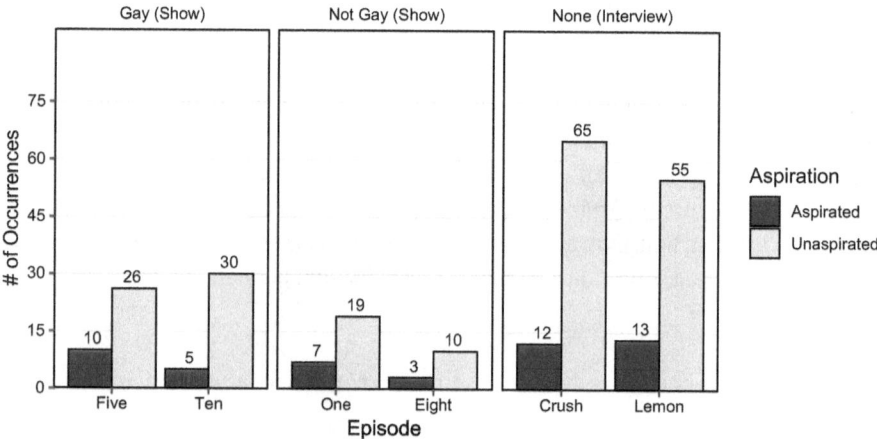

Figure 2: Rates of Word-Final Released /t/ by Episode & Episode Theme (Raw Numbers).

Figure 3 shows the rates of pitch accents H* and L+H* by Episode & Theme. In all categories, H* was used more frequently than L+H*. Between the Gay and Not

Gay categories, there was more use of L+H* in the Gay category, but differences were not significant by Episode Theme.

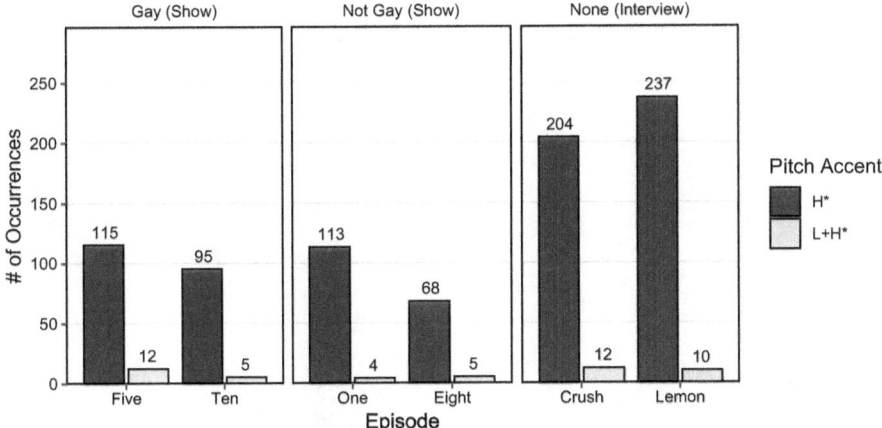

Figure 3: Rates of H* and L+H* by Episode & Episode Theme (Raw Numbers).

Table 3: Proportion of CCR, Aspirated /t/ Release, and Pitch Accent by Episode Theme & Video Type.

	CCR	Aspirated /t/ Release	Pitch Accent
Episode Theme	*Reduced*	*Aspirated*	*L+H**
Gay	.56	.21	.07
Not Gay	.57	.34	.05
None	.61	.17	.05
Video Type	*Reduced*	*Aspirated*	*L+H**
Interview	.61	.17	.05
Show	.57	.23	.06
Overall Mean	.59	.20	.06

3.3.2 Pitch range

Pitch range was analyzed using simple linear regression, with video type, episode theme, and interview as independent variables in three separate tests. Average pitch measurements do not include instances of creaky voice but do include falsetto. Video type was found to have a significant main effect on pitch range (F(1, 568) = 76.16, p < .0001) with an R^2 of .1182. Pitch range was predicted to be 64.42Hz larger in the *Unbreakable Kimmy Schmidt* episodes ('Show' type). Episode theme and interview were not found to be significant. Figure 4 provides average pitch measurements (in Hertz) by video.

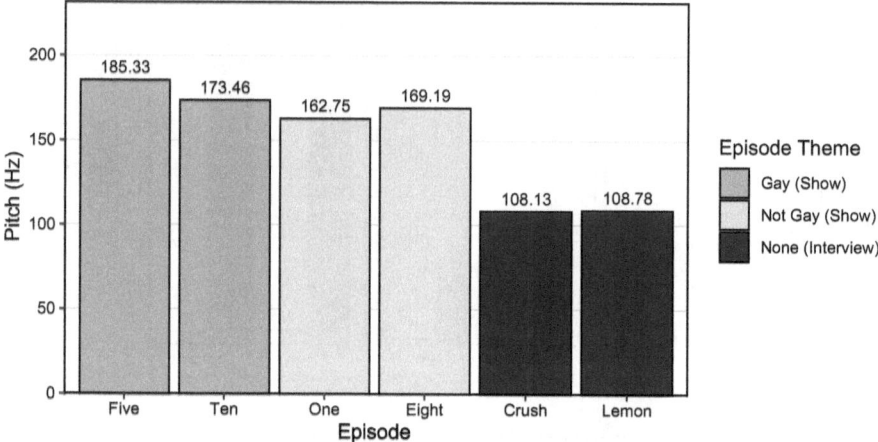

Figure 4: Average Pitch Measurements (in Hz) by Video.

3.3.3 /s/ measurements

Duration of /s/ was measured in milliseconds and analyzed using a simple linear regression. There were no significant differences in /s/ duration found based on video type, episode theme, or interview.

Center of gravity was measured in Hz and analyzed using a simple linear regression. Video type was found to have a significant effect on center of gravity ($F(1, 83) = 14.87$, $p < 0.0001$) with an R^2 of 0.1418. Center of gravity was predicted to rise 838.60Hz in the *Unbreakable Kimmy Schmidt* episodes ('Show' type). Episode theme and interview were not found to have a significant main effect on center of gravity measurements. Figures 5 and 6 provide a summary of /s/ measurement results, with Figure 5 showing average /s/ duration (in milliseconds) and Figure 6 showing average /s/ center of gravity (in Hertz) by video.

3.3.4 Phonation type

Phonation type was analyzed using a Chi Square Test of Independence, with phonation type analyzed as two categories: modal and non-modal, which included

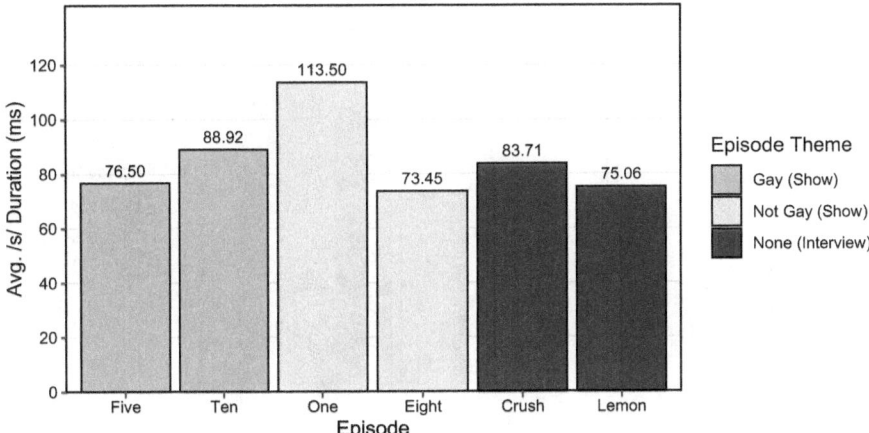

Figure 5: Average /s/ Duration by Video.

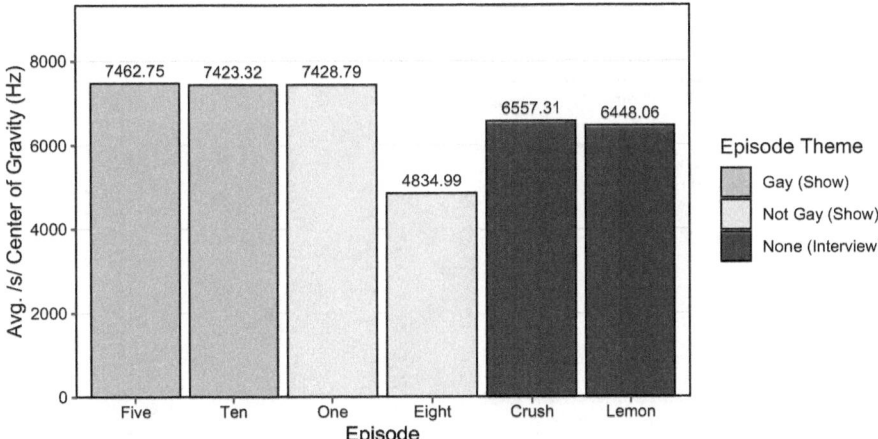

Figure 6: Average /s/ Center of Gravity by Video.

falsetto and creak. Since there were only a few instances of falsetto and creak, they were collapsed into one category to better compare rates of occurrence to modal voice. Differences between modal and non-modal phonation type were not found to be significant based on video type or episode theme. Figure 7 provides the raw counts of occurrences of modal and non-modal phonation type by Episode & Theme. Table 4 provides the proportions of phonation type by independent variables *Episode Theme* and *Video Type*.

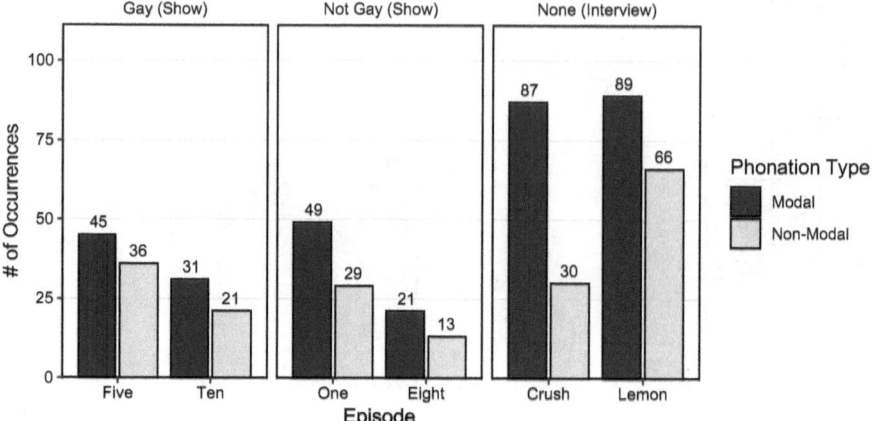

Figure 7: Phonation Type by Episode & Theme (Raw Numbers).

Table 4: Phonation Type by Episode Theme & Video Type (Proportion).

	Phonation Type
Episode Theme	*Non-Modal*
Gay	.43
Not Gay	.38
None	.35
Video Type	*Non-Modal*
Interview	.35
Show	.40
Overall Mean	.38

3.3.5 Grammatical features

Andromedon did not use any grammatical features of AAVE in the examined episodes. Burgess used only one, negative concord, in a single utterance during the *Late Show* interview with Stephen Colbert.

3.4 Summary of results

All features, with the exception of grammatical AAVE features, were present in the episodes and interviews, partially supporting hypothesis I. Video type was a significant main effect in pitch range and /s/ center of gravity, with pitch range being wider and /s/ center of gravity being higher in the Show category than the Interview category, supporting hypothesis I. AAVE features did not vary based on video type, thus not supporting hypothesis I. None of the examined features were found to be significantly affected by episode theme, thus not supporting hypothesis II.

These results suggest that there are systematic differences in speech style between Burgess and Andromedon, particularly in the use of GSS. In the examined episodes, episode theme did not appear to have a systematic effect on which language style was used by Andromedon (hypothesis II), though features of GSS were used more frequently overall (hypothesis I). This suggests that, at least in these episodes, AAVE is not being used to portray aspects of Andromedon's identity. Similarly, Burgess does not appear to manipulate AAVE features, nor does he seem to manipulate GSS to a large degree.

4 Discussion

The manipulation of GSS features but not of AAVE features in this data suggests that in Andromedon's case, gay identity is being performed linguistically, using features that are salient to viewers. Despite the fact AAVE features occur at all could be seen as performing Black identity, Burgess and Andromedon don't use them contrastively. This suggests that Black identity is not being performed linguistically, at least not using the features examined here. The pointed use of GSS could be, and likely is, motivated by Andromedon's characterization as a feminine gay man. His gay identity often acts as comedic relief in scenes, even when he isn't present, as in the first episode where he's first described as "single, but very gay" by his landlord Lillian. Andromedon's gay identity is performed through features like wider pitch range and is made visible through his mannerisms, facial expressions, and clothing. These visual cues are identified as a "performance" of gayness in a way that does not occur in the same way for Andromedon's racial identity (Kohnen 2016). In other words, the fact that Andromedon is a Black man is immediately visible to the viewer, even in the absence of certain linguistic and behavioral cues. This is potentially a contributing factor in why GSS varies between show types, but AAVE doesn't.

Andromedon's characterization as a *feminine* gay man could be acting as further motivation to push his language closer to MUSE and GSS than to AAVE, which has been found to index masculinity, as seen in research on the construction of white masculinity through the use of AAVE by high school teen boys and the frequent use of Mock AAE in media to undermine white masculinity (Bucholtz 1999; Bucholtz & Lopez 2011). At the same time, adherence to more standardized forms often serves as an index of femininity – specifically *white* femininity (Barrett 2017, p. 46). The impression of GSS as not just (hyper)standard but also as *white* reinforces the dichotomy between GSS, MUSE, whiteness, and femininity on one side and AAVE, Blackness, and (hetero)masculinity on the other. This relationship is particularly clear in the juxtaposition of AAVE and white women's speech found in the performances of African American Drag Queens (Barrett 2017).

It's important to recognize some limitations of comparing Burgess and Andromedon. This research uses the two interviews as a sample of Burgess' "natural" speech but recognizes that interview speech is also a performed style. Additionally, *Unbreakable Kimmy Schmidt* is a scripted show, and a scene may be filmed more than once, potentially leading to even less natural speech as lines are repeated. However, though Burgess doesn't have control over the lines that are written for him, he does have control in the way he decides to perform those lines.

While it's not possible to know the exact motivations behind the linguistic choices Burgess makes, especially when in character as Andromedon, Burgess does differ linguistically from Andromedon in ways that suggest there's a conscious manipulation of language, and perhaps a different style in use altogether. At the same time, there are features (for example the phonological AAVE features) that remained stable across the Show and Interview categories, suggesting that these were not consciously manipulated in the same way as suprasegmental and grammatical features.

One goal of a show like *Unbreakable Kimmy Schmidt* is to create characters that feel authentic to an audience, and it is in the best interest of the scriptwriters to have that be reflected in the language characters use (Bednarek 2010; Queen 2015). The choices the *Unbreakable Kimmy Schmidt* writers and Burgess make in creating Andromedon, even if not entirely authentic, provide examples of what people think a Black gay man would sound like. These expectations may overlap with features linguists have observed in gay identity performance, such as differences in /s/; whether they *do* overlap can provide further topics of research into language and identity performance.

5 Conclusion

This research contributes to previous work on persona-based style shifting, as well as the idea of "stylistic bricolage" being used to linguistically index identity (Eckert 2008; Podesva 2007). Though Burgess' performance as Andromedon is a far more dramatic style shift than is typically assumed in sociolinguistic research (in that he's pretending to be a completely different person), the fact that he manipulates features already present in his speech does mirror findings in style shifting research. Additionally, this study provides evidence that scripted media can be used in sociolinguistic research to investigate questions of identity performance. The choices actors and scriptwriters make about how a character should sound reflect previously existing expectations within a society, while also reflecting assumptions about an audience's own beliefs and expectations. Examining this relationship between creator and audience can provide information on the role stereotypes may play within a television show, what things are expected of character types, and what things are linguistically salient to people who are outside of sociolinguistics.

While intersectionality theory does provide a useful framework to examine the complexity of identity, in future work on Black queer language, a stronger application of the theory to linguistic methodology may prove fruitful. One potential approach may be through the application of *dynamism* and *mutual constitution*, two features of intersectionality theory that position social identity as neither stable nor universal, but as constructed within specific, heavily interdependent contexts (Levon 2015, 297–298). In many ways, this framing of identity as dynamic and mutually constituted has already been applied in sociolinguistics through work on indexicality, personae, and stance. Levon (2015) argues, for example, that in Campbell-Kibler (2011), [iŋ] does not act as a direct index of gay male identity, but as an index of competence tied to a "highly educated competent gay man" image that was then used by participants to "constitute what it means to sound gay" (302). Levon asks us to consider "not only how sexual [or other] personae are linguistically materialized . . ., but also why those variables participate in their emergence in the ways that they do" (2015, 303).

One goal of this study was to purposefully apply a categorical, dichotomous understanding of linguistic identity performance to a speaker that fell "between" the categories. While it was expected that features of AAVE and GSS would occur, it was also expected that it would be possible to identify which identity was being performed depending on which features were present. Following Levon (2015), rather than positioning GSS and AAVE as two separate linguistic categories, future research could potentially challenge the idea that GSS and AAVE are stable linguistic categories in the first place. This kind of framework, in addition to increased representation of different kinds of Black and gay speakers, will allow sociolinguists to broaden our understandings of how Blackness and gayness can sound.

References

Barrett, Rusty. 1998. Markedness and style switching in performances by African American drag queens. In Carol Myers-Scotton (ed.), *Codes and consequences: Choosing linguistic varieties*. 139–161. New York: Oxford University Press.

Barrett, Rusty. 2006. Queer talk. In Keith Brown (ed.), *Encyclopedia of language and linguistics* (2nd edn.). 316–323. Elsevier.

Barrett, Rusty. 2017. *From drag queens to leathermen: language, gender, and gay male subcultures*. 33–54. Oxford: Oxford University Press.

Bates, Douglas, Martin Mächler, Ben Bolker & Steve Walker. 2015. Fitting linear mixed-effects models using lme4. *Journal of statistical software* 67(1). 1–48.

Beckman, Mary E. & Gayle Ayers Elam. 1997. Guide to ToBI Labelling-Version, 3.

Beckman, Mary E., Julia Hirschberg & Stefanie Shattuck-Hufnagel. 2006. The original ToBI System and the evolution of the ToBI framework. In Sun-Ah Jun (ed.), *Prosodic typology: The phonology of intonation and phrasing*. 9–54. Oxford: Oxford University Press.

Bednarek, Monika. 2010. *The language of fictional television: drama and identity*. Continuum International Publishing Group. Retrieved from https://ebookcentral.proquest.com

Benor, Sarah B. 2004. *Second style acquisition: The linguistic socialization of newly Orthodox Jews*. Stanford: Stanford University dissertation.

Boersma, Paul & David Weenink. 2018. Praat: Doing phonetics by computer (Version 6.0.43) [Computer software]. From http://www.praat.org/

Bucholtz, Mary. 1999. You da man: Narrating the racial other in the production of white masculinity. *Journal of sociolinguistics* 3(4). 443–460.

Bucholtz, Mary. 2001. The whiteness of nerds: Superstandard English and racial markedness. *Journal of linguistic anthropology* 11(1). 84–100.

Bucholtz, Mary & Qiuana Lopez. 2011. Performing blackness, forming whiteness: Linguistic minstrelsy in Hollywood film. *Journal of sociolinguistics* 15(5). 680–706.

Campbell-Kibler, Kathryn. 2011. Intersecting variables and perceived sexual orientation in men. *American Speech* 86(1). 52–68.

Cartei, Valentina. & David Reby. 2012. Acting gay: Male actors shift the frequency components of their voices towards female values when playing homosexual characters. *Journal of nonverbal behavior* 36(1). 79–93.

Cohen, Cathy J. 1997. Punks, bulldaggers, and welfare queens: The radical potential of queer politics?. *GLQ* (3). 437–465.

Cornelius, Brianna R. 2016. Gay Black men and the construction of identity via linguistic repertoires. *Texas linguistics forum* 59. 39–48.

Cornelius, Brianna R. & Rusty Barrett. 2020. "You Met My Ambassador": Language and Self-monitoring at the Intersection of Race and Sexuality. In H. Samy Alim, Angela Reyes & Paul V. Kroskrity (eds.), *The Oxford Handbook of Language and Race*. 314–341. Oxford: Oxford University Press.

Craft, Justin T., Kelly E. Wright, Rachel E. Weissler & Robin M. Queen. 2020. Language and discrimination: Generating meaning, perceiving identities, and discriminating outcomes. *Annual review of linguistics* 6(1). 389–407.

Crenshaw, Kimberlé. 1989. Demarginalizing the intersection of race and sex: A black feminist critique of antidiscrimination doctrine, feminist theory, and antiracist politics. *University of Chicago legal forum 1989* (1). 139–167.

Duggan, Lisa. 2003. *The twilight of equality? Neoliberalism, cultural politics, and the attack on democracy.* Boston: Beacon Press.

Eckert, Penelope. 1989. *Jocks and burnouts: Social categories and identity in the high school.* New York: Teachers College Press.

Eckert, Penelope. 2004. The meaning of style. *Texas linguistic forum* 47(1). 41–43.

Eckert, Penelope. 2008. Variation and the indexical field. *Journal of sociolinguistics* 12(4). 453–476.

Eckert, Penelope & Sally McConnell-Ginet. 2003. Language and gender. Cambridge: Cambridge University Press.

ELAN (Version 5.0.0-beta) [Computer software]. 2017, April 18. Nijmegen: Max Planck Institute for Psycholinguistics. Retrieved from https://tla.mpi.nl/tools/tla-tools/elan/

"Episode List." 2015. Retrieved, October 30, 2018, from https://www.imdb.com/title/tt3339966/episodes?season=1ACC10/30/18-episodelist

Epstein, Alex. 2006. *Crafty TV writing: Thinking inside the box.* New York: Henry Holt & Company.

Flores, Nelson & Jonathan Rosa. 2015. Undoing appropriateness: Raciolinguistic ideologies and language diversity in education. *Harvard Educational Review* 85(2). 149–172.

Gal, S. 1995. Language, gender, and power. In Kira Hall & Mary Bucholtz (eds.), *Gender articulated: Language and the socially constructed self.* 169–182. London: Routledge.

Gaudio, Rudolf P. 1994. Sounding gay: Pitch properties in the speech of gay and straight men. *American speech* 69(1). 30–57.

GLAAD. 2014. *Where we are on tv report: 2014–2015 season.* (Report no. 9). Retrieved from http://www.glaad.org/files/GLAAD-2014-WWAT.pdf

Holliday, Nicole. 2016. *Intonational variation, linguistic style and the Black/Biracial experience.* New York: New York University dissertation.

Holliday, Nicole & Dan Villarreal. 2020. Intonational variation and incrementality in listener judgments of ethnicity. *Laboratory phonology: Journal of the association for laboratory phonology* 11(1). 3.

Johnson, E. Patrick & Mae G. Henderson. 2005. Introduction: Queering Black Studies/"Quaring" Queer Studies. In E. Patrick Johnson & Mae G. Henderson (eds.), *Black Queer Studies: A Critical Anthology.* 1–18. New York: Duke University Press.

Jun, Sun-Ah & Christina Foreman. 1996. Boundary tones and focus realization in African American English intonations. *The journal of the acoustical society of America* 100(4). 2826.

"Kimmy Goes Outside." 2015. Retrieved from https://www.imdb.com/title/tt3651920/?ref_=ttep_ep1

King, Sharese. 2020. From AAVE to AAL. *Annual Review of Linguistics* 6. 285–300.

Kohnen, Melanie. 2016. *Queer representation, visibility, and race in American film and television: Screening the closet.* London: Routledge.

Labov, William. 1972. *Sociolinguistic patterns* (No. 4). Philadelphia: University of Pennsylvania Press.

Ladefoged, Peter. 2003. *Phonetic data analysis: An introduction to fieldwork and instrumental techniques.* 104–137. New York: Wiley-Blackwell.

Lanehart, Sonja L. 2009. Diversity and intersectionality. *Texas Linguistic Forum* 53(7). 1–8.

Lanehart, Sonja L. & Ayesha M. Malik. 2015. Language use in African American communities: An introduction. In Sonja L. Lanehart (ed.), *The Oxford handbook of African American Language.* 1–20. Oxford: Oxford University Press.

Levon, Erez. 2007. Sexuality in context: Variation and the sociolinguistic perception of identity. *Language in Society* 36(4). 533–554.

Levon, Erez. 2015. Integrating intersectionality in language, gender, and sexuality research: Integrating intersectionality. *Language and Linguistics Compass* 9(7). 295–308.

Lippi-Green, Rosina. 1997. What we talk about when we talk about Ebonics: Why definitions matter. *The Black scholar* 27(2). 7–11.

Lippi-Green, Rosina. 2012. *English with an accent: Language, ideology, and discrimination in the United States*. London: Routledge.

Martin, Alfred L. 2015. Scripting Black gayness: Television authorship in Black-cast sitcoms. *Television & New Media* 16(7). 648–663.

McLarty, Jason. 2011. *AAE and EAE pitch accent types and frequencies: An apparent time perspective*. Raleigh: North Carolina State University thesis.

McLarty, Jason. 2018. African American Language and European American English Intonation Variation Over Time in The American South. *American Speech: A Quarterly of Linguistic Usage* 93(1). 32–78.

Morgan, Marcyliena. 1996. Conversational signifying: Grammar and indirectness among African American women. In Elinor Ochs, Emanuel A. Schegloff & Sandra A. Thompson (eds.), *Interaction and grammar*. 405–434. Cambridge: Cambridge University Press.

Munson, Benjamin. 2011. The influence of actual and imputed talker gender on fricative perception, revisited (L). *The journal of the acoustical society of America* 130(5). 2631–2634.

Niedzielski, Nancy. 1999. The effect of social information on the perception of sociolinguistic variables. *Journal of language and social psychology* 18(1). 62–85.

Podesva, Robert J. 2007. Phonation type as a stylistic variable: The use of falsetto in constructing a persona. *Journal of sociolinguistics* 11(4).478–504.

Podesva, Robert J. & Sakiko Kajino. 2014. Sociophonetics, gender, and sexuality. In Susan Ehrlich, Miriam Meyerhoff & Janet Holmes (eds.), *The handbook of language, gender, and sexuality*. 103–122. New York: Wiley-Blackwell.

Podesva, Robert J., Sarah J. Roberts & Kathryn Campbell-Kibler. 2002. Sharing resources and indexing meanings in the production of gay styles. In Kathryn Campbell-Kibler, Robert J. Podesva, Sarah J. Roberts & Andrew Wong (eds.), *Language and sexuality: Contesting meaning in theory and practice*. 175–189. Stanford: CSLI.

Queen, Robin. 2015. *Vox popular: The surprising life of language in the media*. New York: John Wiley & Sons.

Revelle, William. 2018. *psych: Procedures for personality and psychological research*. Northwestern University, Evanston, IL. https://CRAN.R-project.org/package=psych

Rickford, John R. & Sharese King. 2016. Language and linguistics on trial: Hearing Rachel Jeantel (and other vernacular speakers) in the courtroom and beyond. *Language* 92(4). 948–988.

Rickford, John. R. & Russell J. Rickford. 2002. *Spoken soul: The story of Black English*. New York: Wiley.

Silverstein, Michael. 2003. Indexical order and the dialectics of sociolinguistic life. *Language & communication* 23(3–4). 193–229.

Spears, Arthur. 1988. Black American English. In Johnetta B. Cole (ed.), *Anthropology for the nineties: Introductory readings*. 96–113. New York: Free Press.

Strand, Elizabeth A. 1999. Uncovering the role of gender stereotypes in speech perception. *Journal of Language and Social Psychology* 18(1). 86–100.

Thomas, Erik R. 2015. Prosodic features of African American English. In Sonja L. Lanehart (ed.), *The Oxford handbook of African American Language*. Oxford: Oxford University Press.

Wickham, Hadley, Romain François, Lionel Henry & Kirill Müller. 2018. dplyr: A grammar of data manipulation. R package version 0.7.6. https://CRAN.R-project.org/package=dplyr

Wolfram, Walt. 2007. Sociolinguistic folklore in the study of African American English. *Language and linguistics compass* 1(4). 292–313.

Zsiga, Elizabeth C. 2013. *The sounds of language*. Oxford: Wiley-Blackwell.

Ping-Hsuan Wang
Identity and desire in gay Indian immigrants' definition of coming out in the U.S.

1 Introduction

Coming out of the closet, or 'coming out' for short, has been studied across disciplines and variably defined. For instance, Herdt's (1997) anthropological work conceives of coming out as a ritualistic "rebirth" from the symbolic death of one's heterosexual identity. Plummer (1995), in sociology, describes coming out as "a complex process of moving from a heterosexual (and confused) identity" and developing a "consistent, integrated sense of self" (1995, 84). Widely cited in the extant literature on coming out is queer theorist Sedgwick's (1990) designation of the closet as "the defining structure for gay oppression in this century" (68). In linguistics, studies have embraced this self-based notion of coming out by defining it as "the act of naming and accepting one's same-sex emotions" (Liang 1997, 291).

Into the 21st century, the proliferating research on language and sexuality sees an expansion of disciplinary approaches within sociolinguistics and an integration that draws from related disciplines such as queer studies and cultural studies (Queen 2014). Contributing to this line of scholarly endeavor, linguistics views coming out as a linguistic and social practice of contesting and negotiating sexuality (e.g., Motschenbacher 2020). Studies on coming-out narratives, in particular, highlight the role of language to be analyzed in detail rather than a mere means of data collection (Wang 2021). Of late, intellectual currents have informed social sciences of issues to be explored in linguistics (Wong, Roberts & Campbell-Kibler 2002), such as ethnicity and nationhood that underlie and intersect with coming out, and the theoretical terms based on which these issues are analyzed.

Among these issues, coming out has largely been discussed in Western terms and associated period-specific identities of gender and self, a premise and limitation that scholars have acknowledged (e.g., Chan 1995; Davies 1992). This leads to my second point: identity has been the primary theoretical lens through which coming out is understood and analyzed. Past studies that rely on Western gay identities to analyze modern sexuality, Rofel (1999) critiques, "have not decentered the universalism of Euro-American notions of what it means to be gay" (472). As such, modern relationships between identity and sexuality in research

Ping-Hsuan Wang, Independent Scholar

strengthen institutional coloniality (Chávez 2013). Finally, coming out, which is built around binarism (Sedgwick 1990), has come to be laden with moral values, fixating individuals in a binary system of regulatory categories (McCormick 2015). Recent problematization of coming out as "normative" (Motschenbacher 2020; Sauntson 2015) has begun to probe into less heeded permutations that question the ideological construct of 'outness' in the spirit of queering linguistics (Barrett 2002) on a theoretical, methodological, and disciplinary level.

Building on the position that sexuality is a contingent formation emerging out of a social moment (Leap & Motschenbacher 2012), this chapter presents a linguistic perspective on such emergence by examining three same-sex desiring Indian immigrants' definitions of coming out in sociolinguistic interviews. I posit an integrative theoretical link between desire and identity that desire becomes intelligible through the naming of recognized social categories, which in turn determines if an identity is legitimate or not. The analysis illustrates the ways some categories referred to by the participants configure their same-sex desire into an intelligible gay identity.

2 Problematizing coming out

How coming out as a process, or its *processuality*, is imagined varies. Rust (1993) rejects conceptualizing this process as consisting of several stages in a linear progression, which assumes that individuals go through life events in a certain order and reach an endpoint of maturity (see also Davies 1992). Gonsiorek (1995) concurs that theories should move beyond discovering an identity that manifests itself over time and, instead, account for larger socio-political forces that occur later in life. In this vein, the social constructionist view that Rust envisions treats coming out as an act of describing one's changing location on the social landscape in relation to sexual landmarks, such as other individuals, groups, and institutions. This is reminiscent of Green's (2008) sociological concept of sexual fields, namely structures of desire, in which sexual practices are systematically stratified according to the extents to which sexual desires are standardized or institutionalized.

One such instance of the changing sexual landscape is migration in the case of same-sex desiring immigrants, who experience and grapple with different sets of vocabulary and constraints related to the construal of sexual practices. Scholars have continued to call for studies that highlight the cross-cultural aspect of sexuality (e.g., Cameron & Kulick 2003; Motschenbacher & Stegu 2013) in that "intersections and interplays between the queer and the intercultural" have been marginal in disciplines such as communication (Chávez 2013, 84). However, as Whitehead

(1981) notes, "cross-cultural investigations of homosexuality have too often been used to support various interpretations of the Western homosexual" (p. 498). Research efforts would make little difference if non-Western populations are treated as "case studies" (Wieringa & Sívori 2013; see also Luther & Ung Loh 2019) without critical reflexivity on the theoretical constructs that are employed.

This reflexivity also pertains to being aware of the moral stance with which coming out has been imbricated. 'Outness' is associated with positive qualities such as courage and honesty, whereas 'closetedness' implies secrecy, shame, and fear. Rasmussen (2004) terms this distinction "the coming out imperative." Such idealization of coming out exerts negative effects of perpetuating heterosexism and developing a sense of shame, thereby obscuring the way heterosexism and homophobia in the U.S. are tied to race, class, and gender relations (Mezey 2008; see also D'Emilio 1983). Trickling into academia, the coming out imperative may lead research to subtle biases of framing *not* coming out as a deviation rather than a variation at the intersection of sexuality and races/ethnicities.

Consequently, attention is required for dismantling disciplinary hegemony that favors White, middle-class, highly educated participants (Guittar 2013; Huang 2021). A queer sensitive approach to coming out, then, questions the legitimacy and normalcy of theoretical assumptions related to outness that is underpinned by multiple layers of binarism. This insight is enriched by ethnographic or sociological works that capture the lived experiences of, for instance, queer Dominican immigrant men, whose gender identity is not understood as verbal disclosure of one's desire but expressed through "tacitness" (Decena 2011). This chapter follows this line of interdisciplinary thinking as well as disciplinary critical reflection to examine how, as Perez (2005) explains, coming out crystallizes same-sex experience into homosexual identity through individuation and self-determination.

2.1 Studying coming-out narratives

Narratives provide contexts and examples with which coming out and other sexual practices are studied and understood. Unlike psychology or sociology, in which coming-out narratives are often a means of data collection that precedes identifying themes or developing stage models (Orn 2011), linguistics adopts narrative analysis to closely examine the structural forms and the social discourses of coming out. Liang (1997), for instance, identifies three narrative components in gay college students' coming-out narratives, including coming out to self, coming out to others, and *processuality* (the notion of coming out as an ongoing process as reflected in narrative structure). She notices that while gay European American speakers tend to dwell on their inner conflict regarding coming out to self, gay Asian American speakers dismiss this part in their stories and, rather, emphasize coming out to others. A later paradigm shift in focus from 'story as an independent unit' toward 'narrative as a situated practice' has led researchers to view coming-out narratives as autobiographical accounts constructed under genre-related conventions for an intended audience (e.g., DiDomenico 2015; Wong 2009).

Thus, analyzing narrative accounts of less discussed aspects of coming out, including reasons for *not* doing so (Plummer 1995), is crucial for appreciating the complexity of sexualities and acknowledging the social, cultural, and institutional contexts that bring about such complexity. Doing so would also clarify the analytical stance and the methodological consideration that determine which narratives are included, analyzed, and presented. For example, in questioning the concept of a "global gay identity," Rofel (1999) contends that studying the accounts by and about participants outside the Euro-American regions "entails examining how they articulate with discursive productions of culture and place" (457). Linguistic studies that deal with coming out have also begun attending to a wide range of practices, including 'not coming out' in queer Latinx individuals' narratives (Cashman 2018), a pragmatically 'soft' strategy of coming out by gay Singaporean men (Pak 2021), and encounters of 'coming back in' for same-sex desiring Indian and Mexican immigrants (Wang, forthcoming). This growing scholarly body of inquires into "the broader realms of the social landscape" into which sexualities are culturally incorporated (Queen 2014, 203; see also Leap & Motschenbacher 2012) and the power relations that constitute normativity and taboo (Wang 2020).

Just as participants navigate sexual practices on the social landscape, researchers likewise engage theories in these realms of the social landscape. Particularly, the telling of coming-out narratives in interview settings are highly institutional in nature (DiDomenico, 2015; Wang 2021). To carry out the critical reflection involved in sociolinguistic interviews (De Fina & Perrino 2011), linguistic research has to be wary of the conditions under which coming-out narratives are told and responded to. In this way, the discursive features observed in the telling of these narratives (e.g., Wang 2017) are not a direct result of the participants' sexuality or cultural background. This degree of reflection works to counter the "disciplinary biases" that, while privileging Western institutions, alienate and dislocate both research participants and researchers in an academic system (Luther & Ung Loh 2019, 8; see also Wieringa & Sívori 2013).

2.2 Rethinking sexual identity

In the discussion of bisexuality, Rust (1996) observes that changes in language afford new ways for the enunciation of one's desires on the sexual landscape. At the time when 'lesbian' and 'gay' were common self-descriptors, the newly-introduced term 'bisexual' allowed individuals to involve themselves in new relationships. This suggests a dialectic wherein new terms hold revolutionary potential for exposing the dynamic nature of sexuality until they are stabilized and popularized into fixed categories. Since the turn of the 21st century, the theorization of identity in language and sexuality has evolved; identities are constructed and reconstructed in discourse, which can be explained along three axes of intersubjective tactics of relationality (Bucholtz & Hall 2004):

Table 1: Intersubjective tactics of relationality.

1.	adequation	positioned as alike
	distinction	focused on differentiation
2.	authentication	discursively verified
	denaturalization	disrupted or fabricated
3.	authorization	ideologically affirmed
	illegitimation	dismissed as inappropriate

Still, as with all theories, the identity approach to language and sexuality has its histories in a particular cultural and geopolitical location. Contemporary understandings of sexuality draw on categories such as homosexual and heterosexual and, in a Foucauldian sense of a historical apparatus, reflect the social and political concerns of a point in the Western history (Orne 2011; see also Chan 1995). The claim that identity is produced and performed hinges on the historical contingency of identity that indicates the socio-political conditions in a specific historical era (D'Emilio 1983) and ideological tradition of individual qualities. Therefore, statements like coming out is "the process of lesbian and gay identity formation" (Rust 1996, p. 65) demand critical interrogation on the ground of how coming out deals with the Western framing of homosexuality (Edwards 2005), wherein outness is taken as the reality (Motschenbacher & Stegu 2013) and leads to what Barrett (2002) refers to as "unanalyzed categories."

Among alternative heuristics to identity in language and sexuality research, Cameron and Kulick (2003), criticize that identity relies unduly on symbolic position based on speaker intention rather than concrete practices that, in Butler's (1990) sense, embody recognizable and iterable conventions (see also Lemke 2008). A complete rejection of identity, however, may be counterproductive. After all, as Seidman (1996) argues apropos of identity in queer theory, "the aim is not to abandon identity as a category of knowledge and politics but to render it permanently open and contestable as to its meaning and political role" (12). Similarly, Gaudio (2005) advises that a fruitful approach is to "problematize and operationalize both concepts for empirical discourse-analytic research" (279). While Cameron and Kulick's call has indeed led to increased publications with reinvigorated theoretical interests, the expression of desire may still be tied to specific identity in language (Queen 2014). This tension allows the possibility for sociolinguistics to align with the sociological study of desire as a social structure (Green 2008). To tease apart the connection between desire and identity, the following section pulls together these key theoretical threads.

2.3 Connecting desire and identity

While sexuality is irreducible to desire (Boellstorff & Leap 2004), it is likewise insufficient to theorize that "coming out is a process of social identity construction rather than simply an expression of physical or sexual desire" (Morrish & Suantson 2007, 54). It is the interconnection between desire and identity as intertextually dependent that engenders intelligible subjectivities (Canakis 2015). To delineate the interrelationships between these two constructs in coming-out narratives, this section incorporates positioning and outlines a triadic formula: the discursive expression of desire facilitates the positioning of a person toward (or way from) an approximate category, from which a corresponding identity is recognized, ratified, or challenged.

In Cameron and Kulick's (2003) postulation, desire denotes feelings such as fear, pleasure, fantasy, which are discursively expressed through "social semiotics," that is, iterable and quotable signs and acts as in Butler's (1990) terms of performativity. These semiotics, including observable physical manifestations and verbal expressions, require conventional forms of language and knowledge of norms and references to be recognized in social interaction, as indexed by social categories (Ochs 1992). Like gender in Ochs' example, sexuality is located in constitutive relations with other categories, against which the self and the other can be positioned. In this way, the creation and reification of categories shape the expression of desire (Valentine 2003) and the discursive positioning can be (dis)empowering depending on associated social values. Because of such categorization, the employment of sexual identity necessarily involves its "normative elements" that represents sexuality as "stable and given" (Spijkerboer 2013). For instance, when Rust (1996) wrote about bisexual identity, bisexuality as a form of desire was relatively newly named and subsequently "normaled" (Hall 2013), from which new indexical relations emerge in discourse. Over time, these relations are incrementally cemented for the discursive construction of a bisexual identity to be increasingly recognizable. Thus, the extent to which some forms of desire can be categorized while others are dismissed constitute normativity.

Figure 1 illustrates these indexical relations: assigning individuals to a particular category on the basis of social attributes or practices gives rise to an identity. In line with the Foucauldian thinking, a comprehensible subject arises when a person is subjected to categories contained in language, wherein sexuality is not the source of this discursive process but the effect of it (Spijkerboer 2013). This view of identity emphasizes, for one, how language constructs identity rather than merely reflects it, and, for another, how sociolinguists play a role in this construction (Barrett 2002). The concept of positioning along categories explains said connection between desire and identity. Discursive expressions of desire serve as linguistic acts that position the interlocutors in a regulatory social script that limits how the acts are uttered and perceived (Pak 2021). In sum, desire, simultaneously an internal psychological status and an external social activity, is sustained or undermined as embedded in identity; conversely, identity becomes intelligible through the recognition and categorization of desire (Figure 1).

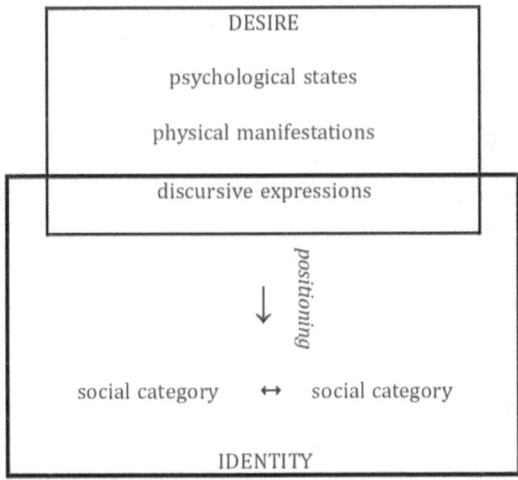

Figure 1: An integrative theoretical link between desire and identity.

This integrative link between desire as the substrate, positioning as the process, and identity as the medium demonstrates how sexuality operates in language, particularly the interactional sociolinguistic approach to sexuality (Gordon & Tannen 2021). The triadic formula also elucidates how identity functions as "a mediating term" between social structures and lived experiences (Lemke, 2008). A compelling example, D'Emilio (1983) details, is how material conditions of capitalism in the 1960s transform previously unnamed same-sex desire into a tangible gay identity, around which individuals can then be politically mobilized.

Such integration directs attention in language and sexuality research to the "historical and cultural-ideological reasons" for which, as Gaudio (2005) discerns, identity pervades in sociolinguistic and anthropology in Western institutions (see also Orne 2011). Coming out, as a linguistic act, produces a performative effect when the context, culturally (e.g., social movements) or institutionally (e.g., academic publications), affords a script for making sense of it. This chapter aims to show that, for the participants in this study, coming-out narratives are scripted both by a sense of outness and by the expectations in sociolinguistic interviews.

3 Data and method

Study participants were recruited through snowball sampling in the Washington D.C. area from 2016 to 2017. This chapter focuses on instances of three same-sex desiring Indian immigrants who, amidst the third wave of Indian immigration in the 1990s, came as companies in the U.S. looked to hire computer specialists from India (Chakravorty, Kapur & Singh 2016). They arrived in the U.S. for employment or higher education, which presupposes, or at times predicts, a socioeconomic status that affords a certain amount of geographical and social mobility (see Table 2).

The study design included one sociolinguistic interview with each participant, consisting of open-ended questions to elicit their coming-out narratives. The interviews were conducted in English, the lingua franca for the interviewer and the interviewees. The interviews were audio recorded and then transcribed for analysis (see Transcription Conventions). All participants quoted herein have been assigned a pseudonym.

Participants were asked to define what it means to come out in the beginning of the interview before recounting personal experiences to substantiate. In line with the interpretive approach to sexuality in communication research (Manning 2013), this method engages participants in open interaction of meaning to avoid imposing researchers' assumptions about coming out (Guittar 2013). This is of particular importance in that in Asia, "coming out is not a common way of asserting one's gayness, and desires do not seem to be framed in terms of political interests" (Kong, Mahoney & Plummer 2001, 249). This approach is to compensate what could be lost when social categories in English are used in the cross-cultural examination of coming out. By adopting a discourse analytic approach to the turn-by-turn development of interaction, this chapter focuses specifically on the participants' definitions of coming out.

Two issues should be noted. First, rather than an objective lens through which linguistic practices are observed, sociolinguistic interviews constitute an interactional context that influences the dynamics in storytelling (De Fina & Perrino 2011). Analyzing narratives produced in interviews should recognize this contextualizing effect and, accordingly, address narrative co-construction between the interviewee and interviewer. Second, my positionality as identifying as gay and having migrated from Taiwan allows the participants to connect over race/ethnicity, cultural background, and sexual orientation. This relationality inevitably imbues language use with a set of expectations, thereby functioning as performative indexicals that simultaneously position the narrator and recipient (Barrett 2002), as the analysis will demonstrate. This chapter treats these conditions in narrative interaction not as detrimental to research objectivity but as fundamental to disciplinary reflexivity in employing positioning between desire and identity.

Table 2: Participants.

Name	Age	Years in the U.S.	Purpose of Traveling
Arjun	38	16	Education
Daksh	36	18	Education
Reyansh	42	17	Employment

4 Analysis

As the participants attend to different aspects of coming out in their definitions, relational and intersubjective positioning vis-à-vis heterosexual others in the narratives allow the narrators' same-sex desire to be translated into a gay identity. The homo/heterosexual binary of social categories is often leveraged to ratify their same-sex attraction. In Excerpt 1, despite Reyansh's repeated utterance of his self-realization (italicized for emphasis), he also relates himself to others in the constructed dialogue of his inner thoughts.

     Excerpt 1
     1. Ping: So, what I wanna ask you is,
     2.   What is coming out (.) to you.
     3.   Like what- what does it mean.
     4. Reyansh: I think coming out- I mean, in my opinion, it never ends.
     5.   You're always coming out.
     6. Ping: Mhm.
     7. Reyansh: Because you will be out to your family, immediate family.
     8.   But not everybody in your family.

9.		You can be out to your<u>self</u>,
10.		Which is a different level of coming out.
11.	Ping:	Mhm.
12.	Reyansh:	And if you join a new job, it's- it's-
13.		Everybody assumes you're straight,
14.		Until you told them otherwise.
15.	Ping:	Mhm.
16.	Reyansh:	So it's you're always perpetually in the closet,
17.		To everybody you meet,
18.		Until you're actually coming out of the closet.
19.	Ping:	Yeah.

Reyansh's definition of coming out, largely in present tense, constitutes a habitual narrative. This narrative form signals regularity, thereby generalizing his coming-out experiences (Wang 2021) and linguistically expressing the *processuality* of coming out. Phrases such as "it never ends" (line 4), "you're always coming out" (line 5) and that a person can be "perpetually in the closet" (line 16) indicate the perceived persistence and ubiquity of heteronormative expectations imposed on him. The first layer of binary is realized relationally in the family (line 8) and the workplace (lines 12–13), where "everybody" is positioned as holding heteronormative assumptions and obstructing the expression of his same-sex desire, thereby *denaturalize* a gay identity. Naming the category "straight" points to the ideological expectations to be challenged (lines 13–14) and requires constant and active attempt to maintain and enunciate (Butler 1990). Coming out, then, becomes a means to *authenticate* a gay identity that is recognizable not only to the story characters but to me, the interviewer whose expectations are conditioned by the research context. This narrative setup reveals the disruptive potential of coming out to destabilize heteronormativity (Leap & Motschenbacher 2012) by which the disavowal of assumed heterosexual desire creates an inversion (Cameron & Kulick 2003) to self-position away from the "straight" category. In sum, the generic form of Reyansh's narrative portrays coming out as an alternative practice that constantly threatens heteronormativity while ratifying his same-sex desire and framing each rupture as part of a common occurrence contributing to a coherent sense of self (Liang 1997). In Excerpt 2, this effect is achieved through relational positioning between a hetero/homo/bisexuality.

Excerpt 2

20.	Reyansh:	So for <u>me</u>, coming out was primarily,
21.		*<u>Me</u> realizing that I am gay.*
22.	Ping:	Mhm.
23.	Reyansh:	And- and everything after that was,
24.		More just another step of coming out.

25.		To me, coming out was when *I realized I was gay*.
26.	Ping:	Mhm.
27.	Reyansh:	And that I wasn't bisexual, wasn't just something,
28.		"Oh, I can be with women at some-
29.		Just have some fun right now,"
30.		"And be with men later on."
31.	Ping:	Yeah.
32.	Reyansh:	Hehehe you know. So *me realizing that, "no I am gay."*
33.		"I cannot possibly marry a woman."
34.		"I'm only attracted to men."
35.		And not just physically but also emotionally.
36.		That even if I somehow (.) marry a woman,
37.		And <u>am</u> able to have sex with her,
38.		Just for the purpose of procreation.
39.	Ping:	Mhm.
40.	Reyansh:	Even then, I would never be straight.
41.		I would always be attracted to,
42.		Physically and emotionally to men,
43.		*Me realizing that* is basically that main coming out.
44.	Ping:	Mhm.
45.	Reyansh:	After that, everything else was just adding on top of it?
46.		But for me coming out was *me realizing that I was gay*.

Parallel to the "straight" category in Excerpt 1, the "gay" category is used and conferred onto Reyansh's understanding of his same-sex desire. As Chan (1995) discerns, for Asians in the U.S., a gay or lesbian identity is achieved by defining oneself through Western cultural concepts. The self-referential phrase of "me realizing I'm gay" conveys Reyansh's reflexivity, akin to the *coming out to self* component in coming-out narratives (Liang 1997), as it symbolizes the peculiarity of one's same-sex desire to be "realized" in the heterosexual matrix. This phrase relates him to other story characters. In his hypothetical narrative, signaled with conditional protases (lines 36 and 40), the idea of being with women (line 28) or marrying them (lines 33 and 36) creates a contrast. At the time when this interview was conducted, same-sex marriage was just legalized in the U.S. but not legally recognized in India. The discrepancy between the two locales hints at the cross-cultural dimension of coming out. His view of marriage is based on reproduction (line 38) and serves as a reference point by which heterosexuality is institutionally sanctioned. Because of the role that traditional, heterosexual marriage plays in Indian society and in the diaspora, resistance to it becomes an emblem of same-sex desire that *authenticates* the construction of a gay identity. His disapproving positioning to marriage as an institutional landmark on the social landscape contributes to the emergence of a gay identity that exists opposite heterosexuality. Reyansh's hypothetical narrative contextualizes the discussion of hetero/homosexual binary and represents the unsaid or repressed desire.

Sexual categorization, as shown in Figure 2, guides Reyansh's understanding of heterosexuality and homosexuality, a delineation between two forms of desire that either *denaturalizes* or *authenticates* a gay identity. The discursive expression of "marrying a woman and having sex with her" denotes a man's heterosexual desire for a woman. Fulfilling this act would supposedly position a man as "straight" when heterosexual marriage legally assures such positioning. However, through repeated self-reference and explicit disavowal of said heterosexual activity (lines 34 and 40) as understood in the social structure, the hypothetical scenario in Reyansh's definition *illegitimates* his presumed heterosexual desire and *authorizes* his homosexual desire. "Straight" sex, for Reyansh, would be purely reproductive, without actual physical or emotional engagement he otherwise has for men (lines 35 and 42). In this regard, the construction of sexual identities hinges on fitting one's desire against conventionally recognized forms of sexual categories.

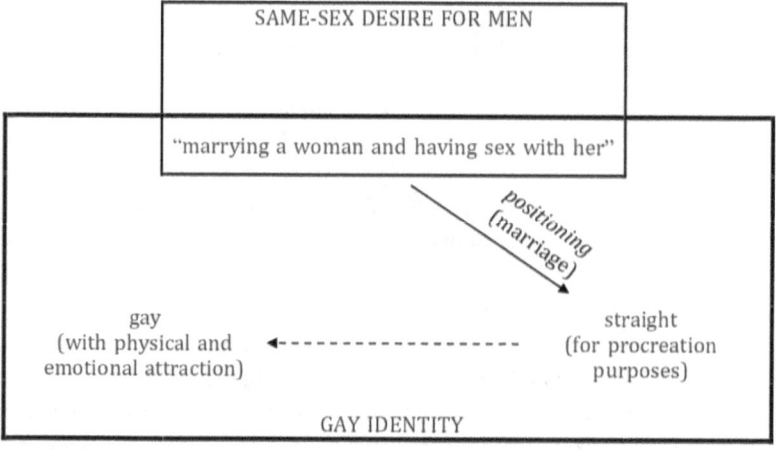

Figure 2: Desire and identity in Reyansh's narrative.

Interestingly, the "bisexual" category is mentioned once and likened to having episodic or sporadic sex (lines 27–30). This creates yet another inversion; in Reyansh's case, heterosexuality is constructed as having sexual desire for women through social and familial obligations while homosexuality is intended to be a committed desire for men. Similar to Rust's (1996) observation that bisexuality is positioned as neither lesbian nor gay, only in reverse, Reyansh's account of not being bisexual affirms his same-sex desire. The designation of same-sex affairs as a sign of bisexuality illustrates the fluid and arbitrary connection between sexual practices and ideological constructs (Wong, Roberts, & Campbell-Kibler 2002).

In the next example, Arjun's description of coming out shows that defining coming out is achieved through relationally positioning others to accentuate that he is "different" from the people around him (italicized for emphasis).

Excerpt 3
1.	Ping:	So, can you tell me something about coming out.
2.		Like what is coming out to you.
3.		What do you think coming out is.
4.	Arjun:	To me, it was, I guess a statement that,
5.		I was making in my circle of friends,
6.		And initially it was just friends, not so much family.
7.	Ping:	Mhm.
8.	Arjun:	Uh, to describe my own- (.) how- how I see myself
9.	Ping:	Yeah.
10.	Arjun:	And how I recognize that- that was *different*.
11.	Ping:	Mhm.
12.	Arjun:	*From um the ways my friends were,*
		Planning their lives out.
13.	Ping:	Mhm.

In defining coming out, Arjun positions himself in relation to other story characters through the voicing of his inner thoughts, indicating that, for him, coming out has an introspective element to be relayed to others. That is, coming out involves a way "to describe himself" and "how he sees himself" (line 8), a reflexivity in which the protagonist, seen externally as an 'other,' is distinguished from the narrator; at the same time, this self-acknowledgement is made among "his friends" (lines 5 and 12) and later "family" (line 6). By making this connection, the idea of being different gains saliency in the telling of sexual stories, wherein identities are marked out of "the other" as defined by the differences and in turn "structure the moral life of culture, group, and individual" (Plummer 1995, 178). By the same token, differences based on binary opposition are not equal as one is always subordinated to the other (Leap & Motschenbacher 2012; Sedgwick 1990). Consequently, differences are never neutral as they make sense through the homo/heterosexual binary and entail divergence from the perceived norms of heterosexuality rather than the other way around.

Comparable to Reyansh's moment of realization, Arjun's cognizance of this difference constitutes a form of disavowal by distinguishing what is not normative. Relational positioning through the mentioning of other story characters, then, verifies Arjun's same-sex desire in order for a gay identity to be *authenticated*. In his framing, coming out means recognizing this *distinction*, in which his same-sex desire is inversely marked. By explaining that coming out makes "planning his life out" different for him from his friends (line 12), this distancing *denaturalizes* his presumed heterosexual identity.

Excerpt 4

14.	Arjun:	When I was first coming out,
15.		I had a conscious sort of thought,
16.		Saying, "I know from this point onward,"
17.	Ping:	Mhm.
18.	Arjun:	"My life is going to be very *different*."
19.	Ping:	Yeah?
20.	Arjun:	*From all the lives of my (.) peers and friends*
21.		*That I grew up with.*
22.	Ping:	Mhm.
23.	Arjun:	And (.) so I had to make that statement.
24.	Ping:	Yeah.
25.	Arjun:	Uh, for my own self, saying,
26.	Ping:	Mhm.
27.	Arjun:	"Yes, this is *different* and this is who I am."
28.		And I think it was just recognizing that,
29.		And- and articulating that *difference*.
30.	Ping:	Mhm.
31.	Arjun:	It was important at some point.
32.	Ping:	Mhm.
33.	Arjun:	Family came sort of later.
34.		Obviously at some point I knew that,
35.		Coming out meant not just coming out to friends,
36.		But family as well.
37.	Ping:	Mhm.
38.	Arjun:	But initially that was not even thinkable,
39.		I mean (.) to come out to (.) my parents, my cousin.

When Arjun recounts the moment when he came out to himself, he stages a conversation to create a performance effect. The tense inflection corresponds to the construction of his inner speech as dialogue, whereby he transposes me, the interviewer, back to the then and there in the past event (De Fina & Perrino 2011). The present-tense dialogue in the story world (lines 16, 18, and 27) is embedded in the past-tense recount in the storytelling event (lines 15 and 23). Furthermore, the time markers contribute to the continuity of his narrative. Starting with "when I was first coming out" (line 14), he notes that it will be a process for him "from that point onward" (line 16). However, in lines 31 and 34, the time "at some point" becomes elusive without a definite point of reference, suggesting that despite an awareness of the eventual disclosure to his family (lines, 33, 36, and 39), Arjun is uncertain when it comes to the execution. The difficulty of coming out to family might seem common, but for Arjun, it is complicated by the need for translating, both literally and figuratively, the concept of coming out into his first language for his family to understand. Therefore, a cultural barrier is implied in his coming-out narrative, leading to the emergence of his Indian identity in his narrative positioning. In contrast, that Arjun is able to elaborate to me in English implies the use of English as lingua franca in "the linguistic construction of non-heteronormative desires" (Leap & Motschenbacher 2012) and its hegemonic role in "international academic practices" (Wieringa & Sívori 2013), thus underscoring both the research context and my positionality as the interviewer.

Arjun's definition of coming out prominently features the consistent theme of *distinction*. The resultant identity is multidimensional. For one, Arjun's remark that having same-sex desire makes him different from "his peers and friends that he grew up with" (lines 20–21) presumably points to the heterosexual majority, as Davies (1992) describes in his study. Still, the positioning away from these people, likely of the same ethnic background, evokes his past of migration from India, during which Arjun was introduced to the concept of coming out in the U.S. Like Reyansh's account, Indian cultural references are mostly implicit: though not foregrounded, his immigrant identity manages to emerge as he highlights this difference. For another, the distance he creates between his family and him because of the potential coming out (lines 38–39) suggests that this positioning entails tension with his Indian friends and family. Arjun's expression of same-sex desire, as opposed to the recourse to explicitly naming the object of sexual desire in Reyansh's definition, underscores the social aspect of coming out and being gay in relation to others. In short, Arjun's narrative reenactment of the perceived differences from his peers *authenticates* an immigrant, gay identity.

In addition to Arjun's migration, the implicitness of "differences" is able to function as a social semiotic of desire also because of the interview context conducted in Washington D.C. with me, as illustrated in Figure 3. First, the study's call for participants and my question requesting information related to his experiences with coming out set the conditions for interpreting Arjun's responses. In his definition, coming out, and being gay in the U.S. by extension, relies on a tacit and shared understanding between the interviewee and interviewer (Wang 2022) that allows for meaning making even with few verbal details available. Through tacitness, though unlike Reyansh's direct citation of the "gay" category, Arjun's designation of his same-sex desire is neither secret nor silent (Decena 2011). Second, my positionality as (East) Asian and gay likewise facilitates such understanding between the interviewee and interviewer. As both the interviewer and the narrative recipient, I play a co-participant role in the interview context, and my knowledge of the topic corroborates Arjun's positioning. In other words, without the particularity of this sociolinguistic interview, the concept of difference alone may be insufficient to deduce his gayness. It is the research setting and the interview dynamics between the two of us that enable Arjun's positioning of his desire toward the gay category, whereby a gay identity is *authorized* interactionally and institutionally.

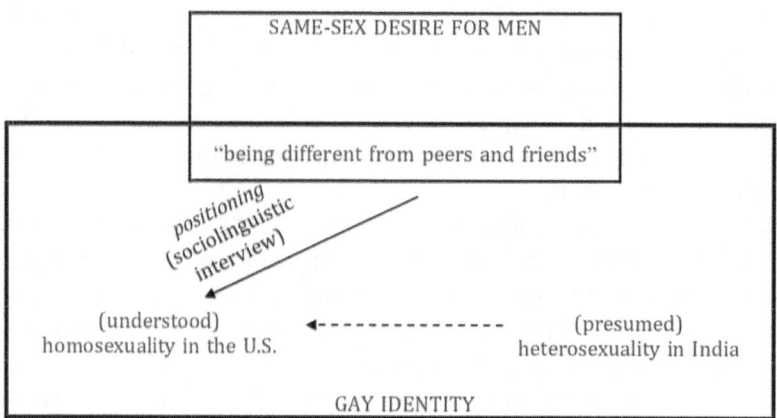

Figure 3: Desire and identity in Arjun's narrative.

In the final example, Daksh's definition of coming out, namely "telling people who he is" (italicized for emphasis), also combines a sense of self and his relationships with others. Besides this feature, Daksh's response to my question adds a layer of morality to the processual quality of coming out.

Excerpt 5
1. Ping: What is coming out.
2. What does it mean to you.
3. Daksh: Uh coming out to me means uh ((tsk)) *telling* (.) *myself*
4. And *People* I interact on a day to day basis *who I am.*
5. That's- that's how I look at it.
6. And that could be anyone.
7. For me, it started-
8. Obviously it started back in my school days.
9. So it was friends and,
10. While I was living with them, my roommates.
11. Ping: Mhm.
12. Daksh: And then it was my brother,
13. And the natural progression was families.
14. That was how it started.
15. Coming out, for me, was *letting them know who I am.*
16. You know, my sexual preferences and what not.
17. Ping: Mhm.
18. Daksh: Yeah. So, and then for me coming out does not stop like,
19. Like it's not like a one time thing.
20. Ping: Yeah.

The commonly noted processual quality of coming out is evinced in Daksh's description that it occurs "on a day to day basis" (line 4), "coming out does not stop" (line 18), and "it's not like a one time thing" (line 19), discursively presenting his coming-out experience as generic, habitual, and processual. The temporal continuity likewise reveals in his narrative order, with the very beginning (lines 7–8) followed by "and then" (line 12) and "the progression" (line 13). Together, these can be seen as a discursive representation that corresponds to the *processuality* that Liang (1997) observes.

Although Daksh lists specific others for coming out to be fulfilled, including friends, roommates, his brother, and family, he does so by emphasizing a sense of selfhood, illustrated by his word choice "who I am" (lines 4 and 15). This exemplifies an inseparable connection between what Liang (1997) calls *coming out to others*, the act of disclosure to people, and *coming out to self*, the reflexivity of an internal being. These two components of coming-out narratives are mutually constitutive: "coming out to others constantly redefine one's notion of self, and the development of a self-identity drives the process of disclosure (Davies 1992, 75). The use of repetition linguistically represents the temporal continuity across the people who he has come out to. Listing these people functions as repetition, whereby the repeated phrase of "telling others who I am" marks the opening and closing of one segment of his definition, threading individual utterances into a unified discourse and, by implication, isolated instances into a coherent life story. Similar to Arjun's example, the relationships with other story characters are built on mutual acknowledgement of his same-sex desire not only as an internal feeling but also as an external and social agreement so that these connections position Daksh toward an 'out' category of homosexuality and thereby *authenticate* his gay identity.

Excerpt 6

21.	Daksh:	Uh. So for me it did not stop just because,
22.		I came out to my family or friends at school.
23.		It was like, it happens every time, uh, I move.
24.		Or I start work. Uh when I went to grad school.
25.		Um different time.
26.		At different time of my life I was coming out.
27.		To people right?
28.		So it's like a thing that continues.
29.	Ping:	It's like an ongoing [process].
30.	Daksh:	[It's an] ongoing process yeah.
31.		And. Uh and it's an ongoing process.
32.		It doesn't become easier.
33.		Uh I would say. It <u>does</u> become easier but it is um,
34.		It feels the right thing to do as- as the years go by.

35.	Ping:	Mhm.
36.	Daksh:	I mean initially you had doubts,
37.		"Ok, I'm coming out."
38.		"Alright I'm not doing the right thing."
39.		But as the years go by, it goes like,
40.		"OH just like a normal thing."

In line 29, I, the interviewer, contribute to the theme of *processuality* in order to demonstrate my understanding of the gist up to this point. Halfway through, Daksh picks up the line and incorporates it into his own account, which illustrates the co-construction of meaning in narrative and the cooperative achievement of textual coherence between the interviewee and interviewer. Also notable in the second part, major life events instantiate the *processuality* of coming out for Daksh (lines 22–24) as the narrated self encounters several social landmarks (Rust, 1993), where coming out is continually necessitated because newly acquainted people come to reinstate heteronormative expectations to be challenged anew. When Daksh's narrative connects these distinct institutional settings, such as the school and workplace, and the people associated with these places, the relations between these elements further reinforce textual coherence in his definition of coming out, with which Daksh then embodies and reenacts the precarious state of being out, or put another way, doing outness. Outness, in this sense, is to be maintained performatively through reiteration (Butler, 1990), so that one's same-sex desire can be recognized and brought into reality. This characterization of coming out resonates with how Reyansh establishes heterosexuality or bisexuality opposite his own desire and how Arjun needs to differentiate himself from others as regards planning his life.

Moreover, the changing landmarks encapsulate how coming out as a form of "social relocation" (Rust 1993) materializes in Daksh's definition as physical relocation. This relates to Perez's (2005) comment that being gay and coming out possess "mobility" and that coming out is a canonized metaphor that expresses "the link between identity and travel" (177). In this regard, moving for education or employment not only necessitates but also facilitates coming out when transnational migration is factored in: the citizenship and nationality afford a new cultural script for Daksh and the other participants to rearticulate their same-sex desire through the coming out discourse in the U.S. (Wang forthcoming). This shows that for these same-sex desiring Indian immigrants, coming out may be construed in a similar way to their gay counterparts in the U.S. Cultural differences, however, may be less definite or clear-cut than a direct correlation to narrative components. As the construction of identity often occurs in plurality, in which multiple social categories may compete with or compromise each other, Daksh's gay identity emerges as he positions himself in named settings, whereas his immigrant identity is eclipsed in his definition of coming out. Transnationality, while it holds the potential for the construction of non-normative desires and identities (Leap & Motschenbacher 2012), remains a subtle contextual clue that becomes perceivable in the requirements for participant recruitment and the use of the English in the sociolinguistic interview.

Finally, coming out in Daksh's definition takes on a moral sense as "the right thing to do" (line 34). A key moment of transition is when he self-repairs in lines 32–33, which yields dual interpretations. On the one hand, that "coming out doesn't become easier" bears a sense of continuity, that is, the performative efforts required to come out remain unchanged. On the other hand, the concept of an increased ease brings out a moral dimension of coming out as someone gets used to outness and its implications. The latter interpretation is supported by Daksh's framing of coming out as "the right thing," echoing the "coming out imperative" that distinguishes between being out as brave and honest and being 'closeted' as hiding and deceiving (Rasmussen 2004). At this juncture, his brief recount charts a trajectory from once having doubts over the motivation for coming out (line 36), which would *illegitimate* an identification as gay, to the ultimate rationalization of coming out as "a normal thing" (lines 38 and 40), which *authorizes* a gay identity as the outcome of an expected course of action. As Daksh borrows the Western coming out discourse around said imperative to express his same-sex desire, his view justifies his decision to come out in the sociolinguistic interview (Wang 2021) and suggests that doing so is no longer debatable. Mapped onto the desire-identity framework, as shown in Figure 4, Daksh's same-sex desire, previously considered questionable, is now warranted by the moral values that outness stands for. This desire, repeatedly expressed and affirmed, is positioned along the continued relocation in Daksh's life, a process that enables the emergence of a gay identity on the basis of social mobility and morality. This signifies the normalization of coming out as an acceptance strategy (Motschenbacher 2020) and reflects the homonormativity that frames certain forms of homosexuality as more normative than others (Motschenbacher & Stegu 2013). In short, while so far the examples have shown that heteronormativity is frequently evoked to communicate one's same-sex desire in coming out, other forms of normativity may also be at work in order for this desire to be identified or even approved in language. Such processes revolving language and sexuality increasingly come under linguistic scrutiny and have become one of the major issues concerning the discursive construction of desire, identity, and normativity that linguistics, as a discipline, is positioned to explore.

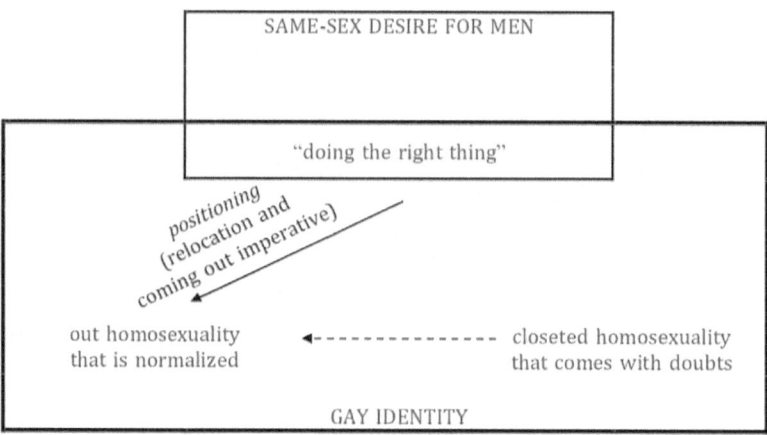

Figure 4: Desire and identity in Daksh's narrative.

5 Conclusion

Using narrative analysis to tease out the microlevel positioning in coming-out narratives, this chapter illustrates how the participants define coming out, whereby their same-sex desire is formulated in ways that an intelligible gay identity emerges in the interview. In terms of methodology, a close examination of coming-out narratives highlights the discourses either acknowledged or contested by the participants. Worth noting is how, in the transcripts, the participants' responses are visibly occasioned to the way I phrase the question (*what is coming out to you*); their definitions are prefaced by the same hedging device of "to me" or "for me," which sometimes persists over a few turns. The participants' strategy to limit the scope in effect qualifies their own understanding of sexuality for sociolinguistic interviews, an underlying yet fundamental element to be reckoned with in the research of language and sexuality (Guittar 2013; Manning 2013). Focusing on participant-centered definitions illuminates the archetype of coming-out discourse, or a meta-narrative that, according to Wong (2009), sustains the construction of the gay imaginary in the U.S.

In terms of discursive features, the examples illustrate that *processuality* is indeed prominent, at times clearly spelled out and other times alluded to with named individuals or places. On the contrary, the concepts of *coming out to self* and *coming out to others* appear highly intertwined and, as a result, neither one easily ascribes to cultural differences as in Liang's (1997) findings. In fact, insisting on culturally correlated differences in participants' perception or expression of sexuality produces a false dichotomy (Huang 2021), which may adversely render non-Western subjects as much as researchers the subaltern outliers (Wang 2022). The participants' Indian/immigrant identity is likewise emergent though often implicit or implied. Rather than restricting immigrants' experiences of coming out in the U.S. to case studies, heightened disciplinary reflection allows for arguments about the transnational circulation and renditions of queerness (Boellstorff & Leap 2004; Chávez 2013).

Finally, this reflection redirects attention back to Western theorization of sexuality and investigates its validity or applicability of the less eventful recounts of coming out (as opposed to well-structured narratives with suspense and a climax, see Wang 2017, for example). While identity is becoming a common analytical tool for sexuality studies across social sciences, the infusion of desire into its linguistic construction may well reinvigorate related studies on language and sexuality. Specifically, it shows how coming out is transformed into a belief system for establishing narrative coherence, namely, a normalizing technique to validate one's same-sex desire. Coming out, and the recount of it, invariably pertains to categories (McCormick 2015), which suppose and sustain normative discourses. Research should meaningfully engage with linguistic categorization (Barrett 2002) to address the queer linguistic concern about how language construct, above all, social difference. A gay identity, in this vein, is carved out of multiple layers of binary exclusion (Wang, forthcoming). For these participants, the perlocutionary effect of coming out to alter social reality as regards their sexuality in relation to others (Liang 1997) holds true, but the speech act is effectuated by categories as an intersubjective reality that comes as a later acquisition in their life. Their accounts, rather than linguistic exceptions, inform the working of desire and identity, which ought not to stay marginalized in the academia but decenter the taken-for-granted theoretical assumptions.

More research is always needed to explore these cross-cultural challenges and norms as illustrated in these narratives. As the examples show, coming out, which seems to contest heteronormativity on a social macro-level, also upholds homonormativity on the local level (Motschenbacher & Stegu 2013): it is recounted to normalize the participants' sense of self and rationalize their acceptance of gayness. In this light, participant definitions can lend insights into lived experiences and theoretical reflections on the interrelationships between desire and identity.

Transcription Conventions

[text]	the start and end points of overlapping speech.
(.)	a brief pause, usually less than 0.2 seconds.
.	falling pitch.
?	rising pitch.
,	a temporary rise or fall in intonation.
-	an abrupt halt or interruption in utterance.
underline	the speaker is emphasizing or stressing the speech.
:::	prolongation of an utterance.
((italic text))	annotation of non-verbal activity.
"text"	reported speech or constructed dialogue

References

Barrett, Rusty. 2002. Is queer theory important for sociolinguistic theory? In Kathryn Campbell-Kibler, Robert J. Podesva, Sarah J. Roberts & Andrew Wong (eds.), *Language and sexuality: Contesting meaning in theory and practice*. 25–43. Stanford, CA: CSLI.

Boellstorff, Tom & William Leap 2004. Introduction: Globalization and "new" articulations of same-sex desire. In William Leap & Tom Boellstorff (eds.), *Speaking in queer tongues: Globalization and gay language*. 1–21. Urbana: University of Illinois Press.

Bucholtz, Mary & Kira Hall. 2004. Theorizing identity in language and sexuality research. *Language in Society* 33(4). 469–515.

Butler, Judith. 1990. *Gender trouble: Feminism and the subversion of identity*. London: Routledge.

Canakis, Costas. 2015. The desire for identity and the identity of desire: Language, gender and sexuality in the Greek context. *Gender and Language* 9(1). 59–81.

Cameron, Deborah & Don Kulick. 2003. *Language and sexuality*. Cambridge: Cambridge University Press.

Cashman, Holly R. 2018. *Queer, Latinx, and bilingual: Narrative resources in the negotiation of identities*. London: Routledge.

Chakravorty, Sanjoy, Devesh Kapur & Nirvikar Singh. 2016. *The other one percent: Indians in America*. New York: Oxford University Press.

Chan, Connie S. 1995. Issues of sexual identity in an ethnic minority: The case of Chinese American lesbians, gay men, and bisexual people. In Anthony R. D'Augelli & Charlotte J. Patterson (eds.), *Lesbian, gay, and bisexual identities over the lifespan: Psychological perspectives*. 87–101. Oxford: Oxford University Press.

Chávez, Karma. 2013. Pushing boundaries: Queer intercultural communication. *Journal of International and Intercultural Communication* 6(2). 83–95.

D'Emilio, John. 1983. Capitalism and gay identity. In Ann Snitow, Christine Stansell & Sharon Thompson (eds.), *Powers of Desire: The Politics of Sexuality*. 100–113. New York: Monthly Review Press.

Davies, Peter. 1992. The role of disclosure in coming out among gay men. In Ken Plummer (ed.), *Modern homosexualities: Fragments of lesbian and gay experience*. 75–83. London: Routledge.

De Fina, Anna & Sabina Perrino. 2011. Introduction: Interviews vs. 'natural' contexts: A false dilemma. *Language in society* 40(1). 1–11.

Decena, Carlos U. 2011. *Tacit subjects. In Tacit Subjects.* Durham, NC: Duke University Press.

DiDomenico, Stephen. 2015. "Putting a face on a community": Genre, identity, and institutional regulation in the telling (and retelling) of oral coming-out narratives. *Language in Society* 44(5). 607–628.

Edwards, Tim 2005. Queering the pitch? Gay masculinities. In Michael S. Kimmel, Jeff Hearn & Robert W. Connell (eds.), *Handbook of studies on men and masculinities.* 51–68. Thousand Oaks, CA: Sage.

Gaudio, Rudolf P. 2005. Language and sexuality and Talking gender and sexuality. *Language in Society* 34(2). 277–282.

Gonsiorek, John C. 1995. Gay male identities: Concepts and issues. In Anthony R. D'Augelli & Charlotte J. Patterson (eds.), *Lesbian, gay, and bisexual identities over the lifespan: Psychological perspectives.* 24–47. Oxford: Oxford University Press.

Gordon, Cynthia & Deborah Tannen. 2021. Interactional sociolinguistics: Foundations, developments, and applications to language, gender, and sexuality. In Jo Angouri & Judith Baxter (eds.), *The Routledge Handbook of Language, Gender, and Sexuality.* 181–196. London: Routledge.

Green, Adam I. 2008. The social organization of desire: The sexual fields approach. *Sociological Theory* 26(1). 25–50.

Guittar, Nicholas A. 2013. The meaning of coming out: From self-affirmation to full disclosure. *Qualitative Sociology Review* 9(3). 168–187.

Hall, Kira. 2013. Commentary I: "It's a hijra!' Queer linguistics revisited. *Discourse & Society* 24(5). 634–642.

Huang, Shuzhen. 2021. Alternatives to coming out discourses. *Oxford research encyclopedia of communication.* Retrieved from https://oxfordre.com/communication/view/10.1093/acrefore/9780190228613.001.0001/acrefore-9780190228613-e-1179.

Herdt, Gilbert H. 1997. *Same sex, different cultures exploring gay and lesbian lives.* Boulder, Colorado: Westview Press.

Kong, Travis S., Dan Mahoney & Ken Plummer. 2001. Queering the interview. In Jaber F. Gubrium & James A. Holstein (eds.), *Handbook of interview research.* 239–258. New York: SAGE Publications, Inc.

Leap, William & Heiko Motschenbacher. 2012. Launching a new phase in language and sexuality studies. *Journal of Language and Sexuality* 1(1). 1–14.

Lemke, Jay L. 2008. Identity, development and desire: Critical questions. In Carmen R. Caldas-Coulthard & Rick Iedema (eds.), *Identity trouble: Critical discourse and contested identities.* 17–42. London: Palgrave Macmillan.

Liang, A. C. 1997. The creation of coherence in coming-out stories. In Anna Livia & Kira Hall (eds.), *Queerly phrased: Language, gender, and sexuality.* 287–309. Oxford: Oxford University Press.

Luther, J. Daniel & Jennifer Ung Loh. 2019. Introduction. In J. Daniel Luther & Jennifer Ung Loh (eds.), *'Queer Asia': Decolonising and reimagining sexuality and gender.* 1–26. London: Zed Books Ltd.

Manning, Jimmie. 2013. Interpretive theorizing in the seductive world of sexuality and interpersonal communication: getting guerilla with studies of sexting and purity rings. *International Journal of Communication* 7. 2507–2520.

McCormick, Tracey L. 2015. Queering discourses of coming out in South Africa. *African Studies* 74(3). 327–345.

Mezey, Nancy J. 2008. The privilege of coming out: race, class, and lesbians' mothering decisions. *International Journal of Sociology of the Family.* 257–276.

Morrish, Liz & Helen Sauntson. 2007. *New perspectives on language and sexual identity*. New York: Springer.

Motschenbacher, Heiko. 2020. Coming out and normative shifts: Investigating usage patterns of gay and homosexual in a corpus of news reports on Ricky Martin. *Sociolinguistic Studies* 14(1–2). 61–84.

Motschenbacher, Heiko & Martin Stegu. 2013. Introduction: Queer Linguistic approaches to discourse. *Discourse & Society* 24(5). 519–535.

Ochs, Elinor. 1992. Indexing Gender. In Alessandro Duranti & Charles Goodwin (eds.), *Rethinking context: Language as an interactive phenomenon*. 335–358. Cambridge: Cambridge University Press.

Orne, Jason. 2011. 'You will always have to "out" yourself': Reconsidering coming out through strategic outness. *Sexualities* 14(6). 681–703.

Pak, Vincent. 2021. Coming out 'softly': metapragmatic reflections of gay men in illiberal pragmatic Singapore. *Gender & Language* 15(3). 301–323.

Perez, Hiram. 2005. You can have my brown body and eat it, too! *Social text* 3(4). 171–191.

Plummer, Ken. 1995. *Telling sexual stories: Power, change, and social worlds*. London: Routledge.

Queen, Robin. 2014. Language and sexual identities. In Susan Ehrlich, Miriam Meyerhoff & Janet Holmes (eds.), *The handbook of language, gender, and sexuality*. 203–219. Malden, MA: Wiley-Blackwell.

Rasmussen, Mary Lou 2004. The problem of coming out. *Theory Into Practice* 43(2). 144–150.

Rofel, Lisa. 1999. Qualities of desire: imagining gay identities in China. *GLQ: A Journal of Lesbian and Gay Studies* 5(4). 451–474.

Rust, Paula C. 1993. 'Coming out' in the age of social constructionism: Sexual Identity formation among lesbian and bisexual women. *Gender and Society* 7(2). 50–77.

Rust, Paula C. 1996. "Coming out" in the age of social constructionism: Sexual identity formation among lesbian and bisexual women. *Journal of Lesbian Studies* 1(1). 25–54.

Sauntson, Helen. 2015. Coming out stories. In Patricia Whelehan & Anne Bolin (eds.), *The International Encyclopedia of Human Sexuality*. New York: Wiley-Blackwell.

Seidman, Steven. 1996. *Queer theory/sociology*. Oxford: Blackwell Publishers.

Sedgwick, Eve K. 1990. *Epistemology of the closet*. Berkeley: University of California Press.

Spijkerboer, Thomas. 2013. Sexual identity, normativity and asylum. In Thomas Spijkerboer (ed.), *Fleeing homophobia: Sexual orientation, gender identity and asylum*. 217–238. New York: Routledge.

Valentine, David. 2003. 'I went to bed with my own kind once': the erasure of desire in the name of identity. *Language & Communication* 23(2). 123–138.

Wang. Ping-Hsuan. 2017. Out of the country, out of the closet: Coming-out stories in cross-cultural contexts. *Southern Journal of Linguistics* 41(2). 173–198.

Wang, Ping-Hsuan. 2020. Negotiating racialized sexuality through online stancetaking in text-based communication. In D. Nicole Farris, D'Lane R. Compton & Andrea P. Herrera (eds.), *Gender, sexuality, and race in the digital age*. 187–203. London: Springer.

Wang, Ping-Hsuan. 2021. "When I came to the US": constructing migration in gay Indian immigrants' coming-out narratives. *Narrative Inquiry* 31(2). 338–357.

Wang, Ping-Hsuan. 2022. Coming out for another: positioning against 'closeted' gay men in Indian immigrants' coming-out narratives. *Journal of Asian Pacific Communication*. Online first. Retrieved from: 10.1075/japc.00092.wan

Wang, Ping-Hsuan. (forthcoming). Querying peripheral identities with penumbral positionings in 'gay' immigrants' 'coming-back-in' narratives. In Yoshiko Matsumoto & Jan-Ola Östman (eds.), *Identity perspectives from peripheries*. Amsterdam: John Benjamins.

Whitehead, Harriet. 1981. The bow and the burden strap: a new look at institutionalized homosexuality in Native North America. In Sherry Ortner & Hariet Whitehead (eds.), *Sexual meanings: the cultural construction of gender and sexuality*. 80–115. Cambridge: Cambridge University Press.

Wieringa, Saskia & Horacio Sívori. 2013. Sexual politics in the global south: Framing the discourse. In Saskia Wieringa & Horacio Sívori (eds.), *The sexual history of the Global South: Sexual politics in Africa, Asia and Latin America*. 1–21. London: Zed Books Ltd.

Wong, Andrew. 2009. Coming-out stories and the "gay imaginary." *Sociolinguistic Studies* 3(1). 1–36.

Wong, Andrew, Sarah J. Roberts & Kathryn Campbell-Kibler. 2002. Speaking of sex. In Kathryn Campbell-Kibler, Robert Podesva, Sarah J. Roberts & Andrew Wong (eds.), *Language and sexuality: Contesting meaning in theory and practice*. 1–22. Stanford, CA: CSLI.

Brenton Watts
Mountain magic
Creating and maintaining community in an Appalachian folk magic social media group

1 Introduction

Appalachia is a sociogeographical and cultural region in the Eastern United States that spans from lower New York State to upper Alabama and Georgia, roughly corresponding to the Appalachian Mountains. The region and its people have long been the source of myths, with outsiders to the region both valorizing and vilifying Appalachian characteristics as it suits their agenda. For example, John C. Campbell described Appalachians as "contemporary ancestors" to the rest of the country, even as he extolled the virtues of the region. Likewise, authors like JD Vance describe the region as suffering from "learned helplessness." As one might expect, little attention has been paid to the effects and consequences that this mythologization has had on the people of the region itself. Appalachian people, then, are left to contend with a broader culture that characterizes them in particular ways, with most unable to partake in re-imagining those characterizations outside of their own communities. As such, it is important that Appalachians tell their own stories and forge their own futures. It was with this intention that this project began, and so it is with this foregrounding that this chapter begins.

Like many Appalachians, my family is a multigenerational one. Growing up, my cousins, aunts, and uncles were all a short walk from my front yard – quite literally just across the road. The holler we lived on was, and still is, our home, and at the center of this home was the woman responsible for it all. Her name was Gertude, but to me she was Nannan. Like she did for all her other grandchildren, Nannan helped my mom raise me. I consider myself the luckiest of her grandchildren because for all my life, she has lived with my mom and me. In fact, the house I grew up in is the very same house that she raised my mom and all her siblings in. Perhaps because she was my most constant companion for most of my formative years, I idolized Nannan as a child. I would often wear her housecoats and slippers around the house in imitation of her. I was especially enamored by the stories she told about her childhood, growing up on a holler just over the hill from the one we lived on.

Brenton Watts, Independent Scholar

https://doi.org/10.1515/9783110742510-005

Born in 1935, Nannan was one of nine children born to her father, an Old Regular Baptist deacon, and her mother, a homemaker. Neither electricity nor indoor plumbing had yet found their way into rural Eastern Kentucky, yet they carved out a living for themselves through agriculture and shared community aid. The hills were alive with frogsong and the stars shone brilliantly in the night sky. Even with all my modern attachments, the hills of my holler still seem so mysterious and powerful, teeming with life and wizened with age; I can only imagine how they must have seemed to my grandma as a little girl. However, as mysterious and beautiful as they may be, they also posed a very real threat to her and her siblings. Aside from the already high child mortality rate, there was the near-constant danger posed by wildlife. For instance, Nannan's little brother Amos, whom she was always fiercely protective of, almost died from a copperhead bite as a child.[1] In addition to the danger of wildlife, one could also never be sure who else was living in the woods and what intentions they might have – other people, too, also posed a potential threat. Dangerous men who were known to "mistreat" women and children were, of course, cause for concern, regardless of whether or not they actually posed an immediate threat. Likewise, there was also the threat posed by those whom they called witches. Witches were seen as a very real threat to the family and community's security. In contrast to the aforementioned "dangerous men," whose identities were not always known, but whose actions were, people knew who the witches were in their community, yet they didn't know how they managed to do what they did. This certainty of identity coupled with the uncertainty of their methods inspired fear in the community. People knew who they were, and they knew not to wrong them lest they should suffer the consequences.

One witch with such a reputation was a man named Ruben Vires. Ruben was a witch when Nannan's mother was a little girl. Everyone said that the Devil had bestowed supernatural powers upon Ruben. Growing up, Nannan's mother had heard tell that Ruben could make a fencepost dance. Another pair of witches, Wiley and Lula McIntosh, terrorized the community when Nannan was a little girl. They were a married couple, who were also said to have received otherworldly powers from the Devil. Whenever Nannan and her siblings walked by their house as they often did on their way to the store, their parents would make sure they had a coin, like a dime, pinned to the inside of their breast pocket with the side inscribed "In God We Trust" against their heart; this was meant to protect them from the witches' doings. After their deaths, Wiley was laid to rest alone at

---

[1] As such, she and her family developed a healthy fear of snakes. Their unpredictable and potentially fatal nature, coupled with their depiction in the Bible, made them a reasonable source of fear, and as such, it was necessary to be vigilant against them.

a crossroads on an isolated hill further up my family's holler–Lula was not buried with or near him. Traditionally, burial at a crossroads was reserved as a penalty for those who had taken their own lives, a punishment which originated from an early English concept known as *felo de se* (Medieval Latin for "felon of oneself"). The idea behind this type of burial was that the spirit of the deceased would become disoriented by the crossroads, thereby ensuring that they would not return to haunt those whom they had left behind (Halliday 2010). While I cannot confirm Wiley's manner of death, it is likely that his status as a witch earned him this kind of burial. Alternatively, it could also be possible that Wiley actually desired a burial of this nature, as *crossroads* themselves are also associated with the Devil, in a mythological tradition that spans from the Greek goddess of magic Hecate to the Yoruba trickster deity Eshu (Hornblower, Spawforth & Eidinow 2012; Pemberton 1975). Therefore, if Wiley truly considered himself a follower of the Devil and/or a practitioner of magic, he may have intentionally wished to be buried in a traditionally "profane" manner in order to symbolize his relationship with his faith even in death. The crossroads have since grown over, and it wasn't until a neighbor began logging near the grave that it was rediscovered. Wiley's grave still stands to this day and serves as a physical reminder of his legend and his legacy, grounding my grandmother's stories in a reality one can both touch and see.

Nannan's stories are important to me for a number of reasons. When I hear them or share them with others, I feel close to her and to our family, and I can begin to imagine a world that I could never truly experience or fully comprehend. Yet they also inspire me to find similar stories and experiences on my own, in my own ways, and with my own Appalachian community. It is this sense of curiosity that led me to Mountain Magic Facebook group. This group, with members numbering in the tens of thousands, is a virtual space dedicated to the sharing and promotion of Appalachian history, culture, and folk traditions, particularly those involving magic and/or witchcraft.[2] The group emphasizes the practice of mountain magic as a means of spiritual expression and as a way to connect to one's cultural heritage. Moreover, it also functions as a general community message board where members can share pictures, stories, ideas and receive advice and input from likeminded individuals. In much the same way the folklore and religious beliefs of my Nannan's youth both informed her worldview and shaped her lived experiences, so too do to they continue to shape the spiritual and community experiences of Appalachians today. Furthermore, in the context of a Facebook group like the one under analysis, the interactions of tens of thousands of members must also conform to

---

2 Within the group, no distinction is made between magic and witchcraft. As such, I use them interchangeably throughout this chapter.

Facebook's terms of use as well as the arbitration of a small group of moderators and administrators (mods and admins). Mods and admins also enforce the group's rules, exercising control over member admissions, bans, restrictions, and removal of disallowed content. As such, the mods and admins, their rules, and the content they post and approve represent a sufficient substrate for the discursive practices and subjects employed within the group and by its members. Herein, I identify and explain the ways in which the group's mods and admins employ discursive strategies in order to enact interactional constraints upon the user base in the interest of achieving the group's broader goals and maintaining a functional and harmonious community. In doing so, I highlight the myriad effects these strategies have as well as their implications for the user base and practitioners of mountain magic in general. In order to understand magic and witchcraft as it is both practiced and imagined by modern Appalachians in a community context, I begin by recounting my family's personal histories of magic and witches alongside the historical context of magic and witches in and throughout Appalachia. Subsequently, I present the relevant theoretical concepts and methodological processes necessary for this analysis. I then review the relevant literature and highlight the interconnectedness amongst Appalachian, rural, and New Age magical traditions, as well as their connections to queerness and folk life, which is then in turn followed by an analysis proper of the "Mountain Magic" Facebook group.

2 Contextualizing mountain magic

Broadly speaking, this analysis is an investigation into the construction of identity. In sociolinguistics, identities are understood as conceptual representations of self and others created and enabled through social interaction (Bucholtz & Hall 2005). Central to this notion is the idea that identities are dynamic rather than static, evolving and changing over a person's lifetime, yet emerging independently within the context of a given individual interaction (Bucholtz & Hall 2005). In short, an individual's identity may be understood as multiple, intersecting facets which comprise a larger entity that we recognize as an individual. An individual may manifest or diminish aspects of these facets and their intersections in order to achieve certain interactional goals within a given interactional context. Interaction is key to this conceptualization of identity, in that interaction involves performance in the sense of Austin (1962). Performative actions are successfully executed, or *felicitous*, when their context matches the speech act. Performative actions, in this sense, are not limited to spoken or signed contexts, though. Communication within virtual, digitally mediated contexts also hinge upon performative actions in ways that directly parallel in-person contexts (Loke & Golding 2016). Judith Butler builds upon this notion of performativity, arguing that gender is also enacted by means of performativity, in that it makes real the very thing it performs. Likewise, other facets of identity, such as race, regionality, and sexuality, may also be understood as being enacted by means of performativity (Hall 1999). It is for this reason that many linguistic anthropologists reject the idea that identity is pre-discursive. Rather, identity, like the social dimensions which constitute it, is understood to be enacted through performance in social interaction. This conceptualization of identity is central to the analysis of the Mountain Magic FB group in that it allows one to interpret the polyphonous, and often contradictory, nature of online, left-leaning, intentionally inclusive, Appalachian witchcraft social media groups, as well as determine the ways in which the polyphonous members of the group, themselves internally polyphonous, enact and negotiate their many identities while co-managing the shared identity of what we might call "Appalachian magic-user."

As Pennycook (2007) describes, performativity is a balancing act in that it must respond to the constraints of both the restrictive pre-existing context and its own potential for (re-)fashioning new futures and possibilities. Gray (2009) establishes the multiple ways in which queer people throughout rural and Appalachian Kentucky manage this balancing act, by working around and through the boundaries of cisheteronormative public spaces. Most notably, Gray (2009) found that online spaces were especially suited to this kind of identity work. For a variety of reasons, online modalities further the potential for breaking pre-existing restrictions and increase the potential for imagining new ways of being. One way that members of the Mountain Magic FB group engage in this is simply by the reclamation and use of "witch" as a self-descriptor. This is in part a reclamation of pre-existing discourses wherein Appalachians are depicted as peripheral, villainous, monstrous, or otherwise dangerous to decent, normative society – e.g., the 1972 film *Deliverance* (Li-Volmmer & Lapointe 2003; Massey 2007).This reclamation is, in a sense, compounded when group members who describe themselves as "witches" or otherwise identify with the subversive character of the Mountain Magic FB group have additional identities that are hegemonically oppressed by Christian, White, cisheteronromative society. For example, Bjork-James (2018) found that a person who overtly claims a queer identity within an evangelical culture will be publicly marked as someone who is incompatible with that culture, and thus face ostracization. For many members, then, the Mountain Magic FB group serves as a found community that allows them to reconnect to their Appalachian heritage in an environment more free from these oppressive pressures. Many may also not have the option to experience this kind of heritage without such an online community. For one, some may be disowned from their Appalachian families on account of their gender or sexuality; while for some, general interest in alternative modes of spirituality, such as magic, is enough to merit disowning from their fundamentalist Christian kin. Still others may have had to distance themselves for personal reasons, such as teenage pregnancy, substance use, politics, or any number of reasons. In short, Appalachian families are not unique in the ways they fall apart. Furthermore, many more may still be on friendly terms with their Appalachian families but belong to the larger Appalachian diaspora and therefore may lack immediate access to Appalachian spaces, communities, and resources. Regardless of the reason, in this context, there is a heavy correlation between non-normative Appalachian outcasts and practitioners of Appalachian magic. Anecdotally, I expect this to be attributable to a shared opposition towards and oppression by hegemonic Christian practices, though I cannot confirm this. In a similar fashion to queer heritage, it is for these reasons that Appalachian heritage is not always so easily inherited. Often, both queer and Appalachian communities must be (re-)found and (re-)communicated. Social media facilitates the extension and maintenance of Appalachian communities across time and space, aiding queer, Appalachian, and queer-Appalachian people alike in (re-)claiming their communities and identities (Watts 2020). Furthermore, the prevalence of online social media communities for Appalachians, particularly magic- or queer-centric communities, complicates the notion of metronormativity, which positions the rural and urban as socially and spatially opposite spheres, and posits urban spaces as the only safe space for queer existence and community (Halberstam 2005). In addition to its anti-metronormative leanings, social media groups like the Mountain Magic FB group also bolster the notion of queer anti-urbanism, by interrogating urbanist and homonormative assumptions about queer (and) Appalachian life (Herring 2007, 2010).

As a queer Appalachian, my queerness and Appalachianness are inextricably linked to one another. I came to understand the world and how it worked at the juncture of these two contexts. As such, I find it necessary to analyze both queer and Appalachian issues through both Appalachian and queer perspectives, respectively. I do this in part because it reflects my lived experiences and represents the nature of my scientific process. Of greater import, though, is that a queer-Appalachian analysis highlights the existence and value of queer Appalachians as a people group and as sources of knowledge and practice. This mode of analysis is based on Crenshaw's (1989, 1991) model of intersectionality, which I adopt here to explain the unique situation of queer Appalachians and others who, whether intentionally or not, find themselves in opposition to Christian hegemony in Appalachia.[3] This is to say, for

---

3 Furthermore, the prevalence of Christian hegemony in Appalachia is central to this analysis in that it represents perhaps the most important constraint shaping the spiritual practices and

example, that the issues faced by queer Appalachians are unique to queer Appalachians; that their oppression is not as simple as "homophobia plus classism," but rather that it is multiplex and compounded by multiple intersecting systems of oppression. Alternative interpretations of intersectionality have also been developed by other theorists, such as Yuval-Davis's (2006) axes-of-difference model or Staunæs's (2003) model of intersectionality as a dynamic process. Methodologically, Fotopoulo (2012) serves as the basis for the hybridized approach utilized in this analysis, wherein my status as someone who is discursively situated within both queer-Appalachian and mountain magic discourse is integral to my analytical approach to the study of those subjects. This hybridized approach is reflected in the interdisciplinary nature of this work. Because the subject under analysis is so intersectionally complex, it is necessary to pull from several pools scholarship in order to produce an equally comprehensive analysis–namely, folklore studies, religious studies, Appalachian studies, linguistic anthropology, queer theory, and feminism, among others.

Importantly, the diversity of magic practice within and outside of Appalachia Magic cannot determine falsifiable truths about our perceived experiences. This, though, is not the point of magic as it is commonly practiced. Roughly defined, magic is the employment of beliefs, rituals, and/or actions with the intent to manipulate natural and supernatural forces (Hutton 2017). Additionally, although it may bear some similarities to religion, such as belief in supernatural forces, magic is traditionally considered a separate entity from religion entirely, though in practice this may not always seem the case. Furthermore, within the context of the group, little difference is distinguished between magic and spirituality. If anything, magic and other traditional Appalachian folk practices are construed as tools to engage with and exercise ones spirituality. Religion, on the other hand, which overwhelmingly means Christianity in this context, maintains a hegemonic hold on the rest of spiritual practice, denoting all that is other as "pagan", "magic", etc. Magic practice is important in that allows its users a sense of control and connection: control of their lives and environments, and connection to their ancestors, communities, and higher spiritual realities. Likewise, as the Mountain Magic FB group demonstrates, it is also no surprise that many modern practitioners of magic are primarily women, Queer, Indigenous, Black, and/or poor. Not only does magic provide a sense of control and connection to these individuals in an otherwise chaotic and increasingly hostile world, but folklore, and especially magic, are the perfect discursive arenas in which controversial social issues may be contested (Ellis 2003). As

---

interactions of Appalachian magic-users. Regardless of whether Appalachian magic-users are Christian or not, the context of Appalachia all but necessitates an orientation with respect to Christianity, whatever that orientation may be, as Christianity is the most significant axis of spirituality within Appalachia.

such, interactions within the realm of folklore and magic may provide ideal substrates for community building and transgressive identity work (Thompson 2017). In short, magic is an alternative way of understanding, creating, and sharing knowledge about the world, while subverting hegemonic pressures and expectations. Indeed, many of the magic practices described by members of the group more closely folk traditions and practices that, due to their emphasis on community or nature, run counter to urbanist and metronormative values.

Additionally, the emphasis on individuality and introspection as core tenets of magic or spiritual practice within the group means that there are essentially as many varieties of mountain magic as there are members of the group. This variety is best described through the lens of polyphony, described by Bakhtin as "a plurality of independent and unmerged voices and consciousnesses" (6–7). In other words, there is not a singular tradition of Appalachian folk magic, but rather multiple, varying traditions of similar and related folk knowledge and practices. Like different ways of playing the fiddle, these traditions may vary not just from holler to holler, but from generation to generation as they are iteratively replicated and reinvented by each new participant. Likewise, magic is far from incompatible with religion in Appalachia; in fact, ritual magic and Christianity in Appalachia are quite compatible with one another. For Nannan's mother Gracie (my great grandmother), they were part and parcel—when anyone contested her belief in witches and black magic, she would reply "Well, *the Bible* speaks of witches, and *I* believe the Bible.". Like prayer as well, many Christian, non-witch Appalachians also practiced or believed in faith healing, and though it was never described as such, it may too be considered a magic practice. In my family for example, it is said to be passed down from generation to generation, always to a person of the "opposite" gender. The effectiveness of the ability is said to be dependent on one's faith in Christ, and although theoretically a person of great faith could heal any ailment with this power, it was more commonly used to treat unwanted warts, skin tags, and very minor injuries. I do, however, believe that in much the same way that folklore and magic can serve as ideological arenas where controversies may be sorted, so too can they provide an appropriate headspace for self-theorizing and self-therapitizing.

Like with faith healing, the character of witches in Appalachia is not always so nefarious. Witches are just as often considered benevolent and wise healers who are integral to the success and health of their communities. For example, in the early 20th century John C. Campbell, an educator reformist, and sociologist known for his surveys of Southern Appalachia, wrote the following about granny witches, a specific kind of Appalachian folk healer:

> There is something magnificent in many of the older women with their stern theology–part mysticism, part fatalism–and their deep understanding of life. Patience, endurance, and resignation are written in the close-set mouth and in the wrinkles about the eyes; but the eyes themselves are kindly, full of interest, not unrelieved by a twinkling appreciation of pleasant things. 'Granny'–and one may be a grandmother young in the mountains––if she has survived the labor and tribulation of her younger days, has gained a freedom and a place of irresponsible authority in home hardly rivaled by the men of the family. Her grown sons pay to her an attention which they do not always accord their wives; and her husband, while he remains still undisputed master of the home, defers to her opinion to a degree unknown in her younger days. Her daughters and her grandchildren she frankly rules. Though superstitious she has a fund of common sense, and she is a shrewd judge of character. In sickness she is the first to be consulted, for she is generally something of an herb doctor, and her advice is sought by the young people of half the countryside in all things from a love affair to putting a new web in the loom. It is not surprising if she is something of a pessimist on the subject of marriage. 'Don't you *never* get married,' is advice that is more than likely to pass her lips. (140)

Despite the exceptionalist biases Campbell presents in this excerpt, echoing his "contemporary ancestor" remarks, it nevertheless represents one of the earliest scholarly accounts of the elevated status of granny witches within their communities. The granny witch persists, though she likely does not adhere to the same cisheteronormative constraints that her predecessors did. The new age granny witch is younger, and may not even be a granny, let alone a mother. Most importantly, she need not be cisgender or straight, and sometimes she may not even be a woman; instead, her status as granny witch is bestowed upon her by the others in her community. As some members of the Mountain Magic FB group describe, a granny witch is "the mom friend", whom others can rely upon for advice and connection to the old ways of doing things, without the old biases and prejudices. Moreover, she likely draws upon multiple folk ways from various cultures. This is characteristic of many New Age spiritual traditions and situates the granny witch tradition and other modern Appalachian folk magics firmly within the realm of New Age traditions, which are characterized by their eclectic and unsystematic natures that seem to evade concrete definition (Kemp 2011). The simultaneous conformist and nonconformist characters of these New Age Appalachian folk traditions allows their practitioners to transgress social norms and forge new ways of being that can walk the fine line between normativity and non-normativity. As such, the socially transgressive nature of these traditions allows queer and other non-normative practitioners to do innovative identity work that otherwise may not be available in more normative circles. This is not exclusive to the Appalachian magic practitioners under analysis here. For example, the radical faeries are a New Age movement created by queer men and centered in the notion of rural utopianism and spontaneous spiritual expression. The movement originated in 1976 when Arthur Evans began a "faery circle" in San Francisco for gay men to regularly meet up and explore radical politics and pagan beliefs (Barrett 2017, 57). The culture of the movement bears many similarities to the culture of the Mountain Magic FB group. For one, they appropriate from a variety of cultural practices. For example, radical faeries celebrate the Celtic Beltane while at the same time employing the Germanic Maypole. Sumerian, Egyptian, and European gods are invoked, and many of the rituals derive from Australian Aboriginal or American Indigenous practices (55). Furthermore, like the radical faeries, the Mountain Magic FB group as a whole does not insist upon a single, unified approach to spirituality and magic use. Although Appalachia is still the foreground for practice, members are encouraged to ask for advice, but to do their own research and come to their own conclusions as their spiritual needs dictate and as their circumstances allow. In this sense, both radical faeries and Mountain Magic members employ an individualistic approach to spirituality which runs counter to traditional interpretations of culture. However, these individualistic and appropriative approaches to spirituality are reflective of white, Christian imperialist ideologies that still may still run the risk of subjugating Black, Indigenous, and other traditions sacred to marginalized people of color (Conroy-Krutz 2015).

The heavy and complex social and identity work visible in online social media groups like Mountain Magic is made possible through indexicality. Indexical signs are signs whose meanings are dependent on the context in which they occur (Agha 1998, 2005; Johnstone 1996, 200; Silverstein 2003) and, for example, allow an individual to communicate specific meanings unique to the context of Appalachia or the Appalachian diaspora, and more specifically Appalachian magic and folkways. The potential for indexical association between regional (ized) differences and other cultural, linguistic, or historical traits associated with a region was first described by Tannen (1984). Following Johnstone (2003), these regional(ized) and/or ethnic(ized) differences can function as a strategic discursive resource. The notion of a discursive resource is an important distinction, in that by describing a form, topic, or feature, as a discursive resource, it allows those not in the community to discuss or use the resource without indexing community membership. In-the-know interlocutors, however, will be able to parse the indexical meaning as intended, and thus allow users to do various kinds of both covert and over identity work. Additionally, by describing something as a discursive resource, it allows for the possibility of use by in-the-know users without asserting any kind of ubiquity amongst all or most of a community.

The meanings indexed by indexical signs are, importantly, of varied types which are not mutually exclusive. Eckert (2008) identifies three levels of indexical meanings: stances, traits, and categories. Stances refer to an individual's emotional or affective orientation towards a given subject within an interaction.

Stances may then index an individual's traits (descriptors about the individual), which themselves may point to the highest indexical order of category. For example, a person yawning within an interaction may index disinterest, which then may index the trait of lazy, especially in conjunction with other indexical signs which point to "lazy." If the person repeatedly exhibits this and similar behaviors, they may then be indexically construed as a slacker, a category of person. The most important feature of indexical orders is that, because indexicality is context-dependent, the same unit of discourse might index any number of meanings, at any indexical level, to any number of people.

Related to the concept of indexical orders is the grouping of indexical signs which point to similar related contexts. These groupings are called *registers*. Signs become indexically linked to context-dependent meanings in a process known as *enregisterment*, which has been described in varying yet similar terms by Labov, Silverstein, and Johnstone (Johnstone, Andrus & Danielson 2006). In keeping with the focus on regional identity and variation, Johnstone's terminology is used for this analysis. As such, I conceptualize indexical signs as being first-, second-, or third-order to describe the extent to which they are enregistered. First-order indexical signs are the least salient and are described as only being correlated with social meaning, such as a high frequency of dialectal features correlating to one's membership to their respective dialect region. For this reason, Labov called them *indicators* (1972). Contrastively, second- and third-order indexicals are available for social identity work. Second-order indexicals (*markers* for Labov) are shaped by ideological constraints and previous discursive experiences. In regional variationist linguistics, the highly salient third-order indexicals reinforce essentialist linkings of place and dialect, although they may also reinforce essentialist linkings of dialect or discursive practice with other elements of identity. As such, Labov called them *stereotypes*. Additionally, in much the same way that registers point to contexts, so too do genres point to speech events. In the context of social media, for example, the inclusion of "lol" at the end of a post might index an informal, light-hearted character. However, it also points to the genre of "informal social media post" or "informal text message" because "lol" is used to index affective stance information that otherwise may not be available due to the lack of embodied emotional information in online interactions. Importantly, although interactions are informed and co-constituted by both genre and register, so too are they constrained by them. Digitally mediated interactions are at least as rich with this kind of indexicality and identity work as in-person interactions, with the near infinite number of mixed-media forms available online allowing for an equally infinite number of communications and subsequent interpretations. This potential is highlighted in McCulloch (2019), which makes the case for social media and other digitally mediated interactions as optimal sites of investigation into human interaction and communication. In Watts

(2020), for example, I examined the ways in which the followers of the Instagram account for a queer Appalachian community organization, as well as the account's managers, co-constructed the Mothman and other folkloric figures as queer Appalachian discursive icons. In doing so, I revealed how orientation to these discursive icons could serve to index identification with queer Appalachianness, in ways that transgress normative discourse about sexuality, regionality, and folklore.

Furthermore, given that this analysis primarily concerns visual and written social media posts, I forego the typical variationist emphasis on lexical and phonological features in favor of an emphasis on discursive topics and icons. This follows the precedent set by Cramer (2013) and Cramer (2016), which established that residents of Louisville, Kentucky, as residents of a linguistic and cultural border zone, have access to multiple (and at times conflicting) regional affiliations, and therein multiple regional(ized) discourses which they may employ in identity work. Walker (2019) also established that discourse subjects with significant indexical links to regional(ized) identities have the potential to influence dialectal shifts in speech production, further bolstering discursive topics and icons as sites with great indexical potential.

This work is situated at the juncture of multiple different strands of scholarship. For one, it pulls from linguistic anthropology and discourse analysis methods in to better understand and better represent a wildly misunderstood and under-researched group, namely Appalachians and Appalachian magic-users. Furthermore, by conducting research in a digital space, this work further highlights the ever-expanding possibilities of digital spaces as sites for community-building, identity work, and social research. Lastly, it also represents the validity of Fotopoulo's (2012) hybridity model as a methodological framework, and the usefulness of analyzing intersectionally complex communities through an equally complex lens and with equally interdisciplinary methods.

3 Into the weeds

The data under analysis here were taken from a Facebook group called Mountain Magic. This is not the real name of the group, as the group has private membership, meaning that only members can see who is in the group and what they post. On Facebook, private membership requires that potential members answer a question or series of questions as a condition for being accepted. The group also employs a strict rule regarding the sharing of posts outside of the group, violations of which result in an immediate ban and blocking. To protect the integrity of the group and the anonymity of its members, I have chosen a false name that conveys a similar meaning as the actual group name. As such, I will also not be sharing any screenshots or images from the group. Instead, I have elected to transcribe posts or photos with text only. The methods I employ to analyze these data represent a multimodal critical discourse analysis (MMCDA) and are drawn from Moran and Lee (2013) and are similar to those used by Machin and Mayr (2012) in their MMCDA of Australian genital cosmetic surgery websites. Broadly defined, discourse is "meaningful symbolic behavior" in any mode. (Blommaert 2005). Discourse is an important subject of study because it creates that which constitutes it: as Johnstone (2018) writes, "[d]iscourse is both the source of this knowledge (people's generalizations about language are made on the basis of the discourse they participate in) and the result of it (people apply what they already know in creating and interpreting new discourse)" (2). Furthermore, as cultural and technological contexts have evolved, multi-modal discourse has become all the more present in public life, and as such, discourse analysts have been drawn to the ways in which information is communicated across multiple, parallel modes of expression (Johnstone 2018, 35). In this analysis, MMCDA involves the parallel iterative processes of identifying themes from both written and visual content (in this case, Facebook posts and other Facebook content) coding for those themes, then re-analyzing the written and visual content together and re-coding for themes once more. This process allowed me to construct a broader picture of the relevant themes present in the Facebook group from which I was then able to extrapolate my findings. As such, this analysis consists of two parts. First, I examine the requirements for entry to the group and the public-facing components of the group visible to non-members. This includes the group's public-facing description, membership questions, and rules. Second, I analyze the moderators and the moderator-endorsed featured posts. By means of this two-part analysis, I aim to demonstrate the means by which Appalachian magic community is created and maintained, as well as highlight the important social identity work being done within this community.

The Mountain Magic FB group's "About" section reads, "Embracing the ways of old. Connecting with the powers of nature, the universe, and ourselves." Although not the most descriptive, these two sentences reflect the group's goal of maintaining the "old" way of doing things. Because the "old" way is not specified, the reader may infer any number of meanings. In conjunction with the name of the group, it might invoke notions of the Appalachian frontier circa the 19th and 20th centuries, and the kind of world that many of the member's grandparents or other ancestors lived in. The description's emphasis on a connection to nature and the broader universe indexes the kind of spirituality associated with many other Neopagan movements, such as the radical faeries, which value nature and rural environs as superior to urban and manufactured settings (Barrett 2017). Again, the vagueness is key, in that it ensures an individualist approach to spirituality; readers and potential members can interpret this description however they like. Although this is characteristic of Neopagan movements, the opacity of the description also ensures that potential members are not scared away by rigid and dogmatic approaches to Appalachian spirituality. This is especially important considering that many members of the group face persecution from mainstream hegemonic Christianity either due to their sexuality, politics, or other personal characteristics deemed incompatible with Christianity's dogmatic belief system. Furthermore, the inclusion of "connection with . . . ourselves" ensures that potential members understand that they will be expected to engage with others in good faith. The community guidelines, which I review later, reinforce this notion of community and encourage, if not enforce, respectful and considerate interaction with other members. However, the reflexive nature of "ourselves" also indexes an aspect of introspection that is integral to the kind of spiritual practice exercised by members of the group. In this sense, "ourselves" also echoes the individualistic nature of Neopagan practices, emphasizing that although potential members will find community in this group, they will also be encouraged to look inward and connect to themselves as a means of connecting to a higher sense of spirituality.

If a Facebook user wishes to join the group, they must either request membership or be invited by a current member. To ensure the integrity of the group and the privacy of its members, many Facebook groups require members to answer questions regarding their interest and reason for joining. The Mountain Magic group is no exception. Oftentimes, the questions also contain a trickier element that tests whether or not potential members have read the group rules before requesting to join. Given the controversial nature of magic use in modern society, the privacy of group members is all the more important. Furthermore, online trolls are ever a constant threat, especially on Facebook. As such, potential members of the Mountain Magic group are required to answer three questions in a sort of vetting process before they are allowed membership. The first question is "Do you understand if you do not answer these questions you will not be approved?". Respondents are only given the choice of "yes" or "no." This question attempts to ensure that the respondent has read the rules and reinforces the importance of rules as both a structure and guiding principles for the operation of the group and the behavior of its members.

The following question is "What path do you identify with?" This question is open-ended and allows the respondent to write their answer in as many or as few words as needed. By asking respondents to describe their "path," the question invites respondents to describe the history with folk magic and their current folk magic practices. For example, when I answered the question to join the group, I described my familial experience with faith healing, which was deemed adequate enough to join the group. Respondents are not given any kind of suggestion for what their path might be, or what their answer should look like. In this way, membership is gatekept to ensure that only in-the-know respondents could accurately respond to this question. Additionally, the choice to describe one's folk magic practice as a "path" is an intentional one. This choice indexes the metaphor of traveling and suggests that the practice of folk magic involves progression from one point to another. This metaphorical description of is of note in that it posits folk magic practice, and in turn one's membership in the FB group, as a journey with a beginning and end.

The third and final question is "Where are you from or what is your connection to Appalachia?" This question ascertains that potential members have a connection, or at the very least a respectful interest or admiration, for Appalachia. Presumably, a response that does not demonstrate either of these qualities would result in denial of membership. Note that the question does not require that people live in or be from Appalachia. Though it is not stated outright, this choice indexes an acknowledgement of and a positive affective stance towards members of the Appalachian diaspora, who are scattered all across the country and indeed the world, and for many of whom, a social media group like this one may be their best chance at (re-)connecting to their culture and those whom they share it with (Guy 2009; Roysdon & Gibson 2014; Teixeira 2008). Furthermore, this question firmly cements Appalachia as the foreground for spiritual and cultural practice within this social media group.

The group's rules, which potential members are required to review and agree to prior to submitting their membership proposal, are as follows (with original emphasis):

1) **ANSWER THE QUESTIONS**
   You must answer ALL the questions to be approved to join the group!
2) **No Hate Speech or Bullying**
   Make sure everyone feels safe. Bullying of any kind isn't allowed, and degrading comments about things like race, religion, culture, sexual orientation, gender or identity will not be tolerated.
3) **Be Kind and Courteous**
   We're all in this together to create a welcoming environment. Let's treat everyone with respect. Healthy debates are natural, but kindness is required.
4) **No Promotions or Spam**
   Give more than you take to this group. Self-promotion, spam and irrelevant links aren't allowed.
5) **Respect Everyone's Privacy**
   Being part of this group requires mutual trust. Authentic, expressive discussions make groups great, but may also be sensitive and private. What's shared in the group should stay in the group.

6) **No posts on race and politics**
   Sorry, but there are other groups that you can join to argue about race and politics. Will not be tolerated in this group. We are all one here.
7) **Sale posts only on Wednesdays**
   We will allow sales posts on items related to the craft only. We will set aside Wednesdays to allow posting. If you try and post sales posts on other days you may be banned. Be careful. Thanks!

The first rule again asks that members answer all the questions in the membership application. Answering all the questions not only ensures that members have a good-faith interest in Appalachian folk magic, but by asking them to describe their personal relationship to both magic and Appalachia, it foregrounds emotional honesty about one's desires, intentions, and background as a core tenet of group interaction. This notion is echoed in the fifth rule, which encourages group members to treat one another with mutual trust and to engage in "authentic, expressive discussions." Again, authenticity is posited as a highly virtuous and desirable trait within the group. Rules two and three also speak to the desirability of mutual trust and authentic expressive discussions, by requiring that members do not engage in hate speech or bullying of any kind and that they act with kindness and courtesy. Both of these rules are included in order to "make sure everyone feels safe" and "to create a welcoming environment." Furthermore, both of these rules are couched in terms of community (i.e., "everyone" or "we're all in this together"). This kind of context characterizes these rules in terms of a moral obligation to a larger community. As part of this obligation, aspects of social identity, namely race, religion, culture, sexual orientation, gender, and in general, "identity," are regarded as protected, which represents at least in part this group's political leanings. However open and accepting the group might be though, rule number six forbids discussion of race and politics because "we are all one here." It's possible that this rule was created to avoid contentious flame wars (a series of excessively disparaging and usually angry comments exchanged by two online interactants). This is even more relevant given the post-Trump context of the group, a political environment where white supremacists are all the more emboldened, not least in a virtual environment where they may face less repercussions for their actions (Beliso-De Jesús and Pierre 2019). Be that as it may, this rule also seems to demonstrate a neoliberal intolerance for difficult discussions, particularly about race. It would seem that, for the predominantly white members, it's easier to avoid these discussions rather than risk any kind of discord in the group. Of course, this too is couched in terms of "oneness" and "togetherness," hearkening back to the aforementioned moral obligation to a larger community. Yet this kind of thinking elides any kind of real political power and falls short of the loftier political goals allegedly held by the group and its members. Lastly, rules four and seven speak to the moderators' desire to keep the group on track to its proposed goals. As such, promotions, spam, and non-Wednesday sales posts are discouraged in order to keep the group focused on Appalachian folk traditions and community building.

Taken together, these rules represent the moderators' attempt at overtly and discursively creating the kind of social environment they believe most beneficial to the group and its members. As such, the second part of this analysis is an examination into the group's moderators, which is also necessary to fully understand the way the group is controlled and the direction it takes to achieve its goals. The moderators control the group's description, membership questions, rules, who gets accepted into the group, as well as punishment or banning for disobeying the group's rules. At the time of writing, there are seven moderators. According to their Facebook profiles, of those seven, six are women and one is a man; likewise, six are from Tennessee and one is from West Virginia. All seven moderators are also white. I share this to help illustrate the demographic makeup of the moderators and to provide some insight into their rules and methods of operation. Further demographic information about the moderators, such as their sexuality, ethnicity, or politics is not available. Given this work's emphasis on intersectional identity and meaning-making, this analysis might be strengthened if that information were present. Regardless, what little information there is available about the moderators, specifically their status as Appalachian and their position as group leaders within this specific group, provides substantial reason to warrant their inclusion in this analysis.

Featured posts are considered to be the most important informational posts and provide useful, supplemental information to the group's members, separate from the rules. At the time of writing, there are eight featured posts. To protect the anonymity of the group and respect the group's most important rule, I will not share the featured posts themselves. Instead, the contents of the featured posts are represented within the below chart, with original spelling and emphasis included. Visual elements, such as emojis or photos, are described textually for ease of accessibility.

Number	Featured Post
1	*(White text against a black background, dotted with blue raindrops. At the top and bottom of the block of text are two lines of emojis, alternating between stop signs, do-not-enter signs, no symbols, and raised hand emojis)*
	"NO SCREENSHOTS No screenshots are to be shared outside of this group! Violaters will be: REMOVED & BLOCKED"

(continued)

Number	Featured Post
2	*(A plain text post.)*
	"Friendly reminder- DO NOT share someone's post on here with another group. It's an automatic ban. You can share memes – but not personal posts! Thank you!"
3	*(A plain text post.)*
	"Starting this Wednesday we will be allowing sales post (on one thread) If you make things to sale or have things you would like to sale, then watch for the post to go up Wednesday! Please do not post an individual post- it has to be on the sales post that we put up. Thank you! *(Red heart emoji)*"
4	*(Accompanied by a meme which features a still from the movie Toy Story. Buzz, a spaceman, has his hand on the shoulder of Woody, a cowboy. Buzz gestures into the distance with a wistful expression while Woody looks on anxiously. White text is superimposed on the top and bottom of the image which reads, "MEMES. MEMES EVERYWHERE.")*
	"Hey yall! Your friendly MOD here. Let's talk about memes. Shall we? We all love memes. They're funny, inspiring, informational. BUT they can also clog up the group, making REAL posts get lost. We do appreciate every contribution to the group, but it's getting a bit out of hand. What we want is your original thoughts/ideas/questions!! When you want to share a meme here, ask yourself the question– Is this RELEVANT to not only witchcraft but to THE APPALACHIAN REGION? This is the focus of our group. There are plenty of generic witchcraft groups on FB. What makes us different is our specific focus Please keep this in mind. And please don't take it personally when your meme post is denied. We are trying to keep the group moving forward in the right direction. Thank you."
5	*(White text against a black background, patterned with grey hearts.)*
	"If anyone sees a post or comment that makes you concerned for another's wellbeing, please tag or message an admin or moderator. We are here to help and support out group, our fellow brothers and sisters. Life is hard. Let's not add stones to their burdens. Let's not burn them at the stake. Let's not walk them to the hanging tree. Don't throw them in the deepest waters to see if they float. We have been persecuted by others for too long. Let's not do it to ourselves. This is our safe space. *(Black heart emoji, sparkle emoji)*"

(continued)

Number	Featured Post
6	*(A plain text post.)*
	"Listen up folks, so many are disappointing us because you cannot scroll by a post that you disagree with. Not everyone is going to see eye to eye. If you are one of those that feel you have to argue every time someone says something, please go somewhere else. We only have a few admins and mods and why you feel we have to sit and babysit everyone, I will never know . . . but do us a favor and leave the group if you cannot be nice or scroll on by when you disagree. We are fed up, and we are deleting people left and right.. but we have lives too! So chill out or get out!!!! Thanks! *(Black heart emoji)* have a wonderful day *(smiling emoji, crying-laughing emoji)*.
7	*(A plain text post.)*
	"This group is not a platform for soap boxes and seeking controversy when there is none. Especially concerning social justice. Taking a post and twisting it to fit your hypersensitive agenda will not be tolerated. This has happened twice today and both members were removed. Some people unfortunately will take the color red and get offended by it. And they feed on any outrage over any topic. Feeders are not allowed. These people do not match the spirit and heart of this group."
8	*(Accompanied by a picture of a smoking smudge stick, comprised of a bundled cone of sage.)*
	"SAGE posts will NO LONGER be approved! The discussions always turn ugly and admins do not have time for refereeing. Each person here is encouraged to do your research, and find your own path."

Two of the featured posts, Posts 1 and 2 in Figure 1, ask members not to share other members' posts, in any form, with people outside of the group. This is particularly in reference to the sharing of posts within Facebook (i.e., sharing to one's own page or to another Facebook group). Both of these featured posts remind members that the breaking of this rule will result in an automatic ban from the group and blocking, ensuring that members cannot rejoin. Again, these posts reinforce the importance of privacy and authentic engagement within the group. This message is echoed by, in Post 1, by the use of a black background, indexing a serious tone, and the use of several different emojis which index "No" or "Stop" as top and bottom borders for the text. The use of all-caps in the first and last lines of Post 1 further emphasizes the serious and imperative nature of the post, as it might in similar online contexts (McCulloch 2019). Likewise, Post 2 also represents a serious command, although the tone and message are conveyed in quite different ways. For one, instead of using text against a patterned background to draw the reader's attention, Post 2 is a plain text post. A plain text post, with no emojis or other embellishments, conveys directness and in doing so indexes a serious tone; as opposed to Post 1 though, Post 2 couches the command in friendlier terms, quite literally describing how they want the post to be received with the first two words: "Friendly reminder." Yet again though, all-caps is used to index a command, as if the writer were yelling or speaking sternly. The more friendly tone of Post 2 is bookended by the moderator's use of "Thank you!" at the end of their post.

Featured Post 3 contains the information for the posting of for-sale items on the weekly sales post thread, again ensuring the integrity of the group and its mission. The use of "Please" and "Thank you!", as well as the use of the red heart emoji, indexes a similar tone as Post 2's: polite but serious. Again, as a plain text post, communication of important information is prioritized over aesthetics or capturing the reader's attention with attractive graphics or backgrounds, further indexing that this post contains a direct and serious message.

Featured Post 4 describes the group's policy on the posting of memes. Memes are of course ubiquitous on social media, but as one moderator relates, they can "clog up the group, making REAL posts get lost." The moderator emphasizes that the group "wants . . . your original thoughts/ideas/questions" and asks that members engage in a little bit of self-moderation; that their memes are "RELEVANT to not only witchcraft but to THE APPALACHIAN REGION" as that is "the focus of our group." The moderator explains that there are plenty of generic witchcraft groups on Facebook, but what makes this group different is their specific focus on witchcraft connected to Appalachia. This post again foregrounds Appalachia as the sociogeographical context for spiritual practice within the group. Furthermore, it is once again another attempt at discursively managing the behavior of the group members and keeping the group "on track." The use of all-caps in certain portions of this post is different from its use in previous posts, though. Here, all-caps is used to emphasize the words the moderator feels are most important, no doubt hoping to draw the reader's attention. Although it could be parsed as yelling or speaking sternly, the context for this post indicates that the use of all-caps here is one pertaining to emphasis. Lastly, Post 4 draws the reader's attention to the meta-discussion of memes by using a meme to convey its message. This not only provides context for the post, but also demonstrates the moderators' in-group status as a literate user of memes, and therefore, a reasonable person to be making a request about meme usage within the group.

Post 5, which is more atypical than the others, asks that if any members see a post or comment from another fellow member that makes them concerned for that person's wellbeing, that they should contact a moderator. The background graphic for this post, a black background patterned with grey hearts, indexes again a serious tone, which is likely intentional as this post is indirectly talking about suicide and self-harm. Instead of a serious command though, the grey hearts help convey that this message is serious in a heartfelt, emotionally honest way. As the moderator explains, "We are here to help and support our group . . . We have been persecuted by others for too long . . . This is our safe space." This post demonstrates a real concern for the community members and acknowledges the struggles that many of them share in being outcast from mainstream hegemonic society. Furthermore, the moderator aligns themselves and the group with an imagined group of historically persecuted witches. This is further reinforced by the moderator asking members to "not add stones to their burdens . . . not burn them at the stake . . . not walk them to the hanging tree." Here, the moderator references historical punishment for witches and others who engaged in counter-hegemonic behavior deemed inappropriate by mainstream Christian society. This establishes the group's members, and by extension Appalachian folk magic practitioners, as inheritors of the legacy left by those persecuted for their beliefs, whether that be the women persecuted in the Salem witch trials or the queer and Black people bashed and lynched by mainstream queerphobic and white supremacist society. The moderator acknowledges the mental damage that living in such a society, while also practicing folk magic, can deal to a person and asks again that members of the group be responsible not just for one another, but to one another as well.

Lastly, there are three featured posts that prohibit discussions of contentious topics. Two of those posts, Post 6 and Post 7, speak to the fact that this group is not supposed to be a "soap box" for those "seeking controversy where there is none . . . especially concerning social justice." According to the moderators, people engaging in this behavior "do not match the spirit and heart of this group." Again, the use of plain text for Posts 6 and 7 is indexical of a desire to communicate information directly rather than draw the reader's attention with graphics. These two posts are of particular interest, in that they simultaneously contradict and affirm the group's rules and mission. On one hand, the group claims to intentionally acknowledge and protect those made most vulnerable by hegemonic society and advises other members to support their fellow folk magic practitioners. On the other hand, members are expressly forbidden from discussing contentious topics, with decisions about what is and isn't contentious left to a group of seven moderators. It's possible that the forbidding of contentious topics is, in part, derivative of a desire to protect members and avoid unnecessary hurt or "drama." However, one can't help but speculate that the taboo on contentious, mostly political or "social justice"-oriented topics is at least in part reflective of a desire to maintain the status quo and restrict more counter-hegemonic ideas from progressing. The threat of immediate removal and blocking, and thus disconnection from this found community, is more than enough to ensure "proper" behavior from group members. However, it is again too reminiscent of the same discriminatory practices that lead many of the members to join the group and engage in counterhegemonic folk magic practices in the first place.

The eighth and final featured post directly names one such type of post that is expressly forbidden. The moderator writes that "SAGE posts will NO LONGER be approved! The discussions always turn ugly and admins do not have time for refereeing. Each person is encouraged to do your research, and find your own path." Here, the use of all-caps is used for emphasis, rather than to convey an emotional state or an imperative. An image of sage, bundled into a cone as a "smudge stick" is also included to draw the reader's attention and give visual context to the issue at hand. Specifically, the issue at hand is that sage use within (primarily white) folk magic communities is one of cultural appropriation and constitutes symbolic violence against indigenous American people and communities. Traditionally, sage is used to spiritually cleanse homes and other places and to purge evil spirits and negative energies. One consensus is that sage use by primarily white folk magic communities deprives native communities from its use in their own spiritual practices, which is where sage as a cleansing tool originated. As such, sage use by white folk magic communities is considered by some to be a continued act of violence against indigenous communities by white settlers (Conroy-Krutz 2015). However, others argue that sage use is a shared practice amongst both native and white communities, and that its use should not be limited to any one group. Furthermore, there is not such a fine distinction between white and native communities, especially in Appalachia, as many people belong to both (or more) ethnicities and seek to honor their ancestors by engaging in sage use. However, as an extension of the group's sixth rule, which bans discussion of race and politics, difficult conversations about serious sociopolitical issues, particularly those concerning race, are completely outlawed, and the individualistic character of Neopagan movements is suggested as an alternative. This is particularly intriguing as it runs counter to the purpose of the group, which is to seek spiritual guidance through community; instead of community connection *and* individual introspection, difficult topics are relegated *only* to the individual. Ultimately, this is a problematic way to handle both sociopolitical and spiritual issues, in that it reproduces the same oppressive hierarchies which privilege the comfort of white people over even the discussion of Indigenous issues, let alone their resolution. Furthermore, it suggests a fractured, inconsistent approach to serious matters within the group, despite attempts at the contrary.

4 Conclusion

These findings are significant for a multitude of reasons. For one, they show how a community too often characterized as backwards and regressive is actively engaging and contending with sociopolitical issues such as race, gender, sexuality, and indigenous belonging, and that these issues are not external to Appalachia, but rather are relevant to the region and its people. Additionally, by virtue of analyzing data generated by Appalachian communities, through my own perspective situated at the intersections of Appalachianness, this work venerates the importance of Appalachians, and other marginalized social groups, being able to claim their own narratives and interpret them for themselves. These findings also validate the importance of interdisciplinarity and hybrid approaches to social analysis. Because the subject of study is situated at the nexus of multiple social dimensions, an analysis lacking an intersectional perspective, either analytically or methodologically, might fail to capture the complexity of the community's discursive practices and social meaning-making. Even this analysis is necessarily limited; further research into online social media communities, particularly those dedicated to regional(-ized) folk magic practices, must contend with the discursive practices of members and practitioners. This work, at least, represents a framework for further investigation into the subject and related areas; by examining the ways in which these communities are discursively engineered by their creators and maintainers, I hope to provide the necessary basis for examining the actual discourse practices of group members and magic practitioners, both online and in-person.

Most importantly, this analysis presents the myriad ways in which Appalachian folk magic practitioners engage in community building, heritage sharing, and social justice in online social media environments. In this way, it also demonstrates how these community members simultaneously engage in both transgressive practices that protect and value socially minoritized people while also engaging in hegemonically normative practices that, despite what moderators might say, further discriminate these people and discourage critical thought and serious engagement with difficult sociopolitical issues. This, in truth, is somewhat to be expected from a group dominated by white members that encourages an individualistic, neoliberal approach to spirituality and community-building. Furthermore, it also provides insight into the ways in which those in charge of these communities discursively create the boundaries and contexts that make these communities possible, as well as highlight how social media platforms like Facebook make such rigid control of these communities possible in the first place. Most intriguingly, it shows that folk magic communities, at least in this context, are not just about magic. More than anything, the Mountain Magic Facebook group demonstrates that the real magic is to be found within the communities and connections that Appalachian folk magic users form with one another as we seek to re-discover our heritages, reclaim our identities, and forge new futures for ourselves and for our communities.

References

Agha, Asif. 1998. Stereotypes and registers of honorific language. *Language in Society* 27(2). 151–93.
Agha, Asif. 2005. Voice, footing, enregisterment. *Journal of Linguistic Anthropology* 15(1). 38–59.
Bailey, Rebecca. 2008. *Matewan before the massacre: Politics, coal, and the roots of conflict in a West Virginia mining community*. Morgantown: West Virginia University Press.
Bakhtin, M. M. 1984. *Problems of Dostoevsky's Poetics*. Caryl Emerson (ed./ trans.). Minneapolis: University of Minnesota Press.
Barrett, Rusty. 2017. *From drag queens to leathermen: Language, gender, and gay male subcultures*. New York: Oxford University Press.
Beliso-De Jesús, Aisha & Jemima Pierre. 2019. Special Section: Anthropology of White Supremacy. *American anthropologist* 122(1). 65–75.
Bjork-James, Sophie. 2018. Training the Porous Body: Evangelicals and the Ex-Gay Movement. *American Anthropologist* 120. 647–58.
Blommaert, Jan 2005. *Discourse*. Cambridge: Cambridge University Press.
Bucholtz, Mary & Kira Hall. 2005. Identity and Interaction: A Sociocultural Linguistic Approach. *Discourse Studies* 7. 585–614.
Campbell, John C. 1921. *The southern highlander and his homeland*. New York: Russell Sage Foundation.
Corbin, David. 2011. *Gun thugs, rednecks, and radicals: A documentary history of the West Virginia mine wars*. Oakland: PM Press.
Conroy-Krutz, Emily. 2015. *Christian imperialism: Converting the world in the early American republic*. Ithaca: Cornell University Press.
Cramer, Jennifer. 2013. Styles, stereotypes, and the South: Constructing identities at the linguistic border. *American Speech* 88(2).144–167.
Cramer, Jennifer. 2016. Contested Southernness: The linguistic production and perception of identities in the borderlands. *Supplement to American Speech* 90. American Dialect Society: Duke University Press.
Crenshaw, Kimberlé. 1989. Demarginalizing the intersection of race and sex: A black feminist critique of antidiscrimination doctrine, feminist theory, and antiracist politics. *University of Chicago Legal Forum* (8). 538–54.
Crenshaw, Kimberlé. 1991. Mapping the margins: Intersectionality, identity politics, and violence against women of color. *Stanford Law Review* 43(6). 1241–99.
Eckert, Penelope. 2008. Variation and the Indexical Field. *Journal of Sociolinguistics*. 12(4). 453–476.
Ellis, Bill. 2003. *Aliens, ghosts, and cults: Legends we live*. Jackson, MS: University Press of Mississippi.
Fotopoulou, Aristea. 2012. Intersectionality, queer studies and hybridity: Methodological frameworks for social research. *Journal of international women's studies* 13(2). 19–32.
Gray, Mary L. 2009. *Out in the country: Youth, media, and queer visibility in rural America*. New York: New York University Press.

Guy, Roger. 2009. *From diversity to unity: Southern and Appalachian migrants in uptown Chicago, 1950-1970*. Lexington: Lexington Books.
Halberstam, Judith. 2005. *In a queer time and place transgender bodies, subcultural lives*. New York: New York University Press.
Hall, Kira. 1999. Performativity. *Journal of Linguistic Anthropology*. 9(1–2). 184–187.
Halliday, Robert. 2010. The roadside burial of suicides: An East Anglian study. *Folklore* 121(1). 81–93.
Herring, Scott. 2007. Out of the closets, into the woods: RFD, country women, and the post-Stonewall emergence of queer anti-urbanism. *American Quarterly* 59(2). 341–372.
Herring, Scott. 2010. *Another country; Queer anti-urbanism*. New York: New York University Press.
Hornblower, Simon, Anthony Spawforth & Edith Eidinow. 2012. *The Oxford Classical Dictionary fourth edition*. 649–651, 688. Oxford: Oxford University Press.
Hutton, Ronald. 2017. *The witch: A history of fear, from ancient times to the present*. New Haven: Yale University Press.
Johnstone, Barbara. 1996. *The linguistic individual: Self-expression in language and linguistics*. Oxford: Oxford University Press.
Johnstone, Barbara. 2003. Conversation, text and discourse. *Needed Research in American Dialects* 88. 75–97.
Johnstone, Barbara. 2018. *Discourse Analysis* (3rd edn.). 235. Hoboken: John Wiley & Sons.
Johnstone, Barbara, Jennifer Andrus & Andre E. Danielson. 2006. Mobility, Indexicality, and the Enregisterment of "Pittsburghese." *Journal of English Linguistics* 34(2). 77–104.
Kemp, Daren. 2011. *New Age, a guide: Alternative spiritualities from Aquarian conspiracy to Next Age*. Edinburgh: Edinburgh University Press.
Li-Vollmer, Meredith & Mark Lapointe. 2003. Gender transgression and villainy in animated film. *Popular Communication* 1(89). 109.
Loke, Swee-Kin & Clinton Golding. 2016. How to do things with mouse clicks: Applying Austin's Speech Act Theory to explain learning in virtual worlds. *Educational philosophy and theory* 48(11). 1168–1180.
Machin, David & Andrea Mayr. 2012. *How to do critical discourse analysis: A multimodal approach*. Los Angeles: Sage.
Massey, Carissa. 2007. Appalachian stereotypes: Cultural history, gender, and sexual rhetoric. *Journal of Appalachian Studies* 13. 124–136.
McCulloch, Gretchen. 2019. *Because Internet: Understanding the New Rules of Language*. New York, NY: Riverhead Books.
Moran, Claire & Christina Lee. 2013. Selling genital cosmetic surgery to healthy women: a multimodal discourse analysis of Australian surgical websites. *Critical Discourse Studies* 10(4). 373–391.
Pemberton, John. 1975. Eshu-Elegba: The Yoruba Trickster God. *African Arts* 9(1). 20–92.
Pennycook, Alastair. 2007. *Global Englishes and transcultural flows*. New York: Routledge.
Roysdon, Keith & Robin Gibson. 2014. *'River' of immigrants from the south shaped Muncie*. Muncie: Star Press.
Shogan, Robert. 2004. *The Battle of Blair Mountain: The story of America's largest union uprising*. Boulder, CO: Westview Press.
Silverstein, Michael. 2003. Indexical order and the dialectics of sociolinguistic Life. In Paul Manning (ed.), *Words and beyond: Linguistic and semiotic studies of sociocultural order*. Special issue, *Language and Communication* 23(3–4). 193–229.

Staunæs, Dorthe. 2003. Where have all the subjects gone? Bringing together the concepts of intersectionality and subjectification. *Nora* 11(2). 101–10.
Tannen, Deborah. 1984. Conversational Style: *Analyzing Talk Among Friends*. New York, NY: Ablex Publishing.
Teixeira, Ruy. 2008. *Red, blue, & purple America: The future of election demographics*. 53. Washington: Brookings Institution Press.
Thompson, Katrina Daly. 2017. *Popobawa: Tanzanian talk, global misreadings* Indianapolis: Indiana University Press.
Walker, Abby. 2019. The role of dialect experience in topic-based shifts in speech production. *Language Variation and Change* 31(2). 135–63.
Watts, Brenton. 2020. The Mothman and other strange tales: Shaping queer appalachia through folkloric discourse in online social media communities. Lexington: University of Kentucky thesis.
Yuval-Davis, Nira. 2006. Intersectionality and feminist politics. *European Journal of Women's Studies* 13(3). 193–210.

Integration

J Calder
Towards a queer and trans sociophonetics
Connecting sociophonetics to a queer and trans linguistics

1 Introduction

Popular discourses have long speculated about the characteristics that make someone "sound queer", and for decades, researchers have sought to pinpoint the characteristics that distinguish the sound of the queer voice. The field of sociophonetics – a branch of sociolinguistic variationism that centers the social factors that contribute to people's voices sounding different from each other – is one field that has focused on the sound of the queer voice. Sociophonetic studies have covered much valuable ground in applying variationist methods to underrepresented populations, in order to identify the phonetic features that are associated with those populations. However, in this chapter I will argue that there is still much opportunity to connect the aims of sociophonetic study with the aims of the fields of queer linguistics and trans linguistics.

Queer linguistics is a field that emerged in the mid-1990s following the poststructuralist turn in the humanities and social sciences. Borrowing from Queer Theory, the aim of queer linguistics is to take a poststructuralist perspective in exploring how language users challenge and negotiate heteronormative discourses (see e.g., Livia & Hall 1997; Milani 2017; Motschenbacher 2011). In other words, how does the exploration of linguistic practice shed light on the construction of larger societal discourses that position cisgender, binary, and heterosexual identities as normal, while positioning other identities as deviant or illegitimate? Queer linguistics seeks to destabilize such cisnormative and heteronormative discourses, and the often taken-for-granted binaries (e.g., male vs female, gay vs straight) that come with them. The relationship between the linguistic practices of queer speaking subjects and these overarching heteronormative discourses that other them is a central site of exploration for queer linguistics.

Queer linguistics emerged as a response to earlier approaches to the study of queer language that framed varieties of queer language as *sexolects*, or discrete language varieties (e.g., "gay language", "lesbian language") that are separate and distinct from those used by cisgender heterosexual speakers. While these earlier approaches have done much to illuminate the differences between the language of

J Calder, University of Colorado Boulder

queer and straight speakers, some have argued that in doing so, they may also serve to reify and essentialize such differences (e.g., Motschenbacher 2011). Rather than taking sexolects for granted as a priori linguistic differences between queer and straight speakers, queer linguistics is concerned with investigating how these differences emerge and how they have the potential to both construct and challenge larger discourses that privilege heteronormative ways of speaking.

Recently, a wave of research has emerged under the umbrella of *trans linguistics*, a disciplinary approach that centers the perspectives of transgender and nonbinary speaking subjects as central to the understanding of gender (Zimman 2020a). In other words, transpeople are not merely outliers relegated to the periphery that serve to reify cisgender understandings of gender as the status quo, but transpeople illuminate how links between linguistic practice and gender identity are socially constructed in general. In addition, in trans linguistics, transpeople are not only objects of study to be speculated upon by outsiders, but they are also collaborators and researchers involved in the knowledge construction enterprise. In this way, trans linguistics is committed to social and epistemic justice for gender non-normative communities, and the field takes trans individuals on their own terms rather than comparing them to how well they conform to cis-normative standards (Zimman 2021). The study of trans speakers can denaturalize cisnormative understandings of sex and gender as essential, disrupting epistemologies rooted in cissexism.

Given the disciplinary goals advanced by queer linguistics and trans linguistics, there is much potential for *queer and trans sociophonetics* to more explicitly connect to these goals. In other words, rather than queer and trans sociophonetics merely being a subset of sociophonetics that examines queer and trans subjects, there remains great opportunity for sociophonetic study to take a critical eye towards the methodological and theoretical norms that are being implicitly (and sometimes problematically) reproduced in the study of queer and trans speakers. Sociophonetic study can also benefit from more explicitly considering the role of cisnormative and heteronormative societal discourses, as the constraining context under which queer voices are embedded, and as the driving force relegating queer voices to the social periphery. Rather than merely describing the phonetic patterns observed among queer speakers, queer and trans sociophonetic studies might instead discuss how and why these patterns result from, or challenge, these overarching discourses. Finally, queer and trans sociophonetic studies should more explicitly consider the role of representation and social positionality, both in terms of the populations being researched as well as the researchers doing the researching. For one, queer and trans researchers should be empowered to study the phonetic practices of queer and trans speakers. And cisgender heterosexual researchers should be explicit in considering their own positionality when interacting with and studying queer and trans populations, in considering how their own positionality might affect the data they are able to acquire, and in considering what their epistemological predispositions are that might lead them to interpret the patterns of queer and trans speakers in particular ways.

In the remainder of this chapter, I start with introducing the fields of phonetic and sociophonetic study, following with a brief review of sociophonetic studies that have focused on queer and trans speakers. As will be illustrated in the review, while early sociophonetic studies sought to pinpoint the phonetic features that differentiated queer and non-queer voices (i.e., the phonetic features of so-called "sexolects" like gay speech and lesbian speech), recent studies are increasingly considering the ways that queer speaking subjects use phonetic variables on the ground to project queer identity in specific, local, and heterogeneous ways. I conclude with some specific suggestions for future research that can serve to facilitate a queer and trans sociophonetics that more explicitly connects with the methodological, epistemological, and social justice goals advanced by queer and trans linguistics more broadly.

2 Phonetics and sociophonetics

The field of phonetics is a branch of linguistic study that focuses on speech sounds as its object of inquiry. Phonetic studies can be acoustic – focusing on the physical and spectral properties of speech sounds – or articulatory – focusing on the ways speech sounds are produced with the articulators like the lips, teeth, and tongue. Phonetic studies can also examine speech production – i.e., the production of speech sounds by speakers – or speech perception – i.e., the perception of speech sounds by listeners. Phonetic studies are traditionally concerned with the language-internal factors that condition the production and perception of speech sounds, often factoring out factors that are said to be external to language. As such, social factors relating to the identity of the speaker or listener, or the situation in which speech sounds are being perceived and produced, are framed as external to the linguistic system, and therefore filtered out of traditional phonetic analysis.

Sociophonetics is a response to this, centering – rather than filtering out – the role of social factors in conditioning the production and perception of speech sounds. Since the introduction of the term in "sociophonetics" in 1974 (Deshaies-Lafontaine), it has been defined in various ways, relating to disciplinary orientation and methodological approach. Most often, sociophonetics is defined as a subset of sociolinguistic variationism (a field concerned with the social factors that condition language variation) that focuses on phonetic variables (see Calder 2020; Podesva &

Kajino 2014; Zimman 2020b for a discussion). Methodologically, like phonetic studies, sociophonetic studies can focus on either speech production or speech perception, exploring the social factors that condition how particular sounds are produced and how particular voices are perceived. In addition, while traditional phonetic studies often prioritize speech data collected in a lab, sociophonetic studies are interested in speech context as a factor conditioning variation and are thus more likely to collect data in a variety of contexts, from a lab, to a formal sociolinguistic interview, to an informal conversation. It has also been argued that sociophonetic study moves beyond traditional variationist studies that focus primarily on categorical phonetic variables by also including the study of continuous variables (Podesva & Kajino 2014; Zimman 2020b). In other words, rather than strictly focusing on variables like (ING) that have multiple, discrete categorical variants (i.e., [IN] and [ING]), sociophonetic analysis also centers the instrumental and quantitative study of variables that are realized on a numerical continuum, for example, pitch (measured numerically in Hz). Whatever the methodological orientation, sociophonetic study is concerned with the ways that variation in speech sounds is related to social factors like identity, stance, speech context and orientation. The field explores the ways that speech sounds connect to the social world.

3 The sociophonetic study of queer and trans speakers

The sociophonetic study of queer and trans speakers[1] has mirrored the trajectory of variationist study at large, as described in Eckert's three waves of variationism (2005, 2012, 2021). Under this description of the way variationism has evolved, first wave studies often start with macro-level demographic differences between speakers, investigating how language variationism reflects these broad differences. In the first-wave perspective, differences in speech are argued to result from demographic differences in identity in a top-down fashion. Second-wave studies zoom in to local communities of practice, exploring how social distinctions that are locally relevant in these communities condition linguistic variation. In other words, second-wave analysis comes with the insight that demographic differences may not condition linguistic variation in the same way in every context. Rather,

---

[1] It is worth mentioning that the sociophonetic study of queer and trans speakers has, by and large, focused on spoken language, and there remains great potential for this field of study to expand to also include signed languages.

specific communities of practice may have their own norms conditioning how phonetic variation corresponds to macro-social differences. Women, for example, may use one feature in one community of practice but another feature in another community of practice, dependent on the norms of those communities. Finally, third-wave studies investigate how linguistic variation contributes to meaning-making on the ground, exploring how speakers use linguistic variables to project certain social qualities, or to construct their identities in particular ways. In other words, rather than a top-down exploration of the ways linguistic variation results from social contrasts, third-wave study explores how linguistic variation serves to construct social contrasts from the bottom-up.

Needless to say, as the analytical foci of variationism have shifted, sociophonetic studies of gender and sexuality have become increasingly concerned with exploring the ways that phonetic variables serve to construct and project gender and sexual identities, rather than merely reflecting pre-discursive identities. In other words, an emic approach has increasingly been implemented, exploring how language users construct and make identities relevant in local interaction.

Whether a top-down or bottom-up approach to identity is taken, connections between linguistic variables and social meanings relating to gender and sexual identities are often framed in terms of indexicality. *Indexicality* is a theoretical concept describing how signs like linguistic variables relate to social meanings like identities. Adopted from the works of Charles Sanders Peirce (1895) and circulating through the fields of linguistic anthropology and sociolinguistics, indexicality refers to a co-occurrence between a particular sign (e.g. a linguistic variable) and an object (e.g., a social meaning like an identity category). For example, when a certain way of saying something is observed to co-occur with a certain type of person, that correspondence can become recognized and feed into social ideologies, such that that way of speaking can later index, or signal, that kind of person. Certain linguistic variables can index, or point to, certain gender and sexual identities. For example, if we observe and recognize men using a particular linguistic variable, that variable will later come to index "men" when we hear it in the future.

Linguists have theorized the ways that linguistic variables can come to index sexual orientation, proposing the idea that sexual orientation is indexed through "gender appropriateness" (Cameron & Kulick 2003). For example, if someone uses language in a way that conforms to what society considers appropriate for their perceived gender, their language may index heterosexuality. On the other hand, if someone uses language in a way that deviates from what society considers appropriate for their perceived gender, their language may index queerness. Ideologies about gender inappropriateness feed into stereotypical assumptions that, for example, gay men talk like women, or that gay women talk like men.

Sociophonetic studies of gender and sexuality have examined both speech production and speech perception to explore the indexical relationship between phonetic variables and queer identity. Production studies are concerned with exploring the ways that queer speakers produce speech sounds, with early studies focusing on how queer speakers' productions differ from those of cisgender, heterosexual speakers; and recent studies have been increasingly exploring how queer speakers can use speech sounds to signal or construct their identities in particular ways. Perception studies explore how the perception of speech sounds relates to a speaker's perceived gender or sexual identity; in other words, these studies examine whether listeners are more or less likely to perceive a person as queer, depending on the phonetic variables they hear that person use.

As will be illustrated in the review of the literature below, studies on the queer voice have overwhelmingly focused on cisgender gay men, likely due to the social salience of gay speech and widely circulating stereotypes in popular ideology about the way gay men speak, like the "gay lisp" (see Calder 2020 for an indepth discussion). On the other hand, queer women have much less often been the subject of sociophonetic research, perhaps due to the "lack of an ideologically grounded linguistic stereotype for lesbians" (Queen 2014, 214). Sociophonetic studies of trans and nonbinary speakers have only really proliferated in the last decade, with much early work on gender either focusing entirely on cisgender speakers or neglecting to mention whether speakers were cisgender or transgender at all. Much early work on trans voices was conducted by speech-language pathologists "who tend to take a medicalized view of the gendered voice that pathologizes non-normative styles" (Zimman 2020b; see also Azul 2013). These studies have often framed the phonetic practices of transgender speakers with respect to how well they conform to cisnormative standards. However, recent studies have explored how transgender speakers use phonetic variables to signal their gender identities and have done much to denaturalize ideological links between particular speech sounds and a speaker's sex assigned at birth. Finally, studies of White English speakers in Western contexts have dominated the field, leaving much opportunity to study non-White speakers, speakers of languages other than English, and speakers in a wider variety of geographic contexts, especially those in the Global South.

In what follows, I provide a review of the sociophonetic studies of queer and trans speakers. Since the study of the fundamental frequency (i.e., pitch) and the frontness of /s/ have dominated much of the literature, I begin with summarizing studies that have been conducted on each of these variables, followed by a discussion of other phonetic variables that have been examined with respect to queer identity. While the review below is admittedly non-exhaustive, it is my aim that it will encapsulate the trends described above, regarding the shifts in theoretical focus and subjects analyzed. That is, while the field was initially concerned with exploring the ways that gay (usually male) speakers' voices differed from straight speakers' voices, studies have increasingly explored how the queer voice is articulated from the ground up, examining the phonetic practices of speakers of an increasingly broad variety of queer identities.

3.1 The fundamental frequency

The fundamental frequency (F0) is one of the most studied phonetic variables with respect to gender and sexuality. F0, or the voice's pitch, is measured in Hz and has been argued to be related to the size of a speaker's vocal tract. It has been reported that cisgender male speakers, typically with longer vocal tracts than cisgender female speakers, exhibit slower vocal fold vibrations as a result, and therefore tend to exhibit lower F0 (Ohala 1984). In simpler terms, overall, women speak with a higher pitch than men. However, there is evidence that F0 can be socially as well as biologically conditioned, as studies have found that gender influences pitch ranges for children, even prior to pubertal changes in vocal tract length (e.g., Ferrand & Bloom 1996; Graddol & Swann 1983). In other words, while the size of the vocal tract can indeed influence vocal pitch, speakers can also manipulate their pitch to achieve social goals or index particular identities (Azul 2013; Podesva & Kajino 2014). Pitch patterns are indeed effective at signaling social meanings related to gender identity, as F0 has been shown in numerous experimental studies to contribute to how feminine or masculine a speaker's voice sounds to listeners (e.g., Guzik 2004; Smyth, Jacobs & Rogers 2003).

Given gender differences in F0, many early studies of queer speakers have examined the pitch of the queer voice, testing stereotypes that perhaps queer speakers sound "gay" because their pitch patterns are more in line with speakers of the "opposite" gender. In other words, a widely circulating social stereotype feeds a hypothesis that perhaps queer speakers' pitch is different from straight speakers of the same sex assigned at birth, and perhaps more like the pitch of straight speakers of the "opposite" sex. However, many studies investigating F0 among gay men and lesbians have either inconsistent or inconclusive results (e.g., Gaudio 1994; Levon 2006; Smyth, Jacobs & Rogers 2003; Van Borsel, Vandaele & Corthals 2013; Waksler 2001). That is, studies either find conflicting results on whether gay speakers' pitch patterns differ from straight speakers', and many studies find no significant difference at all between the pitch patterns exhibited by gay and straight speakers. In other words, despite the stereotype that gay men speak with a higher pitch than straight men and lesbians speak with a lower pitch than straight women, these ideologies have not been empirically borne out in a consistent way across studies. Admittedly, many more of these studies have explored pitch among gay men than among lesbians, however.

Much like the inconclusive results borne out in such production studies, perception studies have found that F0 doesn't reliably and consistently determine how gay a male voice sounds to listeners (e.g., Campbell-Kibler 2011). However, it does affect gayness ratings for women, with lower-pitched female voices being more likely to "sound gay" than higher pitched female voices (Barron-Lutzross 2010). Interestingly, the stereotype that lesbians exhibit lower pitch than straight women is leveraged in high performance contexts, with female actresses using lower F0 when portraying lesbian characters than when portraying straight characters; however, empirical studies comparing the pitch of actual straight women and lesbians find no significant differences between the two groups (Waksler 2001).

Moving beyond these early studies that sought to pinpoint F0 patterns that differentiated the speech of queer men and lesbians from their straight counterparts, later studies explored how F0 can be used in particular contexts to accomplish social goals, indicate stances toward certain topics, or portray oneself as a particular kind of queer individual. For example, Levon (2011) probed the effect of conversational context on the pitch of queer speakers, finding that queer women in Israel exhibited wider pitch ranges when talking about gay-related topics than non-gay related topics. And Podesva (2006, 2007) explored how gay men's pitch ranges varied by situation, with some gay men exhibiting wider pitch ranges in informal gatherings with friends than in formal professional situations. Such studies have illuminated that particular ways of phonetically doing queerness can become more foregrounded in certain social situations, or when talking about certain socially relevant topics.

Finally, while F0 patterns have been varied with regards to speaker sexual orientation, studies of transgender speakers have uncovered more robust results. In one study, Zimman (2013) probed the effects of testosterone therapy on the pitch of the voices of trans men, finding that trans men's vocal pitches dropped over time, but not always in ways that could be solely predicted by the effects of testosterone. In other words, while testosterone therapy did indeed condition F0 for many of the trans men in the study, it wasn't the only conditioning factor, suggesting a social explanation for some of this phonetic variation. In another study, Gorham-Rowan and Morris (2006) found that trans women's F0 was overall significantly higher than that of cisgender men, despite the fact that estrogen therapy has no effect on vocal tract size. And recent studies have begun to explore F0 patterns among nonbinary speakers, with Schmid and Bradley (2019) finding that nonbinary speakers' F0 ranges fell between those of cis men and cis women. Such studies of trans speakers all lend support to the fact that the relationship between gender and F0 is not strictly biological, but in many cases is strongly conditioned by social factors and can be used to project or index gender in a variety of more agentive ways.

3.2 /s/ frontness

The /s/ sound is likely the most robustly studied phonetic variable in studies of language, gender, and sexuality. The voiceless anterior sibilant is articulated by placing the tongue against the alveolar ridge behind the top teeth and passing air over it, with the air hitting the top teeth creating a hiss sound. The closer the tongue is to the top teeth, the higher frequency the hiss sound (Flipsen, Shriberg, Weismar, Karlsson & McSweeny 1999; Jongman, Wayland & Wong 2000). Given the fact that the space between the tongue and the top teeth is manipulable and not entirely constrained by a speaker's vocal tract, it has been argued that the frequency of the /s/ hiss is socially rather than biologically conditioned (Stuart-Smith 2007; Zimman 2013, 2017).

Various acoustic measures have been used to capture the frequency of this hiss, and therefore to correlate with the frontness of the articulation of /s/. Center of Gravity (COG) represents the mean in Hz of where spectral energy is focused, with a higher COG corresponding to a fronter /s/. Peak frequency, representing the spectral peak with the highest prominence, also correlates with /s/ frontness, with a higher peak representing a fronter /s/ (Jongman, Wayland & Wong 2000). And spectral skew, representing the amount of spectral energy above or below the mean, correlates inversely with /s/ frontness, such that a lower skew corresponds to a fronter /s/ (Forrest. Weismar, Milenkovic & Dugall 1988). Whatever the specific measure examined, the frequency of /s/ has been shown to pattern with speaker gender, with (cisgender heterosexual) women producing a fronter /s/ with a higher frequency than (cisgender heterosexual) men in many production studies (e.g., Flipsen, Shriberg, Weismar, Karlsson & McSweeny 1999; Fuchs & Toda 2010; Hazenberg 2012; Podesva & Van Hofwegen 2014, 2016). The perception of the /s/ sound has been linked to speaker gender as well, with Strand (1999) finding that listeners expect women to produce /s/ at a higher frequency than men, thus influencing how they categorize speech sounds like /s/.

The articulation of /s/ is one of the most salient phonetic features that indexes sexual orientation in the popular imagination, especially for men, with the "gay lisp" being a widely circulating stereotype in English-speaking contexts, both in academic study and in popular culture (see e.g., Bowen 2002; Mack and Munson 2012; Schulman 2015; Van Borsel, De Bruyn, Lefebvre, Sokoloff, De Ley & Baudonck 2009; Van Borsel & Van de Putte 2014). Sociophoneticians have probed the articulation, acoustics, and perception of /s/ and how it relates to sexual orientation, in an effort to uncover the phonetic source of the "gay lisp" stereotype (see Calder 2020 for a review). Perhaps due to this salient stereotype, many sociophonetic studies of the /s/ sound have focused on gay men.

Numerous production studies have shown how queer men and women differ from straight men and women with respect to /s/ production, with gay men often being found to produce fronter /s/ than straight men (e.g., Hazenberg 2012; Podesva & Van Hofwegen 2014, 2016), and queer women being found to produce a more retracted /s/ than straight women (Podesva & Van-Hofwegen 2014, 2016). In addition, the frequency of the /s/ sound has been shown to contribute to how gay male voices sound to listeners, with male voices with higher frequency /s/ being rated by listeners as sounding more gay (e.g., Campbell-Kibler 2011; Munson 2007). In one study, listeners also expected lesbian voices to articulate an /s/ with a lower frequency than straight women (Munson, McDonald, DeBoe & White 2006). Interestingly, recent work has suggested that indexical connections between /s/ frontness and perceived gayness are language specific, with /s/ indeed contributing to how gay a voice sounds to English listeners, but not to French and German listeners (Boyd, Freuhwald & Hall-Lew 2021). Such discoveries suggest promise in enriching the field's theoretical understandings of the indexical connections between phonetic variables and social meanings, through the increased study of languages other than English.

All of these findings, taken with the findings for straight men and women, suggest that a fronter /s/ (in English) can index femininity, or – when coming from a voice perceived as male – queerness; and that a backer /s/ can index masculinity, or – when coming from a voice perceived as female – queerness. Recently, studies have explored how speakers can use /s/ frontness to project gender and sexual identity in particular ways. The indexical potential of /s/ with respect to gender is borne out in studies of transgender speakers, with trans men and women exhibiting /s/ patterns that reflect their gender identities, rather than their sex assigned at birth (e.g., Hazenberg 2012; Zimman 2012). Fronted /s/ as a marker of femininity and queerness has been shown to be taken up by drag performers as well. In a San Francisco study, drag queens (who were assigned male gender at birth and perform femininity through their drag personae) were shown to produce fronter /s/ than other male-assigned people in Northern California, including other queer individuals (Calder 2019b). In addition, as these queens visually transformed into their feminine-presenting personae using makeup, wigs, and costuming – that is, as they increasingly embodied visual femininity – their articulation of the feminine-coded fronted /s/ became louder in relation to other segments. In other words, they used amplitude to acoustically foreground a variable indexical of femininity and queerness as their visual presentation became more feminine (Calder 2019a).

Finally, studies of nonbinary speakers have called into question binary assumptions that fronted /s/ always patterns with femininity and backer /s/ always patterns with masculinity. In a Columbus, Ohio study (Steele 2019, 2021), nonbinary speakers' production of /s/ was not shown to pattern with self-rated femininity or masculinity in expected ways, with Black non-binary speakers actually exhibiting a fronter /s/ if they identified as more masculine. Another study comparing non-binary drag queens in two San Francisco neighborhoods found that those whose visual presentation was more in line with conventional ideals of femininity actually exhibited a more retracted /s/ than those whose visual presentation was less conventionally feminine (Calder forthcoming). These studies of gender non-normative individuals suggest that some queer communities deploy phonetic variables in ways that disrupt cisnormative expectations, revealing that for non-cisgender populations, fronted /s/ doesn't always correspond with a feminine identity and retracted /s/ doesn't always correspond with a masculine identity (Calder & Steele 2019, forthcoming).

3.3 Other phonetic variables in studies of queer language

While F0 and /s/ frontness have largely dominated the sociophonetic study of queer speakers, a number of other phonetic features have also been explored with respect to queer identity. Some studies have probed correlations between vowel space dispersion – i.e., how far apart the articulations of different vowels are from each other in the mouth – and sexual orientation, finding that queer men exhibit larger vowel spaces than straight men (Pierrehumbert, Bent, Munson, Bradlow & Bailey 2004; Rogers & Smyth 2001). In other words, queer men pronounce vowel sounds that are more distinct to each other than straight men in many studies, perhaps leading to stereotypes that gay men speak "clearer" than straight men (see e.g., Munson, McDonald, DeBoe & White 2006). Other research has suggested that the pronunciation of vowel sounds in a way that is consonant with the California Vowel Shift – a local sound change taking place in California – may be part of particular gay male linguistic styles (Podesva 2011).

Another feature that has been linked to performances of queerness is stop release – i.e., the audible puff of air after articulating sounds like /t/ – with greater rates and greater amplitudes of stop release being linked to male queerness (e.g., Crist 1997; Podesva 2006; Podesva, Roberts & Campbell-Kibler 2002; Smyth & Rogers 2002). The use of this feature perhaps also contributes to the stereotype of gay men speaking with more "clarity" than straight men.

Phonation, or voice quality, has been examined in a number of studies as well, with both falsetto (Podesva 2007) and creaky voice (Zimman 2013) being linked to the performance and perception of queer male identity. In other words, performances of male queerness may involve more falsetto and more creak than normative performances of cisgender, straight male identity. It has been argued that certain queer styles can employ both falsetto – which results in a higher F0 – and creak – which results in a lower F0 – contributing to an overall wider pitch range that can serve to project certain types of over-the-top queerness, like a gay male "diva" persona (Podesva 2007).

A prosodic feature that has been linked to gayness in both production and perception studies is phrase-final syllable lengthening, with studies showing that gay men produce longer phrase-final syllables than straight men (Calder, Eckert, Fine & Podesva 2013), and that male voices with longer phrase-final syllables are perceived as sounding more gay (Esposito 2020).

Finally, a variable which has been shown to pattern with respect to gender is the (ING) variable. Foundational sociolinguistic studies of cisgender speakers have shown that men tend to produce higher rates of [IN] than women, and women tend to produce higher rates of [ING] than men (e.g., Fischer 1958; Hazen 2008; Tagliamonte 2004; Trudgill 1974). In a study of non-binary speakers, Gratton (2016) found that non-binary speakers exhibited (ING) patterns that serve to distinguish them from their sex assigned at birth, suggesting a degree of agency in the linguistic articulation of gender identity using phonetic variables.

4 What should a queer and trans sociophonetics look like?

While phonetic studies of the queer voice have done much to advance sociolinguistic understandings of the phonetic differences between queer and straight voices, as well as the ways that queer individuals can deploy phonetic variables in agentive ways, there still remains much opportunity for future studies in queer and trans sociophonetics to connect with the broader disciplinary aims of queer and trans linguistics. In the remainder of this chapter, I conclude with some suggestions for researchers in queer and trans sociophonetics to consider in addressing some shortcomings of previous work and in facilitating a more socially and epistemically just representation of the queer and trans speakers under analysis. My suggestions fall under three broad themes: representation, methodology, and theoretic orientation.

As mentioned previously, the sociophonetic study of queer speakers has gone from searching for phonetic markers that result from demographic gay identities, towards probing the performance of queerness that construct a wider range of identities. Despite these shifts, most research on the sound of the queer voice has been focused on cisgender, White, English-speaking individuals, especially White cisgender gay men. While this important work has illuminated much about the phonetic markers of the gay voice, the overrepresentation of certain queer identities in linguistic research brings into question who we as linguists construct as the prototypical queer speaker. While sociophonetic studies of transgender, non-binary, BIPOC, and non-English-speaking queer speakers have started to appear in the last decade, these identities still remain relatively underexplored and underrepresented in the literature. Queer and trans sociophonetics can benefit from representing speakers from a wider range of queer identities from a wider range of geographic contexts, and who speak a wider range of languages. Many of the phonetic patterns that have been observed (e.g., that a fronter /s/ is indexical of femininity and AMAB queerness) are based on studies of primarily White, English-speaking individuals, and studies of other communities – including communities of color – have shown that these patterns aren't necessarily universal and generalizable beyond those White, English-speaking contexts from which they were gleaned. For example, multiple studies have shown that for speakers of color (e.g., Calder & King 2020, 2022; Steele 2019, 2021), and non-English speakers (e.g., Boyd, Freuhwald & Hall-Lew 2021; Mendoza 2021) phonetic variables and gendered social meaning don't always align in the same ways as they do for the White, English-speaking individuals dominating much sociolinguistic research. This suggests that the inclusion of a wider array of speakers can shed much light on the indexical connections between phonetic variables and performances of queer identity, in more complex ways that has been previously assumed. Intersectional analysis (Crenshaw 1989; Levon 2015) that considers how multiple co-constitutive dimensions of identity – like gender, sexuality, race, and place – contribute to phonetic variation could prove fruitful in moving toward this goal. Relatedly, there is a dearth of sociophonetic research on intersex speakers, with important recent work like Dauphinais's (2021) dissertation on women with Turner syndrome in Brazil demonstrating the potential for further exploration on the phonetic articulation of intersex identity.

In addition, a central aim of trans linguistics is to center the perspectives and experiences of transpeople (see Zimman 2020a). In this vein, representation becomes important for queer and trans sociophonetic study, not only in terms of the speakers being analyzed, but also in terms of the researchers conducting the analyses. Given that a person's social epistemology is shaped by their own social positionality, a wider range of researcher perspectives can do much to broaden sociolinguistic understandings of what phonetic variables mean to different types of communities. In other words, individuals who have been positioned as queer through their lived experiences, who have a nuanced understanding of the social constraints and consequences that come from being positioned in such a way, and who have a nuanced understanding of the ways that queer communities leverage linguistic resources to negotiate these constraints, may be able to lend an analytical lens towards the practices of queer communities that more accurately reflects the socially meaningful nuances that are relevant to those very communities. And non-queer researchers conducting analyses on queer communities may develop more accurate, nuanced, and epistemically just arguments in interpreting the patterns of queer speakers if they more explicitly consider the role of their own social positionality, and how this positionality may affect predispositions to interpret patterns in particular ways, exhibited by communities who are socially positioned in very different ways from them.

Queer and trans sociophonetics also has the potential to address some important conversations around methodology in the field. One criticism often leveraged against queer and trans linguistics is that the field's aims are often abstract and theoretical, without tangible grounding in applicable empirical methodology (see Motschenbacher 2011 for a discussion). However, given the instrumental and often quantitative approach employed in sociophonetic study, there is much potential for queer and trans sociophonetics to combat these mischaracterizations of the field and to ground the theoretical aims of queer linguistics in empirical methodologies. A queer and trans sociophonetics can facilitate an exploration of how micro-level linguistic practices (e.g., fine-grained measurable phonetic differences in linguistic form) are both constrained by, and feed into, macro level discourses about gender and sexuality. A mixed methods approach – one that combines the quantitative analysis of the variation of fine-grained linguistic form with qualitative analyses of macro- and micro-level discourses that make these fine-grained distinctions socially meaningful – has much potential to advance the larger aims of queer and trans linguistics and to relate the ground-level phonetic practices of speakers to larger social structures that privilege heteronormativity.

Despite the advantages of leveraging an empirical, quantitative approach, there are some important pitfalls that should be avoided in queer and trans sociophonetic study, as not to mischaracterize, misrepresent, or do epistemic harm to the speakers we analyze. For example, as previously discussed, some research has illuminated how patterns in vowel articulation may differ between queer and straight speakers (e.g., Pierrehumbert, Bent, Munson, Bradlow & Bailey 2004; Podesva 2011; Rogers & Smyth 2001). However, current methods for measuring and analyzing vowels overwhelmingly utilize normalization methods that depend on speakers being placed by researchers into binary gender categories. Recent work (e.g., miles-hercules & Zimman 2019) has shown how such normalization methods not only fail at representing nonbinary transgender speakers but may also produce different vowel measurements entirely for the exact same speaker, depending on which binary category is selected for them. In a similar vein, trans linguistics researchers (e.g., Zimman 2019; Conrod 2019) have critiqued the overly simplistic ways that speaker demographic information is collected and categorized for quantitative analysis, with traditional data-collection methods leading researchers to make assumptions about speaker demographic identity in binning them into binary gender categories that can be easily applied to statistical analysis. In other words, under such methods, transgender speakers may be grouped into a binary gender category they don't identify with, or excluded from analysis entirely, in order to maintain a simplified binary model of gender. While I don't believe any of these emergent arguments mean to suggest that quantitative analysis should be done away with entirely, they do shed light on the fact that dominant methods of categorization should be more nuanced than forced binary choices, in order to more accurately represent and account for speakers whose identities aren't binary and cisgender.

Finally, queer and trans sociophonetic work can benefit from integrating local queer epistemologies into the theoretic interpretations of the phonetic patterns observed in those communities. The phonetic practices of queer speakers are often compared to their cisgender, heterosexual counterparts, with trans speakers especially often being framed as failing at their intended articulation of gender if their manifestation of phonetic variables diverges too much from manifestations exhibited by cis speakers of the same gender. As mentioned previously, many early studies of the phonetic practices of trans speakers, though important in illuminating the phonetic features trans speakers use to index their identities, were conducted by speech language pathologists (e.g., Gorham-Rowan & Morris 2006) who implicitly pathologized the speech of trans speakers who diverged too far from cisnormative standards. Rather than merely describing how queer speakers "fail" to conform to cisgender standards, a queer and trans sociophonetics should explicitly discuss the dominant cisgender perspective this perception of "failure" emerges from. In other words, a sociophonetics in line with the aims trans linguistics should investigate how trans speakers navigate or reject pressures to be normative, (Konnelly 2021) and how the navigation of these pressures relates to the phonetic patterns of trans people that either conform to or diverge from normative patterns exhibited by cisgender communities. In other words, it is not only important to describe phonetic differences between queer and non-queer speakers, but it is also important to connect local phonetic practices with larger heteronormative ideological discourses, facilitating the aims of queer linguistics. Taking community epistemology into account in interpreting practices of trans speakers (see e.g., Calder 2021) can shed much light on the salient distinctions and social goals that may be relevant to trans speakers, beyond merely conforming to dominant binary models of gender.

Research in trans linguistics has also illuminated the insight that the linguistic articulation of gender is more complex than one-to-one essential connections between single variables and manifestations of identity. Traditional phonetic research on gender carries (and constructs) the implicit assumption that for any given variable (e.g., F0), variant x maps in a one-to-one way to femininity (e.g., high F0) and variant y maps in a one-to-one way to masculinity (e.g., low F0). Therefore, the assumption is that those who wish to project gender identity in a particular way must use whatever phonetic variable is currently being analyzed in a way that is indexical of that gender identity. However, research in trans linguistics has challenged this assumption, arguing for an analysis of the gendered voice as stylistic bricolage (Zimman 2017), a stylistic combination of resources, rather than a single property conveyed by an individual linguistic variable. For example, despite the social salience of F0 in indexing gender identity, studies have shown that trans women may be perceived as female even with a low F0 (e.g., Günzburger 1995) or perceived as male with a high F0 (e.g., Gelfer & Schofield 2000). This suggests that, for some speakers, something other than F0 is doing the work of indexing gender. That is, it isn't a singular variable that does the work of indexing gender in a one-to-one fashion, but it is instead collections of signs that do this work. And in these collections of signs, different variables may be contributing gendered meaning to the overall gendered style for different speakers. For example, some speakers who phonetically position themselves as masculine may use a low F0 do to so, but others may use a more retracted /s/, and it is not necessary for every masculine speaker to exhibit both variables to accomplish the social work of positioning themselves as a masculine subject (Zimman 2017). In addition, it may not be a specific linguistic variable that does the work of indexing gender for a particular speaking subject, but it may be another semiotic modality entirely. For example, one study has shown that AMAB nonbinary drag performers that are evaluated as feminine by their peers do not exhibit /s/ patterns that have been argued in the literature to be indexical of femininity; instead, it is their visual presentation – one that allows them to visually pass as women – that contributes the indexical meaning of femininity to their overall styles, a meaning that is recognized and ratified by their interlocutors (Calder forthcoming). Such work, and other work in queer linguistics (e.g., King 2020) foregrounds the importance of the body in articulating gender and sexuality. Recent work has shown how the body can dictate the gendered indexical potential of variables (Calder 2019b), the phonetic realization of variables (Calder 2019a,) as well as the indexical role of phonetic variables in the overall style (Calder, forthcoming), suggesting much promise for the consideration of the indexical role of the body in sociophonetic studies of queer speakers. In other words, because queer voices emerge from queer bodies, and those bodies may be positioned relative to standards of heteronormativity and cisnormativity in particular ways, there remains great opportunity to integrate the phonetic study of the queer voice into multi-modal analyses that illuminate how queer individuals articulate their identities across a range of linguistic, visual, and embodied modalities.

References

Azul, David. 2013. How do voices become gendered? A critical examination of everyday and medical constructions of the relationship between voice, sex, and gender identity. In Malin Ah-King (ed.), *Challenging popular myths of sex, gender, and biology*. 77–88. Cham: Springer.
Barron-Lutzross, Auburn. 2010. You sound like a lesbian: stereotypes of lesbian speech. Amherst: Hampshire College thesis.
Bowen, Caroline. 2002. Beyond lisping: Code switching and gay speech styles. Accessed at https://www.speech-language-therapy.com/index.php?option=com_content&view=article&id=62:code&catid=11:admin&Itemid=101
Boyd, Zac, Josef Fruehwald & Lauren Hall-Lew. 2021. Cross-linguistic perception of /s/ among French, German, and English listeners. *Language Variation and Change* 33(2). 165–191.
Calder, Jeremy. 2019a. The fierceness of fronted /s/: linguistic rhematization through visual transformation. *Language in Society* 48(1). 31–64.
Calder, Jeremy. 2019b. From 'sissy' to 'sickening': the indexical landscape of /s/ in SoMa, San Francisco. *Journal of Linguistic Anthropology* 29(3). 332–358.
Calder, Jeremy. 2020. From 'gay lisp' to 'fierce queen': the sociophonetics of sexuality's most iconic variable. In Kira Hall & Rusty Barrett (eds.), *The Oxford Handbook of Language and Sexuality*. Oxford University Press.
Calder, Jeremy. 2021. Whose indexical field is it?: the role of community epistemology in indexing social meaning. *Proceedings of the 20th Meeting of the Texas Linguistic Society*. 39–55.
Calder, Jeremy, Penelope Eckert, Julia Fine & Robert J. Podesva. 2013. The social conditioning of rhythm: the case of Post-Tonic Lengthening. Paper presented at the Annual Meeting of the Linguistic Society of America, Boston, MA.
Calder, Jeremy. Forthcoming. 'Harsh' SoMa and 'Beige' Castro: the cross-modal construction of queer femininity in two San Francisco neighborhoods. Unpublished manuscript.
Calder, Jeremy & Sharese King. 2020. Intersections between race, place, and gender in the production of /s/. *Penn Working Papers in Linguistics* 26(2). 31–38.
Calder, Jeremy & Sharese King. 2022. Whose gendered voices matter?: race and gender in the articulation of /s/ in Bakersfield, California. *Journal of Sociolinguistics*. Online first.
Calder, Jeremy & Ariana Steele. 2019. Gender in sociolinguistic variation beyond the binary. Paper presented at the Annual Meeting of the Linguistic Society of America, New York, NY.
Calder, Jeremy & Ariana Steele. Forthcoming. Accounting for the nonbinary speaking subject in sociolinguistic variationism. Unpublished manuscript.
Cameron, Deborah & Don Kulick. 2003. *Language and Sexuality*. Cambridge: Cambridge University Press.

Campbell-Kibler, Kathryn. 2011. Intersecting variables and perceived sexual orientation in men. *American Speech* 86(1). 52–68.

Conrod, Kirby. 2019. Language, gender, and harm. Retrieved from https://kconrod.medium.com/title-language-gender-and-harm-e2491de4cf42

Crenshaw, Kimberle. 1989. Demarginalizing the intersection of race and sex; a black feminist critique of discrimination doctrine, feminist theory and antiracist politics. *University of Chicago Legal Forum* (8). 139–167.

Crist, Sean. 1997. Duration of onset consonants in gay male stereotyped speech. *University of Pennsylvania Working Papers in Linguistics* 4(3). 53–70.

Deshaies-Lafontaine, Denise. 1974. *A socio-phonetic study of a Quebec French community: Trois-Rivieres*. London: University College London dissertation.

Dauphinais, Ashlee. 2021. *Guerreiras: linguistic and social practices among women with turner syndrome in Brazil*. Columbus: The Ohio State University dissertation.

Eckert, Penelope. 2005. Variation, convention, and social meaning. Paper presented at the Annual Meeting of the Linguistic Society of America. Oakland, CA.

Eckert, Penelope. 2012. Three waves of variation study: the emergence of meaning in the study of sociolinguistic variation. *Annual Review of Anthropology* 41. 87–100.

Eckert, Penelope. 2021. Gender and the third wave of variation study. *Gender and Language* 15(2). 242–248.

Esposito, Lewis. 2020. Linking gender, sexuality, and affect: the linguistic and social patterning of phrase-final posttonic lengthening. *Language Variation and Change* 32(2). 191–216.

Ferrand, Carole T. & Ronald L. Bloom. 1996. Gender differences in children's intonational patterns. *Journal of Voice* 10(3). 284–291.

Fischer, John L. 1958. Social influences on the choice of a linguistic variant. *WORD* 14. 47–56.

Flipsen, Peter Jr., Lawrence Shriberg, Gary Weismer, Heather Karlsson & Jane McSweeny. 1999. Acoustic characteristics of /s/ in adolescents. *Journal of Speech, Language, and Hearing Research* 42(3). 663–677.

Forrest, Karen, Gary Weismer, Paul Milenkovic & Ronald N. Dugall. 1988. Statistical analysis of word-initial voiceless obstruents: preliminary data. *Journal of the Acoustical Society of America* 84(1). 115–123.

Fuchs, Susanne & Martine Toda. 2010. Do differences in male versus female /s/ reflect biological or sociophonetic factors? In Susanne Fuchs, Martine Toda & Marzena Zygis (eds.), *An Interdisciplinary Guide to Turbulent Sounds*. Berlin: DeGruyter Mouton. 281–302.

Gaudio, Rudolf P. 1994. Sounding gay: pitch properties in the speech of gay and straight men. *American Speech* 69(1). 30–57.

Gelfer, M. P. and K. J. Schofield. 2000. Comparison of acoustic and perceptual measures of voice in male-to-female transsexuals perceived as female versus those perceived as male. Journal of Voice 14(1), 22–33.

Gorham-Rowan, Mary & Richard Morris. 2006. Aerodynamic analysis of male-to-female transgender voice. *Journal of Voice* 20(2). 251–262.

Graddol, David & Joan Swann. 1983. Speaking fundamental frequency: some physical and social correlates. *Language and Speech* 26(4). 351–366.

Gratton, Chantal. 2016. Resisting the gender binary: the use of (ING) in the construction of non-binary transgender identities. *Penn Working Papers in Linguistics* 22(2). 51–60.

Günzburger, D. 1995. Acoustic and perceptual implications of the transexual voice. Archives of Sexual Behavior 24(3), 339–348.

Guzik, Karen. 2004. Acoustic analysis of phonetic parameters of less masculine sounding German speech. *Arbeitsberichte des Instituts fuer Phonetik und Digitale Sprachverarbeitung Universitaet Kiel* 36. 15–29.

Hazen, Kirk. 2008. (ING): A vernacular baseline for English in Appalachia. *American Speech* 83. 116–140.

Hazenberg, Evan. 2012. Language and Identity Practice: a Sociolinguistic Study of Gender in Ottawa, Canada. St. John's: Memorial University of Newfoundland thesis.

Jongman, Allard, Ratree Wayland & Serena Wong. 2000. Acoustic characteristics of English fricatives. *Journal of the Acoustical Society of America* 108(3). 1252–1263.

King, Brian. 2020. Language and embodied sexuality. In Kira Hall & Rusty Barrett (eds.), *The Oxford Handbook of Language and Sexuality*. Oxford: Oxford University Press.

Konnelly, Lex 2021. Nuance and normativity in trans linguistic research. *Journal of Language and Sexuality* 10(1). 71–82.

Levon, Erez. 2006. Hearing 'gay': prosody, interpretation, and the affective judgments of men's speech. *American Speech* 81(1). 56–78.

Levon, Erez. 2011. Teasing apart to bring together: gender and sexuality in variationist research. *American Speech* 86(1). 69–84.

Levon, Erez. 2015. Integrating intersectionality in language, gender, and sexuality research. *Language and Linguistics Compass* 9. 295–308.

Livia, Anna & Kira Hall (eds.). 1997. *Queerly Phrased: Language, Gender and Sexuality*. Oxford: Oxford University Press.

Mack, Sara & Benjamin Munson. 2012. The influence of /s/ quality on ratings of men's sexual orientation: explicit and implicit measures of the 'gay lisp' stereotype. *Journal of Phonetics* 40(1). 198–212.

Mendoza, Christopher. 2021. That /s/ tiene tumbao: investigating acoustic correlates of queer femme-ness in bilingual Latinx Miami. Miami: Florida International University thesis.

Milani, Tommaso. 2017. Language and sexuality. In Ofelia Garcia, Nelson Flores & Massimiliano Spotti (eds.), *The Oxford Handbook of Language and Society*. Oxford: Oxford University Press.

miles-hercules, deandre & Lal Zimman. 2019. Normativity in normalization: methodological challenges in the (automated) analysis of vowels among nonbinary speakers. Paper presented at New Ways of Analyzing Variation 48. Eugene, OR.

Motschenbacher, Heiko. 2011. Taking Queer Linguistics further: sociolinguistics and critical heteronormativity research. *International Journal of the Sociology of Language* 212. 149–179.

Munson, Benjamin. 2007. The acoustic correlates of perceived masculinity, perceived femininity, and perceived sexual orientation. *Language and Speech* 50(1). 125–142.

Munson, Benjamin, Elizabeth C. McDonald, Nancy L. DeBoe & Aubrey R. White. 2006. The acoustic and perceptual bases of judgments of women and men's sexual orientation from read speech. *Journal of Phonetics* 34(2). 202–240.

Ohala, John J. 1984. An ethnological perspective on common cross-language utilization of F0 of voice. *Phonetica* 41(1). 1–16.

Peirce, Charles S. 1895. Of reasoning in general. Reprint in Nathan Houser, Andre De Tienne, Jonathan R. Eller, Albert C. Lewis, Cathy L. Clark & D. Bront Davis (eds.), *The Essential Peirce: Selected Philosophical Writings (1893–1913)*. 11–23. Bloomington: Indiana University Press, 1998.

Pierrehumbert, Janet B., Tessa Bent, Benjamin Munson, Ann R. Bradlow & J. Michael Bailey. 2004. The influence of sexual orientation on vowel production (L). *The Journal of the Acoustical Society of America* 116(4). 1905–1908.

Podesva, Robert J. 2006. Phonetic detail in sociolinguistic variation: its significance and role in the construction of social meaning. Stanford: Stanford University dissertation.

Podesva, Robert J. 2007. Phonation type as a stylistic variable: the use of falsetto in constructing a persona. *Journal of Sociolinguistics* 11(4). 478–504.

Podesva, Robert J. 2011. The California Vowel Shift and gay identity. *American Speech* 86(1). 32–51.

Podesva, Robert J. & Sakiko Kajino. 2014. Sociophonetics, gender, and sexuality. In Susan Ehrlich, Miriam Meyerhoff & Janet Holmes (eds.), *The Handbook of Language, Gender, and Sexuality*. 103–122. Malden, MA: John Wiley & Sons Ltd.

Podesva, Robert J., Sarah J. Roberts & Kathryn Campbell Kibler. 2002. Sharing resources and indexing meanings in the production of gay styles. In Kathryn Campbell-Kibler, Robert J. Podesva, Sarah J. Roberts & Andrew Wong (eds.), *Language and sexuality: contesting meaning in theory and practice*. 175–189. Stanford, CA: CSLI Press.

Podesva, Robert J. & Janneke Van Hofwegen. 2014. How conservatism and normative gender constrain variation in inland California: the case of /s/. Paper presented at New Ways of Analyzing Variation 42. Pittsburgh, PA.

Podesva, Robert J. & Janneke Van Hofwegen. 2016. /s/exuality in smalltown California: gender normativity and the acoustic realization of /s/. In Erez Levon & Ronald Beline Mendes (eds.), *Language, Sexuality, and Power*. 168–188. Oxford: Oxford University Press.

Queen, Robin. 2014. Language and sexual identities. In Susan Ehrlich, Miriam Meyerhoff & Janet Holmes (eds.), *The Handbook of Language, Gender, and Sexuality*. 203–219. Malden, MA: John Wiley & Sons Ltd.

Rogers, Henry & Ron Smyth. 2001. Vowel reduction as a cue to distinguishing gay- and straight-sounding male speech. Paper presented at the Annual Meeting of the Canadian Linguistics Society, Ottawa, Ontario.

Schmid, Maxwell & Evan Bradley. 2019. Vocal pitch and intonation characteristics of those who are gender non-binary. *Proceedings of the 19th International Conference of Phonetic Sciences*. 2685–2689.

Schulman, Michael. 2015. Is there a 'gay voice'? *The New Yorker*, July 10. Accessed at http://www.newyorker.com/culture/culture-desk/is-there-a-gay-voice

Smyth, Rob, Greg Jacobs & Henry Rogers. 2003. Male voices and perceived sexual orientation: an experimental and theoretical approach. *Language in Society* 32(3). 329–50.

Smyth, Rob & Henry Rogers. 2002. Phonetics, gender, and sexual orientation. *Proceedings of the Annual Meeting of the Canadian Linguistic Association*. 299–301.

Steele, Ariana. 2019. Nonbinary speech, race, and non-normative gender: sociolinguistic style beyond the binary. Columbus: The Ohio State University thesis.

Steele, Ariana. 2021. Enacting new worlds of gender: nonbinary speakers, racialized gender, and anti-colonialism. In Kira Hall & Rusty Barrett (eds.), *The Oxford Handbook of Language and Sexuality*. Oxford: Oxford University Press.

Strand, Elizabeth A. 1999. Uncovering the role of gender stereotypes in speech perception. *Journal of Language and Social Psychology* 18(1). 86–100.

Stuart-Smith, Jane. 2007. Empirical evidence for gendered speech production: /s/ in Glaswegian. In Jennifer S. Cole & Jose Ignacio Hualde (eds.), *Laboratory Phonology*. 65–86. New York: Mouton de Gruyter.

Tagliamonte, Sali. 2004. Someth[in]'s go[ing] on!: variable ing at ground zero. In B. L. Gunnerson, L. Bergström, G. Eklund, S. Fidell, L. H. Hansen, A. Karstadt, B. Nordbergd, E. Sundergren & M. Thelander (eds.), *Papers from the Second International Conference on Language Variation in Europe, ICLAVE 2*. 12–14.

Trudgill, Peter. 1974. *The Social Differentiation of English in Norwich*. Cambridge: Cambridge University Press.
Van Borsel, John, Els De Bruyn, Evelien Lefebvre, Anouschka Sokoloff, Sophia De Ley & Nele Baudonck. 2009. The prevalence of lisping in gay men. *Journal of Communication Disorders* 42(2). 100–106.
Van Borsel, John, Jana Vandaele & Paul Corthals. 2013. Pitch and pitch variation in lesbian women. *Journal of Voice* 27 (5).656.e13–656.e16.
Van Borsel, John & Anneleen Van de Putte. 2014. Lisping and male homosexuality. *Archives of Sexual Behavior* 43. 1159–1163.
Waksler, Rachelle. 2001. Pitch range and women's sexual orientation. *Word* 52(1). 69–77.
Zimman, Lal. 2012. Voices in transition: testosterone, transmasculinity, and the gendered voice among female-to-male transgender people. Boulder: University of Colorado Boulder dissertation.
Zimman, Lal. 2013. Hegemonic masculinity and the variability of gay-sounding speech: the perceived sexuality of transgender men. *Journal of Language and Sexuality* 2(1). 1–39.
Zimman, Lal. 2017. Gender as stylistic bricolage: transmasculine voices and the relationship between fundamental frequency and /s/. *Language in Society* 46(3). 339–370.
Zimman, Lal. 2019. Listening to trans+ voices: trans-inclusive theory and practice for research on sex, gender, and the voice. Paper presented at the Linguistic Society of America annual meeting, New York, NY.
Zimman, Lal. 2020a. Transgender language, transgender moment: toward a trans linguistics. In Kira Hall & Rusty Barrett (eds.), *The Oxford Handbook of Language and Sexuality*. Oxford: Oxford University Press.
Zimman, Lal. 2020b. Sociophonetics. In James Stanlaw (ed.), *The International Encyclopedia of Linguistic Anthropology*. New York: John Wiley & Sons Inc.
Zimman, Lal. 2021. Beyond the cis gays' cis gaze: the need for a trans linguistics. *Gender and Language* 15(3). 423–429.

Bryce McCleary
Queer+ Trans folk linguistics
Language regard, identity, and drag performance in Oklahoma

1 Introduction

At the 2019 annual meeting of the Linguistic Society of America, a panel titled "New Directions in LGBTQ+ Linguistics" presented linguistic research and perspectives centering Queer and Trans speakers' language and experience. A motivation for this panel was the commemoration of the special interest group on LGBTQ+ issues in linguistics and the sharing of how much has changed within the field – methods, interests, and gaps. Lal Zimman (2019), panelist for this session, made one particular bullet point that caught the attention of a number of members in the audience: a note that trans people are "natural linguists".

While the vast majority of the room seemed to nod or otherwise project agreement, some skepticism, even pushback, on this point was discussed and tweeted about shortly after the presentation, and it seemed motivated by two ideas: That linguistics is a discipline which requires training and therefore no one is "naturally" inclined to the discreet and technical information across levels of linguistic analysis; and/or that everybody employs language in ways that reflect identity/self in society and interactions, thus rendering everyone, to some extent, "naturally" inclined to think about language and its effects.

Regarding the first point (the technical instruction required to be a "linguist"), one need not look further than oft-cited work within Folk Linguistics (e.g., Preston 1996) to be reminded that non-linguists frequently have and employ, in rich detail across all sorts of levels of language, meta-linguistic knowledge. In some cases, this awareness is granular and comparable to things learned in courses in phonetics, morpho-syntax, sociolinguistics, etc. This fact may seem to support the second argument (that everyone is, in this sense, a "linguist"), but that would be missing the nuance – and the point – of Zimman's comment.

It is an understatement to say that trans and nonbinary people across the world, certainly within the US, remain under attack by certain socio-political ideologies (e.g., "Don't Say Gay" legislation, Texas' urge to report gender-affirming care, prohibiting trans children in sports leagues, and more recently, specifically anti-drag and anti-trans legislation all across the South and in Oklahoma.). Linguistically,

Bryce McCleary, Rice University

https://doi.org/10.1515/9783110742510-007

trans people have to make critical decisions about how they present, linguistically and otherwise, for risk of certain consequences in the social world.

Trans people are not the only "natural linguists" out there; many people of different situations, cultures, heritages, regions, and experiences rely on language to navigate tenuous circumstances. But it is the case that trans and nonbinary folks (and some queer people more broadly) are at risk of discrimination and violence for being themselves, and this very fact can often contribute to a nuanced awareness of language that, by and large, is not demonstrated comparably in predominantly cisgender (and perhaps also predominantly white) communities. The experiences of trans and non-binary people, in fact, often include acts of linguistic violence (e.g., misgendering, misrepresentation; see Jones 2022), and the fact that these linguistic experiences are often overlooked or glossed over in a broader Queer Linguistics has influenced a need for expanding, even the development of a trans linguistics. It is for this reason, Zimman (2020) proposes just such a subfield, which, in addition to calling for more trans and non-binary researchers in the field, attunes itself "not only to oppressive language but also to agency in, through, and beyond language". Experiences of ethno-racial category placement, racialization, and class-based oppression can also render this sort of awareness important or necessary. Intersectionality (Crenshaw 1989, 1994, 2016) plays a crucial role here. These various experiential and identity-related categories are often at play *along with* gender and sexuality.

This chapter introduces a research paradigm focused on studying language regard – ideas, attitudes, beliefs, reactions, etc. on language – exhibited by queer and trans drag performers in Oklahoma. It positions language regard data within the purview of identity in interaction and thus connects metalanguage, presupposition, and implication with sociocultural realities of the performers. Drag is an artform dependent on language (i.e., in presentation of a drag character, mouthing words during lip-sync musical performances, hosting shows, interacting with members of the audience, etc.). Additionally, Oklahoma is not a state known for supporting its LGBTQ+ communities,[1] and it's often because of tenuous and/or dangerous situations through which trans and queer people are forced to navigate that they crucially rely on language (awareness) in order to survive. While the research presented here is not intended to contend with (or take seriously) the criticisms of Zimman's point above, the framework for a Queer+ Trans Folk Linguistics assumes – and hopefully demonstrates – some of the truths in Zimman's point.

---

[1] At the time of this writing, the current Governor sign a bill making any nonbinary distinctions on birth certificates illegal. Earlier this year, he and the Oklahoma houses banned trans athletes from competing in women's sports, and in 2021, he also signed a bill banning any mandatory training at public universities on race and gender/sexuality. More information on LGBTQ+ discrimination in OK later in the chapter.

2 Folk linguistics

Folk Linguistics, as a cohesive subfield of linguistic science, inevitably begins Hoenigswald's (1966) proposal at the 1964 UCLA Sociolinguistics Conference. Of course, this wasn't the first instance of interest in non-linguists' beliefs, attitudes, and ideas towards language (e.g., Polle 1904; Grootaers 1959; and later Daan 1970; Inoue 1977). However, Hoenigswald's (1966) proposal conceptualized the subfield's attention to production of language, perception of language, and (automatic) responses to language.

Bloomfield (1944) is cited in the discussion, particularly regarding his taxonomy of the types of responses to language. This taxonomy accounts for general language production ("primary responses"; e.g., any sort of talk) as well as the production of language about language ("secondary responses"; e.g., talk on the "origin" of language, or the evaluation of a dialect, etc.). Bloomfield's specific characterization of the third taxonomic category is rather odd and reveals his critical view of non-linguists' beliefs about language.

Einar Haugen calls Bloomfield's point of view on these responses "definitely negative" (21), and it's easy to see why. Bloomfield's depiction of non-linguists' ideas about language is one of a stubborn, ignorant, and simple-minded make-believe. It is unfortunate that this sort of coloring of non-linguists' language regard is still present, though hopefully not quite as robustly.

This sort of condescension is reflective of the limited idea of who the "speaker" is. Additionally, when you consider how often Bloomfield (1944) refers to non-linguists, the general public, and their ideas as "simple," this writing is also reflective of the elitism that can accompany discussions of what non-linguists can/do know about language.

The latter portion of the discussion revolves around Labov's idea of the "poverty-stricken" vocabulary of non-linguists (23), ultimately working towards a proposed goal of folk linguistics to dichotomize the things people do and the things people say they do. This is still an interest of folk linguistics today, but it also (mis)represents ideas about folk, their linguistic/cognitive abilities, and about the aims of the field.

Labov examples the poverty-stricken vocabulary of non-linguists with his observations of the use of the label "nasal" for both strongly nasalized and strongly denasalized speech. This interaction was of critical interest to Preston (1996), who demonstrated that, if you interpret the label "nasal" to mean "inappropriate amount of nasality", then the issue of accurate vocabulary is rather trivial, "simply a difference between the folk vocabulary and the technical one" (43). Put more directly, non-linguists may be much more adept at talking about their observations of language than linguists are willing to give them credit. In fact, Plichta (2005) found perceptions of the "nasal" quality of Northern Cities vowels to be, at least sometimes, based on an acoustic reality. Plichta & Preston (2005) found that listeners were able to accurately place voices along a North-South continuum using only degrees of monophtongized /ay/, and that these perceptions were strongly rooted in stereotypes – stereotypes readily employed in perception tasks.

Listening-perception studies within Folk Linguistics provide yet further evidence for the tie between beliefs and perceptions. Niedzielski (1999) found that Detroiters were able to comment on Northern Cities vowels, which many participants employed, even though they sometimes struggled to distinguish those vowels from more "standard" Peterson & Barney-like (1952) vowels when asked to identify which ones sounded most like their own. Additionally, Kristiansen (2009) asked respondents from Denmark to name the Danish varieties they liked most, and most named their own local varieties. However, when given a verbal-guise test and presented with other varieties, the "Modern Copenhagen" was preferred. This last study demonstrates the levels of awareness (see Preston 1996; Silverstein 1981) are likely strongly affected by elicitation conditions, and perhaps from a particular sociocultural perspective (i.e., Bucholtz & Hall 2008) demonstrate the dynamic nature of identity construction in various sociolinguistic tasks.

Language Regard: Methods, variation and change (Evans, Benson & Stanford 2018) constitutes a collection of more recent studies on language regard. In it, Preston (2018) and the other authors exemplify the ways that regard can aid understanding the goings-on behind language variation and change. For example, Alfaraz (2018) re-examines Cuban immigrants' perception of pre- and post-revolution-Cuban dialects, with high regard for the former and low regard for the latter, even effecting listeners' low scores for "correctness" assigned to both standard and nonstandard utterances when listeners were told the speakers were residents in Cuba. Bayley et al. (2018) find that older signers of Black American Sign Language, in some cases, were more likely to choose standard forms taught in ASL classes than either younger black signers or white signers of any age; the researchers propose that this could be a result of an association between their own variety with "problems they encountered in inferior schools" during segregation (179).

These two examples (Alfaraz 2018; Bayley et al. 2018), in a way, allude to two sides of language regard that I take to be of critical importance in a queer+ trans folk linguistics: sociocultural ideas and beliefs about people, places, and time can affect related ideas and beliefs about language; conversely, personal experience and positioning of the self with regard to language-related issues can equally affect language production and perception.

Still, little-to-no language regard work has considered the question of sexual orientation or gender identity, nor any work at all considering gender beyond the binary. Moreover, almost no folk linguistic/language regard research has specifically investigated queer populations (with a few exceptions, e.g., Mann 2012, 2016). This work tends to operate on oversimplified views of gender treating demographic labels as static and deterministic and ignoring intersectionality altogether.

Finally, region has clearly been an important social factor in folk linguistic research so far, as have other social variables like class, ethnicity, education, and age. And while some related research has been done in Oklahoma (Bakos 2013), no studies in this region have considered LGBTQ+ populations and their regard for language. Below I outline why this is a particularly useful endeavor for a place like Oklahoma and discuss in more detail the role that language regard studies can play in LGBTQ+ language research.

3 Oklahoma

Linguistic research in Oklahoma has largely been dialectological. Southard's (1993) analysis includes the consideration of the various waves of settlers who took part in the stealing of indigenous peoples' lands, where these settlers came from, and how they differed across ethnic, regional, and class backgrounds. The mix of Midlanders, Southerners, and Midwesterners to Oklahoma contributed to the state's participation in language variation associated with both Southern and Midland/Midwestern speech. For example, lexical items such as *y'all* appear in Oklahoma (Tillery & Bailey 1998). And though the Southern-associated PIN/PEN merger has been widespread as far back as the 1930s (Bailey, Tillery & Wikle 1997; Weirich 2013), so is the Midwestern COT/CAUGHT merger (Bailey, Tillery, Wikle & Sand 1995).

Along with the mixture of linguistic influences, cultural and ideological influences on language also pervade the state. Hall-Lew & Stephens (2012) write about the label "country" and its ties to ideas of rurality in places like the border of Texas and Oklahoma (41). This is consistent with the findings of the Research on Dialects of English in Oklahoma (RODEO 2019-) Project, some of which appear in Bakos (2013); when he asked 100 undergraduate student respondents to describe 'typical Oklahoma', 'country' was the most frequently occurring label, followed by 'friendly', 'cowboy', 'farm(er)', 'redneck', 'hick', 'conservative', 'laid-back', and 'nice'. These labels either index archetypal images (e.g., cowboy) or otherwise index rurality (e.g., farmer) and attitudinal features (e.g., redneck, nice). In other words, the ideas of 'country' and 'rural' appear ubiquitous in folk and sociolinguistic studies of Oklahoma.

The idea that 'typical Oklahoma' is 'rural Oklahoma' is not only evident in undergraduate student responses (Bakos 2013), but is also an understandable notion given the vast areas of rural landscape across the state. There are about 600 cities and towns in Oklahoma; more than 400 of them are populated by 1500 people or less (US 2010 Census).

Of particular relevance here are sociocultural ideas related to LGBTQ+ populations, especially when considering the way that rural/urban and city/country constructs appear in narratives of experience and identity politics (see Weston 1995). Oklahoma has a history of sociopolitical conservativism that is often, at the very least, antagonistic to LGBTQ+ peoples. UCLA's School of Law's William's Institute, a research center studying public policy concerning sexual orientation and gender identity across the US, has published research that found employment discrimination against LGBTQ+ people in Oklahoma (Mallory, Herman & Badgett 2011; Mallory & Sears 2015). More recently, they have released more expansive research that details LGBTQ+ Oklahomans face economic instability, harassment, housing discrimination, and a lack of relatively any legal protections for people discriminated against on the basis of sexual orientation or gender identity (Mallory & Sears 2019). Thus, LGBTQ+ Oklahomans, regardless of their urban or rural upbringings, have significant sociocultural and political hurdles to traverse.

Though virtually no sociolinguistic work on any LGBTQ+ populations has been done in Oklahoma, other historical and sociocultural accounts of some of the LGBTQ+ communities has. Bacchofer (2013) writes that Oklahoma City boasted a growing underground community of gay and bisexual men by the 1960s, but the following decade was riddled with police violence, heavily monitored gay-associated areas of the city, and rough treatment of queer Oklahomans by police forces. This led way to a liberation movement seeking to parallel that of the movements in larger US cities during the 1970s, much of which rallied around the area of Oklahoma City known as the 39th Street District, a cultural center that nearly all gay Oklahomans who participated in the RODEO project frequented and the seat of the drag community which this chapter studies.

3.1 Some findings from gay RODEO respondents

My work with the Research on Dialects of English in Oklahoma Project (RODEO) began in 2014, and when I started fieldwork, I specifically targeted openly gay men from different parts of Oklahoma in hopes of capturing perceptual dialect boundaries from a population yet unstudied in Oklahoma – in fact, unstudied in most perceptual dialectological research. Seeking what these non-linguists thought about "typical Oklahoma" and "gay speech", I included questions that pertained more to social dialect boundaries in addition to those that pertained to region.

Nine respondents are included here; see Table 1 for the respondents and their hometown designations as either rural (R) or urban (U).

These respondents completed the standard RODEO folk-/sociolinguistic interviews (e.g., word list, reading, and interview tasks), focusing on sociolinguistic situations across Oklahoma. A set of supplemental questions was implemented (Table 2 below) to target LGBTQ+ language interests.

Table 1: Gay RODEO respondents with age, hometown, and population.

Respondent	Age	Ethnicity	Hometown	Population
Ernest	25	White	Oklahoma City	*631,346* (U)
Levi	27	White/Indigenous	Tulsa	*403,505* (U)
Darren	24	White/Indigenous	Owasso	*34,542* (U)
Patrick	33	White	Sand Springs	*19,783* (U)
Chance	23	White	Idabel	*7,007* (R)
Marcus	25	White	Marlow	*4,594* (R)
Jim	24	White	Kingston	*1,632* (R)
Pepper	23	Indigenous	Westville	*1,567* (R)
Francis	28	White/Indigenous	Quapaw	*906* (R)

These supplemental questions specifically targeted the folk linguistic insights of "sounding gay," about what that means in Oklahoma in particular, and asked about the compatibility of gay and Oklahoma speech styles. The semi-structured interview design allowed for participants to further elaborate and tell stories about being gay in Oklahoma; all of them did.

Table 2: Supplemental RODEO questions for gay cisgender male respondents.

- Are you able to tell if someone is gay based on how they talk?
- If so, what gives it away?
- Do you think you sound gay?
- How would you describe "sounding gay"?
- Is there a way to sound gay *and* Oklahoman? Are they compatible?
- How do you feel about those ways of talking?

Much of this investigative work centered on comparative models of analysis, looking at the gay respondents and comparing them to the 100+ other RODEO interviews collected. As sociolinguistics and folk linguistics has a history of this sort of thing (i.e., men vs women, Southern vs Northern), this is not unexpected, but it is also not necessarily the best way to understand this data and can be riddled with problematic assumptions. Prior to this work, nobody had thought to ask RODEO participants about their sexuality. To assume that everyone who had been interviewed before was definitively heterosexual (or cisgender for that matter) would be presumptuous at best. Furthermore, to assume that there *would* be differences based on such things could easily push the researcher to "see" differences regardless of the data. Hence, despite this perspective's employment in my earlier work (McCleary 2016), I no longer endorse the comparative model and thus turn to a reanalysis of the regard data as equally influenced by the elicitation conditions and as representations of identity in interaction.

There are still some traditional methods that elicit rather fascinating responses in folk linguistic interviews. One of the most iconic tasks is that borrowed from Preston (1981): the draw-a-map task. This task has been used quite productively at getting broad patterns of language regard that non-linguists' hold toward regional varieties. There were remarkable and important similarities among the maps produced by these non-linguists (see Figures 1–4 below), not least to say that they all display a level – or a particular granularity (Preston 1996) – of detail regarding their awareness of linguistic variation throughout Oklahoma.

One important fact was that certain regions were almost always identified. For example, the southeast corner is always separated, sometimes referred to by its colloquial name "Little Dixie" and sometimes referred to in terms of stereotypical associations with more Southern-sounding speech (e.g., "trashy," "ugly," "uneducated," etc.). In all maps the two biggest cities (Oklahoma City and Tulsa) are marked as separate from the rest of the state. Perhaps most important is the fact that all respondents display awareness of the linguistic diversity throughout the state, though not necessarily when they are asked explicitly to comment on it.

3.2 "Typical" Oklahoma, "sounding gay", and developing queer folk linguistics

These respondents were asked about their descriptions of "typical" Oklahomans, and elsewhere alluded to "typical" or "stereotypical" ideas about Oklahoma throughout their interviews, offering characteristically similar descriptions. This is both a problematic component of the interview framework and an interesting piece to reflect on. The literature above shows a mixture of dialectological influence in Oklahoma. All respondents reflected awareness of this with a great amount of perceptual dialect regions in their map-drawing tasks. Yet, when the interview question prompted them to think about "typical" Oklahoma, the abstraction of common features/stereotypes to address a (mostly fictional) homogenous "typical Oklahoma" speech is quite fascinating.

Queer+ Trans folk linguistics —— 147

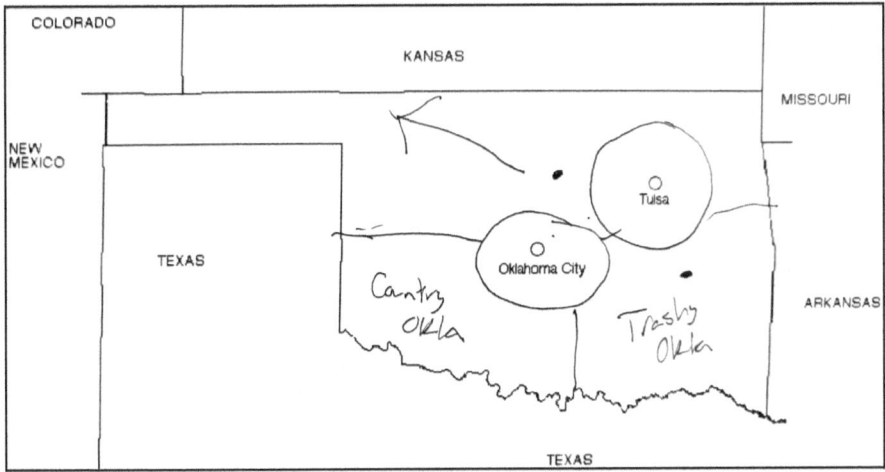

Figure 1: RODEO hand-drawn maps from two Oklahoman respondents from urban hometowns. Darren, 24.

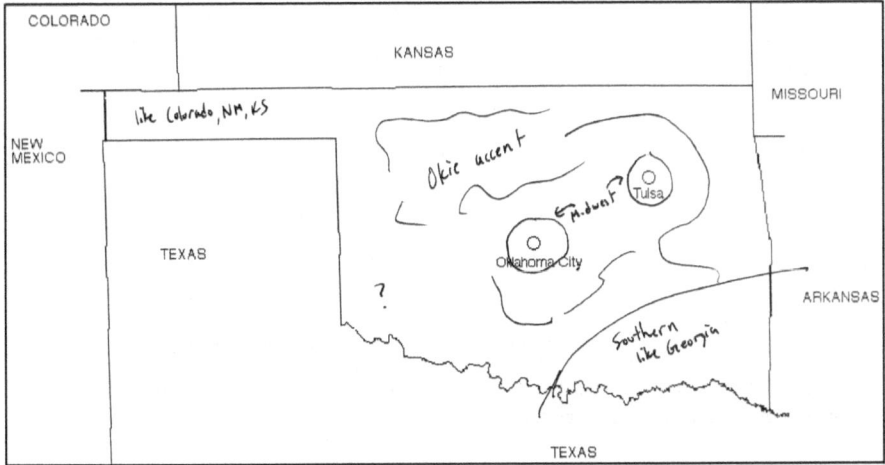

Figure 1a: RODEO hand-drawn maps from two Oklahoman respondents from urban hometowns. Patrick, 33.

Excerpt 1. *Pepper on gendered expectations in Oklahoma*
1 I think um just because like I said it always goes back to my small town
2 experiences but um I would say that women tend to not have as much of the
3 stereotypical Oklahoma [speech] but there's such like this pressure on Oklahoma men to
4 just be like country and strong and so they kinda tend to fall more into the stereotypes

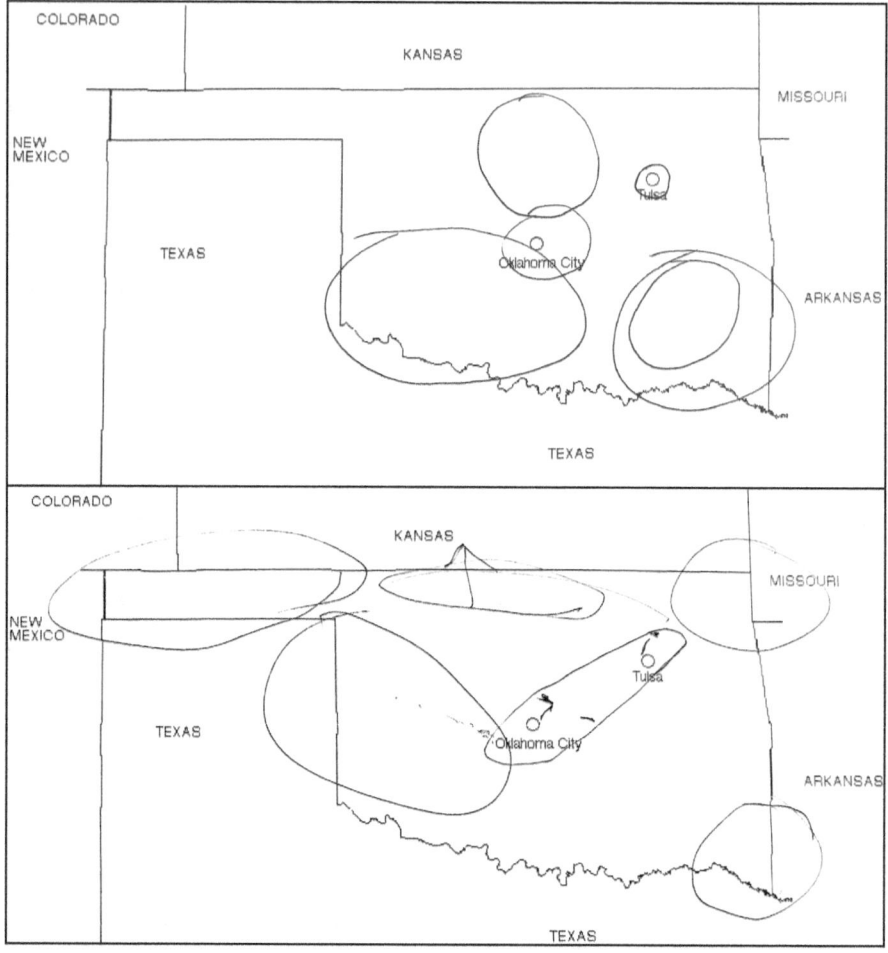

Figure 2: RODEO hand-drawn maps from two Oklahoman respondents from rural hometowns. Marcus, 24 (above) and Francis, 28 (below).

Pepper easily connects his response and his opinion to his "small town" experience. The awareness of stereotypes in discussing Oklahoma language variation (and ideology) is prominent among responses. When asked whether they thought they talked like other Oklahomans, a pattern emerged which distinguished most rural respondents from most urban respondents (see Table 3).

No urban respondents claimed to talk like other Oklahomans, save one who said he only talks like other people from his city (Tulsa) and made efforts to distinguish that from anywhere else in the state. All but one rural respondent claimed

Table 3: Speakers' responses to whether or not they think they talk like other Oklahomans, and if they think that they "sound gay", organized by rural/urban hometown.

	Respondent	Oklahoman?	Gay?
Urban	Ernest	No	Yes
	Levi	No (Tulsans)	Not really
	Darren	No	No
	Patrick	Not Anymore	Not Anymore
Rural	Chance	Yes	Yes
	Marcus	Probably	Yes
	Jim	Yes	No
	Pepper	No	Yes
	Francis	Yes	Yes

that they speak like most other Oklahomans, and that one outlier linked his not *being* like anyone from Oklahoma to be a cause of that – an understandable sentiment for someone who had been harassed for being/sounding/looking "too gay" in his small hometown.

The results of the question "do you sound gay?" produced similar results: all but one urban speaker said "no" and all but one rural speaker said "yes". Intuition might have encouraged the expectation that urban respondents would embrace gay identity (and speech) to further distance themselves from stereotypical (and rural) Oklahoma. This is not the case. Just as the inexistence of a homogenous "Oklahoma dialect" didn't stop respondents from talking about "typical Oklahoma", when asked to describe gay speech, there was an overwhelming similarity here: everyone said "feminine," "effeminate," or "flamboyant". Of course, there's no such thing as a unified, singular "gay style," but because the question frames the information in such a way, respondent accommodation to the interview setting allowed them to make the same move towards abstraction, drawing on common associations for "gay speech," even if they couldn't name any features which made gay speech feminine.

This re-analysis of the patterns found in the data suggest an interpretation that is more complicated than what at first seems to be urban-distancing and rural-aligning with gay and Oklahoma speech styles. Rural speakers aren't just different because they are from small towns. Most of them discuss having left hometowns to escape discrimination, only to find themselves being made fun of for *sounding country* in the cities they moved to. They appear to be both more aware of linguistic variation and more sensitive to the issue (and consequences) of labelling people.

Urban speakers are still aware of the social consequences for sounding/being "too gay" (as one respondent put it). In this sense, urban speakers appear to distance themselves from both rural and gay styles as a preemptive measure to avoid negative socio-cultural reactions for being gay in Oklahoma, and for being Oklahoman elsewhere. Rural speakers problematize the categories without necessarily rejecting them for themselves.

This more nuanced understanding – which came from a more sensitive approach to the discourse in the interviews – prompted another look at some of the stories and experiences shared by the urban speakers. Ultimately, 3 of the 4 urban speakers mention conscious style shifting as a deterrent from being outed – being "too gay" in an unsafe space. They each claim not to sound gay when asked directly, and yet they describe conscious practices to make them sound "less gay".

Thus, urban and rural speakers might not be as different as they first appear. Perhaps in some of these elicitation conditions, urban speakers were thinking about the abstracted stereotypical ideas related to the styles, and perhaps repercussions for using those styles too openly led them to answer the way that they did. Yet, they seem to consciously employ styles which at least *vary* in their indexing of gay identity (categories). In this light, the situation is much more complicated, but the biggest difference between the two groups appears to be in the (in)directness of the responses in relation to the problems, labelling, and consequences of being gay in Oklahoma.

Sociocultural, queer linguistic frameworks are necessary for the kind of sensitivity and respect that ought to be given this regard discourse – particularly for a population which cannot be understood without an intersectional approach to identity in discourse. Once that is built into this analysis, it becomes clear that different questions, tasks, and contexts can motivate speakers to think or process information in particular ways. For example, the map-drawing task seems to encourage more detailed granularity of dialectal variation throughout Oklahoma, but the questions about "typical" style encourage abstraction and more wide-ranging stereotypical ideas of the state.

This latter approach allows for the rural/urban divide to provide a clearer look at the most common patterns of distinctiveness. The stories told, the experiences shared, and at identity-in-interaction, show that most rural respondents have the *experiential factor(s)* of victimization by being made fun of for being gay in their hometowns and then again for being "country" when they left. Additionally, while urban respondents tended to answer in line with what they probably thought the question wanted of them, rural respondents – most of whom having already experience discrimination in their hometown then again in an urban area for being *country* – directly problematized this. That is, the *perceived acceptability* of the questions, or of their sociolinguistic premises, appears to be different for rural and urban speakers.

Thus, I realized that at least a few main theory-methodology components are needed within a new, queer+ trans folk linguistics – namely, a connection between regard data and identity, and the inclusion of *experiential factors* and *perceived acceptability* to the factors that can contribute to folk linguistic awareness (see Preston 1996). This revisiting of the data and the reformulation of a queer folk linguistics helped shape a new project investigating language, performance, and identity among a community of drag performers in Oklahoma City (OKC).

4 Drag in Oklahoma

Nearly all observations and recorded sessions for the data in this section occurred in an area with a rich history and a meaningful presence as a protected space for queer Oklahomans. The 39th St. District, what so many performers call the "Gayborhood" or "the strip", has remained a safe space. Even for younger queer Oklahomans who are not aware of its histories, it serves as a protected place away from the rest of the city/state.

The following data comes from a 4-year long ethnographic study in the 39th St. District, interviewing over two dozen performers, aspiring performers, and workers in the drag entertainment industry in Oklahoma City. It began with ethnographic observation, unrecorded interviews, and later recorded interviews and group discussion questions. Table 4 offers a look at some of the recorded participants whose responses will be covered here; note that their descriptions of their ethno-racial identities and gender identities are conveyed in the same language written by respondents, as are years of experience, age, and drag styles.

Table 4: Selected participants of drag language and culture study.

Performer	Experience (years)	Age (years)	Ethno-racial Identity	Gender Identity (performer)	Drag in a few words
Kelly	19	41	Caucasian	Male	"Glamour for the masses"
Foxxi	10	31	African American	female	"Booty"; "drag is my outlet"
Gizele	9	30	Black	Cis-Male	"Give zero fucks"
Rae	2	30	Black/ AA	Transgender	"Ravishing"
Guin	< 1	25	Caucasian	Transgender Woman	N/A
Alexander	> 1	22	White	Male	"Emo pretty boy"
Celeste	< 1	49	white	Male	"Rocker Chick"

The following section briefly addresses the language used to describe the scene, the industry, and the experiences of these drag performers. While this is not explicitly language regard data, lessons learned in the mal-interpreted results of other LGBTQ+ language regard studies require that we situate the speakers, their language regard, and their identities/experiences within this community before attempting to make sense of how speakers talk about language.

4.1 Oklahoma drag: *Old school* and *cut-throat*

The increasing global popularization of drag performance today cannot be understated, especially given its potential to affect local drag scenes in places like Oklahoma. Everyone I spoke to for this project remarked on the widespread fandom of shows like *RuPaul's Drag Race* and social media-based entertainment offered by famous drag performers. While this is sometimes celebrated, local performers exhibit a complicated relationship with the spread of drag culture.

Two emerging patterns in respondents' descriptions of the scene shed some insight here. There is a lingering presence of "old school" drag – a style which is connected both to drag performance prior to the vast spread vis-à-vis pop-culture and to styles which are perhaps especially associated with white performers. And secondly, that the industry is "cut-throat" and thus very difficult for new talent to find regular jobs. A tension among old and new, establish and up-and-coming, and even racialized treatments of certain styles of drag are very real and critically at work in the language regard data.

Wider exposure to drag adds to the pop-cultural relevance and, perhaps as a result, the value of drag endeavors. In other ways, it pits them against big-budgets, Hollywood, and digital venues that can take away from the regionality of drag entertainment. Performers in Oklahoma very frequently express a willingness to discuss the spread of drag culture, and they are all willing to express their characterization of Oklahoma drag specifically as it is differentiated from an otherwise "mainstream" drag scene. In the excerpt below, Foxxi, a performer with over a decade of experience in the OKC drag circuit, references some of the defining characteristics of this scene.

Excerpt 2. *Foxxi describing drag in Oklahoma*
1 Interviewer: so, how would you describe drag, in Oklahoma
2 Foxxi: ooh [u:w], honey that's a long conversation too, I mean Oklahoma drag has
3 changed, ever since, like I first saw drag, I felt like it was more, of the upscale
4 which is you know you wanna be pretty, and polished, which you should always
5 wanna be, but it was more, it was like, old school drag, you know

Foxxi's very first response ("a long conversation") alludes to the complex place Oklahoma drag finds itself today. She recalls the OKC drag scene back then as "upscale" and "pretty and polished". These two concepts, i.e., class and beauty, both concern appearance and performance, but they are not the primary concerns of all performers in today's drag scene, something Foxxi only implies here with her label "old school drag" but on which she elaborates in excerpt 3 below. She characterizes Oklahoma drag today as still having some "old school" aesthetics, calling attention to "costumes", "big hair", and "stone", which correspond to tailored outfits, higher-quality wigs, and lots of jewels, respectively.

Excerpt 3. *Foxxi unpacking old school drag*
1   Foxxi: Oklahoma is very old school, they want jewels, they want costumes, they want big
2   hair, they want stone, and that's fine, but every person don't wanna do that, some
3   people wanna come out, in a, trash bag or, or something different that's not glam,
4   and that's fine, cause I don't do that all the time bitch I do ratchet hood, sultry sexy
5   or, my creativity is, either doin some Nicki Minaj or some Cardi B, you know with
6   some colored hair, colored outfit, you know something crazy

Foxxi distinguishes "old school" Oklahoma drag from her own approach by using terms like "ratchet" and "hood" descriptors which index associations with African American culture and identity but which also have class-based associations. *Ratchet* has been described as a word which indicates behavior deemed inappropriate in public (Weinraub 2015). Both *ratchet* and *hood* are associated with the language of hip-hop music and culture (Alim 2004, 2009; Jones 2015; Pichler & Williams 2016).

Foxxi's comparisons of "old school" aesthetics and the styles she additionally enjoys performing lend some insight into the privilege granted to the styles of white drag performers (i.e., traditionally country and Broadway/showgirl numbers) over music and performances that are indexical or celebratory of non-white music and culture.

Foxxi, an African American performer who identifies openly as a woman – she talks in interviews about how drag led her to her coming out as trans – and who performs female-presenting drag, also mentions "doin some Nicki Minaj or some Cardi B.", referencing that she lip-syncs to the music of two well-known female rappers of color. As the comparisons of "old school drag" and newer drag rely on more personal experience and explanation from Foxxi, she demonstrates how intricately woven are her ideas about class, identity, race, and artistic ambition. These ideas are integral to understanding the cultures and ways of speaking in the Gayborhood, both for Foxxi individually and for the community.

Foxxi's unpacking of the "old school" label is informative and complex – she is hardly the only performer to use these words to characterize the scene – but one subtlety in her initial response is that Oklahoma drag *has changed*. "Old school" describes a drag performance aesthetic that was pervasive in much of the history of drag in the Gayborhood, and which can still be seen in some parts of the community today. The change, then, stems from younger performers who in the last decade or two have begun to break away from the more traditional styles of performance, partially a result of pop culture's influence.

Kelly, a Caucasian, cisgender male performer of female-presenting drag with nearly two decades of experience, also characterizes parts of the scene as *old school*. She[2] remarks that 39th St. and the venues there have become somewhat predictable, at least in terms of the performers who are regularly booked. She alludes to the fact that drag shows in OKC were scarcer in the past and that, because of their more infrequent occurrences that they felt more special ("kind of an amazing thing"). On the one hand, you would expect the rising frequency of drag shows to be something to be celebrated for a performer – or even for an advocate of queer representation and culture. On the other hand, while the number of shows has grown in the scene, Kelly suggests that this does not necessarily mean that the number of entertainers performing is so much greater.

Excerpt 4. *Kelly on some changes in the gayborhood*
1　Kelly:　used to, if you got to see a drag show it was, uh, kind of an amazing thing, it was
2　　　　　cool, you know there were just a few a week, now there's a show at every bar
3　　　　　every night, um, I don't work a whole lot of Oklahoma City anymore, just because
4　　　　　of that fact, I know if I want to see a certain drag queen I can go to a certain bar
5　　　　　every night, it's always the same queens

Considering Kelly's position as another performer, however, highlights another important component of this scene. Her attention to the increase of popularity, frequency, and regularity of drag shows remind us that to be a headliner,[3] and particularly one who is employed,[4] is to have one of the most prestigious positions within this community. And to be employed at such a venue is to perform there regularly. Not everyone in these positions is equally praised or admired by the rest of the community, but these regularly employed performers often carry some clout in the decisions made about who gets booked at various amateur gigs and shows in their employer's venue.

It's probably not too difficult to imagine how this system can lead to problems in diversification of performances, particularly considering relationships among

---

2 The tradition of referencing performers pronominally defaults to the gender they present in drag, despite gender identity outside of drag performance; most performers still use these pronouns outside of drag as well.
3 i.e., a host or someone who's name is published in large text on a show's advertisement.
4 i.e., not contracted on an event-to-evet basis.

performers. Foxxi mentioned in one conversation, for example, that "every club has their token black girl."

Alexander, a drag king[5] with less than a year of experience performing in the Gayborhoods, also noted the problem of diversification. At the time of Alexander's recording session, many younger performers and queer people were open about the problem of diversity in performers and performance styles within the scene, and in ways that caused tensions within the drag community.

> Excerpt 5. *Alexander on lack of diversity in OKC drag*
> 1 Alexander: oh god yeah, here lately, some clubs have been called out for some stuff, now
> 2 I'm not, gonna get too deep into that because, I'm not about, the drama or
> 3 anything but . . . I'm constantly scrolling through Facebook looking you know,
> 4 <Q who's getting booked, who do I wanna go see tonight, oh it's the same
> 5 people, every night Q>

Alexander's sensitivity to the rising tension on the issue of diversification is revealed in his otherwise ambiguous reference to "some stuff" for which "some clubs" have been "called out". His decision not to offer more details or opinions on the matter speak to the gravity of community-straining tensions within this little queer bubble of OKC.

Gizele, a performer who has nearly a decade of experience doing female presenting drag in the scene, hints at similar perceptions in citing that OKC drag used to be even less diverse than it is today, what she calls "very cookie cutter" drag. She acknowledges that the few changes in casts have been good, and Foxxi claims that "if you do your research" you might see some diversity in terms of race and background compared to previous eras of the OKC drag scene. But both comment that there is clearly room for more progress.

Both Alexander and Rae in a group discussion referred to the scene as "cut-throat"; this was not an uncommon response to the question of how one would characterize the scene. New performers often have such a difficult experience finding shows that their characterizations of the entire industry reflect that. And while the newer performers appear to demonstrate a more direct characterization of Oklahoma City's drag community as cut-throat, they are not alone. Below in excerpt 6, Kelly describes some of the experience she has had as a long-time performer in the scene; that same excerpt offers (below Kelly; separate interviews) Foxxi's comments on competition in the scene.

---

5 i.e., male-presentation of drag; Alexander openly identifies as a While Male and also talks of his being assigned female at birth and how drag led to his realization that he is a trans man.

Kelly's use of the term "cut-throat" is first used as a reason for needing "thick skin" in this community, something she mentions elsewhere that this relates to *throwing shade* – ritual insults that tend to focus on drag appearance and performance. *Throwing shade* has its roots in African American Language and culture as well, looking much like *the dozens*, which Smitherman (1994) characterizes as being used "to test not only [players'] verbal skills but also their capacity to maintain their *cool*" (100). Kelly references competition with other queens, offering personal experience of her own that, presumably, demonstrates the types of cut-throat or competitive behaviors in the community. This competitive coloring of the community is consistent across every participant in this study, though not all talk about it in the same contexts.

Excerpt 6. *Kelly on her experience; Foxxi on competition; "cut-throat"*
1   Kelly: you have to have thick skin, cause it is cut-throat . . . competition with, more
2   established queens, they can be really cut-throat . . . it's really hard to get into the
3   shows . . . my first, 13 years of drag, I was in any show that I wanted to be in
4   Oklahoma City, then I quit drag for two years . . . when I came back, the entire scene
5   had changed, and people who were my friends, that I worked with all the time, had
6   moved on to other bars or had finally gotten their own shows, and would not book me
7   Foxxi: it's so cut throat cause it like either they feel competition, so they wanna like
8   either try to bring you down, break you down to make you feel inferior or,
9   unconfident but that, they doin that because they know that you're competition

Foxxi, for example, uses the term "cut-throat" to refer to the competitive nature of critique, shade, and the arguments various performers get into. She describes the surface motivation for such criticisms as seeking to make someone feel "unconfident" or to "break [them] down", but offers a nuanced understanding of them as well. For both Kelly and Foxxi, the cut-throat nature of the scene is tied to the competitive situation that almost all performers find themselves in. It is at least implied that Kelly lost friends over this sort of phenomenon, while Foxxi explains and certainly contextualizes the types of language-related "cut-throat" behavior that occurs.

These insights help offer a better understanding of the overall characterization of Oklahoma City drag, particularly as it pertains to the work it takes to be successful (or to get noticed and hopefully be able to make money) in the scene. This becomes important in the overview of two critical types of data surveyed below: Explicit regard (metalanguage) and implicata (especially socio-cultural relevance of language).

4.2 Explicit regard: "Drag slang"

Of the questions asked in interviews with drag performers, one of the earlier ones was "Is there such a thing as a *drag style* of speech?" The purpose of this question was two-fold: On the one hand, it offers one way of asking about the speech of drag performers in this community; more importantly, however, there are possible implications for a drag-language connection as well as an implicit bias resulting from the yes/no question.

Compared to some other questions (e.g., "What does it mean to talk like a drag queen?"), this question also tended to focus respondents' answers around explicit metalanguage. For example, most respondents immediately either asked clarifying questions or gave clarifying responses such as the following.

Excerpt 7. *Selected responses to "Is there such a thing as a drag style of speech?"* (**emphasis**)
1 Guin: do you mean **slang**?
2 Alexander   drag style of speech, we have like our own little **slang**
3 Kelly   I mean there's, so many terminologies- yes, it's – there's **drag slang** of course
4 Gizelle   I'd definitely say there is, um, there's a um, I feel like that we have a **code**, and a lot
5   of people wouldn't understand it sometimes

The responses were likely influenced by the packaging of the question, namely the yes/no format and the implication that there might be a language-connection with drag performance. Having said that, it also seems to be the case that there is a popular cultural awareness of language related to drag–perhaps especially for in-group members of a local drag community.

In addition to thinking about "drag slang" in responding to this question, respondents also had a very easy time offering examples of the types of lexical items potentially categorized as slang. Among them, the most commonly mentioned were: *jush*,[6] *throwing shade, sickening*,[7] *fierce*,[8] *boots*,[9] "getting/giving (me) *life*",[10]

---

[6] [ʒʌʃ]; a word which at least appears to be potentially related the word zhoozh, which some credit to the gay British dialect Polari (see Baker 2002; Lucas 1997), suspected to be borrowed from Romani.
[7] i.e., "incredible", what Calder (2017) calls "a positive evaluation of drag".
[8] See note 14.
[9] A modifier or intensifier that can mean "to an excessive degree" or "to an impressive degree"; common collocations occur in phrases like *"read* you *boots"*, meaning someone *read* or critiqued you harshly or possibly intimately.
[10] i.e., to be entertained or excited by something, typically of performance or appearance. Can also be expressed as *"living* (for NP)".

werk,[11] *yas/yaass*,[12] *read(ing)*.[13] See Table 5 for a frequency count within the transcribed sections of the interviews.

Table 5: Popular "slang" items by frequency.

Slang	frequency
bitch	152
tea	30
shade	27
tongue pop	21
live/living	15
jush	14
wig	11
read	10
boots	10
glitz/glam	9
werk	7
ya:s	6
beat	6
snatch	5

Additionally, the word *bitch* was mentioned by almost all of the respondents, somewhat surprising given that this is not a word typically thought of as slang. Using the regard data from this particular question, a simple frequency count was calculated in a transcript of a little over 25 thousand words covering most of the interviews and discussions before and after these two questions (i.e., "drag style of speech" and "talk like a drag queen"). The results are somewhat surprising but also help to explain some of the more surprising findings. Most notably, *bitch* occurs far more than any other word in this transcript.

This sort of methodology allows for interesting work with metalanguage, which can then be checked against language use in certain data, but the most interesting piece of the "slang" component to this data comes when comparing it to the more implicit responses. More specifically, it's certainly the case that *bitch* is used extensively in this community – very rarely as a pejorative (e.g., "you're a bitch") and most often as an in-group label for another ("this *bitch* is fierce!") or for the self ("a *bitch* [I] don't know no country by heart"), and sometimes as an enthusiastic or responsive interjective ("*bi:tch* what did she say?"). However, there appears to be a new usage of

---

11 A celebratory exclamation, typically used as a cheer or message of encouragement. Its popularity is often attributed to RuPaul's 1993 song "Supermodel (You Better Work)".
12 Similar to *werk*; a variation on the word "yes".
13 Ritual insult and/or critique. Similar to *throwing shade*.

this word. While time and space don't permit more discussion here, there is reason to suspect that *bitch* might function for some speakers as a discourse marker.

4.3 Implicit regard: "Talking like a drag queen"

Unlike the responses in the previous section, many of the performers in this section differ in the ways that they discuss what it might mean to "talk like a drag queen". The second question (Q2) reviewed in this chapter elicited discourse which primarily relied on presupposition and implicature. That is, this question encouraged thought and reflection on more archetypal, or perhaps stereotypical, if not ideological levels (see Table 6). Part of this is intentional, knowing that the wording and the premise of Q2 implies or presupposes a way of talking associated with drag queens,[14] a phenomenon of association that I believe to be already well in place, at least in this community. Still, Q2 also encourages generalization in presuming that one is able to "talk like" any category. The results from this, across all speakers, are therefore not considered to be the most detailed and accurate depictions of the scene. Rather, they can reveal well-established ideologies and beliefs about being queer (and performing drag) and the relationship that has to language.

Table 6: Questions 1 and 2 with examples of implicata/presupposition in the question.

Order	Question	Implicational/Presuppositional Detail
1	Is there such a thing as a drag style of speech?	*Drag-style of speech; drag-language connection*
2	What does it mean to talk like a drag queen?	*Drag queen language; you can "talk like" a category*

Foxxi's response to Q2 is equally as complex and nuanced as the responses covered in the previous section, but here, she offers popular characterizations of the ways drag performers perform, entertain, and behave. She delivers a quotative-performative example here with a *tongue pop*,[15] a very marked and well-known feature of queer speech styles associated with drag speech. Foxxi continues this

---

[14] Because of the attention given to female-presenting drag artists, this question intended to rely on the heavy exposure to such drag and on the already existing ideas about drag queens and language.
[15] This is the community term for this sound. It is a lingual ingressive, typically a palatal click [ǂ].

performance with a phrase "okay how you durn", a pronunciation of "doing" probably associated with certain African American Language varieties (e.g., often performed by Tyler Perry's Madea character). It's worth noting that, because of the popularization of African American Language and culture within this community, this example that Foxxi is offering is interesting in that white queens very often employ highly caricatured versions of AAL varieties.

Excerpt 8. *Foxxi on talking like a drag queen*
```
1  Foxxi:  talking like a drag queen is all that you know, <Q ((TONGUE POP)), okay how you durn Q>
2          you know like just extra . . . everybody have they own flavor you know they own, their own
3          interpretation of drag, so you have that, for instance pageant queen, don't really say too
4          much but gives little snick comments or little side eyes or little glances, and then you have
5          that one queen that's loud and speaks her mind and, says everything in the gay dictionary in
6          about five seconds . . . I wouldn't say you're required to be funny, but you have to have a sense
7          of humor . . . if you, never hung out with a gay person or hung out with a drag queen you gone
8          take it, predominantly half the time offensive cause you don't know what the hell she sayin,
9          so, if you don't know the scene and you step out there you gone be culture-shocked as hell
```

The opening of this response is the closest we get to explicit regard in this particular response; the rest of the discourse addresses more directly the *ideas* behind language use and communication. For example, she goes on to say that this speech (or perhaps the speakers) are *extra*,[16] a notion that fits with the idea that drag queens are somehow *more* queer than their non-entertainer community peers. Despite the encouragement to generalize, though, Foxxi does note that everyone has their own *flavor*, their own "interpretation of drag". In a way, it takes back some of the generalizable discourse she initially offers in her response, another potential indication of her nuanced understanding of this community and its patterns of language use.

Foxxi's offering of different types of drag performers further characterizes the "club queen" (juxtaposed with the image of "pageant queen" who largely participates in drag beauty/talent pageants instead of working in night clubs) includes an even more interesting characterization: someone who "says everything in the *gay dictionary* in about five seconds". This "club queen" character is someone who is embracing queer culture and performing it *in excess* (or perhaps in a way that is *extra*), and in ways that parallel the seemingly ubiquitous perception of drag performers (of this type) as excessively queer.[17]

---

16 i.e., "dramatic", "excessive", or even "inappropriately expressive".
17 It's also worth noting that Foxxi's prepositional modifier "in about five seconds" seems to be commenting on rate of speech, and talking fast specifically. This is an interesting comment in a place like Oklahoma where, like many areas of the US South, speakers are told they speak slow.

In the course of this response, Foxxi mentioned that some specific performers do this (i.e., talk like "that one queen") in order to be funny. I still find her elaboration on this pensive and intriguing: "I wouldn't say you're *required* to be funny, but you have to have a *sense of humor*". This line is poignant for a couple reasons: it alludes to something Kelly mentions about needing to have "thick skin" because of the ritualistic *shade* throwing and *reading* practices. More specifically, Foxxi explains that a drag performer doesn't have to be a comedian to be successful. One can get along without telling jokes. The implication here is that one cannot be successful, or survive as an artist, in this community without a *sense of humor*. Performers need to be able to take a joke, perhaps especially about themselves, in order to make it in this community. It's worth noting that Foxxi's standing in the community, her experience as an African American performer in a place like Oklahoma City, and her success in the scene renders her responses extensions of such experience – and of her identity.

Excerpt 9. *Guin on talking like a drag*
1 Guin: talk like a drag queen, I mean I don't know I've always been gay as hell, so, I've always,
2   I guess kinda talked like that, but I guess just like use terminology and know what it
3   means where it comes from . . . like whether it's a straight friend who has never been out
4   before or like, someone who's like new to coming out, or anything like that like to hear
5   them say stuff, you're just kinda like <Q ope Q>, @@@, <Q no that's like that, that's
6   not how you use that girl like that's not right like hang on just second Q>, but, so to like
7   know and have that meaning and like . . . any kind of gay way like that

Guin reflects on her long-held queer identity and links talking-like-a-drag-queen to "always" having been "gay as hell", then uses the conjunction *so* (in its own intonation unit). This *so* looks like the conjunction that implies consequence, an interpretation supported by the follow-up line "any kind of gay way [of talking] like that". She emphasizes this with the additional prescriptive requirement that you have to know the meaning of your slang (a statement almost all newer performers reported). She gives a quotative performance of someone getting in-group language wrong and offers an example of how she might correct them.

This is exact sentiment is expressed in a group discussion that occurred with drag king Alexander and his drag sister, Rae. In their discussion, a blending of the "drag slang" and "talking like a drag queen" topics emerged when the subject of the popularity of drag culture came up.

Excerpt 10. *Drag siblings Alexander and Rae on prescriptive usage of "drag* slang"
1 Alexander: a lot of these are coming out into, normal speech, for, most of, most everyone
2 Rae: [yeah]
3 Alexander: [because] of RuPaul's, um, but I'm tired of people comparing, drag, close to
4   them, to RuPaul's, so like they'll come up they'll see one of us in drag and be

5		like, <Q werk Q>, and it's like <Q you don't even know what that means, fuck
6		off, thank you, bye: Q>
7	Rae:	if you don't know the slur, don't say it, okay, just
8		rewind that again, <Q if you don't know the slur, do not say it Q>
9		<Q say it again for the people in the back Q>
10		<Q if ya don't know the slur, do not say it Q>

Alexander's portrayal of the situation paints pop-cultural influences like *RuPaul's Drag Race* as an instigator in the spread of drag language (and presumably drag overall), something he takes up issue with because of the misuse of such language. Rae joins in with Alexander, which results in their playful banter back and forth (in a linguistic performance reminiscent of call-and-response; see Smitherman 1996) emphasizing that people who "don't know the slur [/slang]" should not be using the language at all.

With this, we now see how newer performers express interest in correcting and policing language far more than the seasoned performers. In fact, this sort of attention to language use is not given much attention at all by them. Gizele's description of talking-like-a-drag queen revolves around "tone", a folk linguistic term that appears to correspond with pitch (contours), amplitude, and/or voice quality (again echoing of the folk vocabulary). However, much like Alexander and Rae made a connection between in-group "slang" and how to use it, Gizele offers another piece of insight that connect "slang" and *where it comes from*.

Excerpt 11. *Gizele on the origins of drag* slang

1	Gizele:	a lot of- I think a lot of it, actually comes, more from *Paris Is Burning*, and, then it's
2		spreading out into mainstream, and *RuPaul's Drag Race* when you see it, now that it's on,
3		in on the screens people are, seeing those words, and now they're rolling out into other,
4		communities now, and a lot of, our slang and stuff, I think a lot of it comes from the
5		South, cause I was watchin, when I was watchin the Housewives of Atlanta, they say a
6		lot of stuff and I'm thinkin like, they got this from the gay community, I was like you
7		know what's funny, I think the gay community got this from the South I think, like "what's
8		the tea" and all that stuff, that's these, Georgia Peaches used to sit down and drink tea, so
9		I think we get that a lot from, Black women

Her attention to the origin of this language, specifically mentioning the African American sociocultural and linguistic roots of this language, is indicative of a different way of thinking about drag-related language from the newer performers. However, Gizele's experience as a performer of color likely plays a role in this. Foxxi, for example, offered an anecdote in which patrons of the clubs will make comments about how funny or cool the slang they hear on "the drag show" (presumable *Drag Race*); her response was that this was language she and her friends use everyday, in the club and in regular life.

That is, language in this communitys – language very frequently appropriated from speakers of AAL varieties – gets spread and appropriated *en masse*. Consider that Kelly Powers, another seasoned queen but one who is white, mentions that the particular things she says in drag would be inappropriate out of drag, or otherwise that she wouldn't feel comfortable with that way of speaking outside of the context of a drag event. After that, however, she claims drag slang is just the same as what the broader "gay community" uses, just more intensified (similar to Guin). Kelly is alluding to the fact that many drag performers' usage of in-group language is both appeasing their audiences and establishing community language norms. But for performers of color like Foxxi and Gizele, the interests and concerns for language use are less about policing, or about meeting the audience needs, or about delineating types of language use on stage vs off stage. For them, the concern is far more about recognition of the origin of the language, of the work they've put in to make it to their levels of success, and to call out the appropriation as they see it.

All of these take-aways from the language regard, it should be noted, would be impossible without ethnographic work in the community and working with respondents to understand their experiences, identity(ies), and goals in their drag- and linguistic endeavors.

5 Conclusions

This chapter reiterates some of the lessons learned in work with language regard amongst LGBTQ+ populations in Oklahoma. It reflects on the ideas that influenced its design, on the data that were collected, and even more on what the process and results mean for future studies. The key ideas covered here are twofold: First is the importance of studying language regard in conjunction with studies of language in general, perhaps especially for sociolinguistic and linguistic ethnographic endeavors, but beyond those concerns, even into theoretical and cognitive directions. People's ideas about language, their ways of organizing their thoughts on it, and the way they deliver those often strongly-held beliefs can inform us not only of the nature of attitudes and beliefs about language but also of facts about sociolinguistic and socio-cultural realities for speakers.

The second point is that, the ability to carry out research on language regard, there must be an understanding of identity and, as shown in this chapter, the ways identity is tied to community and relational roles. People are almost always performing, in one way or another, and performance is dictated more by the complex roles people perform than by any single demographic factor typically relied on to predict variable choices in sociolinguistics. These stand out as two of the most significant lessons learned in this Queer+ Trans Folk Linguistic approach.

To some extent the two points made here are unoriginal, particularly in that they focus on interests either long-held or otherwise recently given attention. The subtle differences, however, lie in their overlap in the study of peoples' (linguists and non-linguists alike) regard for language and in the study of language variation and change. With more attention shifting to marginalized voices, however, methodological and theoretical questions arise, suggesting that many of the basic assumptions made in more traditional socio-/folk linguistic research are influenced by privileged and limited perspectives on the collection of data and the people that data come from. This point attempts to highlight where this study has attempted to be more aware of those privileges – though it will inevitably fall short in some ways – and how that has led to methodological and interpretive insights for the study of language in identity.

This chapter is intended to function as a starting point for the theorization and formulation of a Queer+ Trans Folk Linguistics. It is my hope that this will be the beginning of important ways of thinking about language regard data, identity, and their potential to shed insight on local and broader ideological realities for queer and trans people, and particularly in ways that are sensitive to the complexity of gender, race, roles, and intersectional approaches to identity. I also hope that this chapter has conveyed two final takeaways related to the introduction of this chapter: 1) that LGBTQ+ peoples do often have difficult terrain to navigate in their social worlds, navigation both dependent on and reflected in language; and 2) that LGBTQ+ people's awareness/regard for language is often strikingly detailed and poignant, and that it often reflects complicated and complex socio-cultural realties in LGBTQ+ communities and in the broader world.

References

Alim, H. Samy. 2004. Hip Hop Nation Language. In Edward Finegan & John R. Rickford (eds.), *Language in the USA*, 387–409. Cambridge: Cambridge UP.

Alim, H. Samy. 2009. Translocal style communities: Hip Hop youth as cultural theorists of style, language, and globalization. *Pragmatics* 19(1). 103–27.

Bachhofer, Aaron Lee. 2006. The emergence and evolution of the gay and bisexual male subculture in Oklahoma City, Oklahoma, 1889–2005. Stillwater: Oklahoma State University dissertation.

Bailey, Guy, Jan Tillery & Tom Wikle. 1997. Methodology of a survey of Oklahoma dialects. *SECOL Review* 2(1). 1–30.

Bailey, Guy, Tom Wikle, Jan Tillery & Lori Sand. 1993. Some patterns of linguistic diffusion. *Language Variation and Change* 5(3). 359–390.

Baker, Paul. 2002. *Polari– the lost language of gay men*. London; New York: Routledge.

Bakos, Jon. 2013. A comparison of the speech patterns and dialect attitudes of Oklahoma. Stillwater: Oklahoma State University dissertation.
Bloomfield, Leonard. 1944. Secondary and tertiary responses to language. *Language* 20. 45–55.
Bucholtz, Mary & Kira Hall. 2008. All of the above: New coalitions in sociocultural linguistics. *Journal of Sociolinguistics* 12(4). 401–431.
Calder, Jeremy. 2017. Handsome women: A semiotics of non-normative gender in SoMa, San Francisco. Stanford: Stanford University dissertation.
Crenshaw, Kimberlé. 1989. Demarginalizing the intersection of race and sex: A black feminist critique of antidiscrimination doctrine, feminist theory, and antiracist politics. *University of Chicago Legal Forum* (8). 538–54.
Crenshaw, Kimberlé. 1994. Mapping the margins: Intersectionality, identity politics, and violence against women of color. In Martha Albertson Fineman & Rixanne Mykitiuk, (eds.), *The Public Nature of Private Violence*. 93–118. New York: Routledge.
Crenshaw, Kimberlé. 2016, October. The urgency of intersectionality [Video file]. Retrieved from_ https://www.ted.com/talks/kimberle_crenshaw_the_urgency_of_intersectionality?language=en
Daan, Jo. 1970 [1999]. Dialekten. In Jo Daan & D.P. Blok, Van randstad tot landrand (Bijdragen en Mededelingen der Dialectencommissie van de Koninklijke Nederlandse Akademie van Wetenschappen te Amsterdam XXXVII), 7–43. (Translated as "Dialects" in Preston (ed.), 1999, 9–30.) Grootaers, W.A. (1959). Origin and nature of the subjective boundaries of dialects. Orbis, 8. 355–384.
Evans, Betsy, Erica J. Benson & James N. Stanford (eds.). 2018. *Language Regard: Methods, Variation and Change*. Cambridge: Cambridge University Press.
Gray, Mary L. 2009. *Out the country: Youth, media, and queer visibility in rural America*. New York: NYU Press.
Hoenigswald, H. 1966. A proposal for the study of folk-linguistics. In William Bright (ed.), *Sociolinguistics*. 16–26. The Hague: Mouton de Gruyter.
Hall-Lew, Lauren & Nola Stephens. 2012. Country Talk. *Journal of English Linguistics* 40. 256–280.
Inoue, Fumio. 1977/8. Hôgen Imêji no Tahenryô Kaiseki [Multi-variate analysis of [dialect image] (part 1). Gengo Seikatsu 311. 82–91.
Jones, Lucy. "'I'm a Boy, Can't You See That?': Dialogic Embodiment and the Construction of Agency in Trans Youth Discourse." Language in society (2022): 1–22.
Jones, Taylor. 2015. Toward a Description of African American Vernacular English Dialect Regions Using "Black Twitter". *American Speech* 90(4). 403–440.
Kristiansen, Tore. 2009. The macro-level meanings of late-modern Danish accents. *Acta Linguistica Hafniensia 41*. 167–192.
Labov, William, Sharon Ash & Charles Boberg. 2006. *The atlas of North American English: Phonetics, phonology, and sound change*. Berlin: Mouton/de Gruyter.
Leap, William. 1996. *Word's out: Gay men's English (JSTOR EBA)*. Minneapolis, Minn.: University of Minnesota Press.
Lucas, Ian 1997. The color of his eyes: Polari and the sisters. In Anna Livia & Kira Hall (eds.) *Queerly phrased: Language, gender, and sexuality*. 85–94. New York: Oxford University Press.
Mallory, Chriaty, Jody L. Herman & M. V. Lee Badgett 2011. Employment Discrimination against Lesbian, Gay, Bisexual, and Transgender People in Oklahoma. UCLA: The Williams Institute. Retrieved from https://escholarship.org/uc/item/79w0b14t
Mallory, Christy & Brad Sears 2015. Employment discrimination based on sexual orientation and gender identity in Oklahoma. UCLA: The Williams Institute. Retrieved from:

https://williamsinstitute.law.ucla.edu/wp-content/uploads/LGBT-Employment-Discrimination-OK-Jan-2015.pdf

Mallory, Christy & Brad Sears. 2019. Discrimination against LGBT people in Oklahoma. UCLA: The Williams Institute. Retrieved from: https://williamsinstitute.law.ucla.edu/publications/lgbt-discrim-ok/

Mann, Stephen L. 2016. Rural 'rednecks' and urban 'bluebloods': The (in)compatibility of sounding gay and sounding southern". In Jennifer Cramer & Chris Montgomery (eds.), *Cityscapes and perceptual dialectology: Global perspectives on non-linguists' knowledge of the dialect landscape*, 73–95. Berlin: Mouton de Gruyter.

McCleary, Bryce. 2016. Between a rock and a hard place: Investigating gay men, Oklahoma dialectology, and language ideology. Stillwater: Oklahoma State University thesis.

Newton, Esther. 1979. *Mother camp: Female impersonators in America*. Chicago: University of Chicago Press.

Niedzielski, Nancy. 1999. The effect of social information on the perception of sociolinguistic variables. *Journal of Language and Social Psychology* 18(1). 62–85.

Niedzielski, Nancy & Dennis Preston. 2003. *Folk linguistics*. New York: Mouton de Gruyter.

Peterson, Gordon F. & Harold L. Barney, 1952. Control methods used in a study of the vowels. *The Journal of the Acoustic Society of America* 24(2). 175–84.

Pichler, Pia & Nathanael Williams. 2016. Hipsters in the hood: Authenticating indexicalities in young men's hip-hop talk. *Language in Society* 45(4). 557–581.

Plichta, Bartlomiej. 2005. Interdisciplinary perspectives on the northern cities chain shift (Order No. 3189729). Available from ProQuest Dissertations & Theses Global. (305424938). Retrieved from http://argo.library.okstate.edu/login?url=https://search.proquest.com/docview/305424938?accountid=4117

Plichta, Bartlomiej & Dennis Preston. 2005. The /ay/s have It the perception of /ay/ as a north-south stereotype in United States English. *Acta Linguistica Hafniensia* 37(1). 107–130.

Polle, Friedrich. 1904. *Wie denkt das Volk über die Sprache?* Leipzig: B.G. Teubner.

Preston, Dennis. 2019. How to trick respondents into revealing implicit attitudes – talk to them. *Linguistics Vanguard* 5(s1).

Preston, Dennis. 2018. Changing Research on the Changing Perceptions of Southern U.S. English. *American Speech* 93(3–4). 471–496.

Preston, Dennis. 2016. "Whaddayaknow Now?" *Babel*. 177–99. doi:10.1017/CBO 9781139680448.010.

Preston, Dennis. 2012. Folk metalanguage. In Adam Jaworski, Nikolas Coupland & Dariusz Galasinski (eds.), *Metalanguage*. 75–102. New York: Mouton de Gruyter.

Preston, Dennis. 1996. Whaddayaknow?: The modes of folk linguistic awareness. *Language Awareness* 5(1). 40–74.

Preston, Dennis. 1981. Perceptual dialectology: Mental maps of the United Stated dialects from a Hawaiian perspective (summary). In Henry Warkentyne (ed.), *Methods IV/Méthodes IV (Papers from the Fourth International Conference on Methods in Dialectology)*. 192–198. University of Victoria, British Columbia.

RODEO (Research on the Dialects of Oklahoma). 2009. An ongoing dialectological and sociolinguistic research program in the Linguistics and Applied Linguistics/TESOL Program of the Oklahoma State University English Department.

Silverstein, Michael. 1981. The limits of awareness. *Sociolinguistic Working Paper No. 84*. Austin, TX: Southwest Educational Development Library.

Smitherman, Geneva. 1994. *Black talk: Words and phrases from the hood to the amen corner*. Boston: Houghton Mifflin.

Southard, B. 1993. Elements of Midwestern Speech in Oklahoma. In Timothy Frazer (ed.) *"Heartland" English – variation and transition in the American Midwest*. The University of Alabama Press: Tuscaloosa.

Stanford, James & Dennis Preston (eds). 2009. *Variation in indigenous minority languages*. Benjamins: Amsterdam/Philadelphia.

Thomas, Erik R. 2001. *An acoustic analysis of vowel variation in new world English*. Durham: Duke University Press

Tillery, Jan & Guy Bailey. 1998. Y'all in Oklahoma. *American Speech* 73(3). 257–278.

Weirich, Phillip. 2013. A study of vowel mergers in Oklahoma. Stillwater: Oklahoma State University thesis.

Weinraub, C., Rousseau, Sylvia G., LeMoine, Noma, & Venegas, Kristan. 2015. Influences of African American English That Contribute to the Exclusion of African American Students from Academic Discourse. ProQuest Dissertations and Theses.

Weston, K. 1995. Get Thee to a Big City: Sexual Imaginary and the Great Gay Migration. *GLQ: A Journal of Lesbian and Gay Studies* 2(3). 253–277.

Zimman, Lal. 2019. Presenter for "New Directions in LGBTQ+ Linguistics: Commemorating the LSA Special Interest Group on LGBTQ+ Issues in Linguistics". Panel for Linguistic Society of America annual meeting.

Lex Konnelly
Transmedicalisms, transnormativities, and semantic authority

1 Introduction

Language is often one of the first grounds on which trans people enact their own self-determination. In recent trans linguistic research, trans communities have received a great deal of recognition for their efforts in mobilizing greater attunement to language, and have been shown to exhibit what many community members already knew about themselves: a high degree of metalinguistic awareness about how gender is diffused across linguistic forms, as well as how these indices can be subverted or manipulated playfully and strategically in the practice of self-expression (Abe 2019; Crowley 2022; Gratton 2016; miles-hercules 2020; Zimman 2019; *inter alia*). However, there is no singular, monolithic Trans Community where values are consistently and homogeneously shared, and how we engage with gendered language and gendered categories (and how they intersect with other aspects of identity) is varied and, at times, fraught. Consequently, there is a need to analyze trans linguistic practices in affirming ways that foreground the joys of our communities without flattening the range of gender-diverse experiences and linguistic practices to a singular category that precludes discussion of the role of power and privilege in norm-building and boundary-making.

For many activists, community organizations, and scholars of trans studies (Bornstein & Bergman 2010; Stryker 1998; Vaid-Menon 2020; *inter alia*), *trans* is an expansive and open category encompassing a fluid range of expressions that actively transcend or transgress cisheteronormative understandings of sex and gender, rather than referring to any specific identity or embodiment. Yet as observed by Sutherland (2021, 1–2), "[a]lthough the trans umbrella is useful in the sense of inclusion, outsider recognition, and social activism for non-cisgender identities, often trans individuals hold radically different understandings of their selves and their relationships to one another." As the boundaries of the trans umbrella have continued to grow, so too have internal debates about the boundaries of membership and what constitutes an authentic or "trans enough" collective identity. The notion of "trans enough" refers to a pressure to justify one's transgender experience through "validation from others [. . .] that one's identity is authentic and 'real'" (Garrison 2018, 618), and often, the measure of this authenticity

Lex Konnelly, University of Toronto

is its consistency with what is deemed *transnormative*: the hierarchy of transness that "privileges trans people who display attributes valued by and thus privileged" in society (Johnson 2016, 466). A core axis of transnormativity is medical, whereby adherence to a medical model of gender variance creates an "unspoken hierarchy" (Bornstein 1995, 67) in which normative transgender identities are so defined through access to medical technologies such as hormone therapy and surgical interventions. This is consequential not only for the resultant impact on societal recognition (insofar as transness is often only legible in broader cissexist society through a lens of medical transition), but also leads to marginalization or rejection from within transgender communities themselves, whose members may deem others to be not trans enough or to be not "do[ing] transgender" correctly in the absence of medical intervention (Sutherland 2021, 2; see also Connell 2010; Garrison 2018; Johnson 2019; Konnelly 2022; Miller 2019).

Not all trans people desire medical support to feel affirmed in their gender identities, but for those who do, the medical model can serve as an "accountability structure" (Sutherland 2021, 2) that privileges some trans identities over others. In order to access hormones or surgeries, clinical texts such as the DSM-V and the World Professional Association for Transgender Health's *Standards of Care* (World Professional Association for Transgender Health 2012) recommend a formal diagnosis of *gender dysphoria*, defined as the "clinically significant distress or impairment related to a strong desire to be of another gender" (American Psychiatric Association 2013, 302.85).[1] *Gender dysphoria* as a salient criterion, if not a prerequisite, of an "authentic" transgender identity is widespread and highly contested – both within medical communities and transgender communities themselves (Johnson 2015, 2019). Belief in

---

[1] It should be noted that in contrast to this diagnosis-based model, the informed consent model of care has recently evolved as an alternative model of access, where the ultimate goal is a collaborative relationship between patient and practitioner. Rather than emphasizing doctoral evaluation of transgender individuals' distress with respect to their gender identity, informed consent requires only that a patient "possess the cognitive ability to make an informed decision about health care," including expressing their understanding of the risks, benefits, and information needed to make an informed decision about their medical care (Informed Consent for Access to Trans Health, n.d.). This paradigm also often entails a linguistic shift to further circumvent the pathologizing nature of medicalized language to describe transgender experience: instead of *gender dysphoria*, informed consent guidelines may advocate for terminology such as *gender incongruence* instead, which more broadly captures a felt sense of disconnect between an individual's gender identity and their embodiment (World Health Organization 2019). However, despite the increasing prevalence of the consent-based model, particularly in large urban centers, the diagnosis-based model remains the mainstream paradigm throughout the world both in practice as well as what is primarily emphasized in diagnostic texts (Cavanaugh, Hopwood & Lambert 2016; Schulz 2017; Spanos et al. 2021).

dysphoria as a defining feature of trans identity is a pillar of *transmedicalism*, an ideology of trans boundary-making which stipulates that both gender dysphoria and strong desire for medical transition are required in order to be genuinely transgender. Often referred to, by themselves and others, as *transmedicalists* or *truscum*, those who subscribe to this ideology ratify medical authority in regulating transgender experience and insist that deviating from the established medical model undermines public acceptance of trans communities and trivializes authentic (i.e., medicalized) trans experiences. In this chapter, I present an analysis of precisely these kinds of negotiations of transgender identity in one such transmedicalist virtual space: the social media sub-forum r/Truscum, an online community that identifies itself as "a place for those who have been cast out of mainstream trans subreddits." Though a subject of discussion within trans communities for some time, transmedicalism has drawn attention in the scholarly literature only recently (Sutherland 2021; Vincent 2020), albeit none yet from a sociocultural linguistic perspective attentive to the specific role of language in intra-community boundary-making. Language is a matter of central concern to transgender communities, and this does not appear to be any less the case in transmedicalist spaces than elsewhere – though how linguistic resources are mobilized and contested there has yet to be explored fully.

In investigating the particular ways under which trans identity – specifically, its authentication and its relationship to medicalization – is made locally meaningful on the site, I show how transmedicalist diagnostics of authentic transness also rely at least in part on language ideologies, or implicit assumptions about what they view as "appropriate" language practices (cf. Crowley 2022): specifically, they reject a neoliberal ethos of linguistic self-determination (Stanley 2014; Zimman 2017a) that prioritizes individual agency and entails that each individual is the ultimate source of authority over their self-descriptions. Instead, members argue in favor of broadly prescriptivist norms that prioritize ascribing fixed meanings to linguistic forms, at times appealing to the necessity of medical-institutional authority to define them.

Both public conversations and analytical attention to the significance of linguistic self-determination for transgender communities has generally operated under a transgender-cisgender binary (though see Zimman 2017a for notable exceptions and implications), where the assumption is that transgender people uniformly and categorically advocate for greater expansiveness in (de)gendered language and understandings of gender identity in an unknowing or hostile cissexist society. This chapter differs in its focus on a particular transgender community of practice where something else is desired: that is, the ultimate goal is not necessarily to create more room, but at times, even less. Through a computer-mediated critical discourse analysis of posts and comments on r/Truscum, I show how the semantic authority (McConnell-Ginet 2018) – in other words, the right to define and determine the true and correct meaning – of transgender identity terms is established in this virtual space, and how this practice troubles one-dimensional and binaristic understandings of normativity wherein one subject position is inherently normative and another inherently subversive, highlighting a fractal recursivity (Irvine & Gal 2000) between normativities that co-exist within marginalized communities.

Transgender transmedicalists on r/Truscum may be considered subversive in relation to cisgender individuals, at least insofar as their trans status diverges from a cissexist norm. But being transgender or transsexual does not necessarily entail a subversive politic, and their alignment with medical-institutional authority can, in its own way, be characterized as a particular normative investment. However, their perception of themselves as an ideological minority in relation to more "mainstream" (i.e., anti-transmedicalist) transgender communities often leads them to consider their views as subversive instead. The relationship between users' discursive practices in this environment must therefore be read through the biopolitics (and indeed, the necropolitics; Snorton & Haritaworn 2013) of the transmedicalist model of transgender healthcare, one node in an interlocking nexus of transnormative standards to which intersections of trans communities may differentially respond.

To situate myself in relation to the community of practice that I describe in the following sections, I want to note that I approach this analysis from my positionality as a white, transmasculine, non-binary graduate student researcher in my early 30s. I come from a low-income background, and have firsthand experience with accessing support for gender transformation in the Canadian public healthcare system and the varying opportunities, violences, and frustrations with medical institutions as a whole. As a non-participant observer of transmedicalist communities – and one who would likely be considered very much an outgroup member – I nevertheless want to be thoughtful and intentional about how I engage with their stories. Talking about points of disagreement within trans communities is difficult and not to be undertaken lightly; like Morgan M. Page (2020), "I do not shit-talk other trans people in public". However, these conversations are crucial to interrogate how transgender and non-binary people engage with institutions of power, who we hold responsible for the persistent dehumanization of gender-variant people, and how we can create more accessible and affirming worlds for our communities. It is also necessary in order to contend with the limits of self-determination which "separates relatively privileged trans people from those whose lives are also shaped by the intersecting violences of cissexism, racism, poverty and classism, ableism and homophobia" (Zimman 2017a, 243). Self-identifications are anything but equal – even with respect to how transgender and non-binary people may regard each other. Further, as trans linguistic practices become increasingly enregistered, they are in turn mapped onto different gender-variant identities and characterological figures (Agha 2007), as salient and identifiable semiotic resources to be leveraged in interactional processes of boundary-making.

2 Digital discourse and communities in context: Transmedicalists, anti-transmedicalists, and *truscum*

The internet has been a crucial site of connection and resource exchange for trans communities since its inception (Whittle 1998): bulletin boards, email listservs, chatrooms, Usenet groups, GeoCities websites, and other early forms of social media were abundant with spaces where trans people could express themselves and explore their gender identities in relative safety to their offline lives. Social media have waxed and waned, with trans communities emerging in notable ways on each. In most recent memory, YouTube, Tumblr, Instagram, Twitter, Reddit, and TikTok have all become venues for various trans technologies (Haimson, Dame-Griff, Capello & Richter 2019): a multiplicity of distinctly trans media and digital cultural strategies such as the transition vlog (Dame 2013), queer and trans erotic content (Fink & Miller 2014), virtual activism and to speaking back power (Zimman 2017a, 240), and expansive and wide-ranging innovation in the trans lexicon (Zimman & Hayworth 2020a, 2020b). Though today transgender and non-binary youth in particular are more likely than ever to know another trans person in real life (Beemyn & Rankin 2011, 63), this is not and has not always been the case, especially for older trans people, rural trans people, or transgender people who have not shared this aspect of their identity with anyone offline. To this end, virtual spaces have been lifelines as much as they have been sites of play and creativity, providing opportunities for learning, identity exploration, and community-building.

Of all potential sites of virtual engagement, Reddit is a greatly facilitative social media space for analysts wishing to study digital discourse, as the design of the website itself intentionally cultivates communities of practice organized around a specific shared interest. Posts to the website are submitted to subreddits, self-contained and user-moderated sub-fora that organize collective engagement according to a particular topic, identity, or activity. In the case of r/Truscum, this shared interest is primarily discussions of gender identity as it intersects with transmedicalist ideas. Posts appear in one of several different formats: a text post, an image or video, an external link, or a poll. Users can interact with posts by commenting and either "upvoting" or "downvoting" them, which expresses (dis)pleasure or (dis)agreement with post content,[2] and also contributes towards the visibility

---

[2] Note that while this is not necessarily Reddit's intended use of the upvote and downvote functions, in practice, it is how they are employed by most users. As noted in the website's Reddit 101 section, Reddit's official stance on upvoting and downvoting is that they should not be used as indicators of approval, but of how well the post generates discussion (whether positive or

of a given post: the higher the number of upvotes, the higher up on the main page of the subreddit the post will appear to other users. Each user gets one vote per post or comment (in other words, a post or comment can only be upvoted *or* downvoted by a given user, though the vote can be changed or removed). The amount of upvotes or downvotes that a user receives from their posts and comments are counted towards their "karma," a number publicly displayed on a user's profile that provides a rough measure of what they contribute to the communities that they engage with. The karma system functions as a form of social control: though Reddit user profiles can be kept largely anonymous, karma is in many respects intended to maintain collegiality (as stated in their *Help* section, Reddit encourages users not to "set out to accumulate karma; just set out to be a good person, and let your karma simply be a reflection of your legacy"). Users who have a negative karma have generally received a large number of downvotes and may be ejected or outright banned from certain subreddits on that basis.

Each subreddit has its own set of rules and guidelines for facilitating engagement and restricting undesirable behavior that would result in bans or downvotes; some are generic and likely shared across multiple subreddits (e.g., "be respectful and civil towards other users," often referred to as "the golden rule"; "no spam," etc.), while others are more directly related to the content of the subreddit itself or its user base. For example, r/Truscum's community guidelines include warnings against spreading misinformation, "stirring the pot" (inciting discord on other trans subreddits and posting to complain about bans or other resultant disciplining) or offering diagnoses (i.e., "minidoctor[ing]"), among others. Several other transgender and non-binary subreddits, such as r/traaaaaaannnnnnnnnns, r/ftm, r/MtF, and r/enby, indirectly or explicitly prohibit expressions of transmedicalist viewpoints in their community guidelines. r/Truscum's aforementioned self-description as a place for those "cast out of mainstream trans subreddits" is likely an allusion to the fact that many users have indeed been banned or (in terms common to Reddit) "downvoted into oblivion" from other transgender Reddit communities. This makes r/Truscum a slightly more insular community of practice relative to other subreddits on gender diversity, with users often regarding themselves as subversive in relation to the ideological orientation of larger and more mainstream trans sub-communities.

Many of the users who participate in r/Truscum and similar virtual transmedicalist communities typically identify as *truscum* or *transmeds*, closely related terms that describe a range of beliefs regarding the essential relationship between transgender identity and medical-institutional criteria. *Truscum* (a portmanteau of *true*

---

negative): "If you think something contributes to conversation, upvote it. If you think it does not contribute to the subreddit it is posted in or is off-topic in a particular community, downvote it."

transsexual + *scum*³) originated on the social media platform Tumblr at an undetermined point in the early to mid-2010s, and at the time of its coining carried strongly pejorative connotations.⁴ Though there was much initial resistance to *truscum* as a term among those labeled with it (many of whom described it as a slur), it has been since been reclaimed within many transmedicalist communities who align with it explicitly and celebrate its use. Thus, for many users, the label *truscum* or *transmedicalist* is central to their understanding of their experience as a transgender or transsexual person, reflecting an understanding of their identity as a primarily (or, for some, exclusively) medical condition.

Though *truscum* are by definition transgender or transsexual, the broader umbrella term *transmedicalist* or *transmed* may refer to individuals who are either transgender or cisgender, but who nevertheless subscribe to a medical-institutional definition of transgender identity. Recently, there has been increased discussion regarding the precise distinction (if any) between the labels *truscum* and *transmed*. Some argue that *truscum* refers to a belief in dysphoria alone as the requisite criterion for trans identity, whereas *transmed* refers to a belief in the necessity of medical transition; others argue that the former is simply a more moderate view than the latter, some of whose stringent dependence on transition and biological essentialism have earned them the specific moniker of *radmed* (from *radical* + *transmedicalist*, indicating particularly extremist or fringe views). Still others maintain that there is no distinction and that the two are fully synonymous. For the present purposes, I treat both *truscum* and *transmedicalist* as terms along the same spectrum of medical-institutional alignment, though individuals' specific positionality with respect to either is likely to vary, and truscum and transmedicalist communities more generally have as much internal variation as any other community of practice (Jacobsen, Devor & Hodge 2021). Both, however, primarily contrast with anti-

---

3 The *true transsexual* portion likely refers to the term originally coined by Dr. Harry Benjamin (1966), who proposed a Sex Orientation Scale representing a continuum of gender variance among gender non-conforming individuals who were assigned male at birth. The scale distinguished between "transsexualism" and "transvestitism", with the "true" variant of the former requiring surgical intervention, and the latter representing a largely sexual desire. The scale is now considered to be quite outdated and has been widely criticized, particularly for its conflation of gender identity and sexuality. However, it has strong associations with a medicalized view of trans identity – likely why it was incorporated as part of the *truscum* nomenclature. The *–scum* morpheme has been suggested to have come from what anti-transmedicalist coiners of the term perceived as an aggressive imposition of medicalist ideas (Jacobsen, Devor, & Hodge 2021: 67).

4 While many have reclaimed the term, this is not universally the case, and *truscum* remains highly emotionally charged in many contexts. For this reason, I instead use the terms *transmedicalist* and *anti-transmedicalist* when speaking generally of these positionalities, restricting the use of *truscum* only for those who actively claim it for themselves.

transmedicalists, who they often label as *tucute,* another portmanteau of "too cute to be cis(gender)". Though also a contentious term, not unlike *truscum, tucute* has also been (re)claimed as an identity label in some virtual trans spaces and may broadly refer to individuals who either reject the essentialism of medical criteria as defining qualities of transness, do not adhere to normative gendered embodiments, or both.

Transmedicalists also disalign themselves from those they describe as *transtrenders,* i.e., individuals whose transgender identity is deemed inauthentic or performative in the absence of medicalized criteria, particularly gender dysphoria. This term is not mutually exclusive with *tucute,* and the two are at times used interchangeably. The *–trender* morpheme in this case also belies transmedicalists' alignment with increasingly clamorous public discourses about the perceived faddishness of transgender identity, and closely associated fears regarding rates of detransition, medical malpractice, and child abuse,[5] implying that those who are anti-transmedicalist are actually cisgender people seeking attention or hopping on a cultural bandwagon. Under a transmedicalist view, not only do trenders' appropriation of transgender identity undermine efforts towards greater acceptance of transgender people (such as through expanding gender subjectivities that cisgender people may not understand or making them so broad as to be meaningless, thus leading society to further evaluate the transgender communities negatively), but they also restrict medical access for those who are authentically transgender, saturating already-limited medical systems and exacerbating the scarcity of access to medical technologies.

With this context in mind, I take as the point of departure the following questions. First, in light of their overall alignment with medical-institutional authority, how is trans identity made locally meaningful in transmedicalist space? Specifically, how is semantic authority over identity terms and license to use certain linguistic forms or practices established? And lastly, from a broader view, how can this be leveraged to better understand how primary trans healthcare and the complexity of trans personhood can be made more expansive? Answers to these questions are ones that transgender and non-binary communities have been grappling with – and will surely continue to grapple with – for quite

---

[5] Consider for example the onslaught of high-profile anti-trans legislation in the United States especially, such as the 2022 bill endorsed by Texas Governor Greg Abbott that calls on educational and healthcare professionals to report parents who support their child's access to gender-affirming care on the grounds that it is considered "child abuse" under Texas law (America Civil Liberties Union 2022). Dozens of similar bills have emerged throughout the United States in the last several years, often targeting young transgender people and their participation in public spaces and activities contingent on their gender identity, such as organized sports.

some time. Rather than claim to resolve these questions outright, my intention here is to share some initial reflections.

Language is a core domain in which trans people's very material existence is championed or challenged, and as such, it is perhaps unsurprising that different subsets of gender-diverse communities would feel differently about which linguistic practices they wish to claim for themselves and how trans linguistic advocacy should be enacted. On r/Truscum, talk about talk increasingly salient trans linguistic practices (such as pronoun sharing or lexical innovation) is a central part of the boundary-making that takes place. However, discussions of language are rarely about language alone. The intention of this chapter is therefore to bring to bear new linguistic insight into how trans discourses of language are mobilized in the maintenance of transnormativities in other words, as a part of the process of authenticating some subjects and not others – and how analysis of transnormative uptakes of trans linguistic practices can facilitate a nuanced understanding into the "tensions, shifting identity politics, and power dynamics that shape intracommunity norms and interactions around who can claim a trans identity" (Sutherland 2021, 2).

3 Data and method

Discussion in this chapter is part of a larger project investigating how transgender people use language in creative and intentional ways to navigate medical gatekeeping, with an emphasis on gender-affirming care contexts specifically. In ethnographic interviews with non-binary people navigating access to this medical care (Konnelly 2021a, 2021b, 2022), a common theme that emerged was digital discourse in online trans communities about who counts as "authentically" transgender or "trans enough" to pursue medical support. Individuals I spoke to reported feeling as much pressure from within trans communities to adhere to a particular way of being as they did from interacting with medical institutions, with some citing transmedicalist communities specifically as a source of anxiety and socialization into the requisite linguistic practices to access care (Konnelly 2021b). However, despite expressing their frustration and disalignment from what they described as transmedicalists' intra-community gatekeeping, my participant-collaborators also largely expressed compassion for the transmedicalist perspective, with some viewing it as resulting from trans people's experiences of harm within the medical system (Konnelly 2021b, 5). It was these conversations that directed me to virtual transmedicalist spaces, and r/Truscum specifically, as a site where trans identity and trans linguistic practices were often challenged and contested.

Data for the analysis were extracted via nard (Gadanidis 2021), a Python script that scrapes Reddit's archive (also known as its Application Programming Interface, or API) according to user-specified parameters. To compile the corpus, nard was directed to download all posts from the r/Truscum subreddit falling between the dates of December 2020–January 2021 (inclusive). The date range was intentionally narrow both to reflect the productivity of posting in the forum and to remain consistent with the timeframe of in-person ethnographic interviews for a concomitant component of the project (Konnelly 2021a, b, 2022). The resulting 1,483 posts and their comments were then loaded into NVivo (QSR International Software 2018) and coded inductively, with a specific attention to metalinguistic commentary.

Coding was supported by topic modelling using Latent Dirichlet Allocation (LDA; Blei, Ng & Jordan 2003) in R to identify major themes in the data set. As a computational linguistic method, LDA probabilistically estimates the mixtures of words associated with a given topic, while also determining the mixture of topics into which a corpus can be categorized. It divides the data into a specified number of topics, returning the top five lexical items most strongly associated with a given topic. The data for this chapter are based on an LDA model of 12 topics, determined through experimentation and qualitative evaluation of each topic generated by the model. Though each topic is assumed to by the model to have internal consistency, they are not mutually exclusive; for example, a topic for which the top five lexical items are *call, term, medical, transgender,* and *condition* overlaps with the topic led by *dysphoria, community, lgbt, label,* and *opinion,* since both pertain to metalinguistic discussion of identity labels, linguistic features, and their relationship to medical criteria, albeit with slightly different semantic fields. And of course, overall, given the nature of the community of practice, most if not all topics pertain to discussion of trans experience more broadly regardless. The modeling itself is therefore best understood as a tool to be used in identifying broad themes in large data sets, and it provides the researcher with entry points to narrow in on overarching discursive patterns, as a precursor to closer textual analysis.

This analysis focuses on a Critical Discourse Analysis (Fairclough 2013) of the top 10 posts that the LDA model selected as most strongly correlated with each topic model, for a total of 120 posts; in the following section, examples from this subset are chosen for illustrative purposes. Concerned with identifying relationships between language and systems of power, CDA's utility lies in exploring the relationship(s) between language and social institutional practices and of 'wider' political and social structures. Trans linguistics, with its critical attention to the broader realm of discourse-level strategies that "characterize trans people's place within structures of power" (Zimman 2020, 10), is a well-suited companion to CDA, and the two interpretive lenses mesh in notable ways. Both can be best understood as perspectives or frameworks rather than methods per se, and scholars of both call for an ethos of research as action with a fundamentally liberatory agenda. In bringing these two epistemic assemblages (King 2021) together, I take a sociocultural approach to CDA that follows foundational studies of language and power (Fairclough 1989, 2013).

4 Gatekeeping, semantic authority, and trans identities

On r/Truscum, posts occur on a variety of topics for a variety of purposes, some of which are likely to be seen in similar forms across transgender and non-binary subreddits: sharing memes, soliciting discussion on coverage of trans communities in the media, seeking support through transphobic encounters in daily life, and at times sharing intimate stories detailing medical harm and familial rejection. Unique to r/Truscum is the active evaluation of language related to gender identity and gender diversity through a transmedicalist lens – specifically, overt discussion regarding the merits of certain linguistic practices and whether individuals should, in their view, be legitimated as transgender based on their use of such practices. Central to intra-community discussions regarding license to claim the *transgender* label is its relationship to medical criteria and interaction with medical systems more generally. Excerpt 1 provides one illustrative view:

> Excerpt 1. *"You don't need dysphoria to be trans" ruins people's lives and the people saying it don't have the experience to prove it's true* (December 3, 2020)
> u/Discodoe | 199 upvotes
> 1   Who is this even for? Why do some people want to squeeze their
> 2   way into this label so bad. 90% of the people making these
> 3   claims never transition the other 10% transition to the opposite
> 4   gender end up regretting it and force themselves to stay in this
> 5   dysphoric genderqueer label for the rest of their lives because
> 6   testosterone did so much permanent damage that they'll never
> 7   truly feel how they were before again. You don't need dysphoria
> 8   to swap around some pronouns on Instagram I could do that
> 9   right now if I felt like it, you do need dysphoria to be trans. And
> 10 most important of all you need dysphoria to alter your body.

The poster questions the denotation of the term *transgender* through denouncing individuals who "want to squeeze their way into [the *transgender*] label so bad" (lines 1–2), which in their view is evidenced by how few members of the imagined inauthentic group continue on to medical transition: they contend that the majority

("90%", line 2) of those who identify as transgender but do not align with medical criteria never pursue medical transition, and the remainder of the same group do, but "end up regretting it" (line 3). Therefore, transition for inauthentic transgender people *causes* dysphoria, rather than *curing* dysphoria, as is the normative trajectory for gender-affirming care, and as would be consistent with an understanding of transgender identity as an inherently medical condition. The poster also makes a strong distinction between linguistic practices (i.e., "to swap around some pronouns on Instagram", line 8) and gender identity: while anyone can change their pronouns, this does not entail that they are transgender. In other words, "you do need dysphoria to be trans. And most important of all you need dysphoria to alter your body" (lines 9–10). For this poster, the uptake of trans linguistic practices – such as a change in self-referential linguistic features like identity labels or pronouns, often among the first acts of linguistic self-determination that trans people make (Zimman 2017a) – are insufficient to lay claim to transgender identity. And further, these kinds of linguistic changes, when done either in the absence of medical intervention or in in the context of ungenuine medical intervention, are inauthentic and can lead to individual harm.

Given increasing public conversations regarding trans-affirming language and trans linguistic advocacy (Zimman 2017b, 2018), it is perhaps unsurprising that metalinguistic discussion would emerge as salient in r/Truscum as in other gender-diverse communities of practice. However, discussion of language is largely critical of trans linguistic innovation rather than advocating for it, as has been described in other transgender and non-binary communities (Crowley 2022; Zimman 2017b, 2018). However, boundary-making with respect to trans identity on r/Truscum is not an exclusively trans or even transmedicalist collaboration: anti-transmedicalists, both cisgender and transgender, also regularly visit the forum to challenge users, an invitation that is often heartily accepted and generates substantial discussion. Given the diverging alignments of the participants, these threads are perhaps the strongest examples of identificatory contestations. In a post entitled *neutral here i have a question* (December 16th, 2021), u/aaaanobees, ostensibly a non-regular user of the forum, asks members to explain why they subscribe to transmedicalism – in other words, "why do you care?"

Excerpt 2. *neutral here i have a question* (December 16th, 2021)
u/aaaanobees | 20 upvotes
1   so hopefully i dont sound like a dick, but my question is literally
2   just "why do you care?" personally i dont care if ppl chose to
3   transition if they dont have dysphoria, if they regret it thats on
4   them. same with labels, if they choose a label i dont understand/they
5   end up not liking i just dont care ??? it doesn't effect me at all, so
6   why should i, yknow?

```
7    ive heard the argument that tucute/mogai⁶/etc make the trans community
8    "look like a joke" several time and while i have taken that into
9    consideration, transphobes are going to be transphobic no matter what.
10   long before mogai or whatever else was even a thing people were
11   transphobic.
12   so i just dont understand the mentality of truscum ??? like why does it
13   matter to you how others choose to live.
```

In lines 2–5, makes their stance of non-alignment explicit at the outset: establishing a contrast to the transmedicalists they address in their post, they describe their own position on individuals who transition without dysphoria, indicating that they are not bothered by others' choices of labels regardless of whether they understand them. While they acknowledge the common transmedicalist concern that anti-transmedicalists incite or exacerbate negative evaluations of transgender communities (i.e., make the trans community "look like a joke", line 8), ultimately, they locate responsibility for this response in transphobic individuals themselves: that is, "transphobes are going to be transphobic no matter what" (line 9).

Respondents to this original postv describe their concerns not strictly in terms of language itself, but in terms of what the implications might be for a growing transgender community in light of existing restrictions to gender-affirming care access – such as continuing to secure rights for dysphoric trans people to access transition under their insurance and continuing to ensure access to medical transition for neuroatypical and low-income trans patients.

Excerpt 3.
u/ReineDeLaSeine14 | 36 upvotes
```
1    My personal concerns are: Continuing to secure rights for dysphoric
2    trans people to access transition under insurance and continuing to
3    ensure medical transition is available to autistic people, who are
4    beginning to lose or never got access to medical transition.
```

Gender-affirming care is variably covered under insurance policies throughout the world, and not all transgender and non-binary people are able to secure access to insurance. Commenters therefore call attention to a common barrier in care access for many gender-diverse people: achieving the financial means to access gender-affirming care. They in turn express concern that disconnection from a diagnostic model might exacerbate the present state of care access in rendering primary gender-affirming healthcare fully elective, and therefore even more financially inaccessible.

---

6 MOGAI: Marginalized Orientations, Gender Alignment, Intersex (MOGAI Wiki 2022).

Excerpt 4.

u/MeliennaZapuni | 6 upvotes

1 If tucutes convince broader society that being trans is a choice, we
2 lose our health insurance. Who the fuck has money for full out of
3 pocket surgeries and a lifetime supply of HRT? Hint: Majority of people
4 cannot even consider it an option.

Yet, rather than locating this precarity in institutions and policies that create (or, as it pertains to potential future systemic adjustments, could create) these circumstances, the blame for inequitable, overcrowded, and underfunded healthcare systems is attributed at least in part with other community members who are perceived as less deserving. This is especially clear in comments like that by u/knepan, who has waited over 4 years for hormone therapy and has an estimated year left before obtaining access:

Excerpt 5.

u/knepan | 8 upvotes

1 I've waited 4+ years in an overcrowded healthcare system and still
2 haven't gotten hormones. I have an estimated year left.
3 This system was failing to begin with as it's not built for the average
4 amount of dysphoric trans people. Now put in the non dysphoric/trenders
5 into this already full system and we have waiting times that went from
6 an average of like 6months-1year to now 2 years.

u/knepan acknowledges that the system was "failing to begin with as it's not built for the average amount of dysphoric trans people" (lines 3–4), circumstances exacerbated by the addition of "non dysphoric/trenders" entering into an "already full system" (lines 4–5). While transmedicalists may ultimately align with the institution in echoing its anxieties about inauthentic transgender and non-binary patients, they simultaneously remain attuned to the precariousness of their access to it. However, a link is drawn between inauthentic identities and scarcity of access, whereby identification with a transgender label in the absence of medical criteria implicates the "non dysphoric" trender in the financial hierarchy endemic to gender-affirming care.

While gender – specifically, transgender identity and gender diversity more broadly – is often the locus of metalinguistic discussion on r/Truscum, transgender and non-binary itself is not the only positionality of relevance, particularly in metalinguistic discussion. Other identities are also vigorously contested as well, and are central to users' challenges to those they deem to be "mainstream" trans linguistic practices. Power and privilege are themselves regular topics of conversation: Class is often invoked at least implicitly, and economic privilege looms large through users' references to the financial accessibility of medical care. But on r/Truscum, racialization is equally relevant to the construction of an authentic trans identity: posters also appeal to various semiotic indices of whiteness to invalidate the ideological positions and linguistic practices of those they deem to be trenders and tucutes, and in the process reject descriptions of their own ideological positioning as privileged. In other words, criticisms of white privilege and power are extended to criticisms of specific linguistic practices or anti-transmedicalist positions more generally. For example, in a thread entitled *It's funny because they're basically saying that cis privilege isn't a thing* (December 6th, 2021), u/NuggetsWhileCrying posts an anonymized image of a (presumably anti-transmedicalist) Twitter user who seems to link transmedicalism to whiteness:

Figure 1: Twitter screenshot shared on r/Truscum (www.reddit.com/r/truscum).

In the tweet, the user – whose account name is obscured by virtual black ink in the original image – expresses dubiousness regarding whether the lack of desire to transition could be considered a privilege, a position often held by transmedicalists, given the financial and temporal barriers to gender-affirming care. Rather than drawing a link between this opinion and transmedicalism, however, the Twitter user in the reposted image instead characterizes this as an opinion associated with white trans people, and likewise a repeat behaviour (as indicated by the use of "at it again"). It is unknown whether this Twitter user is themself also white, but it is also not wholly relevant to those responding to the post, many of whom assume as such in their replies, interpreting the tweet creator's invocation of whiteness not as a trans of color critique, but rather as indicative of an endemic whiteness among anti-transmedicalists more generally.

Excerpts 6–11.

u/Archonate_of_Archona | 35 upvotes
    Tucutes stop acting as if PoC transmeds don't exist challenge

u/1933bootyeater | 21 upvotes
1   Man YALL are the white people who are saying that shit lmao. There are
2   thousands more POC truscum. This one probably just discovered they're
3   5% Italian

u/BigTransThrowaway | 5 upvotes
1   LOL riiiiiiight because only *white* trans people face the barriers of
2   medical transition. /s
3   Every single trans person of color I know is truscum/transmed.
4   Tucutes are overwhelmingly white.

u/ crustydustys0ck | 1 upvote
    Guess I'm white now lol

u/sufferingisvalid | 9 upvotes
1   I would actually argue that white privilege and the need to stay there
2   relevant as a young white person motivates a lot of tucute behavior.
3   [Lines removed for identifying information]
4   their disregard for appropriating trans experiences and not
5   respecting trans people who have it much worse than them is possibly
6   inspired by white privilege. Because they likely grew up in
7   environments where they learned that dabbling in other
8   cultures/religions/etc is ok, they probably don't inherently believe
9   is anything wrong with playing trans or recklessly using that label.

Users ascribe various behaviours to the Twitter user based on their statement that are stereotypical of white privilege, such as acting as if they "just discovered they're 5% Italian" (u/1933bootyeater, lines 2–3). u/sufferingisvalid draws a direct link between the perceived whiteness of anti-transmedicalsts, white privilege, and cultural appropriation, suggesting that "disregard for appropriating trans experiences" (line 4) is "possibly inspired by white privilege" (lines 5–6), because they "likely grew up in environments where they learned that dabbling in other cultures/religions/etc is ok" (lines 6–7). This indexical link between whiteness, colonialism, and "cringe" appropriative behaviour (Markbreiter 2022) draws a universal outrage on r/Truscum, but undergoes a different uptake when received by self-identified white transmedicalists and transmedicalists who self-identify as people of color. For users who are not white, this description is tantamount to their erasure from yet another transgender and non-binary; again, they are inscribed outside their community's boundaries and assumed not to be present (as described by u/Archonate_of_Archona, they "[act] as if PoC transmeds don't exist"). But for self-identified white users, it is taken as evidence that racism is truly located in the behaviour of others – specifically, amongst the anti-transmedicalists from whom they strongly disalign. Through the bivalent semiotic link on r/Truscum between whiteness (with its associated qualities of false victimhood and racism) and an anti-transmedicalist ideology (with its evaluation as inherently rooted in inauthenticity and appropriation), white members of r/Truscum simultaneously legitimate themselves as specifically *good white people* at the same time that they construct themselves to be *authentically trans*. In other words, criticisms of white privilege and power are extended to criticisms of specific linguistic practices or anti-transmedicalist positions more generally. This eagerness to locate whiteness as not relevant to their own transgender or non-binary positionality may, at least partly, explain why r/Truscum seems to indeed be a primarily white community of practice. For example, in a poll entitled *Time to break a stereotype; Are you a POC?* (December 11, 2021), 74% (N=681) of the 911 users who responded with their racial self-identifications indicated that they were white.

The demographics of r/Truscum may be as much an artifact of the demographics of Reddit itself and may not necessarily be generalizable to all transmedicalist communities. However, it is notable that both transmedicalists and anti-transmedicalists use whiteness as a means to discredit the others' ideological positioning. Whether this assessment originates in trans of color critique or in white transgender and non-binary people's desire to deflect away from the relationship between their transness and their own whiteness is an open question, and the answer is most likely both. As indicated in the responses by users who themselves identify as people of color, rather than straightforwardly critiquing white supremacy within trans communities, these assumptions also reify it. The characterological figure (Agha 2007) of the transmedicalist is, to anti-transmedicalists, inherently white; likewise, the characterological figure of the anti-transmedicalist is, to transmedicalists, also inherently white. Thus in each case, the canonical representative is a white one, flattening the presence of trans people of color in either community. The fact that the poll did not in fact break any stereotypes was not lost on users either; as noted in one comment, *We been knew that the majority of y'all is white.*

Though not about medicalization per se, this thread is in many ways a window into the heart of transmedicalist and anti-transmedicalist tension: how gender-diverse communities engage one another with their differing levels of access, material resources, and societal recognition, and how these asymmetries inform how we relate to one another – and who we wish to shelter with under a mythological trans umbrella.

5 Discussion and conclusions

As is often the case in performances of identity, members of r/Truscum define themselves by what they are not as much as by what they are. And what they are not, in the terms of the community itself, is *trenders* or *tucutes*. As an often-performed and discussed characterological figure (Agha 2007), the non-dysphoric trender stereotype is invoked in a constellation of semiotic processes related to trans identity and is invoked by forum members to delineate the boundary between supposedly "authentic" and "inauthentic" trans identities. It also acts as a representative for users' fears regarding scarcity of access to medical technologies and social recognition within a legal rights-based framework for trans liberation (Spade 2015). Yet rather than direct their consternation solely the institution itself, users also share their fears of being adequated (Bucholtz & Hall 2005) with trenders in the minds of cis gender subjects who hold the balance of power. And, at least in the context of r/Truscum, the figure of the trender is defined in large part by their "linguistic appropriation" of terminology that is, for transmedicalists, referentially dependent on medical criteria.

In discussing what it means to be transgender and non-binary on r/Truscum, diagnostics are, at least in part, linguistic, and anchored in appeals to a referentialist language ideology (Hill 2008; Silverstein 1979) that rejects an ideology of self-identification (Zimman 2017a). Crowley (2022: 9) describes the ideology of self-identification as the recognition within transgender communities that "as trans people themselves are the ones who best can know and determine their own gender experience, [they] thus are the people who can linguistically name and label this experience." Instead, on r/Truscum, words have fixed meanings and can be used rightly or wrongly, and the correct language usage lies in understanding the referential content of forms themselves. Indeed, a common refrain in the community is that "being trans means something" – so central is this sentiment that it is the slogan for the community, appealing on its homepage banner along with the medical cross superimposed over a gradient color palette suggestive of the trans flag.

Figure 2: r/Truscum homepage banner (www.reddit.com/r/truscum).

Therefore, the right to identify as transgender resides not in the individual, but in the institutions that regulate transgender identities. And incorrect use of linguistic forms – that is to say, identification with transgender identity labels and use of unlicensed trans linguistic practices that defy such institutionally-reified denotations – causes material harm to gender-diverse communities at large.

Normative enforcement and identity-based gatekeeping are highly impactful for trans communities, particularly for transgender and gender-diverse people who either want to access gender-affirming care but who do not align with normative medical expectations (Garrison 2018; Konnelly 2022), or who have no desire to access gender-affirming care at all. To this end, much of the discourse circulating in r/Truscum and similar spaces is certainly worthy of challenge and invites nuance. It also raises the question as to why community members might choose to align themselves so strongly with a system when it is, by their own descriptions, failing them. It is worth noting that the narratives on r/Truscum are often presented in the context of users' own experience of harm in the medical system, and the community anxieties teased out by critical discourse analysis suggest that identity-based boundary-making is closely linked to institutional constraints on transgender and non-binary expression; and in fact, it could be argued that the medical model that transmedicalists so vehemently subscribe to is actually the origin of the same precarity of access that they fear.

r/Truscum is a complex domain that defies a homogenous categorization: it is both a space of mutual support and solidarity for its members, while also strongly delimiting the boundaries of membership, vehemently (and at times, derisively) disaligning from those deemed to be outside of them. It is also, therefore, exemplary of the fractal recursivity (Irvine & Gal 2000) that exists between normativities within communities of practice. As first proposed by Hall, Levon, and Milani (2019) in their *Language and Society* special issue on normativities, rather than a singular universal normativity that is oriented to by all individuals, there exist multiple intersecting normativities that are relevant for different subsets of individuals "each with their own relevant social epistemologies" (Calder 2020, 45). Fractal recursivity involves "the projection of an opposition" (Irvine & Gal 2000, 38) from one level to another, often through the practice of defining the self against an imagined Other. In the case of r/Truscum, the projection of linguistic difference is projected onto category membership, whereby inauthentic trans subjects are associated with certain linguistic practices (and vice versa). It is precisely this fractal recursivity that enables users to construct r/Truscum as subversive in relation to the "mainstream" transgender community, despite their alignment with a transnormative medical model of trans identity.

However, it is important to not only consider these conversations in terms of their discursive moves, but also their material effects. In the case of r/Truscum, it is necessary to understand *why* resistance to linguistic self-determination arose in the time and place that it has, and how this is inseparable from the broader context of trans necropolitics (Mbembe 2019; Puar 2007; Snorton & Haritaworn

2013). As analysts, it can be tempting to level the 'doing' of normativity as a charge against individuals, sometimes even in judgement. Yet describing something as simply "normativity" or as "language ideology" would itself be insufficient, as neither constitute analyses in their own. The process of documenting and interrogating the practice of normative moves must also entail diving deeply to understand where the systemic is operating through the individual (or, from another vantage point, how the individual works to enact the systemic), and how these individual moves are constituted in collective identifications and the invocation of cultural scripts, particularly within marginalized communities.

Medically-based, normative understandings of sex and gender place undue restrictions on the autonomy of many (if not all) transgender and non-binary people, and the effects of these medicalized narratives are diffused throughout institutions (Johnson 2015; Vipond 2015). As visibility for transgender communities in public space and public policy continues to grow, many anti-transgender advocates have claimed that the increased number of openly transgender people – especially youth and young adults – is grounds for scepticism or even outright denial. Rather than attribute the expansion of transgender communities to sociocultural shifts that have made it more possible for many trans people to come out (including linguistic innovation that has provided many with the means to describe their identities in ways that may not have previously been possible or accessible), gender diversity has been characterized as a social contagion whose spread must be slowed or stopped altogether. Particularly in the US where much of Reddit's userbase is located, an overwhelming response to increasing transgender visibility has been to erode rights and protections for gender-variant people. In many ways, users of r/Truscum rigorously evoke the limitations of visibility: as observed by Ciszek, Haven & Logan (2021), we must take note of "gaps that strategies of visibility leave unfilled, drawing attention to symbolic and material resources that are needed for generating effective change," and that visibility-based strategies to social inclusion "can be instrumental in producing an inequitable distribution of power and exacerbating the burden of representation that complicates transgender communicators' ability to navigate organizational politics." Through their metalinguistic identificatory moves, r/Truscum users highlight some of the many ways that visibility alone is insufficient for trans communities and thrive; at the very least, it is not the resource in shortest supply. With visibility also comes surveillance – not just from the cisgender gaze, but from each other as well.

Transgender identity on r/Truscum is defined primarily in its relation to medical criteria – specifically the presence of acute gender dysphoria. However, an experience of dysphoria (at least as it is outlined in medical texts) does not resonate with all transgender and non-binary people. Some orient to *euphoria* instead, eschewing medical authority and understanding changes in embodiment and social recognition as moving towards joy and ease rather than away from discomfort or distress. Others consider their relationship to their gender identity to be fluid, not distillable to a medicalized narrative. And regardless, an experience of dysphoria does not necessarily entail a desire for medical transition. In an essay entitled *Have we got it wrong on dysphoria?*, Abigail Thorn (2022) muses on whether intra-community boundary-making through the lens of dysphoria can be attributed to different epistemological relationships to dysphoric affects:

> The philosopher Gilbert Ryle tells a story about a man who goes to Oxford and sees the colleges and the students and the library and then asks, "Yes but where is the university? You must show me that!" He has made what philosophers call a category error – he thinks "the university" is some extra thing, but it's just a word for the things he's seen already.
>
> In the years of denial before I realized I was trans I often thought, "I am jealous of women, especially trans women. I wish I had features X, Y, and Z, and I am sad that I do not, so sad that I often wish I was dead. But I do not have dysphoria." In hindsight this was a category error: those feelings – jealousy, sadness, wishing – were 'dysphoria.'
>
> [. . .] What is it about these feelings that makes them different when a trans person feels them? What is it about these medical interventions that makes them different when a trans person needs them? Most importantly, why are those treatments so much harder to get for trans people? (n.p.)

It may very well be that the transmedicalist and anti-transmedicalist dispute is less about presence vs. absence of dysphoria, and much more to do with how dysphoria itself is understood and experienced. r/Truscum users disalign from those they deem to be *trenders* and *tucutes* who identify as transgender or pursue medical transition without dysphoria – but rather than an absence of dysphoria, it would appear that anti-transmedicalists simply do not share transmedicalists' definition of it, or do not understand their identities quite as centrally in terms of moving away from dysphoric suffering. In short, for many, *transgender* and other related gender identity labels no longer carry inherent connotations of dysphoria or desire for medical intervention – but amidst the generative and shifting landscape of linguistic innovation and advocacy within gender-diverse communities, many are revisiting age-old and at times uncomfortable questions. What does it mean to be transgender or non-binary? Who, if anyone, has the authority to define what's in a term? And why does it matter?

Though analytical attention to linguistic self-determination within transgender communities has generally assumed a cisgender-transgender binary, the analysis presented in this chapter serves as a reminder that transgender communities are not homogenous, and they are not inherently subversive in their linguistic practices; they can resist language change, even social change. As the discursive tools necessary to access medical settings have become salient and circulated throughout gender-diverse communities themselves, so too has the evaluative component, whereby transgender and non-binary people themselves metalinguistically evaluate each others' language (and identities) for legitimacy. However, positions may also arise from experiences of profound vulnerability and institutional harm. While critical considerations of intra-community linguistic ideologies is necessary and important, instances where transgender and non-binary people are themselves engaged in acts of prescription also highlight the diversity of tactics that arise in cissexist conditions that demand conformity and legibility, and, to which gender-diverse people of different social positions and variable levels of financial and material access differentially respond. Nevertheless, it also indicates that access to care and recognition of the complexity of transgender and non-binary personhood must continue to grow and become more expansive, not less.

References

Abe, Hideko. 2019. Indexicality of grammar: The case of Japanese transgender speakers. In Kira Hall & Rusty Barrett (eds.), *The Oxford Handbook of Language and Sexuality*. Oxford: Oxford University Press.

Agha, Asif. 2007. *Language and social relations*. Cambridge: Cambridge University Press.

America Civil Liberties Union. 2022. Doe v. Abbott. Accessed at https://www.aclu.org/cases/doe-v-abbott.

American Psychiatric Association. 2013. *Diagnostic and Statistical Manual of Mental Disorders: Diagnostic and Statistical Manual of Mental Disorders* (5th edn.). Arlington, VA: American Psychiatric Association.

Beemyn, Genny & Susan Rankin. 2011. *The Lives of Transgender People*. New York: Columbia University Press.

Benjamin, Harry. 1966 *The Transsexual Phenomenon*. Ann Arbor: Julian Press.

Blei, David M., Andrew Y. Ng & Michael I. Jordan. 2003. Latent Dirichlet Allocation. *Journal of Machine Learning Research* 3. 993–1022.

Bornstein, Kate. 1995. *Gender Outlaw: On Men, Women, and the Rest of Us*. New York: Routledge.

Bornstein, Kate. 1998. *My Gender Workbook*. New York: Routledge.

Bornstein, Kate & S. Bear Bergman. 2010. *Gender Outlaws: The Next Generation*. New York: Seal Press.

Bucholtz, Mary and Hall, Kira. 2005. Identity and interaction: a sociocultural linguistic approach. *Discourse Studies* 7(4–5): 585–614.

Calder, Jeremy. 2020. Language, gender and sexuality in 2019: interrogating normativities in the field. *Gender and Language* 14(4). 429–454.

Cavanaugh, Timothy, Ruben Hopwood & Cei Lambert. 2016. Informed Consent in the Medical Care of Transgender and Gender-Nonconforming Patients. *American Medical Association Journal of Ethics*. Accessed at https://journalofethics.ama-assn.org/article/informed-consent-medical-care-transgender-and-gender-nonconforming-patients/2016-11.

Ciszek, Erica, Paxton Haven & Nneka Logan. 2021. Amplification and the limits of visibility: Complicating strategies of trans voice and representations on social media. *New Media & Society*. 1–21.

Connell, Catherine. 2010. Doing, Undoing, or Redoing Gender? Learning from the Workplace Experiences of Transpeople. *Gender and Society* 24(1). 31–55.

Crowley, Archie. 2022. Language ideologies and legitimacy among nonbinary YouTubers. *Journal of Language and Sexuality* 11(2). 165–189.

Dame, Avery P. 2013. "I'm your hero? Like me?": the role of 'expert' in the trans male vlog. *Journal of Language and Sexuality* 2(1). 40–69.

Fairclough, Norman. 1989. *Language and Power*. London: Longman.

Fairclough, Norman. 2013. *Critical Discourse Analysis: The Critical Study of Language*. New York: Routledge.

Fink, Marty & Quinn Miller. 2014. Trans media moments: Tumblr, 2011–2013. *Television & New Media*, 15(7). 611–626.

Gadanidis, Tim. 2021. *Nard: A data downloader for Reddit*. Retrieved from https://gitlab.com/gadanidis/nard.

Garrison, Spencer. 2018. On the limits of 'trans enough': authenticating trans identity narratives. *Gender & Society* 32(5). 613–637.

Gratton, Chantal. 2016. Resisting the gender binary: The use of (ING) in the construction of non-binary transgender identities. *University of Pennsylvania Working Papers in Linguistics* 22 (2). Article 7. https://repository.upenn.edu/pwpl/vol22/iss2/7.

Haimson, Oliver, Avery Dame-Griff, Elias Capello & Zahari Richter. 2019. Tumblr was a trans technology: the meaning, importance, history, and future of trans technologies. *Feminist Media Studies* 21(3). 345–361.

Hall, Kira, Erez Levon & Tommaso Milani. 2019. Navigating normativities: gender and sexuality in text and talk. *Language in Society* 48(4). 481–489.

Hill, Jane H. 2008. *The Everyday Language of White Racism*. Hoboken: Wiley-Blackwell. Informed Consent for Access to Trans Health. n.d. *Informed Consent for Access to Trans Health*. Accessed at http://www.icath.org.

Irvine, Judith & Susan Gal. 2000. Language ideology and linguistic differentiation. In Paul V. Kroskrity (ed.), *Regimes of Language: Ideologies, Polities, and Identities*. Santa Fe, New Mexico: School of American Research Press.

Jacobsen, Kai, Aaron Devor & Edwin Hodge. 2021. Who Counts as Trans? A Critical Discourse Analysis of Trans Tumblr Posts. *Journal of Communication Inquiry* 46(1). 60–81.

Johnson, Austin H. 2015. Normative accountability: how the medical model influences transgender identities and experiences. *Sociology Compass* 9(9). 803–813.

Johnson, Austin H. 2016. Transnormativity: a new concept and its validation through documentary film about transgender men. *Sociological Inquiry* 86(4). 465–491.

Johnson, Austin H. 2019. Rejecting, Reframing, and Reintroducing: Trans People's Strategic Engagement with the Medicalisation of Gender Dysphoria. *Sociology of Health & Illness* 41 (3).517–32.

King, Brian. 2021. Biopolitics and intersex human rights: a role for applied linguistics. In Christian Chun (ed.), *Applied Linguistics and Politics*. London: Bloomsbury.

Konnelly, Lex. 2021a. Nuance and normativity in trans linguistic research. *Journal of Language and Sexuality* 10(1). 71–82.

Konnelly, Lex. 2021b. Both, and: Transmedicalism and resistance in non-binary narratives of gender-affirming care. *Toronto Working Papers in Linguistics* 4(1). 1–15.

Konnelly, Lex. 2022. Transmedicalism and "trans enough": linguistic strategies in talk about gender dysphoria. *Gender and Language* 16(1). 1–25.

Markbreiter, Charlie. 2022. "Other Trans People Make Me Dysphoric": Trans Assimilation and Cringe. *The New Inquiry*. Accessed at https://thenewinquiry.com/cringe/.

Mbembe, Achille. 2019. *Necropolitics*. Durham: Duke University Press.

miles-hercules, deandre. 2020. "A Way to Lift Each Other Up": Blackfemme-ininities and the Materiality of Discourse. Santa Barbara: University of California Santa Barbara thesis.

Miller, Jordan F. 2019. YouTube as a Site of Counternarratives to Transnormativity. *Journal of Homosexuality* 66(6). 815–37.

McConnell-Ginet, Sally. 2018. Semantics and pragmatics: Blurring boundaries and constructing contexts. In Kira Hall & Rusty Barrett (eds.), *The Oxford Handbook of Language and Sexuality*. Oxford: Oxford University Press.

MOGAI Wiki. 2022. *MOGAI*. Retrieved from https://mogai.miraheze.org/wiki/MOGAI.

Page, Morgan M. [@morganmpage]. 2020. *This seems like a good time to remind people of the rule I gave myself a few years ago that has really helped me immensely: I do not shit-talk other trans people in public - if I truly have a problem that must be addressed, I speak to them directly*. Twitter. Accessed at https://twitter.com/morganmpage/status/1212852732652077058.

Puar, Jasbir. 2007. *Terrorist Assemblages: Homonationalism in Queer Times*. Durham: Duke University Press.

QSR International Software. 2018. NVivo 12 for Mac. Burlington: QSR International.

Schulz, Sarah L. 2017. The Informed Consent Model of Transgender Care: An Alternative to the Diagnosis of Gender Dysphoria. *Journal of Humanistic Psychology* 58(1). 72–92.

Silverstein, Michael. 1979. Language structure and linguistic ideology. In Paul Clyne, William F. Hanks & Carol L. Hofbauer (eds.), *The elements: A parasession on linguistic units and levels*. Chicago: Chicago Linguistic Society.

Snorton, C. Riley & Haritaworn, Jin. 2013. Trans Necropolitics: A Transnational Reflection on Violence, Death, and the Trans of Color Afterlife. In Aren Aizura & Susan Stryker (eds.), *The Trans Studies Reader 2*. New York: Routledge.

Spade, Dean. 2015. *Normal Life: Administrative Violence, Critical Trans Politics, and the Limits of Law*. Charlotte: Duke University Press.

Spanos, Cassandra, Julian A. Grace, Shalem Y. Leemaqz, Adam Brownhill, Pauline Cundill, Peter Locke, Peggy Wong, Jeffrey D. Zajac & Ada S. Cheung. 2021. The Informed Consent Model of Care for Accessing Gender-Affirming Hormone Therapy Is Associated with High Patient Satisfaction. *The Journal of Sexual Medicine* 18(1). 201–208.

Stanley, Eric A. 2014. Gender self-determination. *TSQ: Transgender Studies Quarterly* 1(1–2). 89–91.

Stryker, Susan. 1998. The Transgender Issue: An Introduction. *GLQ: A Journal of Lesbian and Gay Studies* 4(2). 145–58.

Sutherland, David Kyle. 2021. "Trans Enough": Examining the Boundaries of Transgender-Identity Membership. *Social Problems*. 1–16.

Thorn, Abigail. 2022. Have we got it wrong on dysphoria? *Trans Writes*. Accessed at https://transwrites.world/have-we-got-it-wrong-on-dysphoria-abigail-thorn-discusses-trans-healthcare/.

Vaid-Menon, Alok. 2020. *Beyond the Gender Binary*. New York: Penguin Workshop.

Vincent, Ben. 2020. *Non-Binary Genders: Navigating Communities, Identities, and Healthcare*. Bristol: Bristol University Press.

Vipond, Evan. 2015. Trans rights will not protect us: the limits of equal rights discourse, antidiscrimination laws, and hate crime legislation. *Western Journal of Legal Studies* 6(1). 1–20.

Whittle, Stephen. 1998. The Trans-Cyberian Mail Way. *Social & Legal Studies* 7. 389–408.
World Health Organization. 2019. *International statistical classification of diseases and related health problems* (11th edn.). Accessed at https://icd.who.int/.
World Professional Association for Transgender Health. 2012. *Standards of Care for the Health of Transsexual, Transgender, and Gender Nonconforming People* (7th edn.). Accessed at https://www.wpath.org/publications/soc.
Zimman, Lal. 2017a. Trans people's linguistic self-determination and the dialogic nature of identity. In Evan Hazenberg & Miriam Meyerhoff (eds.), *(Re)Presenting Trans: Linguistic, Legal, and Everyday Perspectives*. Wellington, New Zealand: Victoria University Press.
Zimman, Lal. 2017b. Transgender language reform: some challenges and strategies for promoting trans-affirming, gender-inclusive language. *Journal of Language and Discrimination* 1(1). 84–105.
Zimman, Lal. 2018. Pronouns and Possibilities: Transgender Language Activism and Reform. In Netta Avineri, Laura R. Graham, Eric J. Johnson, Robin Conley Riner & Jonathan Rosa (eds.), *Language and Social Justice in Practice*. New York: Routledge.
Zimman, Lal. 2020. Transgender language, transgender moment: toward a trans linguistics. In Kira Hall & Rusty Barrett (eds.), *The Oxford Handbook of Language and Sexuality*. Oxford: Oxford University Press.
Zimman, Lal. 2021. Beyond the cis gays' cis gaze: the need for a trans linguistics. *Gender and Language* 15(3). 423–429.
Zimman, Lal & Will Hayworth. 2020a. How we got here: Short-scale change in identity labels for trans, cis, and non-binary people in the 2000s. *Proceedings of the Linguistic Society of America* 5 (1). 499–513.
Zimman, Lal & Will Hayworth. 2020b. Lexical change as sociopolitical change in talk about trans and cis identity labels: New methods for the corpus analysis of internet data. *University of Pennsylvania Working Papers in Linguistics* 25 (2).Article 17. https://repository.upenn.edu/pwpl/vol25/iss2/17.

Institution

William Leap
Queer language before
Linguistics research, assessments of fitness for military service, and the allure of Eugenics

1 Introduction

This chapter addresses the discussions of language, gender and sexuality *before* the recent fluorescence of inquiry associated with lavender language studies, queer linguistics, trans linguistics as well as critical sexuality studies.[1] I use the term *recent* deliberately here, paralleling the temporal referencing in Umbal and Takhtaganova remarks:

> In *recent* years, we have seen *a paradigm shift* in the scholarship of language, gender, and sexuality. Greater recognition of gender diversity has challenged traditional models of gender identity that assumed static and binary categories. . . . *Recent* work has provided theoretical frameworks that engage with the fluidity of gender identities more rigorously. . . . Much of these expansive discussions of gender identity have taken place *in the last decade* (e.g., 2010–2020) (Umbal & Takhtaganova 2022, 2, emphasis WLL)

Umbal and Takhtaganova's remarks imply that *recent work* is somehow different from what *work before,* in that *work before* oriented around ". . . traditional models of gender identity that assumed static and binary categories". This chapter shows that in some instances linguistic research aligned with ". . . models . . ., identities and categories" supporting agendas for societal improvement advocated by Eugenics and Social Darwinist movements. In fact, this paper will show, studies of language and homosexuality *before* influenced homosexual men's admissions to the U.S. Armed Forces during World War II Military during subjects in public settings like the Armed Forces, though not with the impacts that we might initially expect.

---

[1] My thanks to David Peterson (U Nebraska-Omaha, for support and critical reading throughout the development of this paper.

William Leap, Florida Atlantic University

https://doi.org/10.1515/9783110742510-009

2 Background: A project based in queer historical linguistics

This chapter's inquiry is part of a larger project exploring language, gender diversity and transgressive sexuality in U.S. locations during the years preceding the late June 1969 "riot" at Manhattan's Stonewall Inn. According to academic and popular U.S. discourse, the events at Stonewall marked the point in time when gay politics and culture, language included, came *out of the closets and into the streets* (Stein 2019; Duberman 1993). The goal of this larger project is to specify what language before Stonewall actually entailed.

As in the larger project, this chapter follows the orientation of a Queer Historical Linguistics (Leap 2020b, and hereafter QHL). At base, QHL refuses to accept self-serving assumptions (e.g., what is" good, . . . right . . . and true" Althusser 1971, 164, 172) about the temporal significance of language, gender and sexuality, or how gendered or sexual language ". . . reveals itself as itself through time (adapting Edelman 2004, 4). Instead, QHL addresses the connections between language, gender and sexuality within specific settings, contexts or *moments* in history.

Such inquiry requires multiple sources of data, assembled into an *archive* through the use of a *scavenger methodology* (Halberstam 1998; Leap 2020, 48–53), along with systematic attention to multiple discursive and textual practices and the social and historical inflections of those practices as displayed within the archive displays. The inquiry also addresses the linguistic and social ideological premises shaping (and sometimes shaped by) those language-related practices and their inflections. Sometimes the inquiry takes shape systematically. Sometimes the inquiry depends on "luck and chance, . . . [on] reading against the grain . . . [on] following your gut and reading creatively "(Tinsley, in Cervini 2022), or through some combination of both options.

Sometimes, too, a QHL project locates previously undisclosed descriptions of language use and evidence of a previously undisclosed language researchers. These discoveries bring into the foreground understandings of linguistic and social experience that haunt the margins and shadows of what is known about *before*. Here, as elsewhere, QHL disrupts understandings of language, gender and sexuality that ignores evidence of alternative voices and that theorize history solely in terms of homogeneous, inflexible formations.

2.1 Two depictions of *language before*: Rosanoff (1927) and Legman (1941)

Rosanoff (1927) and Legman (1941) are two often-cited discussions of language, gender diversity, and transgressive sexuality before. A careful reading of each paper, paying attention to information on language use(s) and language user(s) that each researcher's commentary provides confirms that language use related to homosexuality was refracted and reflected against social diversities, and not tied to a single gendered/sexual binary.

2.1.1 Rosanoff (1927)

Rosanoff's (1927, 202–204) remarks about the "special slang expressions of the (male) homosexual" are often cited because of what appear at first reading to be references to a "secret code" (Katz 1983, 438–440; Cameron & Kulick 2003, 79). Rosanoff's comments indicate that these special slang expressions are used by men, not women; homosexual is a male-bodied reference in this discussion. As further reading shows that "secret code" is only one of many observations about language *before* presented in Rosanoff's discussion. Rosanoff's references to "special" expressions of the "secret code" is not an appeal to linear historical narrative, e.g., what was "secret" before will become "more accessible, more public" in some recent time. And to read Rosanoff's paper in such developmental terms distracts attention from a more significant portion of his argument.

For example, Rosanoff insists that the "special slang expressions of the (male) homosexual" (1927, 202) are not a single formation but are further inflected along the line set by the "considerable social discrimination" (1927, 203) within the group. He contrasts those male homosexuals who do no cruising with those who solicit strangers in the manner of a prostitute (1927, 203). Given the time frame (1920's) of his commentary, this contrast could be a statement about class differences, a reference distinguishing the language use of conventional from cross-dressing homosexual subjects, or even a misleading inclusion of MTF trans subjects under the category male homosexual. However, explained, those who use the "special slang expressions" are not a single category, even though Rosanoff refers to them with inclusive terms like "clannish" and as "elite". So "special slang usage" marks privileged status, but privileged status is not expressed uniformly.

And these non-uniformities are indicated once Rosanoff's wordlist (1927, 203) is compared to the entries in Legman's "Glossary of Homosexual slang" (1941, discussed below) and other sources indexing non-standard English usage from the early 20th century (Irwin 1931). These comparisons show that Rosanoff's list shares similarities with the language use of sex workers, with the slang of male prison inmates, with vernacular usage of hobos and tramps, as well as with derogatory usage which mainstream US associated with foreigners – including phrases that identified members of the German Alliance during World War I. Apparently, the "special slang expressions" contain expressions drawn from outside of the "elite" domain and likely to be recognized and understood by outsiders. Such features are *not* evidence of the gnostic usage characteristic of a secret code.

But these features are evidence that the homosexual elites who used these special slang formations were not uniformly clannish. Some elites interacted with outsiders – including with the *Fairies* in the less elegant, entertainment venues within the Bowery (Chauncey 1994) or with others who ". . . will and do opt to live outside of reproductive and familial time as well as on the edges of logics of labor and production . . . .and [often] outside of the logic of capital accumulation" (Halberstam 2005, 10). Some frequented the roadhouses on the outside of town, or the more elegant, naughty places like the Parisian venues in Paris associated with courtesans and the can-can during the French Belle-Époque. Some elites avoided all such interactions, although, by Rosanoff language data, they interacted with those who did explore the demimonde in all of these forms.

Rosanoff is not referring to a vernacular language use related to gender diversity and transgressive sexuality. Yet as his word list indicates, the language users that Rosanoff described had enough interaction with vernacular language (s) and their users to allow them to accumulate vernacular expressions into privileged discourse. Rosanoff's discussion leaves us wanting to know more about the vernacular usages (and users) who were the sources for some of these gendered and sexualized references. But what his paper displays argues against reducing his discussion to a monolithic claim about secrecy (Cameron & Kulick 2003, 79).

2.1.2 Legman (1941)

Legman's (1941) essay addressing "the language of homosexuality" was another discussion of language, gender diversity and transgressive sexuality that foregrounded connections between language users and privilege as well as language, social diversity and discord.

Legman's essay was one of the Appendixes included in the first edition of the final report on the *Sex Variants Project* (Henry 1941); the essay was deleted from subsequent editions of that report. Legman's essay benefited from his close collaboration with Thomas Painter, who had assembled linguistic data and other materials for a study of gay male prostitution (also never published). With Painter's consent,

Legman expanded Painter's linguistic archive, adding resources from slang dictionaries and other sources documenting the language use of "harassed [subjects within the urban] demimonde" (Davis 2019, 50). The result was a discussion of gay men's esoteric language and related customs and attitudes

> that was so thorough that many decades later, historians [citing Chauncey 1994] would use it as a source on the gay world of the 1930s and 1940s (Davis 2019: 50).

Legman's essay included a 372 entry "Glossary" of relevant words and phrases. to illustrate his observations about language use. A careful reading of the glossary shows that the "language of homosexuality" is not a linguistic isolate but connected to multiple sources of linguistic practice. By my tabulation, 15% of the 372 entries in the glossary were associated with the language use of hobos/tramps, criminals, prisoners, (female) prostitutes [sic], sailors, or Negroes [sic]. The remainder of entries in Legman's glossary (85%) had unnamed (or unmarked) social associations, and more than 50% of these entries were widely attested throughout vernacular US English as a whole. So, all told, as many as 65% of Legman's "language of homosexuality" was likely to be familiar to language users who were not specifically of gender diverse or transgressive sexual backgrounds. This group included language users/social subjects from various segments of the demimonde as well as subjects connected to some combination of stable employment, permanent residence, lawful behavior and/or Whiteness.

Once again, the language of homosexuality was not a "secret code", but: embedded within public circulations, and that the language users were in frequent contact with social/sexual subjects from diverse locations and backgrounds. Tellingly here, a contrast between backgrounds of privilege and backgrounds where opportunities and resources were less accessible once again was reflected in language use and meanings.

As Davis indicates (2019, 50, footnote 69), one helpful source for clarifying the profiles of diverse language use presented in Legman's glossary is Chauncey's Gay New York (1994). Here Chauncey describes the privileged, same-sex desiring, male subjects (the "queers") in 1930's Manhattan who moved between protected sites of residence and employment uptown and the less restrictive, gender-diverse, sexually transgressive venues in the Bowery.

Chauncey's discussions of language and mobility highlighted the connections between language, gender, sexuality, and concealment and disguise. He describes the freedom of movements of privileged subjects, whatever their gendered or sexual details, adding that once these privileged subjects found (or could claim) seclusion, the acts of *passing* that enabled concealment and disguise in public settings, were often suspended.

But Harlem Renaissance authors like Hughes, McKay, Thurman, Larsen, and Nugent saw the movements of downtowners to and from Harlem's Cotton Club and other main street venues as part of a larger spatial/racial dynamic that included the movement of Harlem residents from uptown to white-dominated social locations downtown (Hughes 1941a; Larsen 1926; Nugent 1926), and the movement of downtowners and Harlem residents between Harlem's main street and back street domains (the speak-easies, the buffet-flats, the rent parties) (McKay 1928; Hughes 1941c). In Hughes's understanding of these movements, Harlem residents were being squeezed out of familiar venues

> {with] all those white folks in the speakeasies and nightclubs, maybe a colored man could find some place to have a drink that the tourists hadn't yet discovered . . . (Hughes 1940c, 228–229)

and that made it a good idea to create

> a get-together of your own where you could do the black bottom without some stranger behind you trying to do it, too (Hughes 1940, 229).

It was also a good idea to create a language of your own, which came to be called *Harlemese* (Hurston 1933, 1942; Thurman 1929) and which did *not* underscore the language user's connections with voluntary displacement and mobility or the forms of privilege displayed in Legman's glossary. By its absence in a subject's language use, Harlemese indicated those whose lived experiences were indebted to those connections.

To illustrate with an anecdote from Van Vechten (1926): Byron, a middle-class Harlem resident, a would-be author, formerly unemployed, has finally found work as an elevator operator in mid-town Manhattan, His co-workers are also Harlem residents, but are from less affluent, less privileged, and Harlem- vernacular backgrounds. Asked by his Harlem friends about his first day on the job, Byron explains that he can "put up with" his coworkers even if they seem to be very different from him. Then he adds:

> . . . but they seem to think I am putting on airs. My clothes or my English are too good. One of them called me an *arnchy* (Van Vechten 1926, 194).

The Harlemese term a*rnchy* indicates a subject displaying elitist pretensions that are inappropriate within the given setting; arnchy also identifies a cis-gendered masculine subject, with cis-gendered, masculinist pretensions, as well. There are no instances of *arnchy* used in reference to an effeminate or same-sex-desiring Harlem resident in my Harlemese archive. So, the co-worker's remark affirms two types of normativity: a subject's hetero-masculine ties and his hyper-elitist privilege.

By those criteria, Legman's glossary is *arnchy*. And to extend support of that point, compared to its rich attestations of men's vocabulary, Legman's glossary includes few terms referring to women or used exclusively by them. All of those terms are specifically marked in the glossary as women's usage; men's-related usage is left unmarked throughout the glossary.

Legman's comments about women's terms are limited (1941, 1155–1156). Usually, his comments simply reiterate his belief that women's language use is incompatible with a language of sexuality: just as women's same-sex attractions are usually more emotional than physical in basis, so women do not express their sexuality in verbal terms. Even when women pursue homosexually-explicit communication, their messaging is unlikely to be audible to others or even to be noticed by them, he argued. Accepting on face value women's dependence on emotional/affective communication, Legman concluded that women's "discourse" of homosexuality had little to contribute to a discussion of the language of homosexuality, an argument that also excluded gender diverse, sexually transgressive female bodied subjects from the subjects associated with the language of homosexuality in Legman's depiction.

3 Language, homosexuality and the admission to U.S. military service during World War II

Contrary to the wording of the essay's title, Legman's "language of homosexuality" is really concerned with approximately 35% of the entries included in his archive. As already explained, 15% of the entries being associated with various forms of vernacular speech, and 50% of the remaining entries being words and phrases that could appear in the language use of any speaker of U.S. English, regardless of topic or speaker socioeconomic background. This limitation, like the instances of derogatory audience reception cited by Van Vechten, underscores the "special status" of the language use in question here; Rosanoff said as much when describing the language use of interest to his essay. As noted, women's language of homosexuality, and other vernacular usages related to homosexual reference(s) are also excluded from these discussions by this argument.

Dynes' (2007) recollections of language before Stonewall as something that "outsiders" found to be a "sealed book" echoes the same position that limits between a homosexuality-related language use to privileged experiences. As Dynes explains. ". . . [t]he argot used by homosexuals fifty years ago, (e.g., in the 1950s) was pretty much a "secret language" and

> [a]s I well recall, those of us in the know could even use the word "gay" without outsiders catching on. If by chance they did suspect, one could always cover oneself by simply saying that they misunderstood. A "gay person" was light-hearted and fun-loving – that was all there was to it [. . .] (Dynes 2007)

"Privilege" here is expressed as gnostic knowledge: things that a select few understand, and the remaining subject s do not, and cannot, comprehend. Privilege becomes a moral judgement, similar to that indicated in Rosanoff's depiction of the "considerable social discrimination" setting the sexual subject in question apart from "others".

This depiction of language, homosexuality and privilege leaves open for discussion what connections may link language and homosexuality for subjects lying outside of privileged social domains. This openness coincides with the understanding of language and homosexuality that helped inform the criteria determining whether same-sex desiring U.S. men called up for military service during World War II were eligible to begin a period of active duty within the US military.

The official government policy stated that confirmed homosexuals were ineligible for admission to military service. So, of the 17 million men who were processed for military admission during World War II, as many as 1.7 – 2.8 million men should have been turned away by local induction centers because of their homosexuality. (These estimates follow popular assumptions that homosexual men always constitute from 10% to 6% of a given male population.) But military sources report that induction centers rejected many fewer candidates; some sources say as few as 5,000. Even though military policy demanded the categorical rejection of homosexual candidates, the lower number of actual rejections reflect the induction center assumptions that homosexual candidates would display their homosexuality through embodiment, vestment, social interaction and language use. If necessary, an in-depth psychiatric interview could prompt the candidate to reveal those displays (Look magazine).

The schedule of activities at the induction center was always tightly compressed, given the number of men who had to be evaluated each day. Ultimately, the schedule allowed for three minutes for purposes of psychiatric evaluation, forcing the psychiatrist to base his evaluation of each candidate for induction on brief impressions during initial encounter. As the military classification officer explained to Don Vining (playwright, editor and social critic) when finalizing Vining's induction center status, if a candidate for service is to be denied admission to the military because of his homosexuality,

> there should be more outward signs, that psycho-neurosis should accompany . . . (cited in Vining 1979: 442)

The problem was, outward signs did not always identifiable to US Military medical staff, as a chief medical officer, assigned to a military hospital unit housing arrested homosexual soldiers awaiting dishonorable discharge from the service, once remarked to his medical ensign. The medical office could not understand how homosexual soldiers newly arrived at the hospital unit could distinguish so easily the homosexual patients from the patients on the ward for other psychiatric reasons. To the medical officer, the homosexual patients displayed no special features; all the patients on the unit, regardless of gender or sexuality, looked and acted in similar ways. Unlike the medical officer, the ensign was same-sex desiring. And unlike the medical officer, the ensign recognized many "outward signs" distinguishing homosexual soldiers from the other patients, starting with language use (Garretts 1980).

Faced with such reports (though probably not always with the comments like the ensign's) military researchers realized that the military needed discovery procedures that would enable induction center examiners to identify these "outward signs" and thereby determine eligibility for military service more efficiently. Gioscia (1950) proposed in the 1940's testing the extent of a candidate's control over his gag-reflex, assuming that a candidate with homoerotic oral experience would have developed greater control over the throat muscles than would a heteroerotically inclined candidate. Other researchers suggested that the homosexual candidate's enjoyment of anal intercourse would stretch and distort the shape and appearance of the rectal opening; if the candidate's physical examination revealed evidence of a patulous (extended) rectum, that evidence would likely mark the candidate as homoerotically and thereby homosexually inclined. Unless the candidate's psychiatric examination provided evidence to the contrary, the candidate would likely be deemed ineligible for service.

Some researchers proposed organizing a list of vocabulary word frequently found in homosexual speech and using the list to monitor each candidate's language use during the psychiatric interview. If enough such entries appear in the candidate's language use, familiarity with the language of homosexuality can be assumed (Due & Wright 1945; Greenspan & Campbell 1945; Loeser 1945).

Importantly, the U.S. military funded Gioscia's gag-reflex study, and also funded language/homosexuality related studies like the ones just listed. And the U.S. military made available to the researchers' subjects to be used as sources for data-gathering: enlisted men who had been admitted to service and subsequently arrested for committing homosexual acts, court-martialed, and now confined to military hospital wards awaiting formal discharge from service.

The Military administration was surely aware of these intended explorations of language and homosexuality. Indeed, reports on these projects' findings circulated within the Military apparatus well before the results appeared in the academic journals. Even so, there is no evidence that any of the language- related findings or recommendations for psychiatric evaluation which these studies produced were incorporated into induction center assessment policies or practices. Instead, just as was the case for the academic linguistic descriptions, Military funded research on language and homosexuality did not produce information deemed relevant to the induction center evaluations of the ". . . outward signs, that psycho-neurosis should accompany . . .".

Interesting to report here, the psychiatric evaluations were to include a language component in their initial formation (Sullivan 1941, 269–271, 274; Binger 1944), but that inquiry was not systematically maintained, because of time restrictions imposed on the interview (initially 12 minutes, ultimately 3 minutes), or other reasons. Hence, as the following anecdotes suggest, examiners reacted differently when candidates displayed homosexual-related messaging during the psychiatric interviews, in some cases (similar to Garrett's anecdote above) showing no understanding (or no interest) of the gender/sexual implications of linguistic practice, in some cases reacting with greater contrast.

First, there is the story of a candidate for induction who wanted to join the army and avenge the death of his cousin, who had been killed in battle the year before. He had prepared carefully word answers to ensure he would successfully dodge questions about his sexuality when he had asked them. But all the examiner asked was 'Do you like girls?" He responded, "yes", because he *liked* girls even though his erotic interests lay elsewhere.

The examiner accepted this one-word response and cleared him for military service induction, ignoring (as the inductee later explained to Bérubé) ". . . my partially bleached, curly platinum blond, my walk, maybe the sissy *S* in my voice – all the things I thought would give me away?'" (adapted from Bérubé 1990, 8).

Then there is the story of a candidate for induction who entered the psychiatrist's office also carefully maintaining a conservative demeanor, only to find a medical officer dressed in full uniform, but (as he later told Bérubé) ". . . a screaming belle – lots of gold braid, but he was a queen if ever I saw one". The officer asked the candidate several personal questions ending with "Did you ever have any homosexual experiences?" The inductee looked the officer in the face and said, "No!" The officer stared right back and said with equal force, "That's good! –" the two of us lying through our teeth", the inductee remembered, with a big smile. (adapted from Bérubé 1990, 24).

But there was also the Induction Center experience of a young man who had moved to Manhattan from Tennessee and found work at a department store just before he was called up for military service (cited in Loughery 1941). He was eager to join the military because, like many American men, he wanted to fulfill his patriot duty. However, his thin and somewhat effeminized demeanor suggested to the physical examination staff that he did not sufficient stamina to withstand the conditions of combat. Complicating the physical assessment, the young man replied: "Why, I like everybody!", when the psychiatrist asked, "who do you like better, boys or girls?". He answered other questions with gendered/sexualized subtext using equally inclusive references.

At the end of that exchange, the examiner brought in a colleague to confirm that the young man ". . . was as cute as [the original examiner] said he was". The candidate remembered being puzzled by that comment but said nothing. The two spoke briefly, then the psychiatrist suggested to the candidate that he forego his hopes for enlistment and accept their offer of an honorable military discharge. After initial objection, he agreed to return to civilian life, although he never understood why he was refused admission to the service.

Thinking now about these anecdotes – the men ready for discharge in the hospital ward whose gay display puzzled the medical officer, the candidate admitted to service despite his platinum blond hair and lisp, the gay candidate who "never" had any homosexual experiences, the ephebic young man from Tennessee who "likes everybody": what evaluation criteria do these stories about evaluation share, if evaluations of evidenced homosexuality is not the common theme?

Richard Bruce Nugent, writing about the taboo status assigned to homosexuality in Harlem during the 1920s, helps answer this question. Nugent observed:

> Homosexuality has always been a dirty word. [. . .] but on the other hand, homosexuality, the practice of it, was not a dirty thing. The dirtyness of it was the flaunting of it. And I use "flaunting" advisedly. Because there is a difference between flaunting it and just not trying to keep it hidden. So if one met the amenities of polite society, who's going to question what your impolitenesses were? (Nugent, cited in Wirth 2003, 21, adjusted).

The criteria determining a homosexual candidate's eligibility for military service were constructed in similar terms. A candidate was deemed acceptable for military service if the candidate showed sufficient evidence of conformity and compliance with "the amenities of polite society", or what military discourse described as consenting to the transformation from "civilian life " into "government issue" (or "g.i.") status, and thereby complying with the obligations of being "an expendable human element . . . in the . . . the mass-produced machine of twentieth-century warfare" (Costello 1985, 75). The evidence for the candidate's consent and compliance could be found within the candidate's language use – not regarding just gender or sexuality, but now regarding additional areas of social practice, too.

4 Language, homosexuality, fitness for service, and Eugenics

From the point of view of the language user, linguistic practices that "met the amenities" could include any number of linguistic options,: the language use that Byron's co-workers termed *arnchy* (Van Vechten 1926), linguistic researchers might associate with the "special slang expressions" of the "clannish elite" when they were not talking about sexuality (or when they were!), Dynes "closed book" and its exceptions, language usage that circulated freely throughout the many social locations within the demimonde, or which associated specifically with a single venue, of group, or social practice there, and more.

But from the point of view of Induction Center examiners, the language use that "met the amenities" invoked considerations that were not necessarily addressed in relationships between language, gender and sexuality – or in the studies of language and sexuality *before*. The central concern here was the socio-racial discourses of *Eugenics*. These discourses had been circulating in U.S. setting since the late 19th century and had been reanimated by resentments over the immigration of "undesirables" into the U.S. during the early 20th century and by the racialized themes strengthening U.S. antagonisms against Germany and Eastern Europe (World War I) and Germany and Japan (World War II).

Eugenics assumes that "human beings came in natural races" each with its own evaluative (e.g., good and bad) social and cultural qualities. These qualities were inherited within the race, the same way that eye color, propensity for Diabetes I, and other genetic traits are inherited. Thus, the aim of eugenics was "the betterment of humankind through the purposeful perpetuation of good qualities over bad ones". Thus "the surest way to improve humanity" given this framework was to encourage the proliferation of the racial characteristics considered to be associated with ". . . the very best kind of people" while discouraging the circulation of less favorable racial characteristics and those associated with them (King 2019, 89). Eugenics calls for deliberate interventions into the processes of natural selection (as outlined by Darwin in his *Origins of Species* [1859] which was like a holy text for many Eugenics practitioners), to ensure that the desired improvements in the gene pool may be obtained.

King offers these remarks to explain early interests in building anti-racist arguments within U.S. anthropology and related academic fields, but his remarks also explain the popularity of Eugenics discourse in the early 20th century United States: As we see here, Eugenics offers practical solutions to problems posed by unwanted immigration and its consequences, and also practical solutions to a second, equally pressing concern: the so-called "Negro problem".

The" problem" in this case does not refer to the Negro elites featured prominently in the success stories associated with the emergence of Harlem as an authentically Black Manhattan (Johnson 1930). The "problem" involves the Negro subject who is "ready at any and at all times to do his share in debasing the blood of the white race in America", to quote R.W. Shufeldt (1905), "a noted doctor with the US Army and a prolific author of eugenic treatises" (Ryan 2022). And it is not only the non-elite Negro men who poses *A Menace to American Civilization* (to quote Shufeldt's [1905] book title). Shufeldt insists that Black women regardless of socioeconomic background are menacing because they are eager to have children with white men. Then,

> [. . .], by virtue of the superior intelligence coming from their white fathers, [these children] will command better positions when they grow up than the pure blacks and [. . .] will powerfully further the interests [. . .] of the African population in this country. (Shufeldt 1915, 124)

For the careful reader, Shufeldt shows how Black women's interests in miscegenation poses a challenge not only to white racial purity but also to long-term continuity of white patriarchal-centered power.

Eugenics' social engineering mandates suggest several remedies to counter the Negro problem's threats to the social, moral and biological authority of white purity. Shufeldt favored the following remedies, Ryan reports (2022): involuntary sterilization to criminal penalties imposed on non-white subjects; tighter controls on prostitution (to decrease the likelihood of race-mixing), tighter bans on interracial marriage and heightened medical control over marriage licenses. Interestingly, while Shufeldt's Eugenics perspectives analyzed homosexuality differently from the "Negro problem", his Eugenics based description of homosexuality will still strike a familiar chord here.

Shufeldt agreed that male cross-dressing, "passive pederasty", and other forms of "sexual inversion" (his terms) potentially posed threats to white social, moral and biological primacy (1905, 389). But he described these subjects as "unfortunates, . . . laboring under the disability of a psychic incubus" (1905, 389), not as subjects intent on a racial advancement at the expense of a more inclusive white achievement. So, Shufeldt argued against incarceration, whippings, and death sentences as remedies for the problems that these "unfortunate . . . sexual inverts" posed. (He was fine with these practices, when needed, as remedies for the Negro problem, he allows). Instead, Shufeldt proposed an agenda closely linked to reproductive engineering as his focus for remediation.

For example, perverts and sexual inverts are unlikely to participate in reproductive sexuality. But were they to do so, or if they had already done so, offspring were likely to inherit the parent's genetic defects. Hence Shufeldt wants to see all proposed marriages tightly scrutinized, this time to prevent inappropriate gender/sexualized miscegenation. (1905, 391).

In addition, Shufeldt proposed more effective instruction for all in the "true principles of sexology", where "true principles" include repeated endorsements of white-centered principles of authority. And Schufeldt proposed the passage of national legislation

> [. . .] to protect or render comfortable the more or less harmless class of sexual perverts in the community and [to] build hospitals and asylums for the dangerous ones where they may be cared for, and scientifically treated. (Shufeldt 1905, 391)

Shufeldt's suggested remedies build on a distinction between the "more or less harmless" sexual perverts, who need only support and protection from surrounding society, and "the dangerous ones" who require seclusion, particular care and scientific treatment. This distinction can be traced to Darwin's distinction between "the better classes" and "the reckless . . . inferior members of society" which anchored Darwin's remarks on the social consequences of genetic inequalities in *The Descent of Man* (1881 [1] 77). In other words, the distinction that Shufeldt expresses here is the longstanding Eugenics doctrine, e.g., transgressive gender/sexuality among "the better classes" is more or less the act of the "harmless," whereas, transgressive behaviors among "the reckless . . . inferior members of society" are potentially the acts of the "dangerous."

As we have seen, Shufeldt's distinction between socially privileged/elite and socially less privileged/ vernacular language users appears repeatedly in the descriptions of language and homosexuality *before* as examined earlier in the chapter. And just as Shufeldt's remarks suggested, those discussions foregrounded the "special slang expressions of the homosexual (elites) "while saying little about vernacular references to sexual sameness, (Rosanoff 1927); or discussed a "language of homosexuality" where language users excluded homosexual women as well as multiple categories of homosexual men, (Legman 1941; Dynes 2007) and also Chauncey (1994) where the language of *queers* reveals only a small part of the language of *Fairies*. And moving even further *before*, Peterson's (2003) studies of Whitman's *Leaves of Grass* (1855) reveal multiple reflections on the intersections between (queer) language and working-class sensibilities, however elite and normative Whitman's own written prose may have been. And Peterson's (2022) recent studies of Ellis [1942], 235) reported recurring associations between the linguistic markings of non-normative gender/sexuality and the linguistic indications of racial and class locations in the life story narratives of his female patients with "non-girl attitude" (Ellis's phrasing).

So, we can take note of these parallels between late 19th and early 20th century discussions of gender variant and sexually transgressive language use (and language users) in linguistics, social psychology and related fields, and Eugenics-centered evaluations of more or less favorably socially inflected gendered and sexualized statuses in discussions of social policy and social engineering. And then, we look for spatial or temporal locations *before* where these parallels between academic and social policy interests could have been expressed and then found space for further cultivation.

As described in this paper, the U.S. military Induction Centers would certainly have provided a workable location to that end. At those sites, the staff were expected to determine the suitability of candidates for admission to service during World War II even though (as the anecdotes examined here confirm) staff were provided with minimal criteria in terms of which to make those evaluations: did the candidate meet the amenities of [military] politeness sufficiently to ensure that any impolitenesses need not be put to the question?

In such a setting, Gioscia's gag-reflex test, like the intrusive invasion of genital privacy required to evaluate a candidate's anal protuberance, posed their own violations of politeness. Initial judgements about vestment or embodiment were equally unreliable, because they mixed assessment with stereotype. What worked? A willingness to speak directly to the examiner's question, without reluctance or hesitancy even if the response had little truth value outside of the specific expectations of the social exchange, e.g., the man in Bérubé's anecdote who insisted that he had had *no* homosexual experiences prior to seeking enlistment. His reply earned a "that's good" response from the "screaming belle" who was conducting the psychiatric examination. Both men knew they were lying, but both men also knew that the young man was showing his willingness to be compliant, to follow the rules in the given setting, rather than his desire to act in some socially inappropriate or "inferior" manner. Compliance, not truth, secured the young man's entrance to the military. The young man from Tennessee who insisted that he "loved everybody" and spoke truth-to-power on every occasion given to him, ended up with a free return trip to Manhattan and a voluntary military discharge.

That there was a mutual influencing of academic studies of language, gender variance and transgressive sexuality(s) and Eugenics-based explorations of an elite/compliant and vernacular/disruptive contrasts within language-homosexuality ties is a topic for additional inquiry. I suspect the erasure of women's language for these discussions for so many years can be explained in part in these terms, and so can the refusal to look outside of white male privileged experiences when studying language and homosexuality.

5 And so...

To say that there was queer *language before* is to invite explorations of the many locations of language use, and the many points of view orienting scholars and practitioners to the understanding of language-as-used in these locations. Rather than get side-tracked by debates over whether queerness applies to temporal periods other than our own, we can more productively ask what *if* queer[ness] did apply to the language use described by Rosanoff? or Legman? or Vining? at the World War II Induction centers? And then we might see where in the archive a pursuit of that *what if* formation then leads.

In this case, such a pursuit leads to a language-centered inquiry – queer historical linguistics – that responds to issues raised in one of Somerville's earlier papers on *scientific racism and the emergence of the homosexual body* (1994). Somerville asks in that paper:

> Is it merely a historical coincidence that the classification of bodies as either "homosexual" or "heterosexual" emerged at the same time that the United States was aggressively policing the imaginary boundaries between "black" and "white"? (1994, 25).

And in a related footnote, Somerville quotes David Halperin suggesting that

> all scientific inquiries into the aetiology of sexual orientation, after all, spring from a more or less implicit theory of sexual races, from the notion that there exist broad general divisions between types of human beings, corresponding, respectively, between to those who make a homosexual and those who make a heterosexual object-choice. (Halperin 1990, 50)

The evidence briefly explored in this paper suggests that the same-time emergence of the sexualized and racialized classifications of bodies to which Somerville refers was no accident (as Somerville's other writings have confirmed). But this paper also suggests that language-centered evidence also contributed to that classification, and so did language-related perceptions of social inequalities and privilege. So, Halperin's claim that scientific inquiries into the "aetiology of sexual orientation" can be traced to an "... implicit theory of sexual races", unfolding along a strict homo/hetero binary, is stated too cautiously. If object-choice is reframed as a focus of linguistic privilege, an object achieved or hindered by mobility, as well as a formation defined by embodiment, then yes – aetiologies of longings, desire, practices, orientations, and social status converge. And as this discussion suggests, the convergence produces unwholesome alliances between scholarship and racist messages about social diversity, the very messages that QHL and other queer inquiry intends to expose and displace.

References

Althusser, Louis. 1971. Ideology and ideological state apparatus (Notes toward an investigation.) *Lenin and Philosophy and Other Essays*. 127–186. New York: Monthly Review Press.
Bérubé, Alan. 1990. *Coming Out Under Fire: The History of Gay Men and Women in World War II*. Chapel Hill: University of North Carolina Press.
Binger, Carl. 1944. How we screen out psychological 4-f's. *The Saturday Evening Post* 216 (28). 19, 75–76.
Cameron, Deborah & Don Kulick. 2003. *Language and Sexuality*. New York: Cambridge University Press.
Chauncey, George. 1994. *Gay New York*. New York: Harper & Row.
Costello, John. 1985. *Virtue under fire: How WWII changed our social and sexual attitudes*. Boston: Little, Brown.
Darwin, Charles. 1859. *Origin of Species*. London: John Murray.
Davis, Susan. 2019. Sex researcher. *Dirty Jokes and Bawdy Songs: The Uncensored Life of Gershon Legman*. 37–64. Urbana: University of Illinois Press.
Duberman, Martin.1993. *Stonewall*. New York: Penguin Press.
Due, Floyd O. & M. E. Wright. 1945. The use of content analysis in Rorschach interpretations 1: Differential characteristics of male homosexuals. *Rorschach Research Exchange* 9(1). 169–177.
Dynes, Wayne. 2007. Migration of gay lingo. *Homolexis*. http://homolexis.blogspot.com/2007/02/migration-of-gay-lingo.html Item posted February 16, 2007. Item accessed May 12, 2016.
Edelman, Lee. 2004. *No Future: Queer Theory and the Death Drive*. Durham: Duke University Press.
Ellis, Havelock. 1942. *Studies in the Psychology of Sex*, Vol. 1, New York: Random House.
Garretts Elwood Burton. 1980. Interview transcript. *Veterans History Project*. U.S. Library of Congress, American Folk Life Center. http://lcweb2.loc.gov/diglib/vhp/story/loc.natlib.afc2001001.43256/transcript?ID=sr0001)
Gioscia, Nicolai. 1950. The gag reflex and fellatio. *American Journal of Psychiatry* 107(5). 380.
Greenspan, Herbert, Lieut. & Comdr. John D. Campbell. 1945. The homosexual as a personality type. *American Journal of Psychiatry* 101. 682–689.
Halberstam. J. 1998. An introduction to female masculinity: Masculinity without men. *Female Masculinity*. 1–44. Durham: Duke University Press.
Halberstam, Judith. 2005. Queer temporality and post-modern geographies. *In a Queer Time and Place*. 1–21. New York: New York University Press.
Halperin, David. 1990. *One Hundred Years of Homosexuality*. New York: Routledge.
Irwin, Godfrey. 1931. *American Tramp and Underworld Slang*. New York: Sears.
Hanson, Dian. 2014. *My Buddy: World War II Laid Bare*. Berlin: Taschen.
Henry, George (ed.). 1941. *Sex Variants*. New York: Paul V. Hoeber.
Hughes, Langston. 1940a. Downtown. *The Big Sea*. 249–255. New York: Hill & Wang.
Hughes, Langston. 1940b. Spectacles in color. *The Big Sea*. 273–278. New York: Hill & Wang.
Hughes, Langston. 1940c. When the Negro was in vogue. *The Big Sea*. 223–232. New York: Hill & Wang.
Hurston, Zora Neale. 1933. Characteristics of Negro expression. In Nancy Cunard (ed.), *Negro: An Anthology*. 24–31. New York: Frederick Ungar.
Hurston, Zora Neale. 1942. Story in Harlem slang. *American Mercury 55*. 84–96.
Johnson, James Weldon. 1930. *Black Manhattan*. New York: Da Capo.
Katz, Jonathan Ned. 1983. *Gay/Lesbian Almanac*. New York: Colophon Books.
King, Charles. 2019. *Gods of the Upper Air: How a Circle of Renegade Anthropologists Reinvented Race, Sex and Gender in the Twentieth Century*. New York: Doubleday.

Larsen, Nella. 1929. *Passing*. New York: Alfred Knopf.
Leap, William L. 2020 a. *Language Before Stonewall: Language, Sexuality, History*. London: Palgrave MacMillan.
Leap, William L. 2020 b. Language, sexuality, history. In Kira Hall & Rusty Barrett (eds.), *The Oxford Handbook of Language and Sexuality*. New York: Oxford University Press. DOI: 10.1093/oxfordhb/ 9780190212926.013.12
Legman, Gershon. 1941. The language of homosexuality: An American glossary. In George Henry (ed.), *Sex Variants*. 1149–1179. New York: Paul V. Hoeber.
Loeser, Lewis H. 1945. The sexual psychopath in the military service (A study of 270 cases). *American Journal of Psychiatry* 102. 92–101.
Loughery, John. 1998. *The Other Side of Silence: Men's Lives and Gay Identities: A Twentieth Century History*. New York: Henry Holt.
McKay, Claude. 1928. *Home to Harlem*. New York: Harper & Bros.
Mead, Margaret. 1935. *Sex and Temperament in Three Primitive Societie*s. New York: New American Library.
Nugent, Richard Bruce. 1926. Smoke Lilies and Jade. *Fire*. 1(1). 33–39.
Peterson, David. 2003. Beyond the body: Walt Whitman's lavender language and "Out of the cradle endlessly rocking". *World Englishes* 17(2). 239–248.
Peterson, David. 2022. I slipped naturally back into my non-girl's attitude": Negotiating normativity in a nineteenth century sexological case history. Paper presented at the 28th annual Lavender Languages Conference, May 23–25, Catania, IT.
Rosanoff, Aaron. 1927. Sexual psychopathies. *Manual of Psychiatry* (6th edn.). 193–208. New York: John Wiley & Sons.
Ryan, Hugh. 2019. How eugenics gave rise to modern homophobia. Washington Post, Outlook. May 28. https://www.washingtonpost.com/outlook/2019/05/28/how-eugenics-gave-rise-modern-homophobia/ Site visited May 23, 2022.
Somerville, Siobhan. 1994. Scientific racism and the emergence of the homosexual body. *Journal of the History of Sexuality* 5(2). 243–266.
Shufeldt, R. W. 1905. The medico-legal consideration of perverts and inverts. *Pacific Medical Journal* 48. 385–393.
Shufeldt, R. W. 1907. *The Negro: A Menace to American Civilization*. Boston: Goram Press.
Shufeldt, R. W. 1915. *America's Greatest Problem: The Negro*. Philadelphia: F.A. Davis.
Stein, Marc (ed.). 2019. *The Stonewall Riots: A Documentary history*. New York: New York University Press.
Sullivan, Harry Stack. 1941. Seminar on Practical Psychiatric Diagnosis: Selective Service System. *Psychiatry* 4. 269–271, 274.
Thurman, Wallace. 1929. Harlemese. In Amritjit Singh & Daniel M. Scott (eds.), *The Collected Writings of Wallace Thurman*, 2003. 64–66. New Brunswick: Rutgers University Press.
Thurman, Wallace & Jordan Rapp William. 1933. Harlem: A Melodrama of Negro Life in Harlem. Reprinted in Amritjit Singh & Daniel M. Scott (eds.), *The Collected Writings of Wallace Thurman*, 2003. 313–369. New Brunswick: Rutgers University Press.
Umbal, Pocholo & Nadia Takhtaganova. 2021. Challenging norms of gender and language. *Toronto Working Papers in Linguistics*, 43(1). 1–3.
Van Vechten, Carl. 1926. *Nigger Heaven*. New York: Alfred Knopf & Co.
Vining, Don. 1979. *A Gay Diary 1933–1946*. New York: The Pepys Press.
Whitman, Walt. 2009. *Leaves of Grass: The Original 1855 Edition*. Orlando: {no press cited}.
Wirth, Thomas H. (ed.). 2002. Introduction. *Gay Rebel of the Harlem Renaissance: Selections from the Work of Richard Bruce Nugent*. 1–61. Durham: Duke University Press.

Tyler Everett Kibbey

The state of Tennessee and the Kingdom of God

Theo-political gender ideology and the emergence of gender transcendentalism in the American South

1 Introduction

Pronouns have been and continue to be an ideological centerpiece of conservative American politics in the 21st century. Acting as a shorthand for perceived social deviancy, only ostensibly based in a prescriptive appeal to grammatical correctness, the greater pronoun debate of our generation has assumed an unprecedented level of importance in contemporary education, politics, and religion. A purely linguistic description of this phenomenon would likely emphasize the role of pronouns, as a grammatical category, in the language ideologies of religious and political groups. However, such an approach would mistakenly equate ideologies about language with language in ideologies. The difference – especially where it concerns the immediate public interest – is significant. It is a difference of equality versus grammaticality, life against language; ideology as a shorthand for identifying a specific social group versus ideology as a semiotic system, rife with its own conceptual and linguistic idiosyncrasies. Yet what began as a nascent discourse on language and sexuality among evangelicals has grown to become a far more all-encompassing theo-political gender ideology.

This chapter seeks to explore these distinctions (i.e., ideology-driven language usage vs ideologies about language) through a case study in Tennessee theo-political gender ideology as it took shape between the Summer of 2015 and the Fall of 2017. I will focus on the relationship between language and ideology as it intersects with the political, the legal, and the religious – starting with the public and legislative denunciation of the University of Tennessee's Pride Center for promoting non-binary pronoun usage and ending with the Council on Biblical Manhood and Womanhood's publication of *The Nashville Statement* (2017). Building from this analysis, I further articulate the emergence of gender transcendentalism and the implicit notion of a gendered soul in this reactionary evangelical tradition, demonstrating how an approach based in but not limited to the study of

---

Tyler Everett Kibbey, University of Kentucky & Humboldt-Universität zu Berlin

language and religion allows for intellectual engagement with language as both an artifact and a cornerstone of ideology.

2 Pre-disciplinary foundations in the study of language and religion

To understand both the significance of gender ideology in contemporary American theo-politics and as a case study in interdisciplinary language science, we must straddle the historiographical and institutional confines of discipline. In the broader Western tradition, theological writing on the nature and origins of language represents a sustained intellectual course of inquiry which spans the entirety of the last two millennia in several distinct religious groups. Admittedly, while the linguistic concerns of a twelfth-century cleric are not entirely intelligible to the modern reader as linguistics, the study of language and issues surrounding the nature of language in the broader context of religion is an ever-present facet of scholarly writing even today. Up until at least the seventeenth century, the careful explication of Aristotle's natural philosophy from theology itself was a frequently condemned, if not explicitly forbidden endeavor (Dear 2009: 14–18). For example, emerging from the writings of the Arabic philosopher Averroës (Ibn Rushd) in the twelfth century, *Averroïsm* argued for the division of Aristotelian natural philosophy from prevailing theological contexts: for Averroës, this meant Islamic theology; for scholars in thirteenth-century Paris and sixteenth-century Padua, when and where interest in Averroïsm caused controversy, this meant Christian theology. For the Christian intellectual tradition, Thomas Aquinas had, in the thirteenth century, argued for the disallowance of such endeavors and alternatively called for the subordination of natural philosophy to theology, a view which quickly became a consensus. As such, when we look at the historical foundations of the study of language and religion, we must keep in mind that "in practice if not always in principle, natural philosophy and theology had become inextricably linked" (15) and, in the case of language science, would remain so until the eighteenth century. As such, much of the extant writing on language even up until the very beginning of the Enlightenment cannot be considered philosophy of language as we know it today, or even as it was first outlined within natural philosophy by Aristotle; rather, such writing on matters of linguistic import is neither definitively philosophical nor entirely theological, and it cannot be freely assumed that these authors would have found such a distinction meaningful in the context of their auxiliary conceptualizations of language. In his introduction to Nicholas Cusanus' *De Docta Ignorantia*, Hawkins (2007) addresses the matter quite adeptly:

> The short answer is that these questions [on the delineation of philosophy and theology] are anachronistic in form and have, as thus expressed, very little bearing upon the main stream of medieval thought. It was in later times that the Christian thinker's need to define his position against various classes of opponents made him lay more and more stress on the distinction between those of his beliefs which could be defended on general grounds of philosophical reason and those for which the appeal could only be to an historical revelation. The distinction was not alien to the medieval mind [. . .] but the emphasis was not the same. The impulse of mediaeval thought was still the faith seeking understanding (*fides quaerens intellectum*) of St. Anselm. (xvi)

The distinction between natural philosophy and theology simply failed to merit explication in the works of many classical and medieval theologians.

With reference to classical and medieval theological writings on language, the critical interpretation of sacred texts, or *exegesis*, constitutes the vast majority of the literature. Of the exegetical works, the primary linguistic concerns of theologians may be broadly grouped as follows: divine predication, metalinguistic literality, and the origins and nature of language. The problem of divine predication specifically concerns whether or not anything true can be said about God or how someone might even begin to evaluate the truth of such propositions. A closely related subject then, metalinguistic literality focuses on contemplation or explication of religious language as either literal or figurative, with variations in the theoretical and theological implications of such inquiries. Thus, as a matter of form, divine predication and metalinguistic literality are frequently debated in parallel. The final subject concerns the origin and nature of language generally, focusing on questions such as whether or not language is a gift from the divine or a natural human faculty, does language have a particular (religious) purpose, and how languages might have changed over time – *change*, here, loosely applied. To better understand the later impulse in the science of language to turn from religion in its entirety, let us consider these areas of thought in more detail.

With respect to divine predication, there is no shortage of texts, theories, and traditions to choose from. The two major theological tendencies in this area of inquiry are *apophatic theology*, also referred to as *via negativa* (i.e., "the negative way"), and *cataphatic theology*, or *via positiva* (i.e., "the positive way"). Forming a dichotomy of sorts, apophaticism represents a manner of thinking about the divine in which only negative statements about the divine are true and is closely associated with mysticism; by contrast, cataphaticism claims that the divine may be understood through positive assertions – *God is* statements – and is closely aligned with literalist interpretations of sacred texts. An exemplar in this area of premodern inquiry, St. Augustine of Hippo argued that true statements could be predicated of God but also conceded that much of Christian scripture, especially Genesis, must be understood as non-literal truths, closely prefiguring modern Conceptual Metaphor Theory (see Gibbs 2017) and representing a stark departure from Augustine's contemporaries studying Rhetoric and Grammar. In *On Genesis: A Refutation of the Manichees*, for example, he writes "No Christian ... will have the nerve to say that [the holy books] should not be taken in a figurative sense, if he pays attention to what the apostle says: *All these things, however, happened among them in figure* (1 Cor 10:11)" (1990, 168). Later, Thomas Aquinas worked to reconcile the cataphatic and apophatic accounts in the *Summa Theologiae* and the *Summa contra Gentiles* where he argued that positive assertions about God were not inaccurate but simply inadequate and that God may only be understood by analogy, thus *via eminentiae* (i.e., "the analogical way", or more accurately " the way of eminence"). Aquinas held that God transcends every species and genus but also that, having created all things can therefore be found within the lesser parallels of creation. For example, if there is goodness in mankind, then God is eminently good by analogy. Within the domain of scriptural exegesis, the Thomistic theory of analogy is by far the most well-formulated as a linguistic theory. Despite Aquinas's staunch belief that natural philosophy is subordinate to theology, Soskice (1985) notes that "Aquinas's theory [can be argued to be] logico-linguistic, as well as metaphysical in intention, and more concerned with determining how we can *speak* of God than with devising crude ontological linkings between finite creatures and infinite Deity" (65). Yet, as he did not write in any substantial sense on matters of natural philosophy separate from theology, Aquinas's inquiries into the nature of language rarely escape the divinity colleges of the modern academy.

These traditions – apophatic, cataphatic, and analogical – broadly represent a pre-modern and highly specialized interest in religious language, in which religious speech is understood in some cases to possess qualities differing from the speech of everyday life. Some contemporary scholars of religious metaphor have even argued that Thomistic analogy and apophaticism represent a natural intersection of theology and cognitive theories of metaphor (Soskice 1985; Feyaerts and Boeve 2018, respectively). Nevertheless, this line of inquiry is only one of many in theology that form the foundations of Western language science as we know it today.

Discussions surrounding the nature and origins of human language, also often appearing within the context of scriptural exegesis, represent another enduring fascination amongst classical and medieval theologians. In the Western world, from antiquity until c. 1750, exegetical writings on Genesis frequently identified Hebrew as the first language, or *primeval language*, of humanity before the assumed confusion of tongues at Babel, despite the fact that no specific language is identified within Genesis (Eskhult 2013). Augustine's *The City of God* [426 AD] presents the most systematic argument for a primeval Hebrew language and the one most highly regarded throughout the medieval period. Although the notion of Hebrew as the first language originates in Hellenistic Judaic texts dating from as early as the mid-second century BCE, Augustine develops a historical-theological theory in which a portion of the Babelites escape the confusion of tongues by virtue of their rightful worship of God and their language, Hebrew, is thus preserved. While Augustine certainly was seen as the pre-eminent authority on the matter within the medieval Christian world, other fringe proposals for the original language of humanity include Johannes Gorpius Becanus's [1518–1572)] argument in favor of Antwerpian Dutch and William Camden's [1551–1623] argument in favor of Welsh (Baker 2019). Accounts interested in a primeval language betray a notion of language as both unchanging and divinely inspired, or that language possesses some objective moral quality by which it can be judged against that of other languages.

While they are easily and quickly dismissed by scholars in the field today, these theological accounts of language nevertheless represent an important period in the development of language science during a time in which natural philosophy and theology were still closely intertwined, as outlined above. So, rather than there being a two-millennia gap in the history of language science following the works of Aristotle, human interest in the nature of language can be seen as continually present from antiquity and the medieval period, continuing unto the present day. In contemporary linguistics, a comparable fascination with primeval language can be observed in Historical and Comparative Linguistics, the efforts of lexicostatistic and glottochronology, and debates on whether the initial emergence of language was monogenetic or polygenetic (for example, Atkinson & Gray 2006, 2005; Barbançon, Evans, Nakhleh, Ringe & Warnow 2013; Crowley & Bowern 2010; Wichmann, Müller, Velupillai, List, Belyaev, Urban & Bakker 2010). While pre-modern accounts of the origins of language were steeped in the theology and religious philosophy of their day, there is nevertheless an unbroken chain of intellectual effort applied to the study of language (and its theoretical dimensions). While almost all of these accounts are centered around outdated theories of humanity and the natural world, they cannot simply be dismissed out of hand because they are expressed in a seemingly antiquated way or because one mechanism is described within a religious framework; while these accounts may tell us little about language, they have much to say about how the modern discipline of linguistics emerged from this sustained inquiry into language.

Yet, what bearing does Aquinas or Averroës have on the contemporary discipline of linguistics and, more so, on this chapter's analysis of Tennessee theopolitical ideologies? In an immediate sense, nothing; in a disciplinary sense, everything. While frequently cited as a convenient start-date for modern language science, Saussure's (1916) *Cours de Linguistique Generale* is but the culmination of a scholarly turn from religion that spans more than a century. It is this divergence, in fact, that prompts Goldsmith and Laks (2019) to begin their monolithic historiography of linguistics with a survey of advancements made not in linguistics but in geology, sociology, biology, and chemistry during the nineteenth century. For them it was simply a matter of time:

> Historical time *exploded* during the nineteenth century: the world went from being a few thousand years old to being much, much older. In large measure, this change occurred because the easy answers once provided by the Bible were no longer sufficient for everyone. Indeed the sense that the Bible was not the final answer to many of these questions had begun with the renaissance; the answers provided in the Bible were no longer consistent with what science was discovering about the physical world. (53–54)

Saussure's position within the history of the discipline is well-deserved, but when taken as such out of context, it obscures many of the motivations for the why the discipline exists as it does in the first place. This is especially true in the case of contemporary approaches to language and religion.

When situated within a greater turn from religion, especially in the context of pre-modern theological inquiry into language as discussed at length above, linguistics as a discipline can be understood as beginning in the late-eighteenth century with Johann Gottfried Herder's (1966 [1772]) *Ursprung der Sprache* in which he offers a full refutation of theological arguments for the divine origin of language. Herder's account of the origin of language was in response to the Berlin Academy's 1769 essay contest, which posed the questions:

> Assuming humans had abandoned their natural faculties, are they in a condition to invent language? And by what means will they arrive by themselves at this invention?[1] (quoted in Sapir 1907, 1, translation my own)

Sapir (1907) took this question to be a pivotal moment in the intellectual climate of the day, where "the burden of proof, in fact, lay upon those who disputed the divine origin of language"; in essence, the question posed was a judgement of human faculties, asking "was the human mind intelligent and resourceful enough to invent so fine a machine, or did the latter require the master-hand of the deity" (1)? After Herder (1772), the burden of proof lay upon those who disputed the natural origins of language. A frequent refrain throughout his essay, Herder argues that language, comprised of natural redundancies and diversity, "is rich

---

[1] Personal Translation of the original French: "En supposant les hommes abandonnées à leurs facultés naturelles, son tils en état d'inventer le langage? Et par quells moyens parviendront-ils d'eux-mêmes à cette invention?"

because it is poor, because its inventors did not have plan enough to grow poor" and asks "[are we then] to believe that the idle inventor of such an outstandingly imperfect language was God" (1966, 154). Following this refutational essay, the study of language diverged more and more from theology until, with Saussure (1914), the linguistic turn from religion was complete. From this point of view, the long(er) nineteenth century of linguistics can be seen as bridging the turn from theological accounts of language, beginning with Herder's *Ursprung der Sprache*, and the formalization of linguistics as a disciplinary science in Saussure's *Course de Linguistique Générale*, as a part of what Goldsmith and Laks (2019) refer to as an *acceleration* of the development of linguistics as a profession in the first half of the twentieth century.

Once linguistics had established itself as a twentieth century discipline, the study of language as it intersected with religion was largely abandoned if not entirely shunned, with any remaining interest in the subject during this period being relegated generally to anthropology. In the latter half of the twentieth century, the subfield of theolinguistics emerged to fill this gap, although it just as quickly dissipated as a defined area of study. Crystal (2018) dates its emergence to the 1960s, when renewed interest in religion and language produced a number of studies on topics such as liturgical language, glossolalia, and religious ritual. It was only later that van Noppen (1981) offered the term *theolinguistics* to reference "the pluridisciplinary field of investigation offered by the linguistic articulation of religious belief and thought" (1). In her survey of the field as it yet remains, Hobbs (2021) articulates an approach to theolinguistics that focuses on discourse analytic methodologies as they are informed by theories from the general study of religion, and more importantly, offers the most comprehensive survey of the subfield to date. Additionally, in the last two decades, another approach to the study of language and religion has coalesced around advancements in cognitive science, combining methodologies and theoretical approaches from both cognitive linguistics and the cognitive science of religion. Given this, a substantial portion of research in this area has focused on cognitivist accounts of religious metaphor in the tradition of Conceptual Metaphor Theory (see for example, Chilton & Kopytowska 2018; Richardson 2013; Richardson, Mueller & Pihlaja 2021; and others). Simultaneously, a new burst of interest in the area is taking place in many aligned disciplines, especially as it concerns language at the intersection of religion and politics (e.g., Byrd 2013; Conroy-Krutz 2015; etc.).

The importance of this history and its subsequent obfuscation within the disciplinary literature of linguistics may best be described as an attempt to naturalize language science. As a discipline, linguistics rests at the boundary of the natural and human sciences, a characteristic essential to the manner in which we conduct research on language. At the very beginning of the American disciplinary project in linguistics, Bloomfield writes:

> The science of language, dealing with the most basic and simplest of human social institutions, is a human (or mental or, as they used to say, moral) science. It is most closely related to ethnology, but precedes ethnology and all other human sciences in the order of growing complexity, for linguistics stands at their foot, immediately after psychology, the connecting link between the natural sciences and the human. The methods of linguistics resemble those of the natural sciences, and so do its results, both in their certainty and in their seeming by no means obvious, but rather, in many instances, paradoxical to the common sense of time. (1925, 1)

I proffer that it is this position between the social and natural sciences that fosters an anxiety within the discipline with respect to religion and anything else that might smack of subjectivity. If we understand disciplines, as institutional projects, to be motivated first and foremost by ensuring the continued existence of each specific discipline, then the perilous positioning of linguistics between two broad realms of scholarly work forces a choice. Do we emphasize the human elements at the expense of a perceived prestige for *hard science*, or do we emphasize the natural elements at the expense of any and all subjective input (Kibbey 2019)? Now, to be sure, this choice between the social and natural sciences as it is forced upon the discipline of linguistics is a false dilemma originating in the institutional structure of discipline itself. Yet, in spite of this, the discipline has largely sought to ascend from the social sciences into the natural sciences, and as a result, has sought in parallel to divest itself of its earlier engagements with religion. As such, all research on language and religion must by necessity look beyond the discipline and read between the lines of our received scientific histories.

3 Politicians, pastors, and pronouns

Religion, as one of the primary institutions of social life, whether ascribed to or intentionally avoided, does not exist entirely apart from institutions such as politics, law, medicine, or education. Even a composite rendering of these institutions (e.g., religion and politics, law and education, etc.) represents a disservice to the ideologies being analyzed. Simply put, the Bible alone does not turn people into bigots and the Constitution likewise does not turn people into conservatives. It is only in their juxtaposition in the social lives of people of shared backgrounds that these more fully developed semiotic systems begin to emerge as a Christian Conservativism or Christian Liberalism, for example. Ideology, when understood as a semiotic register and not simply a convenient by-line for a particular group or system of beliefs, should therefore serve as an analytic framework for the study of language and religion and may allow us access to a more comprehensive understanding of both.

Without ideology as a framework for analysis, it would be difficult to account for any of the driving forces behind co-occurring religious and political events. At first glance, a public outcry over a pronoun chart, an amendment on legal interpretations of gendered language, and a theological treatise on gender identity (or the alleged non-existence thereof) have seemingly little in common aside from a shared animus towards gender and sexual diversity. Yet, following the *Obergefell v. Hodges* decision in the Summer of 2015, a series of public as well as political and theological debates occurred in the state of Tennessee surrounding issues related to gender and sexuality, all stemming from a shared theo-political ideology. Nearly a century following the 1925 Scopes "Monkey" Trial in Dayton, Tennessee (Larson 1997), much remains the same: public debate still centers on the role of theo-political ideologies in legislation as well as the role that such ideologies should or should not play in public education. Only now, instead of Darwinism and evolution, Tennessee pulpits ring out with sermons against "transgenderism" and gender identity. The two principal events that I will focus on here are the 2015–2016 Pronoun Crisis at the University of Tennessee – Knoxville and the publication of *The Nashville Statement* by the Council on Biblical Manhood and Womanhood in 2017.

Following Obergefell v. Hodges, the University of Tennessee Pride Center published on their website an otherwise entirely innocuous chart showcasing the use of the "gender neutral" pronouns they/them/their, ze/hir/hirs, ze/zir/zirs, and xe/xem/xyr alongside the more familiar "gender binary" pronouns she/her/hers and he/him/his. Formatted as white text against a solid UT Orange background, it is unlikely that many individuals, let alone students, who were not actively looking for that specific webpage would have stumbled upon it. Nevertheless, by the end of the Spring of 2016, the Tennessee State Legislature used the pronoun chart, which had since been removed from the university's website, as a justification to defund the Pride Center and drastically reduce funding for the Office of Diversity and Inclusion. In the following Spring of 2017, the Tennessee State Legislature capitalized on their previous success in publicly censoring the LGBTQ+ community at the University of Tennessee by passing the "Natural and Ordinary Meaning" Amendment into law in an effort to limit interpretations of words such as *wife/husband* and *mother/father* as gender-neutral *spouse* or *parent*. The final text of the amendment, as it was passed into law, reads:

> As used in this code, undefined words shall be given their natural and ordinary meaning, without forced or subtle construction that would limit or extend the meaning of the language, except when a contrary intention is clearly manifest. (TN General Assembly 2017)

Then, in August of 2017, the Council on Biblical Manhood and Womanhood published *The Nashville Statement*, which was composed of fourteen articles outlining the Council's theological interpretations of marriage, gender, and sexuality. Signatories of the statement at the time of its publication numbered in the hundreds and included not only ordained ministers and members of the lay clergy but also professors, attorneys, and media personalities. This document stands as an exemplar for the theo-political ideology in question and as such, will be the focal point of our discussion. It should be noted however that *The Nashville Statement* is not in any way a political treatise or document of that kind – its concerns are purely theological. It is only within the wider social context of Tennessee in 2017 that it is possible to understand the statement's importance as a legitimization of the theological foundations for anti-LGBTQ+ and, specifically, anti-transgender legislation. While the statement itself is preceded by the Council's founding document, *The Danvers Statement* (1987), *The Nashville Statement* itself prefigures the anti-LGBTQ+ legislative initiatives being undertaken in the state of Tennessee within a defined religious context.

The Nashville Statement, in its preamble, frames the document in terms of the decline of "Western culture". The statement specifically makes the claim that *post-Christian Western culture* – as they refer to it – has "embarked upon a massive revision of what it means to be human". While the statement is ostensibly focused on marriage, the preamble instead emphasizes a perceived desecration of binary gender as a divinely mandated aspect of what it means to be human, presenting what the authors of the Statement refer to as a "counter-cultural witness" to post-Christian notions of humanity. Following the preamble, the statement presents fourteen articles, each a pair made up of an affirmation followed by a denial, which address marriage, gender, and sexuality. Of the resulting twenty-eight individual statements, only five refer to marriage, while twelve make references to sexuality and nineteen refer to gender and/or sex.

The core element of *The Nashville Statement* is not in fact gender, surprisingly, but is rather the self-referential gendered object. This object is frequently called the *soul* or an ephemeral *self*, but the authors instead use the language *self-conception* – which in this case is a misnomer as they do not indicate that the self, the individual, is any more involved in their *self-conception* than as a mere consequence of the act of being *self-conceived* by God. Bjork-James (2018, 8) notes that "this construct of an idealized receptive self permeates evangelical ideology . . . [and that *The Nashville Statement*] expresses these values as central to evangelical morality". In her wider analysis of the evangelical conceptualizations of sexuality and personhood, she extrapolates the notion of a *porous self* from her analysis of ex-gay testimonials in which sexuality is a cornerstone of spiritual identity and the self can become more or less receptive to the divine depending on how one lives their life. Returning to our wider discussion of ideology as a semiotic system expanding beyond any individual social institution, Bjork-James concludes with the final observation that "claiming an LGBT identity isn't seen as an act of sin . . . it is seen as a form of personhood incompatible with evangelical porosity" (9). It is this "incompatibility", as Bjork-James phrases it, that is of the greatest concern when we begin to expand our understanding of religious ideologies to also include political and legal elements, among others.

The Nashville Statement formalizes three overarching aspects of divinely ordained self-conception: 1) that physical characteristics forming a male/female categorical binary are indicative of but distinct from gender self-conception, 2) that biological sex and self-conceived gender possess a *God-ordained link*, and 3) that gendered language essentially reflects these relationships between sex and gender. Here, I will briefly delineate these themes as they are presented in the statement.

Article 1 ostensibly outlines the scope of the Statement, affirming a belief in marriage as a cisgender, heterosexual, and monogamous covenant and denying that marriage is a purely secular institution.

Article 1

WE AFFIRM that God has designed marriage to be a covenantal, sexual, procreative, lifelong union of one man and one woman, as husband and wife, and is meant to signify the covenant love between Christ and his bride the church.

WE DENY that God has designed marriage to be a homosexual, polygamous, or polyamorous relationship. We also deny that marriage is a mere human contract rather than a covenant made before God.

While this first article frames the impetus behind the statement, specifically as a reaction to marriage equality in the United States, it quickly becomes clear that the majority focus is on gender and, incidentally, sexuality.

Article 5

WE AFFIRM that the differences between male and female reproductive structures are integral to God's design for self-conception as male or female.

WE DENY that physical anomalies or psychological conditions nullify the God-appointed link between biological sex and self-conception as male or female.

Article 6

WE AFFIRM that those born with a physical disorder of sex development are created in the image of God and have dignity and worth equal to all other image-bearers. They are acknowledged by our Lord Jesus in his words about "eunuchs who were born that way from their mother's womb." With all others they are welcome as faithful followers of Jesus Christ and should embrace their biological sex insofar as it may be known.

WE DENY that ambiguities related to a person's biological sex render one incapable of living a fruitful life in joyful obedience to Christ.

Both Article 5 and Article 6 relate to the group's notions of biology, physiology, and psychology as it relates, principally, to *biological sex*. Article 5 stresses the link between *reproductive structures* as conceptualized in a sexual binary and a divinely ordained *self-conception*, denying that *physical anomalies* contradict or contravene such a relationship. Article 6 further clarifies that while those *born with a physical disorder of sex development* still possess a divinely ordained link to a self-conception consistent with a binary *biological sex*, insofar as such a sex can be determined for said individuals.

Article 7

WE AFFIRM that self-conception as male or female should be defined by God's holy purposes in creation and redemption as revealed in Scripture.

WE DENY that adopting a homosexual or transgender self-conception is consistent with God's holy purposes in creation and redemption.

Article 7 moves to the subject of *self-conception*, which is given as mirroring its less ephemeral counterpart in *biological sex*. It offers an affirmation that self-conception is ordained by God and a denial that opposed self-conceptions are consistent with God's design. Of note here is that self-conception is not limited to gender identity.

Article 11

WE AFFIRM our duty to speak the truth in love at all times, including when we speak to or about one another as male or female.

WE DENY any obligation to speak in such ways that dishonor God's design of his image-bearers as male or female.

Article 11 is the only article that specifically engages with (gendered) language. Here, they conceptualize misgendering practices as non-hostile and highlight the importance of an essentialist linguistic *truth*.

Article 13

WE AFFIRM that the grace of God in Christ enables sinners to forsake transgender self-conceptions and by divine forbearance to accept the God-ordained link between one's biological sex and one's self-conception as male or female.

WE DENY that the grace of God in Christ sanctions self-conceptions that are at odds with God's revealed will.

Finally, Article 13 rounds out this triadic relation between gender, sex, and self-conception by stating that self-conceptions can change, specifically from sinful self-conceptions based on an individual's idea of the self to holy self-conceptions as predetermined by the divine agent God.

When taken together – the Pronoun Crisis, the Natural and Ordinary Meaning Amendment, and *The Nashville Statement* – a coherent system of thought begins to emerge. Specifically, a system of thought concerned with the relationships between gender, sexuality, and language and the articulation of those relationships, especially at intersection of the political and the religious. This system of thought possesses particular characteristics which induce the analyst to assign it to "ideology" rather than some accidental association of socio-cultural moments in twenty-first century Tennessee. First, it has a coherent, internal logic that contends with challenges to said logic in a consistent and predictable way. For example, when presented with intersex identities which physically challenge the divinely-ordained binary of gender, as in Article 6, the contradiction is explained away as a disorder of the body which has already been accounted for by revealed scripture (i.e., Matthew 9:12). Thus, the contradiction is re-interpreted as supporting evidence for the core logic, that of a metaphysical binary, at the expense of a hard binary where the physical sex of the body and the metaphysical gender of the soul have a one-to-one correspondence. Second, as an ideology, it possesses a commitment to unifying the world of ideas with the world of reality, even if only implicitly. For the writers of *The Nashville Statement*, this means altering federal and state legal codes to reflect the revealed law of their wider belief system: in the case of sex and gender, this means aligning laws related to reproduction, marriage, family, and education, among other things, with the internal logic of the ideology, which is understood to reflect the laws of God. And finally, as an ideology, it is engaged with as a function of social identity to the effect that those who hold that ideology believe themselves to be linked by shared values and beliefs with other people who also hold that ideology, or at least a version of that ideology which is mutually intelligible and non-contradictory. In short, if one person is motivated to change the world to align it with the internal logic of their belief system, then they have a personal philosophy; if they recruit another person to their belief system and then proceed to identify, as a group, with that belief system, then the two share an ideology. While there is extensive debate on what is fundamental to ideology as a category (see Flannery 2016; Lukin 2019 for further discussion), these three features – (1) a coherent internal system of logic, (2) a commitment to actions that align the ideological world with the experiential world, and (3) a linking of ideology and identity as it extends to group identity – are essential for our analytical purposes moving forward. In this sense, the Pronoun Crisis, the Natural and Ordinary Meaning Amendment, and *The Nashville Statement* are extensions and expressions of this particular ideology: unique in that as linguistic artifacts of this, they make the ideology analyzable. The ideology itself is not confined to the state of Tennessee and is not a static system of belief: like any other semiotic system, it is continuously changing with and reacting to those who participate in it.

4 Legislating evangelical gender transcendentalism

For evangelical gender transcendentalism, as we will refer to it, language then is not only a vehicle of ideology but a salient, ideology-driven feature of theopolitical identity. It is for this reason that researchers should avoid characterizing conservative Christian perspectives on gendered language as a kind of *language ideology*. Rather, gendered language represents a crude ontological link between essentialist notions of biological sex and a divinely-formed soul in the theopolitics of Southern evangelicals, which has assumed a certain orthodoxy following Obergefell v. Hodges. As such, language is both necessary and incidental to such an ontology.

Yet the shift to using language to justify an implicit link between biological sex and a gendered soul is a relatively new ideological innovation. This shift is perhaps best exemplified in contrasting the focal verse of the Council on Biblical Manhood and Womanhood's *Danvers Statement* (1987) – "So God created man in his own image, in the image of God he created him; male and female he created them." (Genesis 1:27) – with the focal verse of the *Nashville Statement* (2017) – "Know that the LORD Himself is God; It is He who has made us, and not we ourselves . . ." (Psalm 100:3). The ideology outlined here diverts the majority of its focus to the metaphysical creation of a human soul, imbued with more abstract qualities such as *gender*, and moves away from an emphasis on biological sex. This is reflected in the contrastive focus of the two verses: where Genesis 1:27 emphasizes the act of creation and what is created by such an act and where Psalm 100:3 emphasizes the creator's role in the act of creation as well as the hierarchical relationship between God and God's creation (i.e., humans). Article's 5 and 6 of *The Nashville Statement* clearly demonstrate this turn in that the authors are forced to concede diversity in biological sex, albeit conceived as anomalous variation. Immediately, this contradicts the purportedly ordained binary instituted by God at the beginning of creation. They even go so far as to revive the outdated social category of *eunuch* rather than concede any intermediate category that would contradict the divine binary (e.g., *intersex*). Instead, Articles 5 and 6 reinforce a metaphysical certainty of gender at the ideological expense of *biological ambiguity*.

Most conceptualizations of the soul, however, do not have such widespread socio-political effects, and the majority of religions rarely engage with the concept of a soul as a means of solving embodied social issues beyond the body's position in before- and after-life-related beliefs (e.g., abortion, burial practices, public acts of mourning, etc.). Sufism, a grouping of mystic Islamic ritual practices and beliefs, emphasizes *light* as a way to conceive of the soul "as a light that could transcend the body, while remaining anchored to it, [and] transforms the human being in his or her entirety into an intermediary between the hidden and manifest worlds" (Abuali 2021, 14). British Quakers frequently conceptualized the soul as a kind of container in which various elements of religious expression could either be present or absent (Koller 2016), similar to Bjork-James' notion of porosity (2017). Religious metaphors related to the LIFE IS A JOURNEY schema in both Christianity and Islam generally treat the soul as a metaphysical reflection of the body (Shokr 2006) and research on inter-religious discourse demonstrates conceptualizations of the soul or metaphysical self as existing in spatial relation to God, where proximity maps to spirituality (Richardson 2012, 2013).

The League of Christian Reformers is one exception to the generally held mutual exclusion of the body from the soul and is worth mentioning here. The League, founded and shepherded by James Larratt Battersby [1907–1955], was a religious community in post-WWII Britain that practiced an emerging messianic fascism centered on the belief that Adolf Hitler was a Christ-like figure or even Christ reborn. In *The Holy Book of Adolf Hitler* (1952), which served as the League's scripture, Battersby creates a systematic framework for messianic fascism, developing an argument for the origins of a Germanic Religion, the nature of a Germanic Soul, an interpretation of Hitler's life as the German Revelation, and finally, a three-chapter plan for global peace and world government, which of course is headed by a German fascist ethno-state. While a theolinguistic analysis of the text could easily fill volumes, the main point of interest here is the conceptual development of what Battersby refers to as the *race-soul*.

> In Adolf Hitler the Aryan peoples of all the world have found their Champion, Redeemer and Saviour. Through him has the race-soul, the eternal striving and aspiration of countless generations of Aryan nations, found its focus and fulfillment [. . .] mere nationality is a minor matter; Race and Spirit is everything. (4–5)

Much in the same way that *The Nashville Statement* represents an attempt to reconcile an evangelical theology of gender with the complexity of biological diversity, *The Holy Book of Adolf Hitler* represents an attempt to reconcile Nazi racial ideology with the strictures of Christianity, the ultimate defeat of Nazi Germany by the Allied powers, and the complexity of human diversity. Shifting ethnicity and race from the physical body to the soul allowed Battersby to imagine a world with neatly delineated boundaries between races, where the worldly ambiguity of race and ethnicity became the theological certainty of a racialized soul. While *The Nashville Statement*'s gender transcendentalism and the *Holy Book of Adolf Hitler*'s ethno-racial transcendentalism emerged in drastically different contexts, the form, function, and motivation of these ideologies belie a shared socio-cognitive foundation, as conceived symbolically and expressed linguistically. The greatest difference between the two, however, is that this particular strain of ethno-racial transcendentalism did not long survive the death of its creator as a distinct theo-political ideology. Evangelical gender transcendentalism demonstrates no such instability.

That being said, the legal and linguistic negotiation of gender transcendentalism in Tennessee has not been as straightforward as we might be led to believe by the apparent domination of the state's politics by the ideology's adherents. In February of 2019, for example, Tennessee Attorney General Herbert H. Slatery issued an opinion on whether or not the Tennessee legal code authorized courts to enhance sentences for hate-crimes committed against transgender individuals (Slatery 2019, Op. Att'y Gen. No. 2019-0). Slatery's opinion answered yes, without reservations:

> For purposes of the hate-crime enhancement, a crime committed against a person because that person manifests a gender that is different than his or her biological gender at birth – i.e. a crime committed against a person because he or she is transgender – is thus necessarily committed because of, at least in part, the person's gender. (2)

This opinion reads within the mainstream line of thought which divides the body into possessing a socially-constructed gender and a biologically determined sex, what Slatery refers to as a *biological gender at birth*. It also represents one of the earliest instances in which a Southern state has extended hate-crime statute protections to transgender individuals. However, immediately following this opinion, state legislators moved to suppress or undermine the attorney general's relative independence from the vagaries of party politics. Specifically, a number of legislators supported an amendment to the Tennessee State Constitution which would require the state attorney general to be approved by the General Assembly following nomination by the Tennessee Supreme Court, whereas previously the attorney general was simply appointed by the Tennessee Supreme Court without the interference of the state legislature (TN General Assembly, 2022a). While the amendment was first submitted on November 13, 2018, it was not until February 21, 2019 – two weeks immediately following the attorney general's opinion on sentence enhancement – that the amendment was put to a vote before the Tennessee Senate, passing easily. The COVID-19 pandemic mostly stalled this legislative effort, but the amendment is still being pursued, with the Senate once again passing the amendment in the 2022 session. While the amendment will not appear on the 2022 ballot as the House adjourned before holding a vote on the measure, it will likely be reconsidered in future sessions.

In a similar vein, the Tennessee State Legislature has passed a constitutional amendment that would remove barriers preventing members of the clergy and lay-clergy from holding public office within the state, an amendment which will be voted on by citizens of Tennessee during the 2022 midterm election (2022b). Currently, Article IX of the Tennessee Constitution bars three categories of people from holding public office: (1) members of the clergy, (2) atheists, and (3) duelists. The sections covering clergy members and atheists are excerpted, here:

> 9.1 Whereas ministers of the Gospel are by their profession, dedicated to God and the care of souls, and ought not be diverted from the great duties of their functions; therefore, no minister of the Gospel, or priest of any denomination whatever, shall be eligible to a seat in either House of the Legislature.
>
> 9.2 No person who denies the being of God, or a future state of rewards and punishments, shall hold any office in the civil department of this state.

Building on the ideological advancement of gender transcendentalism in the state of Tennessee, this amendment represents a concerted effort on the part of the legislature to further erode the final, ostensible boundaries between church and state. Considered on its own, this amendment may be interpreted as mere posturing; but within the larger semiotic system of Tennessee theo-politics, it is hardly exceptional.

Gender transcendentalism, as a theo-political ideology emerging in the wake of Obergefell v. Hodges (2015), has proved to be the foundation for contemporary evangelical politics in Tennessee. While the state's actions against the University of Tennessee's LGBTQ+ community for disseminating information on gender-neutral pronouns in 2015 and 2016 may have been largely reactionary, the publication of *The Nashville Statement* (2017) only a year later formalized what was until then an indistinct semiotic system. In only five years, Tennessee gender transcendentalists have managed to incorporate their ideology into the state's political architecture, such as with the 'Natural and Ordinary Meaning' Amendment (2017), and moved to secure their position and limit dissent, such as with the Remove Religious Minister Disqualification Amendment (2022b) and the Selection of Attorney General Amendment (2022a), respectively. While not all of these may be immediately recognizable as an extension of this ideology, these legislative actions represent the minimum steps for securing the state for more extensive implementation of gender transcendentalism in and through the law. Language and its entailments are then not only the structuring force behind gender transcendentalism but also the principal mechanism for its enforcement.

5 Concluding thoughts

Newly coalescing ideologies at the intersection of religion and politics – such as gender transcendentalism among Tennessee evangelicals – represent a challenge to both the study of language and the safety of LGBTQ+ individuals. For the linguist, gender transcendentalism entails language usage that creates ontological linkings between a sexed body and a gendered soul that are implicit to (non-)gendered language but not necessarily, or at least easily, accessible to discourse analytic frameworks. For LGBTQ+ individuals, linguist and non-linguist alike, gender transcendentalism constitutes an existential crisis which is slowly, steadily growing around the political architecture of the United States. While I solely engage with gender transcendentalism as it has manifested in Tennessee theo-politics, similar trends – of law and ideology – are easily observed elsewhere, domestically and internationally.

The interdisciplinary approach explored in this chapter shows that linguistics alone, both in its disciplinary pursuits and in its historiographical foundations, is ill-suited for research at the intersection of language, religion, and politics. Even when working across and beyond disciplines, borrowing from the various literatures as a meager substitute for substantive research in this area, *theo-political ideology* leaves much to be desired. Nonetheless, as interest in the study of language and religion continues to grow and advancements are made in the scientific study of religion, across disciplines, our methodological and theoretical tools will undoubtedly continue to improve. It is my enduring hope that they will have improved in time enough to be of benefit to the upcoming generation of LGBTQ+ youth who will come of age in a time when ideologies such as gender transcendentalism are no longer new but commonplace, a time when these ideologies have become entrenched within the institutional architecture of the law, a time which is fast approaching.

References

Abuali, Eyad. 2021. Visualizing the soul: Diagrams and the subtle body of light (jism latif) in Shams al-Din al-Daylami's *The Mirror of Souls* (Mir'at al-arwah). *Critical Research on Religion*. 1–18.

Atkinson, Quentin & Russell D. Gay. 2005. Curious parallels and curious connections: Phylogenetic thinking in biology and historical linguistics. *Society of Systematic Biologists* 54(4). 513–526.

Atkinson, Quentin & Russell D. Gay. 2006. How old is the Indo-European language family? Illumination or more moths to the flame? In Peter Forster & Colin Renfrew (eds.), *Phylogenetic methods and the prehistory of languages*. 91–109. Cambridge: McDonald Institute for Archaeological Research.

Augustine, St. of Hippo. 1990. On Genesis: A refutation of the manichees. In J. E. Rotelle (trans.), *The Works of St. Augustine: A Translation for the 21st century*. New York: New City Press.

Baker, David W. 2019. Etymology, antiquarianism, and unchanging languages in Johannes Gorpius Becanus's *Origines Antwerpianae* and William Camden's *Britannia*. *Renaissance Quarterly* 72(4). 1326–1361.

Barbançon, François, Steven N. Evans, Luay Nakhleh, Don Ringe & Tandy Warnow. 2013. An experimental study comparing linguistic phylogenetic reconstruction methods. *Diachronica* 30(2). 143–170.

Battersby, James L. 1952. *The Holy Book of Adolf Hitler*. German World Church in Europe.

Bloomfield, Leonard. 1925. Why a Linguistic Society? *Language* 1(1). 1–5.

Bjork-James, Sophie. 2018. Training the porous body: Evangelicals and the ex-gay movement. *American Anthropologist*. 1–12.

Byrd, James P. 2013. *Sacred Scripture, Sacred War*. Oxford: Oxford University Press.

Chilton, Paul & Monika Kopytowska (eds.). 2018. *Religion, language, and the human mind*. Oxford: Oxford University Press.

Conroy-Krutz, Emily. 2015. *Christian imperialism: Converting the world in the early American republic*. Ithaca: Cornell University Press.

Crowley, Terry & Claire Bowern. 2010. *An introduction to historical linguistics*. Oxford: Oxford University Press.

Crystal, David. 2018. Whatever happened to theolinguistics? In Paul Chilton & Monika Kopytowska (eds.), *Religion, language, and the human mind*. 3–18. Oxford: Oxford University Press.

Dear, Peter. 2009. *Revolutionizing the sciences: European knowledge and its ambitions, 1500–1700*. Princeton: Princeton University Press.

Eskhult, Josef. 2013. Augustine and the primeval language in early modern exegesis and philology. *Language and History* 56(2). 98–119.

Fayaerts, Kurt & Lieven Boeve. 2018. Religious metaphor at the crossroads between apophatical theology and cognitive linguistics: An interdisciplinary study. In Paul Chilton & Monika Koptytowska (eds.), *Religion, Language, and the Human Mind*. 52–88. Oxford: Oxford University Press.

Flannery, Frances L. 2016. *Understanding apocalyptic terrorism: Countering the radical mindset*. London: Routledge.

Gibbs, Raymond W. 2017. *Metaphor wars: Conceptual metaphors in human life*. Cambirdge: Cambridge University Press.

Goldsmith, John & Bernard Laks. 2019. *Battle in the mind fields*. Chicago: University of Chicago Press.

Hawkins, J.B. 2007. Introduction. In Nicolas Cusanus, *Of Learned Ignorance*. Germain Heron (trans.). ix–xxviii. Eugene, OR: Wipf & Stock Publishers.

Herder, Johann Gottfried. 1966. *Essay on the Origin of Language*. Alexander Gode (trans.). In John H. Moran & Alexander Gode (eds.), *On the Origin of Language*. 88–166. New York: Frederick Ungar Publishing Co.

Hobbs, Valerie. 2021. *An Introduction to religious language: Exploring theolinguistics in contemporary contexts*. London: Bloomsbury Academic.

Kibbey, Tyler. 2019. Transcriptivism: An ethical framework for modern linguistics. *Proceedings of the Linguistic Society of America* 4(1). 1–13.

Koller, Veronika. 2017. The light within: Metaphor consistency in Quaker pamphlets, 1659–2010. *Metaphor and the Social World* 7(1). 5–25.

Larson, Edward J. 1997. *Summer of the gods: The Scopes Trial and America's continuing debate over science and religion*. Cambridge, MA: Harvard University Press.

Lukin, Annabelle. 2019. *War and its ideologies: A social-semiotic theory and description*. New York: Springer.

van Noppen, Jean-Pierre (ed.). 1981. *Theolinguistics*. Studiereeks Tijdschrift Vrije Universiteit Brussel, New Series No. 8.

Philo, of Alexandria. 2016. *The Works of Philo: Complete and Unabridged*. C.D. Yonge (trans.). New York: Henderson Publishers.

Pseudo-Dionysius, the Aeropagite. 1990. *Dionysius the Aeropagite: On the Divine Names and The Mystical Theology*. C.E. Rolt (trans.). Christian Classics Ethereal Library.

Richardson, Peter. 2012. A closer walk: A study of the interaction between metaphors related to movement and proximity and presuppositions about the reality of belief in Christian and Muslim testimonials. *Metaphor and the Social World* 2(2). 233–261.

Richardson, Peter. 2013. *A closer walk: A cognitive linguistic study in movement and proximity metaphors and their impact on certainty in Muslim and Christian discourse*. Birmingham: University of Birmingham dissertation.

Richardson, Peter, Charles M. Mueller & Stephen Pihlaja. 2021. *Cognitive linguistics and religious language: An Introduction*. New York: Routledge.

Sapir, Edward. 1907. Herder's "Ursprung der Sprache". *Modern Philology* 5(1). 109–142.

de Saussure, Ferdinand. 1998. *Course in General Linguistics*. Chicago: Open Court Classics.

de Saussure, Ferdinand. 1916. *Course in general linguistics*. trans. Roy Harris (1983). Chicago: Open Court.

Shokr, Mohamed S. A. 2006. The metaphorical concept 'Life is a Journey' in the Qur'an: A cognitive-semantic analysis. *Metaphorik.de*. 94–132.

Slatery, Herbert. 2019. Op. Att'y Gen. No. 2019-0, Tennessee.

Soskice, Janet. 1985. *Metaphor and Religious Language*. Oxford: Clarendon Press.

TN General Assembly. 2017. 'Natural and Ordinary Meaning' Amendment.

TN General Assembly. 2022a. Tennessee Selection of Attorney General Amendment.

TN General Assembly. 2022b. Remove Religious Minister Disqualification Amendment. TN Senate Joint Resolution No. 178 (111th) & Senate Joint Resolution no. 55 (112th).

Wichmann, Søren, André Müller, Viveka Velupillai, Johann-Mattis List, Oleg Belyaev, Matthias Urban & Dik Bakker. 2010. Glottochronology as a heuristic for genealogical language relationships. *Journal of Quantitative Linguistics*. 1–16.

Nicholas Mararac
Queering the military
Heterosexual performativity in leadership

1 Introduction

The United States Armed Forces' compulsory heterosexuality (Rich 1980), predicated on the historic exclusion of women from combat occupational specialties and the historic discrimination against lesbian, gay, bisexual, and transgender service members, is the result of Congressional hearings and debates among politicians in the United States that reflects public discourse and opinion. Thus, understanding gender and sexuality in the military lends insight to understanding contemporary opinion and ways to affect social change. In this chapter, I draw on queer theory to unveil and challenge the ways heteronormativity is (re)produced as a normalizing lens through which social and cultural practices are understood. Broadly, queer theory has been used to elucidate hegemonic masculinity – i.e., "the most honored way of being a man" (Connell & Messerschmidt 2005, 832) and heterosexualities in various institutions, such as queering international relations (Thiel 2018), queering public administration (Lee, Learmonth & Harding 2008), queering organizational management (Rumens, de Souza & Brewis 2019), and queering higher education (Marine 2017). In this vein, I contribute to the scholarship of queering institutions by bringing the queering to the U.S. military, focusing on the U.S navy.

In an effort to understand how ideologies of gender and sexuality shape communicative practices in the U.S. military, I apply a queer linguistics approach (Motschenbacher & Stegu 2013) to the analysis of the leadership discourse of two naval officers. I define leadership as a discursive process predicated on power being tethered to social identities to achieve a specific goal. In this way, I see leadership as not only a performative identity that can be examined as such, but also an identity that should be examined in conversation with other identities – such as gender and sexuality – with a contextualized understanding of the institution. The data for this chapter come from a larger study in which I examined leadership style of naval officers in navy "sea stories" (Mararac 2019). For this study, I provide three excepts in which the participants, a queer identifying, lesbian, cisgender woman ("Kim") and a heterosexual cisgender man ("AJ"), describe other leaders who they worked with while serving on board a U.S. warship during

Nicholas Mararac, Georgetown

https://doi.org/10.1515/9783110742510-011

"Don't Ask, Don't Tell," (DADT) the discriminatory law that prohibited lesbian, gay, and bisexual service members from serving openly. To analyze the data, I draw on Bucholtz and Hall's (2005) sociocultural linguistic approach, specifically their discussion of indexicality (Ochs 1992, 1993; Silverstein 1985) and Kristeva's (1986) notion of intertextuality, to elucidate how ideologies of gender and sexuality shape how the participants construct a leader identity; primarily through the production of evaluation and positioning in stance-taking (Du Bois 2007). Indexicality brings attention to the "semiotic links between linguistic form and social meanings" (2005, 594) and intertextuality draws focus to both the accumulative meanings and the sociocultural history attached to a text. Further, as discussed by Bucholtz and Hall, through stance-taking – i.e., evaluating and then positioning oneself vis-à-vis a "figure" (following Kiesling 2019) – speakers index identities. In my analysis, I am specifically attuned to the employment of discursive features, such as contrastive discourse markers (Schiffrin 1987) and involvement strategies (i.e., details and constructed dialogue by Tannen 2007) that facilitate stance-taking. By examining leadership discourse in this way, I apply a discourse analytic approach, specifically interactional sociolinguistics (Gumperz 2015; Schiffrin 1996; Tannen 2008a), to queer linguistics and uncover how masculinity shapes heterosexual performativity in the U.S. military.

This analysis, in line with queer linguistics, demonstrates not only how ideologies of gender and sexuality affect leadership discourse, but also shows how the participants are *subjugated to* hegemonic masculinity and *operate within* compulsory heterosexuality. Further, because of the historical discrimination against women and LGBT individuals, heteronormativity, following Coates (2015), not only sets heterosexual relationships and practices as the norm but also "others" gay men as feminine and women (regardless of sexual orientation) as masculine – thereby conflating notions of gender and sexuality. When examining the discourse of the participants, my findings reveal ideologies of gender and sexuality pervading the indexical construction of leader identities. In Kim's discussion of a female leader whom she admires, Kim reveals mitigating one's authenticity and femininity as a strategy to subvert the "heterosexual marketplace" (Eckert 2000) dominated by men, while her discussion of a male leader reveals how mocking gay men both maintains military hierarchy and male solidarity through a simulated homosexual act. AJ, who discusses his ship handling ability, reproduces military hierarchy based on epistemic authority and demonstrates how military masculinities can be contested through his negative evaluation of his captain. In each discussion, masculinity not only shows to privilege men, but also emerges to signal group membership in the military's compulsory heterosexuality.

This chapter proceeds as follows; in the next section, I begin my discussion of the theoretical background with a brief history of gender exclusion and sexuality regulation in the U.S. military that I understand as compulsory heterosexuality. I then turn to relevant definitions and frameworks in queer theory that I employ to disentangle and understand how the U.S. military conflates notions of gender and sexuality in the historic discrimination against both women and homosexuals. Lastly, I discuss the linguistic theoretical frameworks – specifically indexicality and intertextuality – that I employ in the analysis. The third section discusses in detail my methods and intentions for recruiting participants who attended the U.S. Naval Academy and served on U.S. warships. The fourth section pertains to the analysis which consists of three subsections. The first section examines Kim's discussion of a female leader whom she admired. The second section examines Kim's discussion of a male leader whom Kim considered a "bad" leader. The last section examines AJ's discussion of himself as a leader and his captain's leadership qualities. I synthesize my findings in the conclusion and provide a discussion about the importance of applying queer linguistics to examining critically gender and sexuality in military institutions to affect, inform, and understand broader social change and (in)justices.

2 Theoretical background

Navigating toward queerness in the military means first unraveling the interconnectedness of gender and sexuality by understanding the ideologies that continue to gender the military as masculine as well as understanding the effects of the military's management of sexuality. Undoubtedly, as Connell (1995) puts it, "Violence on the largest possible scale is the purpose of the military; and no arena has been more important for the definition of hegemonic masculinity in European/American culture (213). Further, as Disler (2008) argues in her exploration of the intersection of language, gender, and the military, the U.S. military is the arbiter of American masculinity and that the historical presence of women in the military has not changed this monolithic view. The U.S. military reinforces gender differences in a number of ways; for example, the differences in physical fitness standards, the past exclusion of women from combat roles, and the continued exclusion of women from selective service (i.e., the "draft"). This gender dichotomy has predicated the debate over how women serve and on what terms since the turn of the twentieth century. Indeed, as Mesok (2022) highlights in the Women's Armed Services Integration Act in 1948, women were not only excluded from combat specialties but also not allowed to exceed 2 percent of the overall U.S. military. This representation is reinforced in popular culture through movies such as "Top

Gun," "Rambo," and "Full Metal Jacket" that valorize men in combat and often depict women in misogynistic ways (Segal 2006).

At the same time, the military has historically discriminated against homosexual and bisexual men and women. During World War II men and women accused of homosexual acts were arrested and sent to military prison (Bérubé 2010). In 1993, President Clinton signed into law "Don't Ask, Don't Tell" which allowed lesbian, gay, and bisexual service members to serve just not openly. The law stated, homosexuality created "an unacceptable risk to the high standards of morale, good order and discipline, and unit cohesion that are the essence of military capability" (10. U.S.C. 654, 2007, 299). However, I agree with Disler (2008) who stated at the time, "it [was] the stereotype of the gay man as a feminized man which threatens the military representation of American masculinity" (12). Arguably, the type of masculinity Disler is alluding to is what Segal (2006) identifies as heterosexual masculinity – a masculinity predicated on the "labeling and policing of gay men" and "defined through the difference from, and desire for, women" (83). In the next section, I turn to how DADT sanctioned heterosexual masculinity and institutionalized compulsory heterosexuality.

2.1 Compulsory heterosexuality in the U.S. armed forces

Important in my discussion about the regulation of military sexuality is Rich's (1980) notion of compulsory heterosexuality and Butler's (1990) conceptualization of a heterosexual matrix. Rich, in her discussion of lesbian existence and female heterosexuality, argues that heterosexuality should be examined as a political institution in which women are subordinated and subjugated to men in terms of "physical, economical, and emotional access" (647). For example, Rich demonstrates the subjugation of women to men in the workplace in her reading of MacKinnon's (1979) study about sex discrimination. Rich states that women "endure sexual harassment to keep their jobs and learn to behave in a complaisantly and ingratiatingly heterosexual manner because they discover this is their true qualification for employment." Further, for women who reject the sexual advances of men, they are "accused of being 'dried-up' and sexless, or lesbian." (642). For closeted lesbians, they are forced to not only hide their sexuality but to alter their behaviors to act feminine. In this way, compulsory heterosexuality reveals how heterosexual women and lesbians are obliged to operate in male-dominated environments. Concomitantly, compulsory heterosexuality presupposes a heterosexual masculinity in which men subjugate and control women.

Guiding my understanding of how heteronormativity as socially construed is Butler's (1990) conceptualization of the heterosexual matrix. It captures the idea that our behaviors and the expectations of our behaviors are linked to our genders, sexualities, and our sexed-bodies. Butler defines it as the "grid of cultural intelligibility through which bodies, genders, and desires are naturalized" (208). From birth, our bodies are assigned a sex and with it a series of mutually constitutive expectations. The assignment of "male" comes with the expectation of a masculine gender (i.e., a man) and the expectation to be heterosexual through the desire of the opposite sex (i.e., a woman). Britton and Williams (1995) observe, "The hegemonic masculine ideal perpetuated by the military conflates soldierliness, masculinity, and heterosexuality" (14). Thus, a military heterosexual matrix might consist of the embodied soldier imbued with a masculinity and heterosexuality unique to the military and acquired through a rebirth in military indoctrination (i.e., bootcamp). How these components of the heterosexual matrix come to be understood as identities can be explained through Butler's theory of performativity in which Butler exemplifies how identities, specifically gender, become "naturalized," meaning, "seen as non-ideological 'common sense'" (Fairclough 1985). By gender performativity, Butler argues that the "anticipation of a gendered essence produces that which it posits as outside itself." They continue, "[it] is not a singular act, but a repetition and a ritual, which achieves its effects through its naturalization in the context of a body" (xv). In other words, the production, or performance, of a specific gender relies on what is already understood as that gender and how that gender should be reproduced. Further, the body becomes a semiotic vehicle when gender performativity is repeatedly produced through the body. Because each component of the heterosexual matrix is mutually constitutive, it is easy to conflate ideas of gender with ideas of sexuality. Indeed, and as pointed out by Cameron and Kulick (2003), our sexed-bodies, our gender identities, and our sexual identities are rarely disconnected and often experienced in connection with one another. Thus, examined through compulsory heterosexuality, how we perform our genders and sexualities is not only reinforced through rituals and repetition, but also institutionalized in different domains of our society.

While Rich's discussion of compulsory heterosexuality addresses the assumption – and enforcement – of heterosexuality upon women, it also resonates with discriminatory practices that exclude and persecute homosexuals. When President Clinton signed into law "Don't Ask, Don't Tell," he reinforced the institutionalization of heterosexuality by prohibiting gay, lesbian, and bisexual service members from serving openly. Through the lens of compulsory heterosexuality, Britton and Williams (1995) state, "The military's refusal to admit gay men and lesbians is an implicit sanctioning of heterosexuality" in which they then ask, "Why does the military prefer heterosexual soldiers?" (11). To answer their question, discrimination against homosexuals was linked to the exclusion of women. In other words, if "gayness is associated with femininity" (Connell 1995, 78), then the justification for prohibiting homosexuals in the military paralleled the same reasons for excluding women – the subjugation of not only women, but also feminine men. Additionally, the sanctioning of heterosexuality through the prohibition of homosexuality – specifically any social acts associated with homosexuality – reinforced hypermasculine ideologies in compulsory heterosexuality. To examine how these masculine ideologies emerge in discourse, I turn to a discussion of indexicality as a theoretical framework for analyzing identity construction.

2.2 Indexicality and the performance of (leader) identities

The study of masculinity in leadership has been largely disregarded because it is understood to be interwoven into the fabric of doing leadership (Sinclair 2005). In my analysis, I draw on Bucholtz and Hall's (2005) sociocultural linguistic approach to identity, specifically their discussion of indexicality, to elucidate how the participants talk about leadership and how leadership is linked to ideologies about gender and sexuality through intertextually (Kristeva 1986). Because the participants talk about individuals they consider leaders, I specifically focus on the employment of evaluation and positioning in stance-taking (Du Bois 2007; Kiesling 2019). In her demonstration of how people construct identities through alignments taken in interaction, Ochs (1992) centralizes the notion of indexicality and states that "the relation of language to gender is constituted and mediated by the relation of language to stances, social acts, social activities and other social constructs" (337). By social, Ochs infers the dependence of mutual sense-making, such as shared knowledge. Ochs further points out that these social constructs can either directly or indirectly index gender. For example, the use of "sir" directly indexes a masculine gender and "ma'am" directly indexes a feminine gender. Holmes (2006), in her research about language in the workplace, highlights examples of interactional styles that index masculinity and femininity. For example, a "supportive" and "collaborative" interactional style can be understood as indirectly indexing femininity. Conversely, a "confrontational" and "aggressive" interactional style can be understood to indirectly index masculinity.

Because evaluation emerges in how the participants talk about themselves and other leaders, I turn to Du Bois's (2007) discussion of stance-taking to examine social stances, specifically the employment of evaluation and positioning, that index masculinity and femininity. Stance-taking in interaction captures how interlocutors position themselves in relation to an object based on their evaluations. Aligning or disaligning in discourse can be considered in Bamberg's (2011) terms of sameness versus difference. Bamberg states, "speakers draw boundaries around themselves – and others – so that individual identities and groups become visible" (105). In this way, stances convey positions that can potentially index identities and signal group membership.

Fundamental to my employment of indexicality is Kristeva's (1986) conceptualization of intertextuality which connects discursive practices to broader social constructs. Kristeva draws on Bakhtin's (1986) discussions of dialogicality where "any concrete utterance is a link in a chain of speech communications" (91) in literary and spoken language. Kristeva, in a similar vein, defines intertextuality as "any text is constructed as a mosaic of quotations; any text is the absorption and transformation of another" (37). It is through this understanding of intertextuality, or repetition (i.e., what Becker [1994] calls "prior texts") that communities form, identities become naturalized, and ideologies are reinforced. Through intertextuality, Kristeva introduced Bakhtin's scholarship to critical studies of language, gender, and sexuality. In her discussion of social meaning and indexicality, Ochs (1992) highlights Bakhtin's notion of voice and calls attention to the "relation of language to gender, where gender may generate its own set of voices" (338). Kiesling (2019), in his discussion of stance, demonstrates that "gay voice" as an enregistered speech style not only indexes a gay identity but also observes that it signals a particular stance [i.e., a negative evaluation] towards a figure, such as a person. In the context of leadership, this lends insight into why an "authoritative voice" might be regarded as stereotypically masculine, especially in masculine gendered institutions like the military.

Important in the analysis of emerging genders and sexualities in a masculine gendered institution is Briggs and Bauman's (1992) theorizing of intertextual gaps in their discussion of genre. Genres can be understood as "generic frameworks" that facilitate interpretation and coherence in conversation or some other communicative means. Their term, intertextual gap, refers to the degree in which a speaker invokes a generic framework. A narrow intertextual gap refers to minimizing the distance between a text or utterance and the generic framework while a wide intertextual gap refers to maximizing that distance. Briggs and Bauman argue that "maximizing and highlighting these intertextual gaps underlies strategies for building authority through claims of individual creativity" (149). Additionally, a wide intertextual gap can also foster resistance to hegemonic discourses and arguably facilitate change.

While the frameworks of indexicality and intertextuality provide insight to examining the relationship between discursive practice and social meanings in identity construction, an understanding of the intertextual gaps help understand how ideologies such as hegemonic masculinities are challenged and how compulsory heterosexuality is/can be compromised. To demonstrate what I mean, I provide a short anecdote from the 2011 Republican Presidential Debate which occurred the day before President Obama's administration repealed DADT. During the debate,

Stephen Hill – a white, masculine-presenting, gay soldier serving in Iraq – appeared via video to ask the Republican candidates if they would reinstate DADT or prohibit LGB service members from serving. Hill, when introduced, was met with applause because of his service. However, when he self-identified as gay and asked his question, the applause turned to "boos." Subsequently, Republican Presidential Candidate Rick Santorum stated he would reinstate the law and argued that homosexuality compromised military readiness. Arguably, Stephen Hill represented the naturalized image of a soldier. But, when he made his sexuality explicit, the intertextual gap widened and challenged Santorum's and the audience's heteronormative expectation. When understood through the intertextual gap, this anecdote exemplifies the injustice (and arbitrariness) of discrimination based on sexuality – it also demonstrates how gay male soldiers are assumed heterosexual until they say otherwise.

3 Data and methods

The excerpts provided in this study come from a larger study examining how leadership style emerges in narratives, or sea stories, told by naval officers. For the study (which was conducted with approval from Georgetown University's Institutional Review Board), I recruited and interviewed 14 current and veteran naval officers from my own professional and personal networks. Each participant commissioned from the U.S. Naval Academy and served as Surface Warfare Officers – meaning they drove ships. Among the seven participants who identified as men, three identified as heterosexual, three identified as gay, and one identified as bisexual. Among the five participants who identified as women, three identified as heterosexual and two identified as lesbian. Among the two participants who identified as transgender, one identified as a gay man and one identified as a lesbian woman. Because each participant attended the U.S. Naval Academy, they underwent the same indoctrination into the U.S. Navy and received similar leadership training while earning a bachelor's degree. Choosing participants who attended the U.S. Naval Academy and served on ships was intentional to not only ensure similar opportunities to leadership but also to ensure that I could elicit similar stories about military service during the interviews.

The structure of each interview was a "semi-structured" conversation (following Tannen 2008b). While I had specific questions prepared, I also allowed the interview to flow as certain themes developed. Because I identify as a gay man and had also attended the U.S. Naval Academy, commissioned as a Surface Warfare Officer, and served on ships, I was very familiar with the experiences of each participant and shared similar adverse experiences from DADT. I spent about one hour with each participant and the interviews took place at a location of their choice. About half of the participants resided at the time in Washington, DC, and I was able to do those interviews in person. I interviewed the remaining half via video conferencing. An important methodological consideration I had during the interview was allowing participants to disclose topics related to their gender and sexuality on their own. In other words, I asked broad questions such as "Did you have any challenging leadership experiences while at sea?" rather than asking questions that implied or presupposed their gender or sexuality had leadership implications.

For the analyses, I provide three excerpts from two participants with the pseudonyms Kim and AJ. Kim identifies as an Asian American and as a queer-lesbian, cis-gender woman. The excerpts were chosen because they included evaluations of other leaders. At the time of the interview, she was in her early thirties. AJ identifies as a Black American and as a heterosexual, cis-gender man. At the time of the interview, he was also in his early thirties. Both Kim and AJ graduated in the same year group at the U.S. Naval Academy and contribute to discussions about their experiences from their first and second ships – which occurred before the repeal of DADT. After graduation from the U.S. Naval Academy, Kim and AJ reported to destroyers – a type of warship which has its own culture – and describe their interaction with other leadership while also discussing their own leadership experiences. In choosing to analyze the discourse of a queer lesbian woman and a heterosexual, cis-gender man, I demonstrate how "queering the military" in a linguistic analysis goes beyond analyzing the discourse of queer people. Instead, it highlights how understandings of leadership in the military context – and how leadership is enacted and described – are shaped by ideologies of masculinity and heterosexuality.

4 Analysis

The analysis includes three sections. The first two sections examine responses from Kim in which she discusses a female leader whom she admired and a male leader who she considered "bad." In Kim's discourse about the female leader, she employs positive evaluations followed by the contrastive discourse marker "but" (Schiffrin 1987) – which demonstrates how being an effective leader and a woman comes with stipulations in which masculinity benefits women differently than men. Her account of a "bad" leader, which included details and constructed dialogue (Tannen 2007), suggests how masculinity when enacted by men facilitates solidarity, maintains hierarchy, and signals group membership. AJ, who provides the perspective of a heterosexual cisgender man, employs details and constructed dialogue to employ evaluations about himself and towards his ship's captain. AJ's account demonstrates how masculinities can be contested through his negative evaluations toward his captain.

4.1 Challenges of being queer, being a woman, and being a leader

In this first section, Kim verbalizes the challenges of being a woman in the military. Kim attended the U.S. Naval Academy during DADT and continued her service as a naval officer throughout the repeal of the law. After Kim graduated, she reported to her first ship. Prior to the first excerpt examined below, Kim shared a narrative about how she was confronted by fellow naval officers who suspected Kim was a lesbian. This discussion led to Kim elaborating on the challenges of being queer, being a woman, and being a leader – specifically in regard to living authentically. As many leadership scholars such as Sparrowe (2005) point out, authenticity, or demonstrating one's true self, is a fundamental quality of leadership. Further, Eagly and Carli (2007), in their scholarship about the challenges women face as leaders, also add that authenticity in leadership is linked with being transparent and being open – a task found challenging by women in masculine gendered institutions. In our discussion of authenticity, Kim noted that it was hard to find a leader to emulate. Following up on that point, I inquired with Kim if she had any leaders who she could emulate during her first few years as a naval officer.

In the following excerpt, Kim highlights the CHENG (Chief Engineer, a department head position on a warship), who she admired as a woman and as a leader. Department heads typically have 6–7 years of service and are navy lieutenants or lieutenant commanders and thus have seniority. On U.S. warships, there are 5–6 department heads. Department heads supervise divisions (smaller units within a department) and report to the executive officer who is second in command to the captain of the ship. An engineering department on a destroyer can have up to 150 sailors who are divided into four divisions, each led by a division officer. Kim, in this instance, is a navy ensign with 1–2 years of service and is a division officer in the engineering department. Thus, she reports to the CHENG.

In this analysis, I highlight how Kim provides social acts that are indexical of female leadership through the employment of a positive evaluation followed by a contrastive idea (introduced by the discourse marker *but*). I then argue that these social acts are atypical leadership qualities that demonstrate how women are subjugated to and operate within the military's compulsory heterosexuality. (See transcription conventions below.)

Excerpt 1.
1. Nick: Did you see any leaders:.. uh during your first tours.. um: or first two tours
2. that you wanted to emulate?
3. Kim: Yeah.. yeah.. There was uh this .. my-my CHENG (2.0)
4. um:: She was an amazing department head.
5. She was really really good-
6. But I could *tell* that in a way she::..
7. She was::.. She seemed very-really closed off to people (.)
8. But I think it was just-It was kinda a defense mechanism-
9. It was like..
10. She knew that as a woman::
11. At least this is my assessment-
12. She's like as a woman-
13. And she was kinda-.. like..s:: weird to say
14. but she was kinda cute (.) you know?
15. So like . . . I think she had to have like *walls up*..
16. You know? So peopl::e-
17. And she was also @@very-
18. She just wasn't personabl::e/ either/..

Without pause, Kim indicates that she wanted to emulate her CHENG which directly indexes the CHENG as a leader. Kim then takes up a stance by providing the following positive evaluation, "She was an amazing department head.. she was really good" (lines 4–5). Kim then describes the CHENG's qualities that are arguably atypical of leaders. Kim first indicates, "But I could *tell* that in a way she:: [. . .] seemed very-really closed off to people" (lines 6–7). Kim then attributes being "closed off to people" to "But I think it was just-It was kinda a defense mechanism" (line 8). Kim introduces each of these statements with the discourse coordinator *but*. Schiffrin (1987) points out, among the different pragmatic uses of *but*, that it can also suggest a contrastive idea or action. Thus, using a "defense mechanism" and being "closed off" can be seen as contrastive, or incongruent, with what is normally expected of an authentic leader identity, as pointed out by Eagly and Carli.

After characterizing the CHENG's leadership, Kim turns to the connection between being a woman and being attractive in the navy. Kim first indexes the CHENG's gender, "She knew as a woman" (line 10) and then evaluates the CHENG's attractiveness, "She was kinda cute" (line 14), and "So like.. I think she had to have like *walls up*" (line 15). By stating "as a woman," Kim evaluates the CHENG in contrast to men which conversely presupposes that men do not have to be closed off. In other words, men can act authentically in their leadership capacities. Further, as a woman in a male-dominated institution, Kim draws attention to the professional challenges of the CHENG's leader identity connected to her gender and attractiveness. The "kinda cute" evaluation appeals to what Eckert (2000) refers to as the *heterosexual marketplace* where individuals acquire value from the opposite sex. Kim's evaluation and mentioning of the CHENG's appearance also suggest that women are involuntarily subjugated to the heterosexual marketplace in ways that compromise their professional capacities. Kim's employment of the metaphor "walls up" illustrates being "closed off to people" as a strategic behavior, or social act, which suggests that the CHENG had to reject the advances of heterosexual men and/or the presupposition of such advances. In doing so, Kim builds on the social acts that are indexical of female leaders in the military in contrast to male leaders.

To be clear, Kim's assessment of the CHENG's appearance suggests that being an attractive woman does not index a leader identity but may (unfairly) undermine it. The strategic behavior of being "closed off" thus conveys a social act that mitigates the subjugation to the heterosexual marketplace based on one's (perceived attractive) appearance. Kim's characterization of the CHENG as being "closed off" suggests the CHENG suppressed her feminine qualities to be seen as an effective leader which indirectly positions her evaluators as belonging to the dominant category in the military – heterosexual men. While this reproduces sexism (and the idea that a feminine person cannot be a good leader), it also serves as a strategy that Kim identifies as worthy of emulation. The suppression of her feminine qualities also suggests the CHENG had to thwart unwanted sexual advances – or the presumption of sexual desire – presumably from heterosexual men in her leadership capacities.

It should also be noted that Kim did not mention the CHENG's sexual orientation and that one could read Kim's description of the CHENG as a "butch" lesbian. Indeed, and as described by Brownson (2014) in her study of women in the U.S. Marine Corps, female marines are not only stereotyped as "dykes" (i.e., butch lesbians), but also as "sluts" or "bitches." These stereotypes reflect the perceived incongruence of being a woman in the military by casting female service members outside heteronormativity regardless of their sexual orientation. During DADT, this incongruence manifested in female service members being disproportionally targeted and discharged for being homosexual. Damiano (1998) identifies the practice of "lesbian bating" where women were accused of being lesbians when they rejected the sexual advances of (or report sexual harassment by) men. In this way, regardless of their sexual orientation, women who serve are subjugated to compulsory heterosexuality in similar ways.

In the following excerpt, I provide the continuation of Kim's response that acknowledges these stereotype categories found by Brownson (2014) and shows how women, specifically the CHENG, operate under the conditions of compulsory heterosexuality by stating that women are either a "bitch" or a whore." This dichotomy intertextually appeals to the female leadership behaviors identified by Baxter (2009) in her discussion of female leadership. Baxter uses the terms "iron maiden" to describe a female leader who demonstrates stereotypically masculine qualities, and "seductress" to describe a female leader who demonstrates stereotypically promiscuous qualities. I continue to highlight Kim's employment of evaluation and the discourse coordinator "but," to show how the CHENG operated within the military's compulsory heterosexuality by indexing masculinity.

Excerpt 2.
19. Kim: *But the reason I* wanted to emulate her was
20. because she was *very* effective at her job.
21. Like.. people didn't really: get to engage with her on a personal level .. or..
22. She was kinda stern/..
23. I don't think that's what her real personality was:/
24. But I think she did it because it was a way of.. being able to..
25. to be good at her job..
26. without people picking her apart as a woman.. you know?..
27. Espec-and-and especially as like-as an *attractive* woman.. so:: . . .
28. It's one of those things I think women(.)a lot of women who are in the military
29. at least in my experience we all say that like if you want to be an effective-
30. Like as a woman in the military you're either known as a *bitch* or basically
31. @@ like a *whore* if you will
32. And I hate to be so grotesque (2.0)
33. But.. it's one of those things that as a woman you have to choo::se . . .
34. to put up some walls.. You know?
35. Nick: mhm
36. Kim: Or be a little bit more masculine.. I guess if you will.

Kim positively assesses the CHENG's leadership behavior; in how she does this, she indexes the normative expectations of leadership while also highlighting how the CHENG seemed to get around them. Again, we see that Kim uses the discourse coordinator *but* which suggests a following contrastive idea – and questions why Kim would want to emulate an individual with the aforementioned qualities that stray from expectations of typical effective leadership. Kim provides the positive evaluation, "she was *very* effective at her job" (line 20). At the same time, the CHENG's effectiveness came with the following stipulations: "people didn't really: get to engage with her on a personal level" (line 21), and "She was kinda stern/" (line 22) which resonates with the masculine "iron maiden" stereotype. Kim also states, "I don't think that's what her real personality was" (line 23). This evaluation regarding the CHENG's "real personality" challenges the authenticity of the CHENG's identity from Kim's perspective. It also highlights the challenges women face and how women navigate a male-dominated institution. Kim notes that her CHENG managed to "be good at her job" "without people picking her apart as a woman" (lines 25–26). "As a woman" again emerges in Kim's discourse which positions the CHENG in contrast to men and brings attention to how women are subjugated to scrutiny because of their gender or feminine qualities.

Next, Kim provides the female leadership dichotomy that she observed in the military – women must either be a "bitch" (line 30) or a "whore" (line 31) – that further demonstrates how women operate within and are subjugated to the military's compulsory heterosexuality. While *bitch* has many meanings, here I argue it is used to disparage a woman, such as an "iron maiden," who demonstrates masculine characteristics (i.e., stern [line 21]) incongruent with heteronormative expectations. This also aligns with Kim's assessment of the CHENG who she observes as being "stern" and "closed off to people." Further, *bitch* maintains heteronormativity by defining, policing, and othering non-normative feminine individuals or to invalidate an individual's masculinity (e.g., when targeting men). Conversely, *whore* maintains heteronormativity by reducing women and their value in the military to their sexual attractiveness – alluding again to the heterosexual marketplace. Additionally, *whore* suggests the presumption that women also commodify their sexed-bodies for personal or professional gain. Kim seems to use these terms with an awareness of their problematic nature, as suggested by the laughter (denoted by "@@") in line 31, and the statement, "I hate to be so grotesque" (line 32). However, by invoking this type of woman leader, Kim identifies a type of leadership behavior predicated on exploiting erotic desire – specifically heterosexual desire. Kim's description of her CHENG's leadership behavior makes clear that the CHENG avoided being categorized as a "whore," and was not so stern to be identified as a "bitch" either. Rather, according to Kim, the CHENG found a way to navigate this impossible dichotomy that worked for her, and which Kim found admirable. Kim's discourse intertextually connects to and indexes these ideologies, and at the same time, it shows how one person successfully navigated the challenges of a male-dominated environment.

Despite the military opening all military specialties to women, Kim's discussion about her CHENG also illustrates how the presence of women both challenges and maintains heteronormative expectations. First, Kim's discourse – specifically the "bitch" versus "whore" dichotomy – demonstrates how heteronormativity is maintained by the "othering" of female service members. Second, and in Kim's view, being an effective leader as a woman involves the rejection or mitigation of one's femininity to thwart the unwanted sexual advances of others (presumably men) or to disavow the presumption that one would commodify their sexuality for professional gain. Kim's description, which emerged through the employment of a positive evaluation + a contrastive idea highlighted these stipulations that women, regardless of their sexuality, face in the military. Thus, while being a woman in the military challenges heteronormative expectations, being an "unfeminine" and "closed off" woman shows how women operate within the military's compulsory heterosexuality. Lastly, if we interpret Kim's description of "stern" as masculine, then we see in Kim's discourse that masculinity for women does not necessarily entail group membership.

In the next section, Kim discusses a "bad leader" and provides one example of how a male leader indexes masculinity by mocking gay men to maintain military hierarchy, solidarity, and group membership.

4.2 Masculinity and male solidarity

After our discussion about the CHENG above, I asked Kim if she had any bad leaders. After stating she had "a lot of those" she describes the "Deck Department Head" – an officer similar in rank to the CHENG. The Deck Department Head (DDH) is responsible for overseeing the management of sailors who work in deck operations, which include the launching and landing of helicopters on the flight deck, dropping the anchor, and maintaining the outward appearance of the ship. Kim noted that the DDH "cared a lot about how the enlisted people saw him" and that "he wanted to be like one of the boys." In the navy, and the military writ large, enlisted service members are subordinate to all commissioned officers. Thus, Kim's observation of the DDH as wanting to be "one of the boys" conveys how masculinity both blurs professional boundaries and excludes those who are not ascribed as masculine.

In the following short excerpt, Kim describes an incident in which the DDH "fake humped" (i.e., simulated sexual penetration of) a senior enlisted chief petty officer (CPO who is a subordinate) in the Deck Department known as "Boats" (a colloquial term for sailors with the military job boatswain). The act of "fake humping," an act of male solidarity, is a common behavior among boys and men and can be unpacked through Ward's (2015) discussion of sex between heterosexual men. Ward juxtaposes the act of anal penetration between men as a form of hazing in the U.S. navy during the "crossing the line ceremony" (when ships cross the equator) with hazing pornography in which actors posing as straight men are hazed into anal intercourse. Ward argues, "the relationship between hetero-masculine and gay approaches to homosexuality recognizes that homophobic disidentification and dramatic displays of repulsion and endurance are what imbue homosexual activity with heterosexual meaning" (185). In the context of a hazing, or what Ward identifies as a "circuit of hetero-masculinity" (189), sex between straight men maintains heteronormativity because it reinforces dominance between men while denouncing homosexuality (through repulsion) and invoking the quality of resilience (through penetration). Likewise (although less extreme), the act of "fake humping" serves heteronormativity because it both mocks gay men (i.e., homophobic disidentification) and is often followed by contestation (i.e., repulsion).

In this analysis, I highlight Kim's employment of details and constructed dialogue to negatively evaluate the DDH and to demonstrate how masculinity emerges the social act of fake humping to mock gay men and reinforce military hierarchy and solidarity at the same time.

Excerpt 3.
1. Kim: And like I think Boats was bent over..
2. And he like fake humped him/
3. And I was like "Why? And like seriously?"
4. And to me it was just so incredibly unprofessional
5. But it was just so indicative of the type of person he was.
6. Especially as an officer like he just was trying to be funny and fit in (.)

Kim offers a stark contrast to how she conveyed the CHENG in the two previous excerpts – she provides a specific event, with relatively specific details, to illustrate her perception of the DDH and index his leader identity. Additionally, in line 3, she uses reported speech, or what Tannen (2007) calls "constructed dialogue" to capture the fact that we recontextualize and reshape the words of others for our own purposes (see also Bauman and Briggs 1990). Tannen describes details and constructed dialogue as "involvement strategies" that not only contribute to the meaning-making process but also evoke emotion in conversation – in other words, they can help convince an audience. In Kim's description, she narrates a specific event in which she constructs DDH as superordinate to Boats. She states that DDH "like fake humped" (line 2) Boats. The social act of "fake humping" indexes masculinity and can be understood as mocking gay men. In doing so, DDH also asserts his institutional authority, or control, over Boats by making Boats the "bottom." At the same time, the act of "fake humping," through its mockery of gay men, also reinforces male solidarity, or what Sedgwick (1985) refers to as homosocial desire.

Kim then uses constructed dialogue capturing her thoughts (it is unlikely she said this out loud), "And I was like "Why? And like seriously?"" (line 3) which conveys her stance and her negative evaluation of the event (and the DDH). It also positions her in contrast to the DDH and suggests her positionality as an outsider in a male-dominated environment. Kim negatively evaluates the event as "incredibly unprofessional" (line 4) and then state, "he just was trying to be funny and fit in" (line 6). In this way, we can understand Kim's observation of a male leader as showing how masculinity emerges in two ways – to reinforce control through the maintenance of military hierarchy and to signal group membership.

In terms of an intertextual gap, Kim's construction of the DDH's leader identity minimizes the intertextual gap and demonstrates how a male leader enacts masculinity –through a homophobic gesture – unproblematically. However, Kim's construction of the CHENG's leader identity maximizes the intertextual gap and shows how being a woman in the military is a delicate balance of not being too masculine (i.e, a "bitch") and not being too feminine (i.e., a "whore"). In this way, we can see how performing heterosexuality is different from Kim's observations of a female leader and a male leader. For the CHENG, she has to perform heterosexuality (as to not be assumed a lesbian and discharged) but also enact masculinity (to subvert the heterosexual marketplace). For the DDH, who is presumably heterosexual, not only does the DDH benefit from enacting masculinity, but he also does so in a way that subjugates gay men. While Kim's observations demonstrate how masculinity operates from the perspective of a queer woman, the next section provides the perspective from a cisgender heterosexual man.

4.3 Competing masculinities in military leadership

In the U.S. military, men benefit from ideals of masculinity that predicate who can be a leader and who cannot. Baker (2014), drawing on Connell's (1995) notion of "patriarchal dividend," points out that men can be seen as "natural leaders" regardless of how much they actually conform to those masculine ideals. As previously discussed, they can act authentically. Further, as Baker also highlights, men who are closer to the ideals of masculinity can contribute to the marginalization of those who do not conform. In this section, I turn to examining how military masculinities emerge in contestation, specifically through evaluations, constructed dialogue, and the provision of details.

In the following excerpt, AJ responds to my inquiry about his Officer of the Deck (OOD) qualification. The OOD qualification is the final requirement before becoming a qualified "Surface Warfare Officer." As the OOD, the officer is responsible for the overall safe navigation of the ship and its various operations. The OOD is a "watch position" in which officers rotate standing while underway at sea. Usually, OOD watches are 4–5 hours in duration and qualified officers stand OOD watch once a day. Additionally, ship captains may have a preferred OOD who they consider their most trusted. These preferred OODs are often designated for challenging operations. Thus, the OOD position is a leadership position in which the designated individual carries out the captain's commands. In this analysis, I examine through the discourse of "watch standing," as a social act, how AJ indexes his leader identity as a naval officer. Additionally, I demonstrate how AJ's positive evaluations of his watch standing ability (i.e., ship handling), as a social stance, reinforces military masculinity through the maintenance of a military hierarchy. Lastly, I show how masculinities can compete through AJ's stance, as constructed through evaluations, towards his captain's watch standing practices. (Note: The bridge refers to the location on the ship where the OOD stands watch and where navigation decisions [changes in speed and steering] are made. The term "ops" is short for "operations.")

Excerpt 4.
1. Nick: What was it like when you were qualified OOD standing watch on the bridge?
2. AJ: I was one of the most trusted OODs on the ship/
3. So.. it was really.. chill? for me/
4. Just because I was a great ship handler::
5. and um:: I had the captain's trust.
6. Like truly had the captain's trust.
7. We:: had a lot of small boat ops.
8. Like we would do some of the most *asinine* stuff..
9. just because my captain had an ego/
10. And.. like he would.. make us do *small* boat ops(.)
11. while doing flight ops(.)
12. a thousand yards from the carrier. (2.0)
13. like "come on man like that's a safety:: hazard in and of itself."
14. Nick: [yeah]
15. AJ: [But] that's just the way he operated.
16. He wanted to do small boat transfers while doing helo (helicopter) ops.
17. I'm like "Okay"..

After I ask about AJ's experience as an OOD, AJ responds by positively evaluating himself. He describes himself in positive terms as, "one of the most trusted OODs on the ship" and as "a great ship handler" (lines 2 and 4). On a U.S. warship, there can be anywhere from 8–15 qualified OODs (depending on the type of ship). AJ's, positive evaluation indexes his leader identity and positions himself vis-à-vis his peers (i.e., above) and his captain (i.e., in alignment). He also provides the evaluation "really.. chill?" which also conveys affective stance that implies confidence or what Kiesling (2018) refers to as a "masculine ease." AJ then reinforces his position vis-à-vis the captain through repetition. AJ states that he had "the captain's trust. Like truly had the captain's trust" (lines 5–6). The repetition and reinforcement of trust suggests that AJ positions himself in alignment with the captain's epistemic authority. Thus, by invoking a specific sociocultural value in the navy, AJ indexes his leader identity via his epistemic stance taking. Further, AJ's indexing of masculinity not only asserts a military hierarchy based on ship handling ability but also establishes group membership among his peers.

After making clear that the captain values him as an OOD above the others, AJ then challenges the captain's leadership and ultimately the captain's version of masculinity. Through details, AJ indicates that the captain ordered the ship to do a variety of operations (e.g., "a lot of small boat ops" [line 7]) which he negatively evaluates as "asinine" (line 8) and he attributes doing these to the captain's "ego" (line 9). AJ elaborates by providing a list of simultaneous operations the captain ordered, "like he would.. make us do *small* boat ops (.) while doing flight ops (.) a thousand yards from the (aircraft) carrier" (lines 10–12). These details serve to support AJ's following negative evaluation which he provides through constructed dialogue to convey his thoughts. AJ states, "Like 'come on man like that's a safety::: hazard in and of itself'" (line 13). The details and constructed dialogue, as what Tannen (2007) calls involvement strategies, add emphasis to the unsafe practices of the captain and intertextually allude to a military masculinity predicated on closeness to danger. At the same time, the negative evaluation directed toward the captain's unsafe ship handling practices and the captain's ego, presupposes AJ's position in contrast to the captain – a position that values safety, which appeals to a military masculinity predicated on good order and discipline. AJ completes his response with the constructed dialogue, "I'm like 'Okay'" (line 17) which shows that, at the time, AJ respected the captain's authority – again reinforcing AJ's good order and discipline military masculinity – and followed the captain's orders.

Observing heterosexual performativity in compulsory heterosexuality through the observations of a heterosexual man lends insight into how masculinity is reproduced unproblematically via a narrow intertextual gap. Similar to Kim's construction of the DDH, AJ's construction of a leader identity demonstrated how masculinity emerges to not only establish group membership (while simultaneously asserting military hierarchy) but also to challenge other versions of masculinity (i.e., his captain's ship handling practices). However, in a close examination of the discourse, we observe that AJ challenges his captain's masculinity as "unsafe" which reflects how hegemonic masculinities are subject to contestation, even within compulsory heterosexuality. Ultimately, as AJ points out, he submits to his captain's orders and performs a masculinity and arguably a heterosexuality that is not his own.

5 Conclusion

In this chapter, I have shown how interactional sociolinguistics as an approach to queer linguistics can unveil how individuals, specifically service members in the U.S. military, are subjugated to and operate within a compulsory heterosexuality institutionalized by the law known as DADT. As demonstrated by the anecdote about

Stephen Hill, who exemplified the archetypical soldier (white, masculine, cisgender man), his identity as a soldier and his service in Iraq were invalidated when he made explicit his sexual orientation. Thus, in line with queer critique, I attempted to explore in leadership discourse how masculinity emerges to perform heterosexuality with attention to whom it benefits, whom it disadvantages, and what purposes it serves.

In my analysis I employed indexicality to explore how leader identities are construed through the provision of evaluations and positioning through discursive features, specifically, the contrastive discourse marker "but" (Schiffrin 1987), details, and constructed dialogue (i.e., what Tannen 2007, calls involvement strategies). In Kim's discussion of a female leader whom she admired; Kim provided a positive evaluation followed by the discourse marker "but" which conveyed that being an effective female leader entailed stipulations. Specifically, Kim's discourse reflected that masculinity served women in order to reject the heterosexuality of men while too much masculinity can result in being perceived as a lesbian. In her discussion of a male leader whom she negatively evaluated; homosexuality, specifically simulated gay sex, emerged as a social act that indexed masculinity and served to create solidarity, reinforce military hierarchy, and signal group membership. However, Kim's reaction demonstrates how such homophobic practices also serve to "other" members who do not subscribe to the same forms of masculinity. In AJ's discussion, he not only conveyed stance of confidence – i.e., masculine ease (Kiesling 2018) – but also positioned himself above his peers to index his leader identity and similarly demonstrate how masculinity reinforces military hierarchy and signals group membership, Importantly, AJ challenging of his ship's captain demonstrated how masculinities can be in contestation. In sum, while masculinity may privilege heterosexual men and signal group membership, women, regardless of the "amount" of masculinity, are disadvantaged and positioned as "other."

Historically, ideologies that construe gender and sexuality have operated as mechanisms for discrimination and oppression. By examining the leadership discourse of Kim and AJ, this study demonstrates how these ideologies also emerge in day-to-day discourse. In this way, these ideologies are pervasive and systemic, and thus call for more attention given the influence of military culture on American culture. Within the queer linguistics approach, this chapter brings attention to the needs of individuals of marginalized genders and sexualities and calls for further research. For example, worth considering is how these individuals operate in a cisgendered, heterosexual, and androcentric institution; how transgender people navigate transitioning in an institution predicated on the gender binary; and how nonbinary people position themselves in this gendered institution. Being able to describe how diverse people use language in military contexts and to analyze it using theories from sociolinguistics and discourse analysis will open the door for deeper critical work to more thoroughly address issues of social (in)justice in the military that arguably reflect contemporary public opinion, especially as related to sexualities and gender identities.

Within the field of linguistics, there is a dearth of research on the U.S. military – arguably the largest and most diverse institution in the United States. The U.S. military consists of 1.3 million active-duty members that represent all 50 states, the District of Columbia, and five U.S. territories. Among Americans, there are approximately 19 million military veterans – while this is less than 10% of adults (Schaeffer 2021), the discourse of this 10% certainly merits research attention. This study has identified some key discursive features used by military members as they talk about leadership and navigate the indexed ideologies associated with it – evaluation or assessment, and "constructed dialogue" and details (Tannen 2007). It thus contributes to our quite limited understanding of the linguistic resources military veterans use in their discourse and sense-making, which connects to and extends sociolinguistic and discourse analytic research focused more generally on identity construction (e.g., Bucholtz & Hall 2005; Ochs 1992, 1993).

Further, this analysis starts to get at the fact that service members and veterans represent a wide and diverse range of backgrounds and (intersecting) identities – racial, ethnic, cultural, socioeconomic, gender, sexuality, religious, linguistic, and so on. As the civilian-military divide continues to expand, a queer linguistics approach captures only a component of the complexities that constitute the military, but also, a broader sense of masculinity and leadership in the sense that, following Disler (2008), the military is arguably the arbiter of American masculinity. It also points to the compulsory heterosexuality that has long dominated the military and has only recently begun to be chipped away. Thus, the implications of research on language and masculinity do not remain confined to the military. This field addresses important issues such as the politization of the military, how the military is represented in popular culture, and military exceptionalism – all of which are predicated on historical discrimination against marginalized identities. Thus, in addition to bringing attention to the omnipresence of ideologies of gender and sexuality in the discourse of those who have affiliations with the military, queer linguistics offers opportunities for better understandings of the U.S. military (and other militaries) while also emphasizing the importance of acknowledging the military's history and status as an institution and of integrating scholarship from multiple fields, including on language and identity, leadership, and gender and sexuality.

References

Baker, Paul. 2014. Two hundred years of the American man. In Tommaso M. Milani (ed.), *Language and masculinities: Performances, intersections, dislocations*. 34–52. London: Routledge.
Bakhtin, Mikhail. 1986. *Speech genres and other late essays*, Carl Emerson & Michael Holquist (eds.), Vern W. McGee. Austin: University of Texas Press.
Bamberg, Michael. 2011. Narrative practice and identity navigation. In James A. Holstein & Jaber F. Gubrium (eds.), *Varieties of narrative analysis*. 99–124. London: SAGE Publications, Inc.
Baxter, Judith. 2009. *The language of female leadership*. New York: Springer.
Becker, A. L. 1994. Repetition and otherness: An essay. In Barbara Johnstone (ed.), *Repetition in Discourse*. 162–175. New York: Ablex.
Bérubé, Allan. 2010. *Coming out under fire: The history of gay men and women in World War II*. Chapel Hill: University of North Carolina Press.
Briggs, Charles L. & Richard Bauman. 1992. Genre, intertextuality, and social power. *Journal of Linguistic Anthropology* 2(2). 131–172.
Britton, D. M. & Williams, C. L. 1995. "Don't Ask, Don't Tell, Don't Pursue": Military Policy and the Construction of Heterosexual Masculinity. *Journal of Homosexuality* 30(1). 1–21.
Brownson, Connie. 2014. The battle for equivalency: Female US Marines discuss sexuality, physical fitness, and military leadership. *Armed Forces & Society* 40(4). 765–788.
Bucholtz, Mary & Kira Hall. 2005. Identity and interaction: A sociocultural linguistic approach. *Discourse Studies* 7(4–5). 585–614.
Butler, Judith. 1990. *Gender trouble: Feminism and the subversion of identity*. London: Routledge.
Cameron, Deborah & Don Kulick. 2003. *Language and sexuality*. Cambridge: Cambridge University Press.
Coates, Jennifer. 2015. *Women, men and language: A sociolinguistic account of gender differences in language*. London: Routledge.
Connell, Raewyn. 1995. *Masculinities*. New York: Blackwell.
Connell, Raewyn W. & James W. Messerschmidt. 2005. Hegemonic masculinity: Rethinking the concept. *Gender & Society* 19(6). 829–859.
Damiano, Christin M. 1998. Lesbian baiting in the military: Institutionalized sexual harrassment under "Don't Ask, Don't Tell, Don't Pursue." *American Journal of Gender, Social Policy & the Law* 7(3). 499–522.
Disler, Edith A. 2008. *Language and gender in the military: Honorifics, narrative, and ideology in Air Force talk*. Amherst: Cambria Press.
Du Bois, John W. 2007. The stance triangle. In Robert Englebretson (ed.), *Stancetaking in discourse: Subjectivity, evaluation, interaction*. 139–182. Amsterdam: John Benjamins Publishing Company.
Eagly, Alice H. & Linda L. Carli. 2007. *Through the labyrinth: The truth about how women become leaders*. Cambridge, MA: Harvard Business Press.
Eckert, Penelope. 2000. *Linguistic variation as social practice: The linguistic construction of identity in Belten High*. New York: Blackwell Publishing.
Fairclough, Norman L. 1985. Critical and descriptive goals in discourse analysis. *Journal of Pragmatics* 9(6). 739–763.
Gumperz, John J. 2015. Interactional sociolinguistics: A personal perspective. In Deborah Tannen, Heidi E. Hamilton & Deborah Schiffrin (eds.), *The handbook of discourse analysis* (2nd edn.). 309–323. Hoboken, NJ: John Wiley & Sons, Inc.

Holmes, Janet. 2006. *Gendered talk at work: Constructing gender identity through workplace discourse*. New York: Blackwell.

Kiesling, Scott F. 2018. Masculine stances and the linguistics of affect: On masculine ease. *Norma* 13(3–4). 191–212.

Kiesling, Scott F. 2019. The 'Gay Voice' and 'Brospeak': Towards a systematic model of stance. In Kira Hall & Rusty Barrett (eds.), *The Oxford handbook of language and sexuality*. 1–20. Oxford: Oxford University Press.

Kristeva, Julia. 1986. *The Kristeva reader*. Toril Moi (ed.). New York: Columbia University Press.

Lee, Hugh, Mark Learmonth & Nancy Harding. 2008. Queer (y) ing public administration. *Public Administration* 86(1). 149–167.

MacKinnon, Catherine A. 1979. *Sexual harassment of working women: A case of sex discrimination*. New Haven: Yale University Press.

Mararac, Nicholas M. 2019. *"I Have the Deck" Power and Style in the Discursive Production of Leadership by Individuals of Marginalized Gender and Sexual Identities in the US Navy*. Georgetown University.

Marine, Susan B. 2017. Changing the frame: Queering access to higher education for trans* students. *International Journal of Qualitative Studies in Education* 30(3). 217–233.

Mesok, Elizabeth. 2022. Combat exclusion policies and the management of gender difference in the U.S. military. In Beth Bailey, Alesha E. Doan, Shannon Portillo & Kara D. Vuic (eds.), *Managing sex in the U.S. military: Gender, Identity, and behavior*. 245–273. Lincoln: University of Nebraska Press.

Motschenbacher, Heiko & Martin Stegu. 2013. Queer Linguistic approaches to discourse. *Discourse & Society* 24(5). 519–535.

Ochs, Elinor. 1992. Indexing gender. In Alessandro Durant & Charles Goodwin (eds.), *Language as an interactive phenomenon*. Cambridge: Cambridge University Press.

Ochs, Elinor. 1993. Constructing social identity: A language socialization perspective. *Research on Language and Social Interaction* 26(3). 287–306.

Rich, Adrienne. 1980. Compulsory heterosexuality and lesbian existence. *Signs: Journal of Women in Culture and Society* 5(4). 631–660.

Rumens, Nick, Eloisio M. de Souza & Jo Brewis. 2019. Queering queer theory in management and organization studies: Notes toward queering heterosexuality. *Organization Studies* 40(4). 593–612.

Schaeffer, Katherine. 2021, April 5. The changing face of America's veteran population. *Pew Research Center*. https://www.pewresearch.org/fact-tank/2021/04/05/the-changing-face-of-americas-veteran-population/

Schiffrin, Deborah. 1987. *Discourse markers*. Cambridge: Cambridge University Press.

Schiffrin, Deborah. 1996. Interactional sociolinguistics. In Sandra Lee McKay & Nancy H. Hornberger (eds.), *Sociolinguistics and language teaching*. 307–328. Cambridge: Cambridge University Press.

Sedgwick, Eve K. 1985. *Between men*. Columbia university press.

Segal, Lynne. 2006. *Slow motion: Changing masculinities, changing men*. New York: Springer.

Silverstein, Michael. 1985. Language and the culture of gender: At the intersection of structure, usage, and ideology. In Elizabeth Mertz & Richard J. Parmentier (eds.), *Semiotic mediation*. New York: Academic Press.

Sinclair, Amanda. 2005. *Doing leadership differently: Gender, power and sexuality in a changing business culture*. Parkville: Melbourne University Publishing.

Sparrowe, Raymond T. 2005. Authentic leadership and the narrative self. *The Leadership Quarterly* 16(3). 419–439.

Tannen, Deborah. 2007. *Talking voices: Repetition, dialogue, and imagery in conversational discourse* (2nd edn.). Cambridge: Cambridge University Press.

Tannen, Deborah. 2008a. Interactional Sociolinguistics. In Ulrich Ammon, Norbert Dittmar, Klaus J. Mattheier & Peter Trudgill (eds.), *Sociolinguistics:* An International Handbook of the Science of Language and Society, 76–88. Berlin: De Gruyter Mouton.

Tannen, Deborah. 2008b. "We've never been close, we're very different": Three narrative types in sister discourse. *Narrative Inquiry* 18(2). 206–229.

Thiel, Markus. 2018. Introducing Queer Theory in International Relations. In Stephen McGlinchey, Rosie Walters & Christian Scheinpflug (eds.), *International Relations Theory*. 97–103. E-International Relations Publishing.

Ward, Jane. 2015. *Not gay: Sex between straight white men* (Vol. 19). New York: New York University Press.

Rusty Barrett and Kira Hall
Closet monsters
Naysayers, gatekeepers, and bullies in queer and trans linguistics

1 Introduction

In the mid-1990s, when we were both in graduate school, Judith Butler's work on performativity was sweeping through academia and challenging long-standing essentialist views of gender as an issue of biological sex. Within language and gender studies, research on lesbian, gay, and gender-variant practices in diverse communities challenged the field's essentialist focus on gendered talk as correlated with the biological sex of the speaker. The excitement of bringing issues of queer theory to linguistic research was dampened by our nervousness about how our work might be received and what the consequences for our careers might be if our research led people to realize that we were queer. Ultimately, a major part of our graduate education involved learning how to navigate academic contexts and their associated closets.

Closets are nothing new to studies of LGBTQ+ language and culture. Even Edward Sagarin's influential sociological text *The Homosexual in America: A Subjective Approach* (1951) was published under the pseudonym Don Cory (an allusion to André Gide's early 20th century queer novel *Corydon*). In this chapter, we are interested in the ability of interactional discourse to create and enforce (and ultimately dismantle) academic closets. In particular, we focus on three discursive patterns that contribute to a cisheteronormative public sphere by suppressing disclosures of queer and trans subjectivity. We first consider "naysayers" who marginalize minority groups through microaggressions that make it clear that certain topics should be kept out of the public sphere. Such microaggressions have a cumulative effect so that repeated actions and insinuations create unwelcoming contexts. We then turn our attention to "gatekeepers" who discursively construct academic disciplines in ways that mark certain topics, research questions, and methodologies as "outside" the disciplinary realm of linguistics. For example, the "this is not linguistics" trope is repeatedly used by linguists to deny LGBTQ+ scholars access to public spaces. The final category is that of "bullies"

Rusty Barrett, University of Kentucky
Kira Hall, University of Colorado Boulder

who overtly attack and undermine the work and careers of graduate students and emerging scholars. In discussing these three types of academic "closet monsters," we do not mean to imply that these categories are clearly distinct or rigidly defined. There is, of course, overlap across categories, and many interactions could fit into more than one category. However, we see the demarcation of these categories as a means of raising awareness regarding various types of closet-enforcing behaviors in our field – an awareness that we believe is critical to the continued growth of queer and trans linguistics in the 21st century.

When discussing various types of closet-enforcing discourse prevalent in the field of linguistics, we use our personal experiences moving in and out of closets in US academic contexts to address current issues in the field. The behaviors that we experienced in relation to our work on language and sexuality persist. Indeed, such behaviors are now enabled by a broad-scale nostalgic return to the biological essentialism that preceded the birth of queer linguistics in the 1990s. Driven by an unlikely partnership between rightwing "anti-gender" politicians across the globe and a brand of feminists in Europe and the Americas identifying as "critical of gender," the discourses arising from this nostalgia find common ground in calling for the marginalization and erasure of transgender identity. Prejudice against trans people has become central to contemporary naysaying, gatekeeping, and bullying, both in linguistics and in gender studies. Our analysis of this disturbing development highlights the importance of forging an intersectional sensibility across lines of abjection in order to confront the discourses that continue to sequester queer and trans perspectives.

2 Theorizing closets

Closets serve to create an illusion of normativity by pushing non-normative identities and practices out of public discourse. Research on language and secrecy has examined the various ways concealment serves to construct and delimit both publics and counterpublics (Warner 2002). In other words, public discourses (and discursive spaces) are defined by what should (not) be said in public (or counterpublic) contexts (see Debenport 2023 for a review). The silencing of marginalized voices, whether enacted in domains of sexuality, gender, race, religion, class, age, ability, or geopolitics, is the cornerstone of normativities.

In her work on concealment and revelation, Debenport (2020) notes that these two practices are always about the formation of social groups. As Sedgwick (1990) discussed in her pathbreaking book *Epistemology of the Closet*, closets emerge whenever there is a binary point of social distinction. The salience of a social opposition is heightened whenever one is faced with deciding whether or not they are located on the marked end of that point of difference. Across interactional moments, individuals align or disalign with one another through shared evaluations and identities. When the evaluation of some stance object (Du Bois 2007) reveals a link to a social opposition, speakers must choose whether to reveal their association with the less normative side of the binary. Revealing one's self to be on the marginalized side of an opposition typically carries consequences. For example, in a study of after hour calls to British healthcare providers, Kitzinger (2005) demonstrates that interactions are problematized or questioned when a caller reveals that their relationship to the patient is anything other than parent-child or husband-wife (cf. Ostermann 2017). Being on the non-normative side of a binary opposition always comes with risks.

Although typically represented as a "before and after" moment, coming out of the closet is not a singular event. As Liang (1997) argued early in the trajectory of queer linguistics, coming out is not an either-or choice between concealment and revelation. Liang notes that the metaphor of coming out has two primary meanings: to recognize and accept one's sexual identity and to reveal that identity to another person. Being "out" varies by degrees, with those who are open about their identity across a broad range of contexts as "more out" than those who are open only in a limited number of counter-public spaces. Narratives about how one comes out of the closet (also known as coming out stories) are deeply enregistered within LGBTQ+ communities. Studies on lesbian and gay speakers in North America and Europe have shown that individuals are socialized to produce narratives that fit a normative generic structure (DiDomenico 2015) emphasizing metaphorical movement that overcomes conflicts through experiences of self-recognition (Chirrey 2020).

Coming out stories typically present revelation as a singular trajectory, but coming out is a recurring event in that one must constantly adapt to interactional contexts that require a choice between revelation and concealment. As Sedgwick writes:

> "Closetedness" itself is a performance initiated as such by the speech act of a silence – not a particular silence, but a silence that accrues particularly by fits and starts, in relation to the discourse that surrounds and differentially constitutes it. (Sedgwick 1990, 3)

Because interactions vary in terms of the risk posed by revealing one's self, LGBTQ+ individuals become socialized to self-monitor their physical and linguistic behaviors across interactional contexts (see Cornelius & Barrett 2020). This means that scholars with marginalized gender and sexual identities also compartmentalize the overt expression of their own subjectivity according to context. The ways in which "not being said" is achieved are quite varied. Some of us, for instance, may engage in clearly conscious acts of self-censorship, such as maintaining distinct versions of our CV for use in different contexts or deciding not to participate in a particular research project for fear of "giving away too much." Yet there are also many cases where a binary point of social difference does not surface in an interaction, so that revelation is irrelevant. Those benefitting from heterosexual and cisgender privilege may later feel betrayed when they come to learn the sexual or gender identity of a colleague who withheld the "secret" across multiple interactions. Lakoff's (1975) now infamous characterization of the use of women's language as "damned if you do, damned if you don't" readily comes to mind for theorizing the closet, except here the discursive paradox arises from the forced choice between concealment and revelation.

In this regard, it is important to remember that the discourses that work to silence individual voices vary widely, so that experiences of "coming out" may also vary widely across contexts (see Decena 2008; Hall 2019; Pak 2021). For example, trans voices may be silenced in ways that are distinct from the silencing of cisgender LGB individuals (see Zimman 2009, 2020, 2021). This brings us to a crucial point in the fight against queer and trans suppression: *closets are multiple and intersectional.* Although the closet is most commonly associated with LGBTQ+ communities, the negotiation of concealment and revelation is relevant for all forms of social opposition. Multiple closets are at play in any interaction, particularly within the context of academia where we are also driven to maintain closets related to age, ethnicity, class, regional identity, geopolitical location, and so on. For example, the "you don't sound Black on the phone" trope, widely reported in studies of racial discrimination (e.g., Baugh 2015; Nenonene, McIntosh & Vasquez 2021; Santamaría & Jean-Marie 2014; Tourse, Hamilton-Mason & Wewiorski 2018), seems to presume that African Americans have some obligation to reveal themselves as such to white people, even in cases where racial identity is entirely irrelevant. The discourses that enforce these various types of closets pose distinct risks and require distinct strategies of concealment. In her work on queer migration politics, queer Chicana feminist Karma Chávez (2013) notes that failure to conceal one's status as an undocumented immigrant may have much worse implications than failing to hide one's sexual identity (see also Seif 2014).

As with other forms of intersectionality, closets are not additive but rather multiplicative (Crenshaw 1989). In other words, the risks of revelation for intersectional identities are more than the simple addition of multiple axes of discursive oppression (for a discussion of this point with respect to the erasure of race in language, gender, and sexuality research, see miles-hercules 2022). As Crenshaw notes, efforts to prevent discrimination against African Americans are typically most beneficial to African American men. Similarly, efforts to stop discrimination based on gender identity tend to be most beneficial to cisgender white women. This means that African American women come to be discursively erased, so that it becomes much more difficult for them to be recognized and protected from discrimination.

For individuals who experience multiple axes of oppression, the exponential force of intertextuality may make public revelation much more difficult. That is, the discourses that enforce closets typically have histories that intertwine normative assumptions about both gender/sexuality and race. For example, Snorton (2017) demonstrates that modern understandings of women's bodies were founded on non-consensual (and non-anesthetized) exploratory surgeries performed on African American women. This means that white discourses of sexual and gender identity came to dominate public discourses specifically because of racist assumptions about normative bodies and behaviors. Similarly, Lugones (2007) has argued that contemporary understandings of gender and sexuality cannot be divorced from colonial domination of indigenous peoples. More recently, Steele (2022) and Pyle (2022) have applied this argument to the linguistic study of nonbinary identification. The continued use of colonialist tropes such as "sodomy" or "perversion" as excuses to justify violence against both ethnic populations and LGBTQ+ groups demonstrates the ways in which heteronormativity cannot be divorced from understandings of whiteness.

If closets emerge from binary points of distinction, as Sedgwick (1990) claims, then an effective way to challenge the power of the closet is to undermine the binary nature of social categories themselves (cf. Zimman, Davis & Raclaw 2014). We often presume that challenging the gender binary depends on the emergence of liminal identities that fall between the categories of female and male (indeed, this presumption was formative to the development of queer linguistics in the 1990s). However, the gender binary may also be challenged by bringing more attention to the intersectional realities of social oppression. The intersectional nature of gender and sexuality means that discourses based on a "truth" of binary gender will always be exclusionary and marginalizing. This is why scholars calling for a return to essentialist understandings of biological sex cannot help but reject intersectionality, since acknowledging the vastly differential social treatments experienced by people assigned female at birth would expose what is wrong with using biology as a singular analytic. The positioning of gender as a binary opposition based in biology inevitably defines that binary in terms of the privileged, erasing the variations in experiences of gender oppression across other social dimensions.

3 The naysayers

The naysayers continually produce microaggressions that make it clear that LGBTQ+ individuals do not "fit in" and aren't welcome in academic contexts. For example, a heterosexual faculty member who warns a lesbian graduate student about being safe in a homophobic fieldwork setting is not expressing legitimate concern. As every queer graduate student knows, homophobia is pervasive in all sociocultural contexts, even so-called "first world" urban ones. Moreover, as a sustained endeavor often requiring intimacy with unknown persons, fieldwork may be dangerous regardless of one's sexuality. Such an utterance therefore has the primary effect of raising a binary point of difference without justification. It is a kind of advice that serves to prevent queers from doing fieldwork, blocking the ambitions of emerging scholars. This is a microaggression. Of course, because the utterance is framed as an expression of concern, it is less likely to be recognized as prejudicial by those who do not experience microaggressions themselves. Indeed, the producers of microaggressions are not always aware of the impact of their utterances.

In his ground-breaking work on microaggressions, Sue (2010) considered microaggressions to include overt derogatory remarks, such as the use of slurs. However, several researchers have argued that this view misses the important distinction between microaggressions and hate speech (di Gennaro & Brewer 2018; Minikel-Lacocque 2013; Nadal et al. 2011). While hate speech is clearly intended to cause immediate emotional harm to the addressee, the intent behind microaggressions is often ambiguous. Indeed, microaggressions may even be structured as compliments. For example, complimenting an African American for being "articulate" (see Alim & Smitherman 2012) or a lesbian for being "pretty" (or worse, for "not looking like a lesbian") positions the addressee as exceptional while making it clear that the speaker believes stereotypes to be true.

Similarly, expressions of concern (such as the above example of warning a student about anti-LGBTQ+ violence in fieldwork) may do little more than emphasize a point of social difference. The indirect nature of microaggressions makes them less likely to draw attention (compared to hate speech). For example, when Nadal et al. (2011) asked LGBTQ+ students about microaggressions, most gave examples of overt examples of hate speech. The slippery nature of microaggressions makes them more likely to continue without comment. As Minikel-Lacocque notes, the ambiguity of microaggressions is the reason they can cause harm:

> The insidious, slippery, sometimes hard-to-name nature of microaggressions is precisely where their power lies to cause damage. It is the "cumulative burden" of these commonplace acts that can have drastic effects for the target (Pierce, 1995). Furthermore, the fact that it is difficult for perpetrators to recognize them as potentially racist offenses contributes to their commonplace nature. (Minikel-Lacocque 2013, 459)

In a linguistic study of microaggressions, di Gennaro and Brewer (2018) present another important distinction between hate speech and microaggressions. Hate speech is directed at an individual because of their membership in a marginalized social group. The marginalized status is the obvious reason for hate speech to occur. In contrast, di Gennaro and Brewer argue that microaggressions need not be directed towards a marginalized individual; rather, microaggressions (re)produce the individual's marginalization within a given social context. In other words, it is the cumulative effect of repeated microaggressions that causes harm. Microaggressions are constant reminders that one is different, unwelcome, and unlikely to ever fit in.

Graduate students are marginalized through multiple patterns of microaggressions, including those related to their status as graduate students, but such microaggressions continue throughout one's academic career. Colleagues frequently express concern over certain research topics being discussed in annual performance reviews or included on one's CV. We have both participated in search committees during the last two decades in which colleagues dismiss male (queer) candidates for being "too social" or "too dramatic" and female (queer) candidates for being "too unfriendly." Women who have an academic female partner are dismissed in ways that potential heterosexual partner hires are not. Queer candidates of color are particularly targeted as "not fitting in." Research on LGBTQ+ topics is openly criticized for only applying to a small subset of the population or lacking empirical rigor. Linguists whose primary research method is thinking of ungrammatical sentences criticize queer scholars for studying "their own communities."

For many LGBTQ+ academics, these microaggressions serve to discursively impose closets in public spaces. Because of their slippery nature, microaggressions often occur without comment; it is difficult to quickly explain why a compliment (for example) is distressing. This makes it exceedingly difficult for discourse analysts who rely on recipients' reactions to study microaggressions within interaction (though see Lobban, Luyt & McDermott 2022 for a conversation analytic perspective). Sociolinguistic work on this topic is nevertheless essential to battling hegemony: it is through microaggressions that we come to accept our marginalization, learn the dangers of breaking cisheteronormative norms, and become trained to remain silent in the face of our own oppression.

4 The gatekeepers

The gatekeepers are those who use their professional status in attempts to control how the field of linguistics is defined and what research "counts" as linguistic scholarship. Bias against language, gender, and sexuality scholars is part of a larger problem of the field's ongoing dismissal of sociocultural questions about language as something other than linguistics. For many years, Chomskyan paradigms served to marginalize minority scholars for being interested in issues that are relevant within their own communities. Throughout the 1990s, the Linguistic Society of America's annual meeting always had one (and only one) sociolinguistics panel with three presentations. The "socio panel" was always scheduled for 10:30 on Sunday morning (with the conference ending when the panel was over). This made it possible for "real" linguists to return home on Sunday morning without missing anything worthy of their interest. The effects of this marginalization continue to be an issue within the discipline as each new generation of minority scholars struggles to have their concerns recognized by others in the field (see Barrett 2014; Bucholtz & miles-hercules 2021; Charity Hudley, Mallinson & Bucholtz 2020; Davis & Smalls 2021; Foster 2021; Leonard 2021; Nascimento & Windle 2021; Rice 2022; Zentella 1996).

One of the primary mechanisms of gatekeeping is asserting control (or expertise) on what "counts" as linguistic research. The phrase "that's not (real) linguistics" is often used to discourage or block research on various topics, a practice originating in Saussure's (1916) focus on *langue* instead of *parole* as "the essential, real linguistics" (Joseph 1995) and revitalized by Chomsky's (1965) call in *Aspects of the Theory of Syntax* to investigate innate language knowledge (competence) instead of actual language use (performance). Indeed, the exclusion of social (and embodied) concerns was widely viewed in the mid-20th century as necessary to the disciplinary establishment of linguistics as a "science" (Goldstein & Hall 2021). One would think that the many influential sociolinguistic critiques of the competence/performance distinction published from the 1970s forward would have brought an end to such dismissals, but the gatekeeping of "real linguistics" continues to figure prominently in the narratives of language, gender, and sexuality scholars (see, e.g., Bucholtz & Hall 2008; Calder 2020; Hall & Davis 2021; Lanehart 2021; Mendoza-Denton 2021, Queen 2017). In fact, for many linguists, any research that addresses concerns other than formal structure is automatically "not linguistics" (for critiques of this position, see Agha 2007; Fromkin 1980; Johnson 2000; Lindblom & Maddieson 1988).

It is therefore of little surprise that our efforts in the 1990s to secure stable academic employment were hampered by Chomsky's own circulation of the phrase "that's not linguistics" on the lecture circuit. One year after Kira began a position at Yale, Chomsky visited the campus to deliver a pair of talks, one of which focused on revisions to government and binding theory set out in *The Minimalist Program* (Chomsky 1995). In the question-answer period attended by some 2,000 faculty and students, a member of the audience asked Chomsky about the Oakland school board's 1996 resolution to recognize Ebonics. The hearable reaction to the question suggested that the audience was expecting a very different kind of linguistics, one attentive to the sociolinguistic perspectives on language and race that had dominated the news cycle for much of the previous year. And why wouldn't attendees expect this, given Chomsky's renowned dual status as linguist and social critic? (His second Yale lecture addressed the sociopolitical topic of "Neoliberalism and the New World Order.") Instead of offering an answer to the question, however, Chomsky responded by drawing a sharp boundary around what counts as linguistic scholarship, erasing the work of numerous sociolinguists who had (bravely) defended the school board's decision before the public: "It's an interesting question, but it's one for sociologists, not linguists." To his credit, Chomsky at least described this U.S. language controversy as "interesting," even if not the purview of linguistics. But the segregation between sociolinguists and "real linguists" is sadly familiar to any linguist (real or otherwise) interested in the relationship between language and society.

All too often, we also find linguists who gatekeep the field by positioning sociolinguistic questions as "impossible to study." For example, when working on his dissertation at the University of Texas at Austin, Rusty was told by a faculty member that the study of gay male language is pointless because there are plenty of straight men who "sound" gay and plenty of gay men who "sound" straight. Rather than seeing the question of why some speakers "sound gay" as interesting, this linguist viewed the slippery nature of gay speech as making it unviable for linguistic study. When such warnings come from mentors whom we depend on to write recommendation letters, they can easily come across as threats. As graduate students, it was quite clear to each of us that writing a dissertation about language and sexuality would end our careers before they even started; we were repeatedly reminded that choosing such a topic would mean that we would never get a job. It is because of this sentiment that Kira never told her department at UC Berkeley about her book contract with Oxford for *Queerly Phrased: Language, Gender, and Sexuality* (Livia & Hall 1997), even though she and her co-editor Anna Livia had strategically invited a chapter by the then president of the Linguistic Society of America. Fortunately, we both found solace in the support of seasoned language and gender scholars, most of them outside our departments, who assured us that our futures could be otherwise, among them Jen Coates, Penny Eckert, Sally McConnell-Ginet, Candy Goodwin, Robin Lakoff, Deborah Tannen, and Keith Walters. Their early encouragement of our work was key to our navigation of an otherwise unfriendly academic hierarchy, reminding us to this day of the critical importance of mentorship to the survival of the field.

Yet gatekeeping can also come from senior scholars in one's own area of research. When Labovian variationism began to move more squarely into the linguistics mainstream, new practices of gatekeeping arose from within the subfield of sociolinguistics itself that excluded work deploying non-quantitative methods (see, e.g., Johnson's 2000 critique of the "inflexible beliefs" associated with "real sociolinguistics"). This development continues to have repercussions for the largely qualitative field of language, gender, and sexuality. Although we view the debates among scholars invested in the superiority of their own methods as important to the advancement of sociolinguistic inquiry, our work in the interdisciplinary subfield of language, gender, and sexuality has taught us the value of approaches that draw from diverse sociocultural linguistic perspectives.

That said, as queer academics, we have also learned never to presume that other queers will be supportive allies. For example, efforts to create a journal associated with the establishment of the International Gender and Language Association in 1999 were hindered by reviews from a senior scholar in the field arguing that there was not enough good research (other than their own?) to justify a journal in the area. This judgment was delivered on the heels of a decade of explosive growth in language, gender, and sexuality research, facilitated by the broad-scale success of four biennial conferences at UC Berkeley which each published extensive proceedings (for a retrospective on this period, see Hall, Borba & Hiramoto 2021a, 2021b). By the end of the decade, all major academic presses were actively publishing research in the area (journal articles, edited volumes, monographs), even commissioning review articles of the field. In one review of scholarship on gay and lesbian language, the author called for a "moratorium" on linguistic research on sexual identity (despite having published such research themselves). Appearing in one of anthropology's most respected journals, this article delivered a major blow to the nascent field of language and sexuality. We want to stress that we strongly believe in the importance of productive critique to academic worldmaking, but extreme acts of gatekeeping such as this, whose goal is to exclude emerging lines of inquiry, serve primarily to silence, not foster, intellectual growth.

5 The bullies

While microaggressions and gatekeeping may be interpreted as unintentional, bullying is often openly and pointedly intentional in causing emotional pain. Forms of bullying and sexual harassment are rampant in academic contexts (see

Debenport 2020; Misawa & Rowland 2015). The competitive nature of academia as a career, where faculty are forced to vie for limited resources, fosters an environment where bullying is welcome and often successful in pushing newer scholars out of the field. As with other forms of closet enforcement, bullying occurs across numerous binary points of social difference. It is especially common for graduate students and recent PhDs to experience bullying from more established senior scholars. As with other forms of closet enforcement, bullying is inherently intersectional (see Misawa 2015). Since gender and sexuality cannot be isolated from other dimensions of social life, bullying will always involve multiple axes of difference.

Bullying contributes to the enforcement of closets through public pronouncements arguing that a certain class of individuals does not have the right to participate in academic discourse, or in particularly reprehensible cases, even to exist (or make their existence public knowledge). Often, bullying makes examples of individuals who are out and vocal as a way of implying that the larger communities they are seen to represent are unwelcome. For example, a very well-known linguist publicly posted the claim that being asked to respect a person's gender identity by using their preferred pronoun was "the most extreme manifestation of prescriptivist Stalinism I have ever encountered." The analogy to Stalinism is typical of the way in which those working to erase trans identities attempt to frame themselves as the victims of some hyperbolic horror. The exchange was largely directed at an individual trans linguist, but the implication throughout presumed that respecting trans people's identities was not a valid concern. In contemporary academia in Europe, North America, and Australia, the most pervasive and insidious form of bullying also targets trans scholars. In particular, academics espousing "gender-critical feminism" produce arguments that attack the basic human rights of trans people, among them the right to identify as trans (and hence to exist). Scholars working within gender-critical feminism are adamant that they are not promoting transphobia but rather introducing a legitimate theory based on (biological) sex instead of (social) gender. In the space remaining, we hope to set out why gender-critical feminism – a perspective overtly discussed by its practitioners as "non-intersectional" – is also unworkable as theory.

The most thorough work on gender-critical theory to date is Lawford-Smith's (2022) book *Gender-critical Feminism*. A controversy emerged regarding Oxford University Press's decision to publish this book during the summer of 2022, despite the author's noted history of hate speech and harassment targeting the trans community. As in other work in this area, Lawford-Smith argues that the oppression of women is a kind of oppression based on biological sex; therefore, feminism should focus exclusively on "biological" women. In this perspective, trans women are seen as men wanting to "erase" women by (among other things) calling for inclusive terminology that (in our view) acknowledges the shared struggles of cis, trans, and nonbinary people under patriarchy. For example, recent decisions by healthcare professionals to recognize trans and nonbinary clients through collocations such as "reproductive rights" and "pregnant people" (revisions made necessary by generational shifts in identity discourse during a time of tightening restrictions on abortion access) are critiqued by gender-critical feminists as examples of "the disappearing woman." One can quickly see how transphobia becomes disguised as a debate over language, making linguists who are sympathetic to this perspective an authorizing source for the spread of hate speech.

There are a number of problems with the assumptions inherent in gender-critical feminism. Here, we briefly point out a few serious issues. First, there is the problem of assuming that oppression is tied directly to biological sex, as this ignores the recursive nature of sexism. Forms of oppression use physical differences as the basis for attempts to control behavior, but these differences gain their meaning from society, not biology. Racists rarely raise objections to skin color itself; rather, they raise objections about things that *index* the racial categories defined by skin color. Similarly, chauvinists do not need women to verify that they have vaginas before acting like sexists; it is the *indexical markers* of femininity that trigger sexism. Sexism becomes recursive when gender distinctions at one level are mapped onto other levels of social distinction (Irvine & Gal 2000). Because of recursivity, gay men may be targeted for conveying non-normative gender, the working classes may be construed as violently masculinist, and entire ethnic populations may be condemned as effeminate.

This brings us to a second, related problem: feminisms that reduce oppression to biological sex (rather than acknowledging broader forms of oppression based on gender) are unable to recognize the interconnecting roots of misogyny, homophobia, and transphobia. Without this recognition, we cannot see the close relationship between (for example) movements against reproductive rights and movements against medical treatments for transgender individuals. Both have emerged from a broader patriarchal process of controlling bodily autonomy, regardless of the genitals attached to that body. In the end, feminisms defined by sex instead of gender run the risk of seeing biology as responsible for social behaviors unrelated to physiology. A theory of oppression based solely on biology cannot be a social theory.

The third problem with gender-critical feminism concerns the broader politics that cohabitate with this position. The reliance on biology not only erases the role of sexism in the oppression of transgender individuals, it places gender-critical feminism in agreement with rightwing fascists who campaign against "gender ideology" (Borba 2022a; see also articles in Baran & Tebaldi 2023). At first blush, the theory's alignment with white supremacist views of "gender ideology" might appear coincidental. Although both discourses invoke biology to circumscribe womanhood, their renderings of what womanhood can and should be are of course very different. But gender-critical feminism's stated incompatibility with theories of intersectionality (see Lawford-Smith 2022, 58) supports white hegemony. Lawford-Smith explains that gender-critical feminism "need not be about multiple axes of oppression (it can be about sex alone) and . . . need not be about the intersections between sex and other axes that create novel forms of oppression (it can be about non-intersectional oppression alone, in this refined sense)" (255). However, choosing to ignore the "novel" forms of oppression experienced by women of color produces a feminism centered on the experiences of cisgender white women, creating what Watkins (2019) calls a "feminism of the privileged." The uncomfortable similarities we find across the discourses of gender-critical feminists and far right politicians make sense once we recognize that both ideologies support and maintain white supremacist worldviews.

Our fourth and final concern returns us more directly to the topic of bullying. Just as fascist movements license hate speech and violence, gender-critical feminism opens the door to direct attacks on trans communities. By making hateful statements about entire classes of people an acceptable part of "feminist" discourse (even to the point of praising such statements as "defending" women), gender-critical feminism not only encourages discursive violence against trans individuals, it lowers academic discourse to be closer to fascist propaganda than to an actual search for understanding the complexity of our world. By treating the oppression of women as an anti-vagina movement, gender-critical feminism reproduces old tropes that have long been used to oppress women, people of color, and queer folks. Thus, the basic tenets of gender-critical feminism are not only ill-conceived, they also directly contribute to discourses that harm women and obstruct the very goals of feminism. Scholars like Lawford-Smith may describe their work benignly as "gender-critical," but a worldview that rejects the right of trans people to exist is the opposite of feminist.

6 Unlocking closet doors

When introducing this chapter, we suggested, somewhat boldly, that gender-critical feminists and neofascist opponents of "gender ideology" share a populist nostalgia for an era when forms of prejudice and discrimination were accepted (and even celebrated). Just as those hoping to "Make America Great Again" long for a time when racial segregation was ubiquitous and women were denied education and professional opportunities (Goldstein & Hall 2017), advocates of gender-critical theory long for a feminism that precedes third wave considerations of racism, homophobia, and transphobia. In such discussions, performativity, multiculturalism, queer theory, and even Judith Butler emerge as anti-heroes who have destroyed feminism for future generations by focusing on "gender ideology" instead of "women." What these discussions miss is that all feminisms, regardless of brand, have failed to make a significant dent in systemic gender oppression. Ethnographers have abundantly shown that the fact of sexism is displayed for younger generations in the everyday actions of cisgender parents, family members, teachers, healthcare workers, politicians, and peers. The decision to "opt out" of a sexist system by identifying as trans or nonbinary is not an act against women, it is an act against oppression.

As linguists who write about the power of language, we view the youth-led movement to contest binary gender as one of the most significant feminist challenges to systemic sexism in the last fifty years. We invite our colleagues to join us in developing a feminism for the future and not the past, one that recognizes the unique intersectional challenges faced by rising generations across the globe. Academics who gatekeep established paradigms are of course also affected by nostalgia; they are nostalgic for the way academia used to be. But as we have seen, nostalgia achieves its powerful effect by erasing civil rights abuses and other social inequalities found in the past. It is as if everything was going well until trans (or Black or lesbian or working class or nonbinary or disabled) people began to talk about their own oppression. Although the stories we have shared in this chapter may appear individualized to particular people, times, and places, we want to emphasize that cisheterosexism is a systemic problem. For this reason, we have tried whenever possible to avoid identifying our closet monsters by name. Viewing their behaviors as systemic, not individual, also helps us understand the common predicament by which one person's bully is another person's ally.

If binary points of social distinction produce closets, as we have argued throughout this chapter, then challenging such binaries is the way forward for the field (see Zimman, Davis & Raclaw 2014). Feminism must be about liberation for all peoples affected by systemic gender oppression, regardless of race or genitalia. Intersectional and transdisciplinary approaches have offered convincing evidence that current understandings of gender and sexuality cannot be divorced from the histories of racism and colonialism in which understandings of gender emerge. Because forms of oppression are always intersectional, the resolution to the oppression of women and queer and trans people must also be intersectional. This is why we must push for a "global allied linguistics," as recently proposed by Borba (2022b), cultivating relationships for social justice with scholars, activists, and especially the communities we research. If we want to pry open closet doors, we must join forces to fight against the mutually enforcing dimensions of homophobia, misogyny, classism, ableism, racism, colonialism, cissexism, and transphobia. If we want to ensure that those doors stay open, we must work to promote the inclusion of all voices that the naysayers, gatekeepers, and bullies seek to silence.

Acknowledgments: We are grateful to Tyler Kibbey for organizing this important volume and to Rodrigo Borba, Mie Hiramoto, Maureen Kosse, and participants at the PRALASE colloquium on "secret language practices" (Paris, 2023) for their insightful comments on the manuscript.

References

Agha, Asif. 2007. The object called "language" and the subject of linguistics. *Journal of English Linguistics* 35(3). 217–235.

Alim, H. Samy & Geneva Smitherman. 2012. *Articulate while Black: Barack Obama, language, and race in the U.S.* New York: Oxford University Press.

Barrett, Rusty. 2014. The emergence of the unmarked: Queer theory, language ideology, and formal linguistics. In Lal Zimman, Jenny L. Davis & Joshua Raclaw (eds.), *Queer excursions: Retheorizing binaries in language, gender, and sexuality*. 195–224. New York: Oxford University Press.

Baugh, John. 2015. Linguistic profiling. In Sinfree Makoni, Geneva Smitherman, Arnetha F. Ball & Arthur K. Spears (eds.), *Black linguistics: Language, society and politics in Africa and the Americas*. 155–168. New York: Routledge.

Borba, Rodrigo. 2022a. Enregistering "gender ideology": The emergence and circulation of a transnational anti-gender language. *Journal of Language and Sexuality* 11(1). 57–79.

Borba, Rodrigo. 2022b. Animating other wor(l)ds: Transformation in language and social justice – Notes on "allied linguistics." Plenary presented at the American Association of Applied Linguistics 2022, Pittsburgh.

Bucholtz, Mary & Kira Hall. 2008. All of the above: New coalitions in sociocultural linguistics. *Journal of Sociolinguistics* 12(4). 401–431.

Bucholtz, Mary & deandre miles-hercules. 2021. The displacement of race in language and gender studies. *Gender and Language* 15(3). 414–422.

Calder, Jeremy. 2020. Language, gender and sexuality in 2019: Interrogating normativities in the field. *Gender and Language* 14(4). 429–454.

Charity Hudley, Anne H., Christine Mallinson & Mary Bucholtz. 2020. Toward racial justice in linguistics: Interdisciplinary insights into theorizing race in the discipline and diversifying the profession. *Language* 96(4). e200–e235.

Chávez, Karma R. 2013. *Queer migration politics: Activist rhetoric and coalitional possibilities*. Urbana: University of Illinois Press.

Chirrey, Deborah. 2020. Metaphors we come out by: how structural metaphors construe coming-out in internet advice texts. *Gender and Language* 14(1). 8–27.

Chomsky, Noam. 1965. *Aspects of the theory of syntax*. Cambridge, MA: MIT Press.

Chomsky, Noam. 1995. *The minimalist program*. Cambridge, MA: MIT Press.

Cornelius, Brianna & Rusty Barrett. 2020. "You met my ambassador": Language and self-monitoring at the intersection of race and sexuality. In H. Samy Alim, Angela Reyes & Paul Kroskrity (eds.), *The Oxford handbook of language and race*. 315–341. New York: Oxford University Press.

Cory, Donald Webster. 1951. *The Homosexual in America: A subjective approach*). New York: Greenberg.

Crenshaw, Kimberle. 1989. Demarginalizing the intersection of race and sex: A Black feminist critique of antidiscrimination doctrine, feminist theory and antiracist politics. *University of Chicago Legal Forum* 1989 (Article 8). 139–167.

Davis, Jenny L. & Krystal A. Smalls. 2021. Dis/possession afoot: American (anthropological) traditions of anti-Blackness and coloniality. *Journal of Linguistic Anthropology* 31(2). 275–282.

Debenport, Erin. 2020. Sexual harassment, speech acts, and public secrets in U.S. higher education. In Kira Hall & Rusty Barrett (eds.), *The Oxford handbook of language and sexuality*. Published at Oxford Handbooks Online.

Debenport, Erin. 2023. Secrecy. In Alessandro Duranti, Rachel George & Robin Conley Riner (eds.), *A new companion to linguistic anthropology*. Hoboken, NJ: Wiley Blackwell. 495–508.

de Saussure, Ferdinand. 1916. *Cours de linguistique générale*. Charles Bally & Albert Sechehaye, eds. Paris and Lausaunne: Librairie Payot & Cie.

Decena, Carlos Ulises. 2008. *Tacit subjects: Belonging and same-sex desire among Dominican immigrant men*. Durham, NC: Duke University Press.

di Gennaro, Kristen & Meaghan Brewer. 2018. Microaggressions as speech acts: Using pragmatics to define and develop a research agenda for microaggressions. *Applied Linguistics Review* 10(4). 725–744.

DiDomenico, Stephen M. 2015. "Putting a face on a community": Genre, identity, and institutional regulation in the telling (and retelling) of oral coming-out narratives. *Language in Society* 44(5). 607–628.

Du Bois, John W. 2007. The stance triangle. In Robert Englebretson (ed.), *Stancetaking in discourse: Subjectivity, evaluation, interaction*. 139–182. Amsterdam: John Benjamins.

Goldstein, Donna M. & Kira Hall. 2017. Postelection surrealism and nostalgic racism in the hands of Donald Trump. *HAU: Journal of Ethnographic Theory* 6(4). 397–406.

Goldstein, Donna M. & Kira Hall. 2021. Darwin's hug: Ideologies of gesture in the science of human exceptionalism. *HAU: Journal of Ethnographic Theory* 11(2). 693–712.

Foster, Michèle. 2021. I've known rivers: A journey through the academy in search of my language, voice and power. *Gender and Language* 15(3). 403–413.

Fromkin, Victoria. 1980. Comments on plenary session on "The Goal of Phonetics." *Phonetica* 37 (1–2). 22–23.

Hall, Kira. 2019. Middle class timelines: Ethnic humor and sexual modernity in Delhi. *Language in Society* 48(4). 491–517.

Hall, Kira, Rodrigo Borba & Mie Hiramoto. 2021a. Relocating power: The feminist potency of language, gender and sexuality research. *Gender and Language* 15(1). 1–10.

Hall, Kira, Rodrigo Borba & Mie Hiramoto (eds.). 2021b. Theme series: "Thirty-year retrospective on language, gender and sexuality research." *Gender and Language* 15 (1–4).

Hall, Kira & Jenny L. Davis. 2021. Ethnography and the shifting semiotics of gender and sexuality. In Jo Angouri & Judith Baxter (eds.), *The Routledge handbook of language, gender, and sexuality*. 93–107. London: Routledge.

Judith T. Irvine & Susan Gal. 2000. Language ideology and linguistic differentiation. In Paul V. Kroskrity (ed.), Regimes of language: Ideologies, polities, and identities. 35–83. Santa Fe, NM: School of American Research Press.

Johnson, Ellen. 2000. Beyond the vernacular. *American Speech* 75(3). 259–262.
Joseph, John E. 1995. Saussurean tradition in linguistics. In E. F. K. Koerner & R. E. Asher (eds.), *Concise history of the language sciences: From the Sumerians to the Cognitivists*. 233–239. Oxford: Pergamon.
Kitzinger, Celia. 2005. Heteronormativity in action: Reproducing the heterosexual nuclear family in after-hours medical calls. *Social Problems* 52(4). 477–498.
Lakoff, Robin Tolmach. 1975. *Language and woman's place*. New York: Harper Collins.
Lanehart, Sonja L. 2021. Say my name: African American Women's Language. *Gender and Language* 15 (4). 559–568.
Lawford-Smith, Holly. 2022. *Gender-critical feminism*. London: Oxford University Press.
Leonard, Wesley Y. 2021. Toward an anti-racist linguistic anthropology: An Indigenous response to white supremacy. *Journal of Linguistic Anthropology* 31(2). 218–237.
Liang, A. C. 1997. The creation of coherence. In Anna Livia & Kira Hall (eds.), *Queerly phrased: Language, gender, and sexuality*. 287–309. New York: Oxford University Press.
Livia, Anna & Kira Hall (eds.). 1997. *Queerly phrased: Language, gender, and sexuality*. New York: Oxford University Press.
Lindblom, Björn & Ian Maddieson. 1988. Phonetic universals in consonant systems. In Larry M. Hyman & Charles N. Li (eds.), *Language, speech and mind: Studies in honour of Victoria A. Fromkin*. 62–78. New York: Routledge.
Lobban, Rosemary, Russell Luyt & Daragh T. McDermott. 2022. (Hetero)sexist microaggressions in practice. *Gender and Language* 16(2). 125–148.
Lugones, María. 2007. Heterosexualism and the colonial/modern gender system. *Hypatia* 22(1). 186–209.
Mendoza-Denton, Norma. 2021. Language, gender, race, politics: How my field and I chose each other and what I learned along the way. *Gender and Language* 15(1). 119–127.
Minikel-Lacocque, Julie. 2013. Racism, college, and the power of words: Racial microaggressions reconsidered. *American Educational Research Journal* 50(3). 432–465.
Misawa, Mitsunori. 2015. The color of the rainbow path: An examination of the intersection of racist and homophobic bullying in U.S. higher education. *Canadian Journal of Educational Administration and Policy* 173. 94–112.
Misawa, Mitsunori & Michael L. Rowland (eds.). 2015. Special issue: Academic bullying and incivility in adult, higher, continuing, and professional education. *Adult Learning* 26(1).
Nadal, Kevin L., Yinglee Wong, Marie-Anne Issa, Vanessa Meterko, Jayleen Leon & Michelle Wideman. 2011. Sexual orientation microaggressions: Processes and coping mechanisms for lesbian, gay, and bisexual individuals. *Journal of LGBT Issues in Counseling* 5(1). 21–46.
Nascimento, Gabriel & Joel Windle. 2021. The unmarked whiteness of Brazilian linguistics: From Black-as-theme to Black-as-life. *Journal of Linguistic Anthropology* 31(2). 283–286.
Nenonene, Rochonda L., Novea McIntosh & Ramon Vasquez. 2021. Faculty of color and collective memory work: An examination of intersectionality, privilege, and marginalization. *Understanding and Dismantling Privilege* 11(2). 1–21.
miles-hercules, deandre. Forthcoming. The real tea: Language at the intersections. In Kira Hall & Rusty Barrett (eds.), *The Oxford handbook of language and sexuality*. New York: Oxford University Press.
Ostermann, Ana Cristina. 2017. "No mam. You are heterosexual": Whose language? Whose sexuality? *Journal of Sociolinguistics* 21(3). 348–370.
Pak, Vincent. 2021. Coming out 'softly': Metapragmatic reflections of gay men in illiberal pragmatic Singapore. *Gender and Language* 15(3). 301–323.

Pierce, Charles V. 1995. Stress analogs of racism and sexism: Terrorism, torture, and disaster. In Charles V. Willie, Patricia Perri Rieker, Bernard M. Kramer & Bertram S. Brown (eds.), *Mental health, racism, and sexism*. 277–293. Pittsburgh, PA: University of Pittsburgh Press.

Pyle, Kai 2022. Queer gender and sexuality in Indigenous language revitalization. In Kira Hall & Rusty Barrett (eds.), *The Oxford handbook of language and sexuality*. New York: Oxford University Press.

Queen, Robin. 2017. When a linguist talks to a dog. Forum Lecture. Linguistic Society of America Summer Institute, Lexington, KY.

Rice, Mskwaankwad. 2022. Power and positionality: A case study of linguistics' relationship to Indigenous peoples. *Proceedings of the Linguistic Society of America Annual Meeting* 7(1). 5295. Washington, DC: Linguistic Society of America.

Santamaría, Lorri J. & Gaëtane Jean-Marie. 2014. Cross-cultural dimensions of applied, critical, and transformational leadership: Women principals advancing social justice and educational equity. *Cambridge Journal of Education* 44(3). 333–360.

Sedgwick, Eve Kosofsky 1990. *Epistemology of the closet*. Berkeley: University of California Press.

Seif, Hinda. 2014. "Coming out of the shadows" and "undocuqueer": Undocumented immigrants transforming sexuality discourse and activism. *Journal of Language and Sexuality* 3(1). 87–120.

Snorton, C. Riley. 2017. *Black on both sides: A racial history of trans identity*. Minneapolis: University of Minnesota Press.

Steele, Ariana J. 2022. Enacting new worlds of gender: Nonbinary speakers, racialized gender, and anti-colonialism. In Kira Hall & Rusty Barrett (eds.), *The Oxford handbook of language and sexuality*. New York: Oxford University Press. Published in Oxford Handbooks Online.

Sue, Derald Wing. 2010. Microaggressions, marginality, and oppression: An introduction. In Derald Wing Sue (ed.), *Microaggressions and marginality: Manifestation, dynamics, and impact*. 3–22. Hoboken, NJ: Wiley.

Tourse, Robbie W. C., Johnnie Hamilton-Mason & Nancy J. Wewiorski. 2018. *Systemic racism in the United States: Scaffolding as social construction*. Cham: Springer.

Warner, Michael. 2002. *Publics and counterpublics*. New York: Zone Books.

Watkins, Susan. 2019. Beating the beadles. Review of Kate Manne's *Down girl: The logic of misogyny*. *New Left Review* 119 (Sept/Oct).

Zentella, Ana Celia. 1996. The "Chiquitiafication" of U.S. Latinos and their languages, or: Why we need an anthro*political* linguistics. In Risako Ide, Rebecca Parker & Yukako Suaoshi (eds.), *Salsa III: Proceedings of the Third Annual Symposium about Language and Society – Austin, Texas Linguistics Forum* 36. 1–18.

Zimman, Lal. 2009. "The other kind of coming out": Transgender people and the coming out narrative genre. *Gender and Language* 3(1). 53–80.

Zimman, Lal. 2020. Transgender language, transgender moment: Toward a trans linguistics. In Kira Hall & Rusty Barrett (eds.), *The Oxford handbook of language and sexuality*. New York: Oxford University Press. Published in Oxford Handbooks Online.

Zimman, Lal. 2021. Beyond the cis gays' cis gaze: The need for a trans linguistics. *Gender and Language* 15(3). 423–429.

Zimman, Lal, Jenny L. Davis & Joshua Raclaw (eds.). 2014. *Queer excursions: Retheorizing binaries in language, gender, and sexuality*. New York: Oxford University Press.

Index

African American (Vernacular) English 7, 35, 37–40, 42, 45–47, 49–51, 56–59
Appalachia 7, 89, 91–98, 100–105, 108–112
appropriation 40, 110, 163, 176, 184, 186
assemblage 179

Bible 21, 96, 220, 222
binary 14, 64, 71–72, 73, 75, 83, 117, 127–130, 132, 142, 171–172, 174, 177, 189, 197, 199, 212, 215, 223–227, 229, 254, 260, 262–264, 269, 272
bisexual 13–14, 17–18, 21, 29–30, 32, 67–68, 73–74, 144, 235–236, 238–239, 242
body 4, 8, 66, 132–133, 179–180, 212, 227, 229–230, 232, 239, 248, 263, 270
boundary 5, 49–50, 93, 111, 144, 169, 171, 177, 180, 184, 186–187, 189, 212, 221, 230–231, 240, 249, 267

category 2, 7, 14, 16, 18–19, 30–32, 51–55, 57–59, 64, 67–74, 77, 79–80, 83, 98–99, 121, 130–131, 140–141, 150, 159–160, 169, 187, 189, 197, 199, 210, 215, 228–229, 231, 246, 259–260, 263, 270
– identity category 31
Christianity 15, 93–96, 98, 102, 109, 216–219, 222, 224, 228–230
cisgender 6, 97, 117–118, 122–125, 127–129, 131, 140, 145–146, 154, 169, 171–172, 175, 180, 189, 225, 235, 244, 251, 254, 262, 271–272
class 4, 35, 40, 65, 140, 143, 153, 199, 202, 210, 260, 262, 269, 272
coming out of the closet 7, 19, 21–22, 24, 63–68, 70–73, 75–83, 153, 161, 261–262
conservative 8, 29, 143–144, 206, 215, 222, 228
critical discourse analysis 101, 171, 187
culture 38, 42, 66, 75, 89, 91, 93, 97–98, 103–104, 125, 140, 151–154, 156, 159–161, 184, 198, 224, 237, 243, 254–255, 259

desire 7, 15, 19, 23–24, 28, 31–32, 64–66, 68–75, 77, 79–83, 104–105, 109, 170, 183, 185, 187, 189, 211–212, 238–239, 246, 248, 250
dialect 99, 141, 144, 146, 149

dialectology 8
digital media 13, 16–17, 35–38, 45, 51, 58–59, 94, 99, 173, 179, 224
– social media 7, 93–94, 98–100, 103, 108, 111, 152, 171, 173, 175
Discipline 1–2, 3, 4, 5, 6, 7, 8, 9, 81, 139, 216, 219–222, 238, 253, 266
– transdisciplinary 5, 8, 272
discourse 8, 19, 21, 31, 45, 65, 67–68, 70, 79–83, 93, 95, 99–101, 111, 117–118, 130–131, 150, 158, 160, 171, 173, 176–178, 187, 198, 200, 203, 207–208, 215, 221, 229, 232, 235–236, 240–241, 243–245, 247–248, 253–255, 259–263, 265, 269–271
diversity 1, 95, 146, 155, 174, 179, 182, 188, 197–200, 212, 220, 223, 229–230
drag 8, 35, 126–127, 132, 140, 144, 151–163
– drag queens 35, 126–127, 158, 160
– drag show 154

embodiment 2, 5, 41, 99, 126, 133, 169, 204, 211–212, 229, 239, 266
enregisterment 99, 241, 261
essentialism 99, 175, 226, 228, 259–260, 263
ethnicity 4, 63, 71, 77, 98, 105, 143, 230, 255, 262–263, 270
evangelicalism 8, 93, 215, 224–225, 228, 230–232
experience 1, 5–6, 7, 8, 14, 16–21, 24, 26, 28–32, 37, 39, 41, 64–65, 69–70, 72, 77, 79, 83, 91, 93–95, 99, 102, 129–130, 139–140, 142, 144, 147–148, 150–156, 161–163, 169, 171–172, 175, 177–179, 184, 186–188, 198, 202–203, 205–207, 211, 242–243, 247, 252, 260–264, 269, 271

femininity 38, 40, 57–58, 123, 126–127, 129, 132, 149, 236, 238, 240, 246, 248, 251, 270
feminism 95, 262, 269–272
folk linguistics 8, 141–142, 145, 150
folk magic 7, 91–98, 100–104, 109–112

gatekeeping 8, 177, 187, 190, 259–260, 266–268, 272–273
gay 13–14, 16–22, 28–32, 35–36, 38–45, 47–50, 57–59, 63–67, 69, 71–75, 77, 79–83, 98, 117, 119, 121–129, 144–146, 149–150, 160–163, 198, 200–201, 204, 207, 225, 235–236, 238–239, 241–242, 249–251, 254, 259, 261, 267–268, 270
gender 1, 5, 7–8, 14–15, 32, 35, 38–39, 41, 43–44, 63, 65, 68, 93, 96, 103–104, 111, 118, 121–123, 125–132, 139–140, 142, 144, 151, 164, 169–174, 176–177, 179–183, 186–189, 197–201, 203, 205–208, 210–211, 215–216, 223–228, 230–232, 235–237, 239–241, 243, 245, 248, 254–255, 259–263, 266–272
gender dysphoria 170, 176, 188
granny witch 96–97

heteronormativity 6, 14, 30–31, 39, 72, 77, 80–81, 83, 117–118, 130–131, 133, 235–236, 238, 242, 246, 248–249, 263
heterosexuality 6–7, 8, 13–17, 19, 21, 24, 29, 31–32, 38, 63, 67, 71–75, 77, 117–118, 122, 125, 131, 146, 212, 225, 235–236, 238–239, 242–244, 246, 248–249, 251, 253–254, 262, 264–265
historiography 2, 216, 232
homonormativity 31, 38, 81, 83, 94
homophobia 8, 31, 39–40, 65, 95, 172, 249–251, 254, 264, 270, 272–273
homosexuality 13–15, 18, 30, 65, 67, 73–74, 79, 81, 197, 199–201, 203–212, 225–226, 236, 238, 240, 242, 246, 249, 254
humanities 5, 117

identity 4, 6–7, 8, 13–21, 23, 29–32, 35–43, 45–47, 51, 57–59, 63–75, 77–83, 90, 92–94, 96–101, 103–105, 112, 117–123, 126–129, 131–133, 139–140, 142, 144, 146, 149–153, 161, 163–164, 169–171, 173–180, 182, 185–189, 197, 223, 225–228, 235–236, 239–241, 245–247, 250–255, 260–263, 268–270
ideology 7–8, 14, 16–19, 29–32, 35, 38–39, 41, 44, 64, 67, 70, 72, 74, 96, 98–99, 121–123, 131, 139, 143, 148, 158–159, 164, 171–172, 174, 182–183, 185–186, 188, 198, 215–216, 219, 222–225, 227–232, 235–237, 239–241, 243, 248, 254–255, 270–271
immigrant 7, 64, 66, 70, 80, 83, 142
indexicality 8, 35, 42, 59, 68–69, 98–100, 109, 121–122, 126–127, 129, 132, 153, 184, 236–237, 240–241, 244, 246, 254, 270
India 7, 64, 66, 70, 73, 77, 80, 83
interdisciplinary 1–2, 5–6, 9, 39, 65, 95, 100, 216, 232, 268
intersectionality 1, 7
intonation 45, 84, 161

lavender language 197
law 8, 14–15, 41, 222–223, 227, 232, 236, 238–239, 242, 244, 253
leadership 8, 105, 235–237, 240–255

masculinity 37–40, 43–44, 58, 126–127, 132, 235–241, 243–244, 247–255
metaphor 8, 80, 103, 218, 221, 229, 246, 261
military 8, 203–207, 211, 235–239, 241–255
– navy 235, 244–245, 249, 252
Mormonism 7, 14–18, 24, 29–31

narrative 7–8, 63, 65–66, 68, 70–74, 76–80, 82–83, 111, 144, 187–189, 199, 210, 242, 244, 261, 266

performativity 5, 7, 68, 70–71, 81, 92–93, 159, 176, 235, 239, 253, 259, 272
politics 2, 6, 8, 29, 64, 67–68, 70, 94, 98, 102, 104–105, 109–110, 139, 144, 177–178, 188, 198, 215–216, 219, 221–225, 227–232, 238, 262, 270
power 8, 26, 66, 96, 104, 172–173, 177–178, 183, 186, 188, 209, 211, 235, 263–264, 272
pronouns 179–180, 215, 223, 231

queer 1, 6–7, 8, 9, 15, 32, 38–39, 59, 63–67, 83, 93–94, 97, 100, 109, 117–120, 122–124, 126–132, 140, 142–144, 150–151, 154–155, 159–161, 164, 173, 197–198, 210, 212, 235–237, 243–244, 251, 253–255, 259–265, 268, 271–272
queer theory 8, 67, 95, 235, 237, 259, 272

Index — **279**

race 4, 7, 35, 38–39, 45, 48, 65, 71, 93, 103–104, 110–111, 129, 153, 155, 164, 182, 208–209, 229–230, 260, 262–263, 267, 272
region 66, 89, 98–99, 111, 140, 143–144, 146
register 99, 222
religion 2–3, 8, 15, 29, 31, 95–97, 103–104, 215–222, 230, 232, 260

Same-Sex Attraction (SSA), identity 7, 14–21, 23–24, 26, 28–32
sex 7, 13–16, 17, 18, 19, 21, 23–24, 27, 29–31, 38, 63–66, 69–75, 77, 79–83, 118, 122–123, 126, 128, 169, 188, 200–205, 224–228, 230, 238–239, 246, 249, 254, 259, 263, 269–271
sexuality 5, 7–8, 13–15, 17, 29–32, 38–40, 44, 63–70, 81–83, 93, 100, 102, 105, 111, 121–123, 125, 129–130, 132, 140, 146, 197–201, 203, 205–211, 215, 223–225, 227, 235–243, 248, 254–255, 260, 262–264, 266–269, 272
slang 157–159, 161–163, 199–201, 208, 210
social sciences 5, 63, 83, 117, 222
society 4–5, 14, 32, 37, 42, 59, 73, 93, 102, 109, 121, 139, 170–171, 176, 182, 207, 210, 239, 267, 270
style shifting 7, 59, 150

transgender 1, 6–7, 8, 9, 39, 117–120, 122, 124, 126, 128–132, 139–140, 153, 169–190, 197, 199, 259–260, 262, 269–272
transmedicalism 8, 171, 180, 183
transnormativity 8, 170
transphobia 9, 39, 179, 181, 269–270, 272–273

www.ingramcontent.com/pod-product-compliance
Lightning Source LLC
Chambersburg PA
CBHW020224170426
43201CB00007B/307